PLAYS AND PLAYWRIGHTS

2001

edited and with an introduction by

Martin Denton

Published by The New York Theatre Experience, Inc.
P.O. Box 744
Bowling Green Station
New York, NY 10274-0744

Visit The New York Theatre Experience on the World Wide Web at:
http://www.nytheatre.com
e-mail: info@botz.com

ISBN 0-9670234-2-4
Library of Congress Card Number: 2001086423

Book designed by Nita Congress
Cover designed by Steven Waxman

PERMISSIONS

reproduction, such as information storage and retrieval systems and photocopying, and the rights of translation into foreign languages, are strictly reserved. All inquiries concerning rights should be addressed to the author at screwyscrawler@aol.com.

ACKNOWLEDGMENTS

Putting on a play, it has often been observed, is one of the most collaborative processes in the arts. The same has to be said for putting on a book of plays. This volume would not have been possible without many, many people whose contributions I gratefully acknowledge here.

First, to the playwrights whose work appears in this book: Julia Lee Barclay, Matthew Ethan Davis, Richard Day, Edmund De Santis, Gary Giovannetti, Elizabeth Horsburgh, Arlene Hutton, Jeff Hylton and Tim Werenko, Joe Lauinger, Jeni Mahoney, Anthony P. Pennino, Craig Pospisil, Adrian Rodriguez, Ben Sahl, Joshua Scher, and Travis Stewart. I am proud and honored to include your plays here; thank you for allowing me to do so.

I am indebted to the following people who helped me discover these plays in the first place: Peter Cromarty, Alice Cromarty, Sherri Jean Katz, David Gersten, Timothy Haskell, C.J. Hopkins, and Brett Singer; and also to John Clancy and Elena Holy (artistic and producing director of the New York International Fringe Festival, where *Velvet Ropes* and *Cuban Operator Please...* debuted); Christopher Sanderson (artistic director, Gorilla Repertory Theatre, producer of *Washington Square Dreams*); Monica Sirignano (artistic director, Screaming Venus Productions, producer of *Fate* and *Word To Your Mama*); and Stuart Warmflash (artistic director, Harbor Theatre Company, producer of the reading of *The Language of Kisses*). And kudos to Jeff Hylton and Travis Stewart for their tireless promotion of their own work.

I thank, from the bottom of my heart, the colleagues who helped put this book together: Nita Congress, who designed and edited the book; Steven Waxman, who designed the cover; Maricel Quintana Baker, who provided invaluable Spanish-language proofreading support; and Rochelle Denton, who held everything together, day in and day out.

There would be no *Plays and Playwrights 2001* if there hadn't been a *Plays and Playwrights for the New Millennium.* I am especially grateful to the following people who, each in his or her own way, contributed indelibly to the success of that first anthology: Fred Backus; Jonathan Bank; Al Benditt; Dan Berkey; Harry Bouvy; Kirk Wood Bromley; John Clancy; Dave Dannenfelser; Edmund De Santis; Jeffrey D. Eiche; Mark Glubke; Michael Gnat; Timothy Haskell; C.J. Hopkins; Judith Jarosz; Rachel Kranz; Lynn Marie Macy; Matt Maher; Matt Oberg; Michael Puzzo; Gary Ruderman; Mike Sears; Rozanne Seelen, Sasha Domnitz, and everybody at Drama Book Shop; Karin Sibrava; Robert Simonson; Brett Singer; Jessica Chandlee Smith; Dave Summers; Ken Urban; Stuart Warmflash; Garth Wingfield; Bev Willey; and Eric Winick.

Finally, there would be no book without someone to write it for. *Plays and Playwrights 2001* is for all future playwrights, wherever they may be; and in particular is dedicated to my favorite future playwrights, Julie and Sarah.

Martin Denton
New York City
January 2001

PREFACE

Many of the shelves of the bookcases that line my apartment walls are devoted to plays, and on the last of them, after the William Wycherley, William Butler Yeats, and Paul Zindel, are the anthologies. A good number of these compendia have titles that begin with the word "new"—*New Plays from the Underground, New Off-Off-Broadway Plays, New Plays from the Black Theatre*, etc.—titles that the publishers and editors no doubt hoped would infect the reader with the exhilarating possibilities inherent in uncovering spanking new plays by unknown playwrights.

The trouble with all these upbeat volumes is their copyrights: 1969, 1970, 1971. In the decades since that fervent era, publishing houses—whether provoked by lack of sales or a perceived lack of interest (theirs and ours)—have largely ceased printing the works of promising dramatists. These days, a playwright is more likely to clutch a Tony or a Pulitzer in his or her hands before he or she thumbs through a bound copy of the work that won the prize.

In such a world, *Plays and Playwrights for the New Millennium*, the 2000 collection of eight plays by nine obscure writers (this one included), and the predecessor of this edition, is an anomaly. The parent of that laudable enterprise was Martin Denton. I have little fear of contradiction when I say there is no one else like Martin in the entire theatre community. This is not a base compliment; it is a simple observation based on the unusual facts that make up his story. Until recently, he was a senior manager, an essential cog in the vast machinery that is the payroll department of the Marriott Hotel chain. But in 1996, Marriott made the mistake of sending him to an Internet class. Inspired, Martin decided to honor his lifelong passion for the stage by creating his own website, "The New York Theatre Experience." The title of the site presented a slight difficulty, vis-à-vis content, as the editor lived in the Washington, D.C., area. Weekly trips to Manhattan, crammed with matinees and evening performances, commenced soon after. After each journey, Martin logged his reviews. He gained nothing from this labor (indeed, he lavished much money and priceless hours on the project); the theatre gained an indefatigable supporter.

I first met Martin in 1998. He was one of the few critics to attend the New York premiere of my play *Café Society*. I was suspicious of the qualifications of an unknown Internet theatre journalist, as only a man who earns his bread through Internet theatre journalism can be. So, my surprise was great when he wrote the most thoughtful, reasoned, and intelligent review my production received. He then did something of which few reviewers make a habit: he remembered my play. Not content with the role of observer, he collected my script and seven others and published them at his own expense as *Plays and Playwrights for the New Millennium*. They were all plays he liked, plays that had stayed with him, plays he didn't want to see disappear into the ether.

They didn't disappear. Speaking only of my own experience, *Café Society* received productions in Boston and Texas as a direct result of the anthology. Perhaps the ultimate test of the book's success is that it has spawned the successor you now hold in your hands. With a little luck and a little money (the necessary industry is already on hand), the Denton anthologies will become an annual event.

Many drama critics, writers, and editors contend that they make a valuable contribution to the art of the stage—and, indeed, by devoting their time, analyses, and words to the art, a few of them do. But Martin's contribution goes a bit further, and may even be called noble. He is putting new comedies and dramas out where directors, producers, artistic directors, and theatergoers can find them. More than that, he is reinvesting the long moribund world of play publishing with vision and enthusiasm. New plays, it seems, are new once more.

Robert Simonson
January 2001

TABLE OF CONTENTS

INTRODUCTION

Martin Denton

Nobody really knows exactly how many new plays get produced in New York each year, let alone how many get written.

But it's a humongous number and it seems to be growing larger all the time: testament to the indomitable creative spirit and, more than that, to the ineffable, magical lure of the theatre itself. There's a renewed energy in the New York theatre scene, one that manifests itself in an explosion of young companies and artists, putting on shows in traditional venues and makeshift spaces all around Manhattan. From a tiny West Village cabaret to a venerable Upper East Side institution; and from a college auditorium in the Financial District to a converted apartment living room in the heart of the Theatre District; in 2000 there was theatre literally everywhere in New York. And a lot of it was quite wonderful.

My job, as theatre reviewer and as editor of what is hoped to be an annual series of *Plays and Playwrights* anthologies, is to root out that wonderful stuff: to find it and quickly spread the word about it on the nytheatre.com website, and then, less quickly but more lastingly, package some of the best of it in this volume. What's in *Plays and Playwrights 2001*? Nine brand-new dramatic works, culled from the myriad productions that opened off- and off-off-Broadway during the past twelve months or so, representing the sharpest, the smartest, and the funniest new writing on New York City's stages. These are plays that show us what's on our minds and in our hearts; plays that make us laugh and make us think about life on this planet at this particular moment in history.

They also serve as introductions to the extraordinary talent and craftsmanship of their creators—the sixteen playwrights (plus the dozens of actors, directors, designers, producers, and backstage personnel who put these shows on their feet) who have heretofore received far less attention and recognition than their work deserves. The plays and playwrights featured in this book are ripe for production in colleges and regional theatres; my greatest hope is that these works will live again on stage as a result of someone reading them here.

What follows is a brief introduction to the nine pieces that comprise *Plays and Playwrights 2001*; and then of course are the works themselves. There is magic in this book: fairies descend on Washington Square Park (*Washington Square Dreams*) and a fairy godfather (of sorts) makes poor deformed John Merrick the star of his own Broadway show (*The Elephant Man – The Musical*). There's also that other kind of magic, the kind that comes from Cupid's arrows: in *Fate*, two strangers are transformed by a mysterious love letter; in *Straight-Jacket*, a closeted gay movie star is transformed by the love of a good man. Father and son reach across time and space to understand each other in *Cuban Operator Please...*, while an estranged mother and daughter bruise and heal one another in *The Language of Kisses*. And more global human concerns—the nature of art, theatre, and pop culture: of America itself—are considered in *Velvet Ropes*, *Word To Your Mama*, and *House of Trash*—in, as you will see, delectably provocative fashion.

⁂

Gorilla Repertory Theatre has been bringing its unique stagings of the classics to New Yorkers for about a decade now. Anchored by their annual summer presentation of *A Midsummer Night's Dream* in Washington Square Park, Gorilla Rep, led by founding artistic director Christopher Carter Sanderson, offers free (and free-wheeling) outdoor theatre that intoxicates and engages audiences. This past year was a particularly good one for this emerging company, including—in addition to the staple Shakespeare plays—a rousing *Pirates of Penzance*, a sharply up-to-the-minute *Ubu Roi*, and—unforgettably and definingly—*Washington Square Dreams*, which is the first play in this volume.

As a program of eight ten-minute plays—thematically linked, but by different authors—*Washington Square Dreams* stands almost without peer: there's simply not a dud in the bunch, and most of the pieces are better than merely good. So on the basis of merit alone, this work deserves a place in *Plays and Playwrights 2001*, as a delightful and diverse collection of compact comedies and dramas celebrating the magic powers of love and, not incidentally, of theatre.

But there's another reason that *Washington Square Dreams* is here. The unifying concept of the eight plays is that they all take place during a performance of Gorilla Rep's *Midsummer Night's Dream*: *Washington Square Dreams* is a loving and entirely appropriate tribute to the mission and the spirit of Gorilla Rep—a mission and spirit, I might add, that is seeping beyond the confines of Manhattan and being embraced by outdoor theatre performances across the country. These plays capture, as much as it's possible to, the very special enchantment that comes from enjoying the revels of Oberon, Titania, Puck, and the rest on a glorious moonlit summer night.

They dazzle with their variety, too. Anthony P. Pennino's *Forgeries of Jealousy* sets the tone for the evening, with Christopher Sanderson himself taking on a pair of disruptive theatre critics who are determined not to enjoy themselves. *Throw of the Moon*, by Jeni Mahoney and Ben Sahl, tells the story of an ordinary Joe from New Jersey who sneaks out of the house to work the lights for Gorilla Rep. Arlene Hutton's *Faerie Tale* is a sweetly impish account of a reunion between a burned-out executive and the sprightly fairy who inspired him when he was in college. Joe Lauinger's delightful *Prepost'rously Befallen* gives us Oberon and Titania themselves, watching *Midsummer* and toying with a couple of mortals along the way. *The Tale of St. Jude and the Donut Queen* is Gary Giovannetti's comic romance of a pragmatic actress and a pixilated dreamer. *Guerilla Gorilla*, by Craig Pospisil, imagines a scary, not-too-distant future where theatre has been outlawed:

> SANDY: It doesn't matter if the law is good or bad. You can be arrested for performing or just watching a play. And they're really serious about prosecuting people. *(Slight pause.)* And it's not like anyone needs theatre anymore. Between cable and the 'Net, people can get all the entertainment they need at home. Safe. Theatres are just places where people might get hurt.

Matthew Ethan Davis's *A Midlife's Dream* juxtaposes a troubled married couple and their idealistic younger selves against the backdrop of Shakespeare's magical comedy. And Jeni Mahoney's *American Eyes* echoes *Midsummer*'s theme of mismatched lovers with surprising inventiveness.

Separately, the short plays in *Washington Square Dreams* illustrate the economy and artistry of eight very different authors. Together they tell the story of a young off-off-Broadway theatre company that has already touched the lives of thousands of theatregoers.

Fate is another very short play, yet it manages to encompass practically the entire spectrum of human relationships within its brief running time. Playwright Elizabeth Horsburgh proves herself a wonderfully deft satirist in this hilarious account of two strangers who meet on a New York street and, thanks to a mysterious letter that one of them finds on the sidewalk, embark on a whirlwind courtship—and breakup—in a matter of moments. *Fate* would be just a gimmicky revue sketch if it weren't so well-crafted: what's remarkable about this play is how complete it feels, despite its compactness, and how thoroughly satisfying it is to an audience.

Horsburgh pokes well-deserved fun at the self-centered Chekhovian caricatures that contemporary urbanites are in danger of becoming. She gets their (our?) voice exactly right:

> WOMAN: I'd love to see some of your poetry.
>
> MAN: I have some from my last relationship. It was so sad. She was in London and I was here and it was such a drag but I wrote her all these poems about how lonely I was. And not just little short ones, either, but pages and pages of misery and heartache. It would be very courageous and intimate for me to show them to you.
>
> WOMAN: I feel honored. I have a few of my poems memorized. I like to say them in my head at certain times of the day to inspire or revive me, kind of like a cup of hazelnut coffee. Or vanilla. Sometimes amaretto.

Shrewdly, Horsburgh moves these two through their paces at breakneck speed, so that we always just keep up with them: her plot sails inevitably and triumphantly to its conclusion before we even realize it.

Fate is a gift to audiences as well as to actors: the Man and Woman who are its only characters offer countless opportunities to young performers everywhere. *Fate* premiered as part of *Kallisti*, a festival of one-act plays from the then-brand-new Screaming Venus Productions, a company that has, in just a year's time, proven to be one of New York's most significant new theatre groups. Horsburgh and Screaming Venus are continuing to collaborate as of this writing; their work definitely bears watching.

⚜   ⚜   ⚜

Joshua Scher, author of *Velvet Ropes*, is another young writer to keep an eye on. Fresh from the Yale School of Drama, Scher is already a prolific and proficient playwright; this play, a daffily surreal comedy about two innocents trapped in a modern art gallery, is a joy. At first glance, *Velvet Ropes* looks like a sarcastic *homage* to *Waiting for Godot*:

even before the play begins, as we read the character list, we get the all-too-broad hint:

CHARACTERS

EVERYONE: Everybody's companion
EVERYBODY: Everyone's companion

Within the script, there's all the babble and banter that you'd expect; there's an insult game; there's even blatant reference to the master when the pair happens upon a sculpture of a leafless tree in the middle of a desert:

EVERYONE: It's a mystery wrapped in an enigma.

EVERYBODY: The point of view is bleak, dark, disgusted.

EVERYONE: The style suggests a pungent fabulous.

EVERYBODY: It illuminates some notion of the acrid cartoon of the story of mankind.

EVERYONE: It is an uneventful, maundering, loquacious piece.

Even if you don't get Scher's inside joke (every one of those lines is taken, or usurped, from Brooks Atkinson's review of the first Broadway production of *Godot* in 1956), the scene is still hilarious; and then Scher feeds us, not one, but two, punchlines:

EVERYBODY: *(Furrowing his brow)* I don't get it. Title.

EVERYONE: *(Reading)* "Didi and Gogo by Brooks Atkinson."

Like the best modern art, *Velvet Ropes* has layer upon layer of meaning: Scher resurrects *Godot*'s spirit (and that of Tom Stoppard's *Rosencrantz and Guildenstern*) by chasing and shifting meaning throughout the play, as his profound innocents consider the nature of comedy, art, and, by extension, life itself. Some of Scher's observations are breathtaking for their insightfulness; almost all of the rest are glorious little gems of epigrammatic wit.

Velvet Ropes is that rarity—a play that reads beautifully as literature, and then springs to life brilliantly on the stage in a whole new way. Matt August's lark of a production of *Velvet Ropes* at the 2000 New York International Fringe Festival was splendidly realized, and I trust that other directors and actors will have fun putting this very playable comedy on the boards.

I suspect that actors will be clamoring to play Zan, Mara, and Blue, the three characters in Edmund De Santis's compelling family drama, *The Language of Kisses*. This beautifully written work is very much an actors' play, offering limitless opportunities to the fortunate artists who perform it. At its center is Zan, a woman in her early forties, whose tenuous but idyllic life with a young man half her age is interrupted by the sudden appearance of her estranged daughter. Mara, away from home for five years, has returned for unspecified (but clearly serious) reasons; when she and Zan reunite, the results are explosive. In a long, dangerous night of recriminations and revelations, unspoken truths about Zan and Mara's pasts emerge, changing mother and daughter—and the young man Blue—forever.

The Language of Kisses is the second De Santis play that we have published: last year, his *Making Peter Pope* appeared in *Plays and Playwrights for the New Millennium*. As the stated mission of this anthology is to promote the work of new playwrights, a word of explanation is in order: *The Language of Kisses* is included here because it is so darn good, it felt right to break a rule or two to get it before the public.

This play breathes! Like the best work of William Inge, it examines the unexpressed passions that simmer just below the skins of homely, everyday people; I love it for that. Watch how De Santis shrewdly exposes his characters in the course of the most mundane conversation, as when Blue meets Mara for the first time:

> MARA: Hi Blue, nice to meet you. *(She extends her hand.)*
>
> BLUE: *(Does a double take to ZAN and back.)* Oh! You! You're the! Daughter! The one who's. You went to be a movie star, right? Pleased to meet you.
>
> ZAN: Mara's going to stay here for a few days.
>
> MARA: I might even apply to college. That should make you happy.
>
> ZAN: I wish you wouldn't do that.
>
> MARA: What, apply to college?
>
> ZAN: No. Anything for my happiness. Blue, mayonnaise or mustard?
>
> BLUE: Depends what the lunch meat is.
>
> ZAN: Turkey.
>
> BLUE: Mustard, please. Thanks, Zan, most people don't ask and you get this sandwich with the totally wrong condiments. *(To MARA.)* Welcome. What's your name again?

Invoking Inge is apt: *The Language of Kisses*, unlike perhaps 70 or 80 percent of all plays written these days, is a naturalistic, well-made drama—the kind that dominated Broadway forty or fifty years ago, when Inge was active. It's nevertheless stunningly contemporary in terms of subject matter, much of which wouldn't have even been whispered about in 1950. De Santis has appropriated and updated a form that suits his material perfectly: *The Language of Kisses*, far from feeling old-fashioned, is one of the most courageous plays of the year.

❧ ❧ ❧

If *The Language of Kisses* represents traditional dramatic form, Julia Lee Barclay's *Word To Your Mama* is firmly entrenched in the world of the experimental and avant-garde. *Word* premiered in Screaming Venus's *Kallisti* festival and then went on to become one of the hits of the 2000 New York International Fringe Festival, where its provocative, shapeless, in-your-face energy was precisely at home, in an edgy, theatre-of-cruelty-type staging by the author.

Now the text rests here, along with some explanatory background material by Barclay, ripe for interpretation by some daring director. I hope many rise to the challenge, because this is rich material. I think of *Word To Your Mama* as nothing less than a summation of the nineties: a spray of hyperlinked sound bites: misremembered information and dislocated data, filtered through Barclay's conflicted, preternaturally active social conscience.

And while the script is a sophisticated distillation of a decade's worth of upheaval and inertia, the play's structure is a tribute (or parody, or *homage*, or all three) to several decades of theatrical experimentation. Everybody from Richard Foreman to Anne Bogart shows up in *Word*. This was made tangible in Barclay's staging, but I think it's also evident in the text: no characters, no stage directions; just a long string of words to say on stage. Barclay used three actors in both of her productions (Monica Sirginano, Nicole Higgins, and Kate Ward, who were brilliant), with whom she developed a set of rigid gestural and performance constructs that worked beautifully. But this is a play decidedly without rules.

On paper, *Word* looks most like Ntozake Shange's choreopoem *for colored girls who have considered suicide/when the rainbow is enuf*; and I think it has some of the same urgent brilliance of that piece:

> No one who is not starving can complain.
> This is The Law.
> This is why Homeless People are so important to us.
> Or "the homeless"... coalitions for life in hell...
> Nomads with carts.
> No one.
>
> Let's see the other names: drug addicts,
> bums,
> mental patients,

troublemakers,
creeps,
dangerous,
families,
the unfortunate,
the lazy,
the stupid,
the unlucky,
the "there but for the grace of God go I" people,
alcoholics,
good for nothing,
Vietnam vets,
unwanted, abused,
set on fire,
left to die,
stabbed in a shelter,
allowed to rot,
smell bad,
look funny,
wish they were gone.

Barclay's way with ironic metaphor is unmatched: "Too many people live in Switzerland," goes my favorite line in this play, which incidentally summarizes the spirit of *Word* about as effectively as I know how.

Cuban Operator Please... is a remarkable first play by a young man named Adrian Rodriguez. Rodriguez is a teacher in the New Jersey public school system and occasional short story writer who will, I hope, continue to work in the theatre. Intelligent, articulate, and wise beyond his years, Rodriguez is an important new voice—the theatre always needs writers like him.

This is a play of almost painful intimacy, about a young man and his memories of his father, who is in a hospital somewhere, dying. Abel, the play's protagonist, looks back on his father's emotionally barren life as a Cuban immigrant—exile, really—living in Union City, New Jersey. Punctuating Abel's reminiscences and his father's rebuttals are scenes from Abel's childhood, centered around the telephone, which was the single (though terribly unreliable) link to the family's homeland:

ABEL: Placing a call to Cuba was a major event, a monumental undertaking. My father never called himself, so my mother had to muster up all of her strength and all of her English words and call. The problem was that there were very few telephone lines open to Cuba and the ones that were available were so poor that you could hardly understand a word that was being said on the other line. So when your call finally went through a shouting match began where few words were intelligible and one hung up never really knowing whether or not the other side heard a thing you said. Cold war politics and third world infrastructure conspired to keep families distant.

The two threads that run through *Cuban Operator Please...* are equally compelling. It's a play about a man transformed by the experience of exile; and it's a play about a father and son struggling to understand one another. It's written in English and Spanish, the way Cuban-Americans speak and live; in performance, even though I don't understand Spanish, the play's meaning came through clearly. (Rodriguez has provided an English translation of the Spanish speeches in the play here as an aid to people like me. My advice: read the play all the way through as it appears, bilingually, and then take a look at the translation.)

As the great-grandson of Europeans who arrived in America at the end of the nineteenth century, I have lived my life with a fairly fixed set of assumptions about what the immigrant experience means. *Cuban Operator Please...* challenged and changed those assumptions; it's that potent. And the play's complex central relationship, quite apart from its unique Cuban-American perspective, should resonate with anyone who's been—or had—a father.

⁂

About a year ago I got an email about a new show at the Greenwich Village cabaret space Rose's Turn called *The Elephant Man – The Musical*. The catch phrase appearing on the materials was "Everything you're afraid it's going to be." Intrigued, I headed over to Rose's Turn with a friend, and was pleasantly surprised to discover that the show, contrary to its own claim, was in fact everything I could ever hope it might be. Deliberately sophomoric in many ways—how many shows boast as many as three songs about the male genitalia?—*The Elephant Man – The Musical* is nonetheless a superbly crafted musical parody. It has a strong book, hummable music, superb lyrics, and—best of all—a point of view.

That point of view is expressed in one of the show's song titles—"Ever'body Wants Their Life to Be a Musical." Delivered with requisite brio by a charismatic producer called Presby Raincoat (think about it), the song gets right to the heart of the matter: there's something about a stage full of dancing cats, or students on a barricade, or a fallen chandelier that's irresistible. *The Elephant Man – The Musical*, which wisely does not attempt to construct a Lloyd-Webber-ish pop opera around the story of John Merrick, is a valentine to theatrical excess, and at the same time a burlesque of some of its most venerable exemplars.

It's also a showcase for several massively talented people, including director James Riggs, co-librettist Tim Werenko, and lyricist/co-librettist/co-composer Jeff Hylton (who also stars as Presby Raincoat). Werenko and Hylton have the take-no-prisoners shamelessness of the young Mel Brooks (indeed, *The Elephant Man – The Musical*, with its relentless shtick and naughty one-liners, feels a lot like, say, *Young Frankenstein*). But Hylton also has the wit and dexterity of a Larry Hart or—dare I suggest—a Stephen Sondheim. I became a Jeff Hylton fan when I heard him perform this impeccably constructed lyric (from "Ever'body Wants…"):

> *Pippin* and *Gypsy* and *Porgy and Bess*.
> *Carousel, Carnival, Carrie* and *Chess*.
> *Cabaret, Camelot, Candide* and *Mame*.
> *Follies* and *Funny Girl, Forum* and *Fame*.

(And so on, for fourteen amazing lines; see page 209.)

And when I finally got a chance to savor the intricate internal rhymes of his Gilbert-ian patter song "A Significant Lecture," I was hooked:

> The fleshy deposit
> Has grown so, what was it?
> The left arm is virtually rot.
> So out of proportion,
> This human distortion.
> What nature should nurture, he's not!

So *The Elephant Man – The Musical* is part of this collection, entirely without apology. If our theatre needs more Adrian Rodriguezes, it also needs more Jeff Hyltons and Tim Werenkos.

※   ※   ※

Trav S.D.'s *House of Trash* is also something of a burlesque, though of a decidedly different stripe than *The Elephant Man – The Musical*. This raucous five-act populist musical is actually an adaptation of a comedy by the Roman playwright Terrence, set in a remote backwater that Mammy Yokum would have thought lowbrow. *House of Trash* proudly celebrates the one group that even in these politically correct times still seems to be fair game—the redneck white trash of the American interior. Hilariously, but with great sophistication, it pokes good-natured fun at the hayseed in all of us—the part that wants to believe that *National Enquirer* articles are true; the part that can't turn off WWF on the TV. I think of *House of Trash* is a wake-up call: a reminder of the double-edged sword of God-fearing family values that made this country what it is today.

I think of it, also, as spectacularly good writing. *House of Trash* contains goofy faux-country tunes with titles like "I Like to Drive My Truck"; daunting revelatory soliloquies that are at once funny and explosive; broad burlesque bits that you hate yourself for enjoying (like the scene in which Preacher Bob Maggot, the garbageman moonlighting as a Baptist preacher who is the play's hero, gives his grandson a frog sandwich to use to polish a telephone, see page 251); an audacious prologue delivered by no less a personage than Jesus H. Christ; and a pair of extraordinary speeches that find the poetry in everyday expression as Preacher Bob honestly and unpretentiously addresses his God:

> You build yourself a new house.
> It's a well-made thing:
> Corners are square, joints are tight, roof and beams is solid
> And everybody says that's Jim Dandy.
> That architect, that carpenter, they did a bang-up job.
> Sold! I'll take it! Where do I sign?
>
> Time passes:
> Along come a man
> To take possession of this great, new beautiful virgin house.
> A laze-about bumstead who warms the sofa cushions all day
> Whilst his mangy pups run feral, flea-covered and foul-mouthed
> about the grounds
> Like hyperactive Hun children
> And commence the long, slow process of depreciation.

Trav S.D. (say it out loud) is, by the way, emerging as something of a Renaissance man of the downtown theatre scene: besides writing the script and the songs (words and music) of *House of Trash*, he also directed it, produced it (with his company Mountebanks), and starred in it at the 2000 New York International Fringe Festival. Some piece of the future of the American theatre rests in his hands, I think; it's time for the word to start spreading.

≈ ≈ ≈

Alone among the plays in this volume, *Straight-Jacket* premiered at an off-Broadway house (Playhouse 91, on the Upper East Side). It's the work of a first-time playwright named Richard Day, a writer who makes his living in television comedy ("Spin City," "Ellen," "The Larry Sanders Show," among others). It sported a first-class production (directed by the author) and featured name actors like Carrie Preston and Mal Z. Lawrence in its cast.

It also garnered reviews in the mainstream media that pretty much ensured its closure after just two weeks on the boards. Which is why *Straight-Jacket* is here: if ever a play deserved a second chance, it's this brilliantly conceived, smartly executed, wholly subversive satire of Hollywood and hypocrisy.

Subversive? Absolutely: so much so that it was grossly misunderstood when it opened. *Straight-Jacket* is a stylish, diamond-sharp comedy about a movie star who falls in love with his screenwriter. The problem: the screenwriter is a man, it's the middle of the 1950s, and the gay movie star is about to take on the leading role in a big-budget spectacular. *Straight-Jacket* recounts this tale with a breezy, brittle, insouciant wit that, at first glance, feels superficial and light-weight.

But wait, something more is going on here—a lot more. *Straight-Jacket*'s movie star hero bears more than a passing resemblance to Rock Hudson. And *Straight-Jacket*'s scenario—scene by scene, line by line almost—is cannily like one of those frothy, soulless comedies that Rock used to make with Doris Day: the dialogue is a succession of witty bon mots, the characters are stock archetypes, the virginal heroine even bursts into song at one point. Day (Richard, not Doris) has taken us beyond parody: he has masterfully deconstructed—and then rebuilt—a vintage fifties comedy à la *Pillow Talk*, fashioning a plastic world where the systemic hypocrisy of the McCarthy-Eisenhower era gets exploded in everybody's faces, especially those of the too-willing audience members.

It's an extraordinary achievement, all the more so because it's so darn funny. Consider this, from a scene in which the movie star Guy Stone tries to avoid sleeping with his new bride Sally, who has become his inadvertent "beard":

> GUY: …Which brings me to rule number three. Separate beds. In fact, separate rooms.
>
> SALLY: But why?
>
> GUY: I just think a man and woman sleeping in the same bed is ungodly.
>
> SALLY: Even once they're married?
>
> GUY: I'm deeply religious.
>
> SALLY: Then we should go to church.
>
> GUY: Which is not to say a fanatic.
>
> SALLY: Can we at least share a bed when we're trying to have children?
>
> GUY: Absolutely. Rule number four: No children.

The script of *Straight-Jacket* published here is different from what was seen in New York in June 2000. Day has spent a significant amount of time revising his play, at once tightening and clarifying the work, and making it friendlier to small theatre companies that might want to stage it (by eliminating some sets and characters). It's in better shape than ever; it's heartening to know that Day believes so much in his play. I do too.

And now, prepare to laugh and cry and to be surprised and provoked as sixteen remarkable playwrights work their own particular magic on you.

Washington Square Dreams
An Evening of Ten-Minute Plays

Gorilla Repertory Theatre

GORILLA REPERTORY THEATRE was founded in 1992 by Christopher Carter Sanderson, who is the company's artistic and producing director. Its mission is to provide the highest quality productions of classical dramatic material, with the flavor of contemporary immediacy, for people where they are, free of charge. Gorilla Rep presents numerous plays every year, including its now-famous annual rendition of Shakespeare's *A Midsummer Night's Dream* in Washington Square Park (which inspired *Washington Square Dreams*). It has also commissioned several original works based on classical source material, such as the musical *Faust* (music by Chris Barron, libretto by Kirk Wood Bromley); *Story of an Unknown Man* (by Anthony P. Pennino, from a novella by Anton Chekhov); and *The Cherry Orchard*, adapted by Leah Ryan. Its official website is at http://www.gorillarep.org.

MATTHEW ETHAN DAVIS (*A Midlife's Dream*) holds BFA and MFA degrees from New York University's Tisch School of the Arts Dramatic Writing Program, and an MA in deaf education from Hunter College. His plays have been produced at Expanded Arts, Emerging Artists, and The Riant Theatre. His screenplay, *Proposing to Steve*, was a finalist in the New York Picture Awards for Best Comedy. He is a member of The Dramatists Guild and is co-founder of The Film Society of Lincoln Center's Deaf and Hard of Hearing Film Program. He thanks Michael for a life of love.

GARY GIOVANNETTI (*The Tale of St. Jude and the Donut Queen*) has had plays performed in many New York City venues, including the Harold Clurman Theatre, Riant Theatre, and Vital Theatre Company. His one-act play *The Canonization of Bill Buckner* was accepted into the Samuel French Short Play Festival and was a finalist in the Strawberry Festival of One-Acts.

ARLENE HUTTON (*Faerie Tale*) is a member of New Dramatists and Circle East. She is resident playwright for The Journey Company, which produced her play *Last Train to Nibroc* at the 78th Street Theatre Lab and at the Assembly Rooms for the Edinburgh Fringe Festival. Moved to the Douglas Fairbanks Theater for a commercial off-Broadway run, *Last Train to Nibroc* received a Best Play nomination from the New York Drama League and was revived a year later by The Barrow Group. Hutton is a two-time winner of the Samuel French Short Play Festival and a Heineman Award finalist.

JOE LAUINGER (*Prepost'rously Befallen* or *Ass-Backwards in Washington Square*) has had plays performed throughout the United States and in India and Australia. He is the author of *Dirty Work*, which won the Los Angeles Drama-Logue Award for Best Writing in 1997; *LYZ!*, a modernization of *Lysistrata* ; *What A Moon!*, a series of one-acts; and *Mother's Day*, which was premiered by Gallery Players in Brooklyn, and has been accepted for development by Rattlestick Theatre in New York City. Lauinger is a member of The Dramatists Guild. He currently teaches dramatic literature at Sarah Lawrence College.

JENI MAHONEY (*Throw of the Moon* co-author; *American Eyes*) is the author of many plays, including *The Feast of the Flying Cow…and Other Stories of War*, which was presented at the 1997 National Playwrights Conference; *Mercy Falls*; *Martyrdom of Washington Booth*; and *Bad Water Juju*. She teaches at Playwrights Horizons Theater School, New York University's Tisch School of the Arts, and is the artistic director of the Seven Devils Playwrights Conference in McCall, Idaho. Mahoney is also associate director of the Mint Theater Company in New York City and an associate member at New York's Rattlestick Theatre. She is married to fellow playwright Ben Sahl.

ANTHONY P. PENNINO (*Forgeries of Jealousy*) is an actor, writer, and director. His plays include *Survivors, Story of an Unknown Man, Contagion,* and *The Casual Comedy,* as well as the radio series *City of Shadows.* He directed Marc Palmieri's *Poorfellas* in New York City and several of the plays in *Washington Square Dreams* at Gorilla Rep. As an actor, he appeared in *Our Town, The Cherry Orchard,* and his own play *Story of an Unknown Man.* He holds an MFA from Columbia University and a PhD from the University of London.

CRAIG POSPISIL (*Guerilla Gorilla*) received his master's degree from New York University's Tisch School of the Arts. His play *Somewhere in Between* won both the FutureFest and InterPlay national playwriting competitions, and has had more than forty productions around the world. Other plays include *The First Date, Months on End,* and *First to Last,* a collection of related short plays, several of which were adapted for radio. Pospisil has also written articles on copyright and intellectual property issues.

BEN SAHL (*Throw of the Moon* co-author) was born in Spain and raised in New York City. He received his BA from Columbia University, where he returns each summer to teach; and his MFA from Indiana University, where his play *The Weight of Breath* premiered. His plays have been produced from New York's SoHo Rep to London's Canal Cafe. He is married to fellow playwright Jeni Mahoney.

Washington Square Dreams was first produced by Gorilla Repertory Theatre (Christopher Sanderson, Artistic Director) on October 30, 2000, at the theatre at 413 West 44th Street, New York City, with the following cast and credits:

Christopher/Tony/Nick/Oberon/Mutton/
Richard/Soso .... Sean Elias-Reyes

Katherine/Midge/Finuella/Titania/Tina/
Olivia/Maka .... Katherine Gooch

Jeff/Bobby/Marvin/Jude/Sandy/Rich/Oberon .... Dale Ho

Ceila /Brittany/Gloria/Susie/Alana/Liv/Edith .... Rachel Jackson

Directed by: Matt Freeman, Anthony P. Pennino, Missy Somers
Stage Manager: Jeff Allen
Dramaturg: John Rue
Publicity: Brett Singer

INTRODUCING *WASHINGTON SQUARE DREAMS!*

Christopher Carter Sanderson,
Founding Artistic and Producing Director, Gorilla Rep

In 1989, a talented group of people came together to help me put on a production of Shakespeare's *A Midsummer Night's Dream* in Washington Square Park, in the heart of New York City's Greenwich Village. It moved from place to place as it went from scene to scene around the southwest corner, near the asphalt hills and bouncing over the playground fixtures there. The actors and a few helpful volunteers lit the show with flashlights.

When I watched that first intrepid audience of fifty or so New Yorkers go running after the actors to get the best spots for the next scene, I knew we were onto something. The show has run every summer since, to audiences numbering in the hundreds each night. I'm so thankful for the blessing of this show. It helped me launch an aesthetic and form a company that is fast approaching its ten-year anniversary.

The high-energy, dynamic acting style and excitement of that first performance of *Midsummer* have inspired everything about Gorilla Repertory Theatre Company, Inc. This includes these short plays, *Washington Square Dreams*, which are all set during a Gorilla Rep production of *A Midsummer Night's Dream* in Washington Square Park.

It was John Rue's brilliant and flattering notion to have Gorilla Rep commission and produce a series of ten-minute plays. And, to have them be about a central aspect of Gorilla Rep seemed like the perfect way to introduce the company as a sponsor of new work, while keeping our mission clear.

Well, again, a talented group of people came together to make *Washington Square Dreams* an absolute success on the stage, indoors in New York's theatre district. It was a moving tribute to the hundreds of others whose hard work and spirit have made Gorilla Rep happen over the years. It was a wonderful taste of the madness of a New York summer's eve with Gorilla Rep in the park!

Please enjoy that flavor and catch some of that madness in the short plays that these fantastic and notable playwrights have woven into *Washington Square Dreams.*

FORGERIES OF JEALOUSY

Anthony P. Pennino

CHARACTERS

CEILA: A critic, twenties
JEFF: A critic, twenties
KATHERINE: An actress playing Titania, thirties
CHRISTOPHER: An artistic director, thirties

SETTING

A summer evening in Washington Square Park, present day.

Lights up. Washington Square Park at night. We are at the beginning of Gorilla Rep's production of A Midsummer Night's Dream. *CHRISTOPHER enters, carrying a large yellow horn. He blows the horn.*

CHRISTOPHER: Good evening and welcome to *A Midsummer Night's Dream.* I'm Christopher Carter Sanderson, and I directed this show. A couple of points to further your enjoyment this evening. This is environmental theatre. That means we move around from place to place. The last line of one scene is the cue line for the next scene. So you need to hustle. If you are the first ones to a new scene, please sit or kneel down so those behind you can see. If you find that you are in a place that you cannot see, please move around to the left or the right until you have a better view. If you find that you are well-lit, this is a playing area. Please just take a step back. We are Gorilla Rep!

(He runs off. Beat. JEFF and CEILA run on. They have a picnic basket and a blanket.)

JEFF: This spot seems relatively dry.

CEILA: We'll set up here.

JEFF: Pass me the blanket.

CEILA: Ah, Jeff, the view is crappy. They're all the way over there on those mounds.

JEFF: Don't worry. They'll be back.

CEILA: Oh. Don't you think… ?

JEFF: Don't I think what?

CEILA: That we should… run after them.

JEFF: No. It's too…

CEILA: Hot?

JEFF: Sultry.

CEILA: Oh.

JEFF: I mean, we can still hear them. And you can see them sometimes through that gap.

CEILA: Uh huh.

JEFF: And they'll be back around here eventually. And when they are…

CEILA: And when they are?

JEFF: ...we'll have front row seats. Again.

(KATHERINE runs on. CEILA says the following under her breath along with KATHERINE.)

KATHERINE: "These are the forgeries of jealousy;
And never, since the middle summer's spring,
Met we on hill, in dale, forest, or mead,
By paved fountain or by rushy brook,
Or in the beached margent of the sea,
To dance our ringlets to the whistling wind,
But with thy brawls thou hast disturb'd our sport.
Therefore the winds, piping to us in vain,
As in revenge, have suck'd up from the sea
Contagious fogs; which falling in the land
Hath every pelting river made so proud
That they have overborne their continents..." *(She runs off.)*

JEFF: See?

CEILA: Gotcha. Sandwich?

JEFF: I don't know. What do you have?

CEILA: Um, let's see, I have black forest ham with imported triple cream brie on a bed of arugala, sliced cherry tomatoes, a hint of honey mustard on sourdough sesame bread.

JEFF: Hmm. I don't know.

CEILA: All right. How about crabmeat salad with cucumber/mango salsa and a slice of a Bermuda onion on Polish potato bread?

JEFF: How boring, Ceila.

CEILA: Boring?

JEFF: Yes. Jejune.

KATHERINE: *(Running back on.)* "Set your heat at rest.

The fairy land buys not the child of me.
His mother was a vot'ress of my order..."

CEILA: Jejune?

JEFF: You heard me.

KATHERINE: "...And, in the spiced Indian air, by night,
Full often hath she gossip'd by my side,
And sat with me on Neptune's yellow sands..."

CEILA: You're accusing my sandwiches of jejune-osity?

JEFF: Indeed.

KATHERINE: "...Marking th' embarked traders on the flood,
When we have laugh'd to see the sails conceive
And grow big-bellied with the wanton wind..." *(She runs off.)*

CEILA: I got them from Dean and DeLuca, you moron.

JEFF: You know my palate is very sensitive. I can't have any coarse or harsh flavors. You remember the lo mein incident.

CEILA: How could I forget?

JEFF: What else do you have?

CEILA: Lightly sautéed ostrich breast infused with balsamic vinegar and virgin olive oil imported from this tiny island off of Sardinia where the mute nuns release only ten barrels of their stock to the world. It is overlaid with cheese from only the finest free-range Argentine llamas. The lettuce is grown in the gardens of Windsor Castle. The bread is baked by Buddhist monks before they observe their daily prayers. In short, Jeff, this is a sandwich's sandwich.

JEFF: Sounds good. I'll have that.

CEILA: You'll have the black forest ham.

JEFF: But...

CEILA: Don't start, Jeff. You're starting. I don't want to hear the Marxist-Leninist dialectic behind why *you* can't have this sandwich.

JEFF: But I hate arugala.

KATHERINE: *(Walking on.)* Excuse me.

CEILA: Yes?

KATHERINE: Our show isn't interrupting your argument, is it?

JEFF: We're not arguing.

KATHERINE: Ah, well, you see that's strange. Because from where I was standing, you were raising your voices to one another and being generally disruptive to the rest of the audience.

JEFF: We weren't arguing. We were debating.

KATHERINE: Oh.

JEFF: On the merits of sandwiches.

KATHERINE: Of course. Look, do you think you could kind of do that someplace else?

CEILA: *(Taking out a sandwich and passing one to JEFF.)* Oh, hey, wow, you're doing a really great job. I love what you are doing with the part. Titania is one of my favorites in Shakespeare, you know.

KATHERINE: Great. Thanks for letting me know. Good to hear. Now I have to get back to work. *(Under her breath as she exits.)* Audience...

CEILA: God, she's awesome.

JEFF: You think she's doing a good job?

CEILA: Of course she's doing... Oh, what, you don't like the show?

JEFF: No! It's dreadful. It's always dreadful. That's why we come every year. Easiest show in New York to trash.

CEILA: I disagree. It's actually quite brilliant in reaching a wide range of possible audiences in New York. And him—he's so dreamy.

JEFF: What? The Jy guy playing Oberon?

CEILA: No, the director. He must be a genius.

JEFF: Please. What has gotten into you?

CEILA: Don't you see, Jeff? He's clearly laid down a foundation of Brecht in his presentation. What is this if not epic theatre designed to reach the proletariat as well as the intelligentsia. There are elements of the Federal Theatre Project living newspaper technique in the production's relevance to contemporary issues. He utilizes RADA techniques for his actors. And what's that? Do I detect a whiff of Peter Brook in the style of the presentation? He has culled only the best principles of these different techniques to the point of synthesis in order to present a compassionate, well-nuanced *Midsummer*.

JEFF: Please, Ceila, spare me the feminist post-modern performance theory.

CEILA: Here we go.

JEFF: What is the matter with you?

CEILA: I want to be an actress.

JEFF: An actress?!

CEILA: Remember when Courtney had that reading and one of her actresses became sick and she asked me to fill in? Well, I really had a good time. I think I might want to try it. Play Titania sometime. Look! They're on the move again! Come on, let's go. I said, "Let's go!"

JEFF: All right. *(Standing up with his sandwich picking the arugala out of it and throwing it on the ground.)*

CEILA: What are you doing?

JEFF: I really hate arugala.

(They run off. Beat. They run back on.)

JEFF: The life of the actor isn't for anyone with half a brain. Look, these entire proceedings are tedious. Not to say insipid and lacking in any sort of intellectual schema. I must confess that Gorilla Rep's tautology here is extremely difficult to determine which leads me to suspect that there is none whatsoever.

CEILA: Oh, don't be silly.

JEFF: What they have failed to do is discover the *übertext*. Now, if we look at this from a New Historicist perspective...

CEILA: Oh, not New Historicism again.

JEFF: Yes, again, it is the only valid way of analyzing literature. With an underpinning of Marxist-Leninist ideology, we can fully explicate any given author's—including Shakespeare's—socio-political intent. "Many signal systems, as we have seen, operate directly, indeed necessarily, within the terms of their more general social and cultural order. But it is also a crucial fact in the development of art that some kinds of signal become internalized, or are indeed quite internally developed, within art forms."

CEILA: Oh, fine, drag Raymond Williams into this.

JEFF: Yes. Isn't it obvious?

CEILA: But what about the multiplicity of interpretation?

JEFF: Not the multiplicity of interpretation. Not the multiplicity of interpretation!

CEILA: Yes, the multiplicity of interpretation. It is all so clear, Jeff, but you continue to wander around in this fog of your precious New Historicist approach. Because there is an author, a director, performers, an audience, we must evaluate the work based that any number of people are involved in how that work is presented. You can be such a simple creature some times.

JEFF: Me? It is you who completely obviate the economic implications of *Midsummer*. How women are treated as nothing more than the possessions of men. How Demetrius is bound in love to Helena through a potion. How the oppressive Theseus manipulates and controls the rude mechanicals. Rude mechanicals, ha! Such a term. As if it could really describe their plebian and repressed state. Why I recall reading of an East German production of the play where they eliminated all of the humor and in so doing eliminated the bourgeois sheen that hid the play's more horrid conceits and exposed them to the true light of day.

CEILA: It's a comedy!

JEFF: Shakespeare's clever, I'll give him that. Now in the East German perspective...

CEILA: Stop with the East German perspective. I don't want to hear about the East German perspective any more. Do you understand me?

JEFF: We never talk any more, Ceila.

CEILA: Well, it's obvious that you hold my literary interpretations suspect. You've never believed in an open approach toward literature. You are closed to any sort of dialogue whatsoever.

JEFF: That is certainly not true. But people can lose sight, lose focus, on what, say, a play is there for. So, you see....

(During the next, CHRISTOPHER enters behind them.)

CEILA: "Art suggests a way for us to see the world in which we live, and, by seeing it, to accept it and integrate it into our sensibility. The open work assumes the task of giving us an image of discontinuity. It does not narrate it; it *is* it. It takes on a mediating role between the abstract categories of science and the living matter of our sensibility; it almost becomes a sort of transcendental scheme that allows us to comprehend new aspects of the world."

JEFF: You're leaving me?

CEILA: It's seems to me the only solution.

JEFF: That's it. Just quote Umberto Eco and walk out of my life. It hardly seems fair.

CEILA: We haven't been happy together for months.

JEFF: So?

(CHRISTOPHER blows the horn behind them. They are startled out of their seats.)

CHRISTOPHER: *(Speaking fast.)* Hello, I'm Christopher Carter Sanderson, artistic director of Gorilla Rep and director of tonight's production of *Midsummer Night's Dream.* Is there anything I can do to help you with the enjoyment of tonight's show because you are clearly not enjoying it.

JEFF: Well, it has to do with your interpretation of the play. It occurs to me that while you may be using the surrealism as counterpoint to the underlying metaphor...

CEILA: Don't try and sweet-talk me. My mind is made up. *(To CHRISTOPHER.)* We're sorry. We'll try and be more quiet.

CHRISTOPHER: My God, you're Jeff Van Hauten and Ceila White.

JEFF: You know us.

CHRISTOPHER: Of course, I know you. *(Pointing at CEILA.)* You wrote in "The Upper West Side Feminist" that my *Twelfth Night* did not fully integrate the psychosexual homoerotic tensions that were inherent in the work. And you... *(Pointing at JEFF.)* ...wrote in "Leninist Literary Quarterly" that my *Macbeth* celebrated the status quo of the existing power structure in that I staged Malcolm's ascension to the throne as a cause of celebration rather than what it obviously was intended to be—the continuing tragedy manifested in Macbeth's hegemony. What the Hell are you two doing here?

CEILA: What do you mean?

CHRISTOPHER: Well, you obviously hate my work. And I mean all of my work. So why are you here?

CEILA: I'm sorry about all of that. I really am. But you know, I think I'm starting to get...

JEFF: Look, we're actually having a bit of a personal situation right now, so if you wouldn't mind...

CHRISTOPHER: No, sir. From eight to ten p.m., Thursday through Sunday, this park is my theatre. You're disturbing my actors and my audience. So it isn't personal.

CEILA: We've just broken up.

CHRISTOPHER: Oh.

JEFF: We didn't just break up. We're having...

CEILA: Jeff. We've broken up.

CHRISTOPHER: Look, I don't know anything about what you two are going through, and, quite frankly, I don't want to know. But there is one thing I can maybe help you with.

JEFF: What's that?

CHRISTOPHER: To try and love the theatre. Because you hate it. I'm just a guy who puts on a bunch of free shows in public parks every summer. But I know that in all of your research, and your graduate seminars, and your search for meaning, signs, and theory—you've missed the point completely. Theatre is supposed to be enjoyed. Even Shakespeare. Especially Shakespeare. Arthur Miller once said that the theatre is for policemen and firemen. And you are supposed to be entertained. Everyone is supposed to be entertained. It's true even for Shakespeare. Especially for Shakespeare.

KATHERINE: *(Off.)* Yes, that's them. Can't you get them to shut... *(She shrieks.)*

CHRISTOPHER: Katherine?!

KATHERINE: *(Entering, limping.)* Damn it. Damn it.

CHRISTOPHER: What happened?

KATHERINE: I tripped on a piece of arugala.

CHRISTOPHER: Are you okay?

KATHERINE: I think I twisted something.

CHRISTOPHER: Katherine, we're only in Act II.

KATHERINE: I know. I know.

CEILA: Excuse me, Mr. Sanderson.

CHRISTOPHER: Yes?

CEILA: I know the part.

JEFF: Ceila!

CHRISTOPHER: You know the part?

CEILA: I'm trying to learn to enjoy the theatre.

KATHERINE: The show's already going. I don't see where we have a choice.

CHRISTOPHER: Ok. You're on. Do you know what to do?

CEILA: I've been trashing you for years. Sure I do. Won't you stay, Jeff, and see me? We could try again.

JEFF: *(Standing.)* I can't... *(Looks at her for a moment, turns and goes.)*

CHRISTOPHER: Here they come. Get ready.

CEILA: Thank you, Mr. Sanderson. I really appreciate this opportunity to bring your vision to...

CHRISTOPHER: Yeah, yeah, yeah. Whatever. You're on.

CEILA: "Come, now a roundel and a fairy song;
Then, for the third part of a minute, hence—
Some to kill cankers in the musk-rose buds,
Some war with rere-mice for their leathern wings,
To make my small elves coats, and some keep back
The clamorous owl, that nightly hoots and wonders
At our quaint spirits. Sing me now asleep.
Then to your offices and let me rest."

(Blackout.)

THROW OF THE MOON

Jeni Mahoney and Ben Sahl

CHARACTERS

TONY: Thirties, mechanic with a secret romantic side.

MIDGE: Thirties, Tony's wife. Loud, witty, crass.

BOBBY: Twenties, Midge's brother. Unemployed. Very.

BRITTANY: Twenties, actress playing Titania, character in *A Midsummer Night's Dream.*

At the top of the play BRITTANY stands holding a flashlight, lighting an outdoor production of A Midsummer Night's Dream. *Occasionally she looks about as if trying to find someone in the crowd.*

TONY enters. He is in a hurry, but furtive: he evidently doesn't want to be seen. He spies BRITTANY and scurries toward her.

Behind TONY are BOBBY and MIDGE also sneaking so that TONY doesn't see them. BOBBY points to TONY approaching BRITTANY.

BOBBY: *(To MIDGE.)* Watch this...

MIDGE: *(Quieting BOBBY.)* Sha! He's gonna see us.

(Tony taps BRITTANY on the shoulder. SHE is clearly excited to see him. HE gestures apologetically but all is forgiven; BRITTANY silences him with a finger to his lips, kisses him on the cheek, then quickly rubs off the lipstick she has left. BRITTANY hands the flashlight to TONY and EXITS. TONY holds the flashlight, lighting some offstage scene from A Midsummer Night's Dream.*)*

BOBBY: What'd I tell ya? The cheatin' bum. Lowlife. Scumbag.

MIDGE: That's my husband.

BOBBY: I'll eat his children.

MIDGE: Those'd be MY children.

BOBBY: I'll tear out his proprietary gland.

MIDGE: With what you big potato? You gonna slash him to death with your *TV Guide?*

BOBBY: *(Deflates visibly.)* Hey! Who followed him around for a week; who figured out where he was goin'? Huh?

MIDGE: *(Stroking his face.)* You're a good brother Bobby. I appreciate all your... sneaking and... snitching. *(She watches TONY holding the flashlight.)* What the hell is he doing?

BOBBY: Yeah!

MIDGE: Yeah what?

BOBBY: What?

MIDGE: What's he doing?

BOBBY: I donno.

MIDGE: Whadya mean you donno? You been followin' him all week.

BOBBY: Yeah I follow him. He comes here.

(MIDGE looks at BOBBY witheringly.)

BOBBY: She—she kisses him. She gives him the flashlight.

MIDGE: Then what?

BOBBY: Then what? Then I go home. I can't follow him twenty-four hours a day.

MIDGE: Why not?

BOBBY: It's not like I'm gonna sit through that whole thing—it's that Shakespeare crap. *(Now he's gonna be witty:)* I like my beer unshaken.

MIDGE: You never stayed?

BOBBY: No.

MIDGE: So this is all you seen?

BOBBY: Gotta get home for *The Simpsons*.

MIDGE: *The Simpsons* are in syndication, moron. Those are repeats.

BOBBY: Nu-uh.

MIDGE: Uh-uh.

BOBBY: I seen new ones.

MIDGE: It's the summer, Bonehead. It's all repeats.

BOBBY: Don't tell me about television. I know all about television—I watch more television than anyone else in the entire family all put together.

MIDGE: Do you know why that is Bobby?

(BOBBY tries thinking...)

MIDGE: Because the rest of us work! Now shut up and let me think.

BOBBY: What're you gonna do?

MIDGE: *(Girds herself to confront TONY.)* This'd be a hellova lot easier if I didn't love the Big Rat.

(MIDGE advances on TONY.)

TONY: *(Surprised, continues to hold the flashlight high above him, but tries to cover.)* Hey, Midge... Bobby? Hey. Whatchu doin' here?

MIDGE: That's funny.

TONY: Yeah?

MIDGE: Cuz that's what I was gonna ask you.

TONY: Me? *(Shrugs; looks to ensure light is still illuminating MSND.)* I ain't doin' nothing. *(Trying to make out that it is a happy coincidence.)* But, hey, wow, this is great. You got Bobby off the couch.

BOBBY: Hey, Tony, why's your hand stuck up in the air?

(TONY looks at his own outstretched arm. Searches for how to explain. At same time struggles to keep light on the offstage MSND scene.)

TONY: What it is, is like... It's like...

MIDGE: The girl in the tutu, Tony? The kiss? Huh?

TONY: Oh, yeah— *(Realizing how that must've looked to MIDGE.)* Oh, yeah, oh... yeah... She was jus' happy to see me is all.

BOBBY: She looked happy.

TONY: See, I was late.

MIDGE: Late?

TONY: Yeah. I shoulda been here earlier?

MIDGE: I know what "late" means Tony, I'm wonderin' what you were late for.

TONY: The play.

MIDGE: The Shakespeare play?

TONY: *(Shrugging.)* Yeah. I'm just helpin' out, you know. Holding the flashlight. See? Lights up the play.

(MIDGE is skeptical.)

TONY: That's it. That's what you wanna know, right? What I been doin' at night. Well, you got me. This is it.

MIDGE: You mean to tell me you've been lying to me lyin' to the guys at the garage—lyin' to Bobby and my whole friggin' family so you could come out here and hold up a flashlight?

(TONY shrugs, embarrassed.)

BOBBY: You ain't gettin' a taste a' the Dairy Queen?

TONY: Fairy Queen. She's the Fairy Queen.

MIDGE: —Oh, that's much better...

TONY: I just hold the flashlight. That's all.

MIDGE: Do I look stupid?

TONY: No, Midge —

MIDGE: You expect me to believe you stand here like the statue of liberty for *fun*?

BOBBY: She got you there grease boy!

TONY: *(To BOBBY.)* Shut up couch monkey! *(To MIDGE.)* Midge, baby, can't we discuss this at home? I'm busy here... I got a commitment.

MIDGE: To the flashlight?

BOBBY: To the flashlight...

TONY: *(Sotto voice to MIDGE.)* I don't wanna talk in front a' your brother, okay. What's between you and me, okay, but your brother...

(MIDGE grabs the flashlight.)

TONY: *(Resisting.)* No, no, no...

MIDGE: Bobby, take the flashlight.

BOBBY: *(Resisting.)* No, no, no...

TONY: He'll screw it up!

BOBBY: Damn right.

MIDGE: Bobby?

(MIDGE puts the flashlight in BOBBY's hand.)

BOBBY: *(Disgruntled.)* I won't screw it up.

(MIDGE and TONY cross to a more private space. BOBBY holds the FLASH-LIGHT looking weary and uninspired. TONY, concerned, keeps an eye on him.)

MIDGE: Hey, look at me.

(TONY looks.)

MIDGE: Now we're alone. I'm waiting.

TONY: Alright, Midge, it's like this. *(Beat.)* It's like this, see... ? *(Beat. Giving up and just coming out with it.)* I like the play.

MIDGE: *(Beat.)* Since when?

TONY: Seventh grade. I don't love you any less. I just also love this play.

MIDGE: But how... ? You can't even... I mean... It's Shakespeare for Christ's sake. It ain't even in English.

(BOBBY's distracted and his arm is starting to droop.)

TONY: It's English— *(Alert to BOBBY's slovenliness.)* Look, he ain't even holdin' it right.

MIDGE: Hold up the goddamn flashlight, you moron!

(BOBBY holds the flashlight up again.)

TONY: He's not getting their faces!

MIDGE: If you do not hold that flashlight right I will come over there and rip your arms off. *(To TONY sweetly.)* Why didn't you just tell me?

TONY: I didn't want you to think I was a… you know… a guy who likes theatre or nothin'.

MIDGE: Well, it's not like your puttin' on lace panties and singin' showtunes… is it?

TONY: No, baby, I just like this play. I like holdin' the flashlight. I like the… I donno—the romance.

MIDGE: You? Like the romance?

TONY: *(In his best Shakespearean.)* "I am your spaniel; spurn me, strike me, neglect me, only give me leave, unworthy as I am, to follow you…"

MIDGE: That's in the play?

TONY: Yeah, and— "You are all the world. I am never alone when you are looking at me." And look— *(Turns her to see the play.)* how could you not like it? Even Bobby's into it.

(Sure enough, BOBBY is happily engrossed, shining the flashlight.)

BOBBY: Hey, Midge—Tony—look—I'm the moon! I'm holding up the moon!— That chick in the tutu is one hot tamale.

(MIDGE turns to scold TONY anew, but TONY preemptively defends himself.)

TONY: I just like holding the moon. I swear. You're the only tamale on my plate.

MIDGE: *(Teary.)* Oh, Tony… I thought you were… Bobby said it was a girl and… *(Hitting TONY playfully.)* You big palookin' moron! Don't scare me like that!

TONY: So… you don't mind? That I got this… romantic-type guy inside?

MIDGE: What? Are you crazy?

TONY: Come on, baby, let's go home. I'll throw some fairy dust your way.

MIDGE: Please, no fairy dust. What about your play?

BOBBY: *(Totally into it now.)* You go ahead. I got it, man.

TONY: See? This play…

MIDGE: Got him off the couch, it must be magic.

(They begin to exit.)

MIDGE: So tell me about the play. What happens?

TONY: Well this dude, he gets all mad at his girlfriend, so he zaps her with this magic potion that makes her fall for this donkey and she's like all over this donkey—

MIDGE: *(A memory of romantic days past.)* — Remember Tijuana?

TONY: Yeah, it's kind of like that. Listen, you won't say nothing to the guys right? Bout me likin' Shakespeare or nothin'…

(MIDGE and TONY exit. BRITTANY enters and notices Bobby holding the flashlight.)

BRITTANY: Where's Tony?

BOBBY: Family emergency. He had to go. But everything's under control. I'm takin' over.

BRITTANY: Okay. Follow me; the next scene is over here.

BOBBY: *(Following.)* Hey, what're you doin' after the show?

BRITTANY: *(As she exits.)* Going home.

BOBBY: *(Calling after her.)* Maybe tomorrow then! Like between Rosie and Oprah! *(No response.)* You can bring your donkey! Yeah… she digs me… *(Shining the light on the scene.)* Wu-wu—I'm the moon!

FAERIE TALE

Arlene Hutton

CHARACTERS

NICK
FINUELLA

A bench in Washington Square Park. Traffic noises at first, which diminish as the play goes on. An outdoor production of A Midsummer Night's Dream *is in progress offstage.*

NICK, who looks about thirty or thirty-five, sits on the bench, staring unhappily into space. He wears a jacket and tie. On his lap is a small black case, probably containing a computer.

FINUELLA (pronounced fin-oo-la) enters. She looks to be in her late twenties or early thirties. She is probably small or thin and dressed in loose clothes in thin green fabrics. Maybe a flowing scarf, some delicate gold jewelry. There is an artsy look to her; she belongs in Greenwich Village. She has a fabric tote bag. She also carries a hand-lettered sign on a stick which says "Fairies have rights, too," on one side and "Midsummer Misrepresents Fairies" on the other. She carries a clipboard with some papers on it.

FINUELLA drops her sign on the bench, startling NICK, who grabs his computer

tightly. She holds out her clipboard, but he does not look at her.

FINUELLA: Sign the petition?

NICK: I don't sign petitions.

FINUELLA: You don't even know what it's for, Nicky.

NICK: I don't sign petitions. *(Beat.)* Do I know you?

FINUELLA: *(Not giving up.)* We're protesting the play.

NICK: What play?

FINUELLA: *Midsummer Night's Dream.*

NICK: You got me. What's there to protest?

(FINUELLA looks at him in disbelief. She turns away from him, looks up and sighs.)

NICK: *(Seeing her looking up.)* Are they injuring the trees?

FINUELLA: Oh, no! Are they?

NICK: I was asking you.

FINUELLA: Oh, no. I didn't think about that. Oh, they mustn't hurt the trees. (*She looks up at the canopy overheard, as if taking this very personally.*)

NICK: What's wrong with *A Midsummer Night's Dream*? It's Shakespeare.

FINUELLA: It's the fairies. *Midsummer Night's Dream* perpetuates the myth.

NICK: (*Not following.*) The myth. The myth of fairies.

FINUELLA: Exactly. When would you ever see a fairy king and queen for instance?

NICK: Well, never.

FINUELLA: Of course not!

NICK: Okay.

FINUELLA: And fairy servants? You'd never see *them*.

NICK: Of course not. I'd never see them.

FINUELLA: The whole class structure is misleading. The mushrooms are always in a circle.

NICK: The mushrooms.

FINUELLA: When you see mushrooms. In a forest. They're in more of a circle. It's a democracy. You don't see a leader, do you? One big mushroom with an audience of small mushrooms. They're always in a circle. Or semi-circle if it's a small meeting.

NICK: (*Figuring out she's putting him on and going with it.*) So you don't think there should be fairies on stage?

FINUELLA: Not these. They're more like, what, oh, I don't know, not sprites or elfs, more like naiads, maybe?

(*Note: FINUELLA pronounces it "elfs."*)

NICK: They looked like aliens to me.

FINUELLA: See? They are not fairies.

NICK: What does it matter?

FINUELLA: (*Taking back the clipboard.*) I can't believe you said that.

NICK: They're just fairies. Come on, it's not like an ethnic group or anything. Who cares?

(*FINUELLA stares at him.*)

NICK: What?

(*She turns away.*)

NICK: What?

FINUELLA: Never mind. (*She starts to go.*)

NICK: What? What is it? Where do I know you from?

(*FINUELLA picks up her sign.*)

FINUELLA: It's important! (*Pointing toward the stage area.*) They look foolish.

NICK: Fairies are foolish sometimes.

FINUELLA: (*Floored by this thought.*) Do you think?

NICK: (*Treading water here.*) Um, sure. Elfs, too.

(*Note: NICK says "elves."*)

FINUELLA: Elfs can be very foolish. Silly.

NICK: Yeah.

FINUELLA: Not as silly as leprechauns.

NICK: (*Humoring her.*) You think?

FINUELLA: Don't you? Leprechauns are the worst. I don't like them. And not just because of all the attention they get in March, either.

NICK: On principal. As a group.

FINUELLA: I've never met a leprechaun I liked.

NICK: Me neither.

(FINUELLA points offstage.)

FINUELLA: There might as well have cast leprechauns in this play.

NICK: Did they cast fairies?

FINUELLA: Of course not.

NICK: I didn't think so.

(FINUELLA starts to get worked up.)

FINUELLA: It's not a dream, it's a nightmare. *(She is about to cry.)*

NICK: It's just fairies. Who believes in that anyway? It's a fantasy. It's not real life.

FINUELLA: What is real life?

NICK: Job, money, house.

FINUELLA: *(After a beat.)* That's all?

NICK: That's all there is. Just work hard to keep up. It's an exploding economy. Got to grab my share while I can.

FINUELLA: Your share of what?

NICK: My piece of the pie.

FINUELLA: Does your pie taste good?

(NICK takes a good look at her for the first time.)

NICK: Finny?

FINUELLA: What?

NICK: You're Finny. You're… Finny.

FINUELLA: Yes.

NICK: I don't remember your real name.

FINUELLA: Finuella.

NICK: Right. Finuella. Finny.

FINUELLA: Hello, Nicky.

NICK: Nick. Yes. Columbia. You were at Columbia.

FINUELLA: Barnard.

NICK: '68. 1968. No, wait. It couldn't have been you. Was it your mom? Your mom, wasn't it? You're not old enough.

FINUELLA: You don't look old enough.

NICK: Boy, do I know it. Don't tell anyone. I've had some work done.

FINUELLA: What kind of work?

NICK: On my face. Don't tell anyone.

FINUELLA: I won't tell.

NICK: You, too, right? You've had some work done, too. Botax? Collagen? A facelift? You look like you're thirty. What's your secret?

FINUELLA: It's a secret.

NICK: Well, not to me. I know how old you are. 1968. Columbia.

FINUELLA: That's right.

NICK: But you don't look that old.

FINUELLA: You don't look that old.

NICK: Well, I've had a facelift.

FINUELLA: *(Surprised and hugely interested.)* Why?

NICK: Why would I have a facelift?

FINUELLA: Yes.

NICK: *(After a beat.)* I work for a dot-com company.

FINUELLA: Oh.

NICK: You have to be young. They want you to be young.

FINUELLA: What's a dot-com?

NICK: It's a... you're kidding me.

FINUELLA: Okay.

NICK: Cute. You're still cute. You were always the cutest...

(She smiles at him. He collects himself.)

NICK: I work for a start-up. I'm the front man representing all the twenty-two-year-olds. Look young, but I can wear a suit and talk to the investors without scaring them off.

FINUELLA: You never wore a tie.

NICK: Things change, Finny. Kids, divorce, custody battles, private schools. My dot-com went belly-up today. It's a battlefield out there.

FINUELLA: You used to fight for change, for peace.

NICK: *(After a beat.)* I'll sign the petition.

(She holds the clipboard for him. He signs it as she watches.)

FINUELLA: Nicholas. I never thought about your name being Nicholas.

NICK: You bring it all back. The '68 riots? The sit-ins? Those days and nights in the math building. The police.

FINUELLA: The bullhorns!

NICK: You bringing us news. And food. You brought us food. And clean clothes. How did you get through to us? There were police everywhere.

FINUELLA: You had to eat.

NICK: Was it the tunnels? Was it the tunnels under campus? I always thought it was, but then I could never find the doors. You were an angel. We couldn't have stayed that long without you. I thought you were a beautiful angel. And then it was all over. And you just—disappeared. I thought I had pictures of you—we took pictures, remember? Group shots to show the world. But I never saw you in the pictures. I even remembered standing with you in one. But I never saw it. I never saw a picture of you and me. Just me and everybody else.

FINUELLA: I don't like having my picture taken.

NICK: That's right! I had my arm around you so you couldn't get away. I had my arm around you. For the photographer. But I never saw a picture with you in it. And I never saw you after. *(Beat.)* You still look like a student. You look... you look so young! What do you do now? Teach yoga, sell vitamins or something?

FINUELLA: I make things...

NICK: Crafts? That's great! That's really big now. What do you make?

FINUELLA: I make things... happen. I travel.

NICK: Craft fairs? Where do you travel?

FINUELLA: *(Uncomfortable, but she is unable to lie.)* Berlin a while back. Moscow. Korea most recently. Washington sometimes. Probably Cuba soon.

NICK: You must have lots of frequent flyer miles.

(She doesn't say anything.)

NICK: Talk to me, Finny! Talk to me! Tell me about yourself.

(She picks up her clipboard. NICK grabs her arm.)

NICK: You brought us food when nobody could get near the building.

FINUELLA: It was important.

NICK: We were kids. I miss those days. I miss protests. Causes. Caring.

FINUELLA: There are still causes to care about.

NICK: You still care. You worry about fairies, of all things.

FINUELLA: They're important.

NICK: *(Swatting a fly away from his face.)* No, they're not. Fairies aren't real.

FINUELLA: Fairies are important! *(Holds up the sign.)* Fairies are important!

(NICK lets go of her to swat the fly. During the following, he takes off his tie, as the gnats buzz around him.)

NICK: Finny, you and I are important! Over thirty years, Finny! How do you do it? You look so—You haven't aged. How do you do that, Finny? Talk to me. Finny, how did you get into the buildings? There

were police everywhere! No one could get in or out. But you. You brought us food. Finny, how did you do that? How can you still be so young? You're over fifty years old! Talk to me, Finny! Stay with me!

(He grabs the sign away from her. There is a thunderclap. NICK looks up at the sky. With the sign, he swats at the insects now swarming around him.)

NICK: Finny, I think it's… [about to rain]

(He turns to look at her. She is gone. The insects are gone as well. Her clipboard remains on the bench. NICK is stunned and looks in all directions.)

NICK: Finny! *(Takes his tie and ties it around his head.)* I believe, Finny! *(Throws his computer bag offstage.)* Finny, I believe!

(NICK stands alone on stage. He picks up the clipboard and sign. He raises the sign high and waves it, holding out the clipboard for the audience to sign the petition. He walks offstage waving the sign.)

NICK: *(As he exits.)* Down with *Midsummer*! Sign the petition!

(Blackout.)

PREPOST'ROUSLY BEFALLEN

or

ASS-BACKWARDS IN WASHINGTON SQUARE

Joe Lauinger

CHARACTERS

OBERON: King of the Fairies
TITANIA: Queen of the Fairies
GLORIA: A girl from New Jersey, twenty-one
MARVIN: A boy from New Jersey, twenty-three

SCENE

Washington Square, NYC, during a performance of *A Midsummer Night's Dream* by Gorilla Rep.

TIME

Summer. The present.

Lights up on OBERON and TITANIA on the grass in Washington Square, drinking champagne. They are a rather well-off NYC couple in their thirties, normal-looking except for the fact that both are wearing plastic antennas on their heads and fairy-wings on their backs. They are attending a performance of Gorilla Rep's Midsummer Night's Dream *and are listening closely.*

PUCK'S VOICE: *(Offstage.)* "Then will two at once woo one.
That must needs be sport alone;
And those things do best please me
That befall prepost'rously.

(OBERON and TITANIA applaud furiously.)

OBERON: Bravo! Bravo!

TITANIA: Author! Author!

OBERON: He's not here like that, my love.

TITANIA: It feels like he is.

OBERON: That's his way.

(Enter MARVIN and GLORIA, a couple in their twenties, visiting the city from New Jersey. They see TITANIA and OBERON and giggle, whispering to each other, pointing. OBERON notices them.)

OBERON: We are not the play. The play has gone over there. *(Pointing.)* There. It moves from place to place. Now shoo! Run along! Trot! Whatever you do to locomote!

(MARVIN and GLORIA explode with laughter.)

TITANIA: Mortals.

OBERON: Let us not be hasty. Immortal essences slum around the Village all the time. I shall examine them.

(He waves his arms magically, and MARVIN and GLORIA freeze in place. OBERON presses his fingers to his eyes in concentration.)

OBERON: Names—Marvin (the male), Gloria (the female). Ages—twenty-three, twenty-one. Occupations—hardly matter. Education—nothing to speak of. Habitation—good God, New Jersey. The female is in menses. The male has recently masturbated. *(Beat.)* So has the female.

TITANIA: Together?

OBERON: No such luck.

TITANIA: What jerk-offs these mortals be.

OBERON *(Still concentrating.)* Secret fantasies— *(Suddenly looks at MARVIN with interest.)* —the male has unacknowledged but powerful bisexual yearnings!

TITANIA: That's promising. How about the bitch?

OBERON: Language, my love. Remember we are guests. Let's see—the female cherishes fantasies about… a shortstop. Derek Jeter?

TITANIA: I like the Mets. We'll make do with Marvin.

OBERON: Make do, my love? Are you suggesting that we—

TITANIA: I never suggest, my dove. I act!

(She claps her hands once, and MARVIN and GLORIA emerge from their trance, in mid-laugh. TITANIA raises a hand; they quiet down instantly.)

TITANIA: Hail, quasi-copulatives! We are drinking champagne. Join us.

(MARVIN and GLORIA giggle.)

GLORIA: Like you're really serious? You'll like just let us have some of your champagne?

OBERON: Bollinger '79. The best your world permits.

GLORIA: That really was like bottled in 1979? I was like born in 1979!

OBERON: A maid so young, a wine so old. So much for time.

GLORIA: Totally!

(She takes the glass he has poured for her. MARVIN has held back. She gestures at him.)

GLORIA: C'mon! It's like real champagne.

TITANIA: Yes, come. Sit with me.

OBERON: Or sit with me.

MARVIN: I think it's like against the law in New York to drink from an open container.

TITANIA: Only if you're poor. Come to me, Marvin!

OBERON: Marvin, come to me!

GLORIA: Yeah, Marv, get your ass over here.

(MARVIN hesitantly accepts a glass of champagne.)

MARVIN: Like how do you know my name?

GLORIA: 'Cause I said your name. I said get your ass over here, Marv. They said come to me, Marvin. That's how they talk. No big deal.

MARVIN: They like said it before you said it.

OBERON: What's in a name? A rose by any other name would smell as sweet.

TITANIA: Wrong play.

OBERON: Same period.

TITANIA: Speaking of period, Gloria, do you have a heavy—

OBERON: *(Quickly interrupting her.)* Isn't the Bard divine under the stars?

MARVIN: Stars? I don't see no stars. And I think it's weird you guys know my name—

GLORIA: My name is Kimberly. Kimberly LaGloss.

OBERON: It's not. It's Gloria Moskowitz. Never lie to a fairy.

MARVIN: I knew he was a fruit!

GLORIA: Hey, it's New York, Marv, okay? Chill. So you guys are fairies. That's cool. Like the outfits! They're really dope.

TITANIA: What outfits?

OBERON: Time to introduce ourselves, my love. I am Oberon, King of the Fairies, and this is my Queen, Titania.

GLORIA: You're married? How, if he's like a fairy and you're like a chick? Oh, I get it! You like embrace a bisexual lifestyle.

MARVIN: Bisexual lifestyle, my ass. This guy's a fucking drag queen. I am outa here, man—

OBERON: *(Putting an arm around him.)* Tut, tut, lad. What's a little poly-

morphousness among friends? Have some more champagne.

MARVIN: Get offa me, man! Married to a fucking drag queen!

TITANIA: Is he referring to me?

GLORIA: I don't know why he's so upset. He likes to wear my panties.

MARVIN: I do not!

GLORIA: He gets up at night when he thinks I'm asleep and puts them on in the bathroom. That's why the elastic always gives out—

OBERON: *(Applauding.)* Bravo, Marvin! Never lie to a fairy—or a girl with open eye. Well, tell us, tell us! What kind of panties do you fancy?

GLORIA: Him or me?

OBERON: I suppose I was assuming you shared the same pair. How deliciously naïve of me!

TITANIA: Marvin, have you tastes in panties that deviate from Gloria's?

OBERON: Thong for her, bikini cut for him?

MARVIN: How about you eat some knuckles, fairy?

TITANIA: Oh, I love it when they get bestial! Strike him, Marvin! Do!

(OBERON smiles obligingly, offering his jaw. Beat. MARVIN draws back.)

MARVIN: I don't hit old guys.

OBERON: Old guys! Marvelous!

TITANIA: I'm disappointed in you, Marvin. Here you were, promising us a display of raw human violence, and what happens? You peter out, go limp. Most churlish. However, I forgive you. Now lie down beside me and place your head in my lap. I want to stroke your ears.

GLORIA: Hey!

OBERON: The boy's got good ears. Big, not too hairy—

TITANIA: They're lovely ears.

MARVIN: Really? Nobody's ever said anything nice about my ears before. I know I have attractive legs—

TITANIA: Gorgeous legs.

OBERON: I admit the legs are good too, but you know what they say about a man with big ears.

MARVIN: No, what?

OBERON: Shall I tell him?

TITANIA: I'll tell him. But he must come to me first so I can pour my distilment in the porches of his ears.

OBERON: Wrong play.

TITANIA: Mind your own business.

MARVIN: What's this about pouring something in my ears?

TITANIA: Honeyed words of sweet affection.

OBERON: My love, I must protest. That is not the Bard, it is Diana Ross and the Supremes.

TITANIA: I use what works.

MARVIN: *(Coming closer.)* Well, I guess words can't hurt.

OBERON: Oh child! Perhaps we shouldn't, Titania. A succulent boy, I grant, but too green, methinks, for our picking.

TITANIA: Green is my favorite color.

MARVIN: Who you calling boy?

TITANIA: You, lovely boy. Sweet, lovely boy! Come!

(MARVIN comes to her, strangely mesmerized.)

GLORIA: Hey! Hey! HEY!

(MARVIN stops, still in a trance.)

TITANIA: *(To GLORIA.)* Leave us, wretch.

GLORIA: As if! Look, Tatiana, I don't know what kind of game you're—

TITANIA: Titania. Tatiana is a heroine in Pushkin, and a mopey little sniveler to boot.

GLORIA: Whatever. That's my boyfriend. Okay? Hands off.

TITANIA: No hands? Delighted. I'll use my toes.

GLORIA: No toes either! Jesus, this is getting freaky. *(Rubs her belly uncomfortably.)*

OBERON: Gloria, my sweeting, come sit with me.

GLORIA: Like that's close.

OBERON: I know a bank where the wild thyme blows. And inhaled judiciously there's nothing like wild thyme for easing menstrual cramps.

GLORIA: Wild what?

OBERON: Thyme.

GLORIA: Wild Time. Is that like some kind of designer drug?

OBERON: Let's just say you have to know how to use it. I do.

GLORIA: Cool.

(GLORIA goes to OBERON and he produces a sprig of wild thyme which he waves under her nose. She instantly relaxes and lies back in his arms; MARVIN crawls to TI-TANIA and lays his head in her lap. She strokes his ears sensuously.)

OBERON: *(To TITANIA.)* You owe me one, my love.

TITANIA: Duly noted, my dove. Such funny creatures these are, up close. When we get back we must tell Will to put them into a play.

GLORIA: Get back? Where you guys from?

OBERON: Fairy Land!

(Music starts.)

GLORIA: Is that in the East Village?

TITANIA: Fairy Land is where the poets live—

OBERON: —and sylvan shades of whirling thought—

TITANIA: —chase words to cheer cold time.

GLORIA: I knew it was the East Village.

OBERON: East meets West there, and up joins hands with down—

TITANIA: —to stride past heav'n and the utmost bounds of hope.

MARVIN: Sounds far.

TITANIA: No place more distant—

OBERON: —and yet it is here.

TITANIA: No place more near—

OBERON: —yet blind to creeping sight.

GLORIA: Golly. How do you get there?

TITANIA: Upon the wings of fairies—

OBERON: —and in the player's voice—

TITANIA: —within the spell of music—

OBERON: —and in the word rejoice.

(Pause; end of music.)

TITANIA: Mine's asleep.

OBERON: Mine's drunk. Did you enjoy his ears, my love?

TITANIA: Best I've had in years, my dove. You were kind to let me. Did you draw any sweetness from your... thing?

OBERON: An ill-favoured thing, but mine own.

TITANIA: Wrong play.

OBERON: It'll have to do in the circumstances.

TITANIA: The problem is always what to do with them after one is finished with them. Will either kills them off—

OBERON: Rather too tragic an ending for this lot, I think.

TITANIA: —or has the lovers marry.

OBERON: A vulgar kind of comedy but a crowd-pleaser.

TITANIA: You know, I almost feel a kind of pity for them. Perhaps we should let them dream forever. They always suffer so when they wake up.

OBERON: I think they call that withdrawal.

TITANIA: I thought they called it life.

OBERON: I know! We'll take them to Fairy Land.

TITANIA: These clowns?

OBERON: The play, my love! It's returning to us.

TITANIA: Of course! They'll wake to the play! Where has it got to? How far are we gone?

OBERON: Shush!

(They listen.)

PUCK'S VOICE: *(Offstage.)* "For night's swift dragons cut the clouds full fast, And yonder shines Aurora's harbinger…"

OBERON: Act 3, Scene 2! Plenty of great stuff left!

TITANIA: Enough to charm the likes of them.

OBERON: The best in this kind are but shadows, and the worst are no worse if imagination mend them.

TITANIA: Right play at last.

OBERON: Position them so they wake in each other's arms. Quickly, my love! The play approaches.

(They do so.)

OBERON: Now! Away!

TITANIA: *(Hesitating.)* Do you truly think they will marry, Oberon? These two?

OBERON: Mortals, Titania. Poof. Who cares? *(Beat.)* Oh, all right… *(Spreads some fairy dust on them.)* If that doesn't do it, there's no hope left for New Jersey.

(They disappear. MARVIN and GLORIA groggily wake up.)

MARVIN: I have had a most rare vision—

GLORIA: I have had a dream past the wit of man to say—

(They look at each other.)

GLORIA: Marvin?

MARVIN: Gloria?

MARVIN: Gloria, thou art translated! Thou art translated!

(They embrace.)

PUCK'S VOICE: *(Offstage.)* "Up and down, up and down, I will lead them up and down. I am feared in field and town. Goblin, lead them up and down."

MARVIN: I guess it's some kind of play.

GLORIA: It feels like magic.

MARVIN: Want to stay and watch?

GLORIA: Do you?

MARVIN: I guess. If you do.

GLORIA: I do.

MARVIN: I do too. *(Notices an unopened bottle of champagne.)* Hey, somebody left champagne!

GLORIA: Who needs champagne?

(They watch the play.)

THE TALE OF ST. JUDE AND THE DONUT QUEEN

Gary Giovannetti

CHARACTERS

SUSIE: A young woman
JUDE: A young man

SETTING

Washington Square Park.

SUSIE is doing stretching exercises and reciting lines to herself. JUDE enters and sets up a camera and tripod.

JUDE: Excuse me, but can you tell me what's going on here?

SUSIE: We're doing *A Midsummer Night's Dream.*

JUDE: Well, you're going to have to stop.

SUSIE: Oh really?

JUDE: Yes. I have something very important going on right now. And I'm going to tape it.

SUSIE: Sir, there's no taping the performance.

JUDE: I'm not going to tape the performance! I'm going to tape Washy.

SUSIE: Washy?

JUDE: Don't tell me you haven't heard of Washy.

SUSIE: Sir, I'm about to go on in a few minutes. I don't mean to be rude, but can you please leave me alone?

JUDE: Washy is the beast who lives in this park.

SUSIE: Excuse me?

JUDE: Sure, it's hard to believe. I know. But I've seen him. Washy is about seven feet tall and hairy. He roams around the park when the moon is right and there's a summer breeze in the air.

SUSIE: Are you saying this Bigfoot-type thing lives in this park?

JUDE: He and Bigfoot are related.

SUSIE: Of course.

JUDE: But they really don't talk much anymore. Some falling out over a will or something.

SUSIE: You honestly believe that this beast can live in a park this small?

JUDE: Sure.

SUSIE: Then how come you seem to be the only one who knows he exists?

JUDE: Well, you have to believe in him. You have to let down your guard to see him. You have to let go of looking at the world through our nine-to-five, daily drudgery eyes. And you have to be very observant. Like me.

SUSIE: Then I'm sure you've observed that I'm busy.

JUDE: Oh. Right. The play. You should be careful. I don't know if Washy will like the fact that you're performing this play. He prefers Shakespeare's history plays.

SUSIE: Well, that's too bad. We're doing *A Midsummer Night's Dream* whether he likes it or not.

JUDE: I see. I've always thought the character of Lysander was based on me.

SUSIE: Shakespeare wrote this play hundreds of years ago!

JUDE: If he were alive, I'd sue.

SUSIE: *(Laughing.)* I don't know about Lysander, but you are some kind of character, alright.

JUDE: Hey, is anyone famous in this play?

SUSIE: Not exactly. I've done some commercials, but that's about it.

JUDE: Really?

SUSIE: Yes. I was the Donut Queen of eastern Kentucky.

JUDE: Excuse me?

SUSIE: From the time I was six years old, I've done commercials for this small chain of donut shops based in Lexington, Kentucky.

JUDE: The Donut Queen, huh?

SUSIE: For most of my life I've had this weird kind of local celebrity. I'd go to the supermarket and people would say, "Oh look! It's the Donut Queen!" That was a lot to give up to come up here.

JUDE: Well, I'm sorry you had to abdicate your throne. And I'm sorry I have to interrupt your play. But you see, Your Majesty, I have a mythical beast to tape so...

SUSIE: And I have masses to entertain, so...

JUDE: Well there's the crux of the problem right there. I am searching for an actual fantasy while you are presenting a pre-packaged one. Which is more important?

SUSIE: Easy. Mine.

JUDE: Why?

SUSIE: We're surrounded by actual fantasies everyday. Whether they're perpetrated on us by the government, religion, corporations... At least Gorilla Rep is being upfront with people and *telling* them it's a fantasy.

JUDE: But isn't there something sublime about finding something fantastical in the mundane? That's what I'm trying to do here. To find something that's extraordinary amidst all of the banality of everyday. That's what proving Washy's existence is all about.

SUSIE: That's what finding love is all about.

JUDE: Um, absolutely.

SUSIE: And that's pretty much what your life is all about, isn't it? Searching for the fantastical in everything?

JUDE: I guess so.

SUSIE: I knew it. What's your name?

JUDE: Jude.

SUSIE: Ah. Saint Jude, the Patron Saint of Hopeless Causes.

JUDE: That's me.

SUSIE: You believe in love at first sight, don't you?

JUDE: Yes.

SUSIE: And you voted for Nader, didn't you?

JUDE: Yup.

SUSIE: Mets fan?

JUDE: Guilty.

SUSIE: I know your type, Jude. You so desperately want to believe in something—anything—that will bring wonder to your life. Your whole existence is a never-ending search for something... perfect.

JUDE: You say it like we're criminals.

SUSIE: Not criminals. Just admired... and pitied.

JUDE: I see. And what's your name, Your Highness?

SUSIE: Susie.

JUDE: Susie the Donut Queen. You think I should be more practical?

SUSIE: No. Practical people need the crazy dreamers like you. We need someone to set off fireworks for us every once in a while.

JUDE: And you consider yourself practical?

SUSIE: Yes.

JUDE: In other words, after rationally and objectively researching every possible career option, you decided the most practical career for you was... acting.

(SUSIE laughs.)

JUDE: Maybe you're not as practical as you think.

SUSIE: Maybe not. But I'm not trying to tape the missing link in the middle of an urban park.

JUDE: Washy is real!

SUSIE: Of course he is.

JUDE: He's hairy, he's irascible, and he speaks in grunts and growls.

SUSIE: Sounds like Friday night at McSorley's. What does Washy eat?

JUDE: It's weird. Parking summonses.

SUSIE: Amazing. And how long has he lived here?

JUDE: Hundreds of years.

SUSIE: Come on.

JUDE: Hey, you try finding a spacious place with a yard in the West Village rent-free. Why would he ever leave?

SUSIE: Jude, it truly has been an... experience talking to you. But my scene is coming up and I'd like to be ready for it when it does.

JUDE: What part are you?

SUSIE: I'm playing Helena.

JUDE: Are you a Method Actress? Did you study for the role?

SUSIE: Yes. I want to a Grecian forest and talked to people who had love spells cast on them by fairies. *(Beat.)* I didn't study much.

JUDE: I should have assumed. You wouldn't believe in things like love spells and fairies and such.

SUSIE: Of course not. If fairies exist than how come I've never seen one?

JUDE: You're from Kentucky.

SUSIE: We should quiet down. People are starting to give us dirty looks.

JUDE: Why?

SUSIE: They want to hear the play. And so do I. That way I can hear my cue.

JUDE: Maybe this is your cue. Maybe your cue is me. Your cue to start believing in the impossible, like the people in the play. Your cue to listen to that voice inside of you.

SUSIE: What voice?

JUDE: The one that's telling you not to be afraid. The same one that told you to move to New York and pursue acting. You have doubts about whether that was the right thing to do, right?

SUSIE: How did you know?

JUDE: You wouldn't be human if you didn't. We spend most of our lives trying to talk ourselves out of doing truly amazing things.

SUSIE: Back home they don't understand why I had to do this. Why I had to come here just to try it. Just to see. They said, "You can act right here."

JUDE: But you can't be the Donut Queen forever.

SUSIE: No! It was fun for a while, but I mean, come on! You're selling jelly-filled and honey-glazed. It's not like there's a whole lot of room for character growth. And believe me, I tried to give her some depth. When they introduced crullers I tried to act as though the Donut Queen was excited, but also slightly ambivalent about these new interlopers in her empire. But that didn't play too well on-screen. Besides, that crown was starting to get a little ratty. So I moved here. I gave up my regional stardom. And now I'm doing one of the greatest theatrical comedies ever in the greatest city in the world and you know what? I don't think I want to *see* a Boston Creme again for as long as I live. *(Kisses him.)*

JUDE: See? I knew you weren't all harsh reality. But now, unfortunately, you have to tell them to stop the performance. It's about time for Washy to make an appearance. It's the second night of a full moon, it's a little past nine, and I just felt that familiar, ominous chill in the air.

SUSIE: Jude, maybe you do have a point about not always being rational and embracing the off-kilter. But there just is no beast in this park!

JUDE: Yes there is! I've seen him! And now I'm going to get proof!

SUSIE: Well, best of luck. But I just don't think—

JUDE: That's weird.

SUSIE: What is?

JUDE: That actor keeps repeating the same line over and over.

SUSIE: Yeah, well, that's my cue. *(Realizing.)* That's my cue! I have to go!

JUDE: *(Looking past SUSIE in horror.)* Wait!

SUSIE: Jude! I have to—

JUDE: Look!

(JUDE indicates the playing area. His eyes widen. SUSIE turns to look and her face suddenly changes to an expression of shock. Screams are heard.)

SUSIE: There's some seven-foot hairy

creature with parking tickets hanging out of its mouth standing behind Sean!

JUDE: Hey, Sean! Look out!

SUSIE: Sean! Behind you! He's not paying attention! He's too busy giving me a dirty look to listen to me! How unprofessional! I told them they should never cast him as Demetrius.

JUDE: Oh no! Washy's raising his paw! For God's sake, Sean! Look—

(A roar is heard and a bloody shirt flies onto the stage. SUSIE picks it up.)

SUSIE: Alas, poor Sean. I knew him, Jude.

JUDE: Poor guy. The camera!

(JUDE runs to turn on the camera. SUSIE grabs him.)

SUSIE: No! We should get out of here!

JUDE: But this is what I've been waiting for. If I can tape him—

SUSIE: Forget that! What about our safety?

JUDE: But if I prove Washy's existence the world will be a better place. Maybe people won't always succumb to the easy, surface judgment. I can force people to look deeper into things and to appreciate the unknown instead of being afraid of it.

SUSIE: Sweetie, this bit of the unknown just took off an actor's head. People *should* be afraid of it. And besides, I want you to take me out of here.

JUDE: What?

SUSIE: I want *you* to take me out of here. You said you believed in love at first sight. Maybe, just maybe, I'm starting to.

JUDE: Really?

SUSIE: You've made me see more in ten minutes than I have in my entire life.

JUDE: Wow.

SUSIE: So I'm offering you my hand.

JUDE: But the Washy footage—

SUSIE: That footage may very well prove to the world that they should believe in miracles and the unknowable. But doesn't every love story prove the exact same thing?

(JUDE stand there for a moment, considering. Finally he takes SUSIE's hand.)

JUDE: People can claim the footage was a hoax. Someone else could have taken pictures already. And besides, you're a lot better looking than Washy.

SUSIE: Let's go.

JUDE: Susie? What about "the show must go on"?

SUSIE: Oh it will go on again. Tomorrow.

(They begin walking offstage.)

JUDE: Hey, this doesn't make me the Donut King, does it?

(Blackout.)

GUERILLA GORILLA

Craig Pospisil

CHARACTERS

SANDY
ALANA
MUTTON
TINA

Washington Square Park in the near future. It is night. Shadows flicker across a park bench and some bushes as a brilliant moon shines through the leaves of the trees.

TINA, a police officer, patrols through the area. She stops, as if sensing something, but after looking over the area she continues on.

A young man and woman, SANDY and ALANA, sneak out from behind some bushes. They look about furtively.

SANDY: Come on. Please. Let's get out of here.

ALANA: No, Sandy. Look, you can go home, but I want to see Danny in this play.

SANDY: The park is dangerous. I'm not leaving you alone here.

ALANA: Well, I didn't ask you to come, or to follow me like some stray dog.

SANDY: This is illegal. We're gonna get caught.

ALANA: No, we're not. The cops don't care. It's a stupid law and they know it. Like jaywalking. No one pays attention.

SANDY: Alana, they bust people all the time for theatre-going. I read on the 'Net

that forty people got arrested in one night last summer for going to a play.

ALANA: Yeah, I read that too. But those people were asking for it. That was stupid, putting on a play in the middle of Central Park. Of course you're gonna get caught. But this group, Gorilla Rep, they move around. They're harder to spot.

SANDY: Hello?! We just missed getting spotted by that cop!

ALANA: But she *did* miss us.

SANDY: This is insane.

ALANA: It's not like it hurts anyone.

SANDY: That's not the point.

ALANA: Of course it's the point. It's stupid to outlaw something that doesn't hurt anyone. Something, in fact, that lots of people enjoy.

SANDY: No, the point is that live theatre is illegal now. It doesn't matter if the law is good or bad. You can be arrested for performing or just watching a play. And they're really serious about prosecuting people. *(Slight pause.)* And it's not like anyone needs theatre anymore. Between cable and the 'Net, people can get all the entertainment they need at home. Safe. Theatres are just places where people might get hurt.

ALANA: How?

SANDY: Lots of ways. Like... fires, or... riots.

ALANA: Riots?!

SANDY: It's happened. And any time people are in the same place there's the chance of the spread of disease, or—

ALANA: Oh, please, you can't believe that stuff! The government just made up all that nonsense because the theatre scares them. It expresses the truths about this corrupt society, and it's something they couldn't control. They tried to kill it by abolishing the NEA, but it kept going. So they passed this absurd law.

SANDY: Alana, are you listening to yourself? You sound like one of those radicals from sixty years ago, or... Oh, I am so stupid. Danny. He fed you all that, right?

ALANA: Hey, Danny's right. Theatre's dangerous to the status quo. It's political and alive. You never know what might happen.

SANDY: I know what's going to happen. We're gonna spend the night in jail.

ALANA: So go home where it's nice and safe and no one's rioting. I'm seeing Danny's play.

SANDY: He's gay, you know.

ALANA: *(Slight pause.)* What does that have to do with anything?

SANDY: It means, he's gay. He likes men. You are a woman. He's not interested in you like that.

ALANA: I just want to see a play.

SANDY: Please! You think I don't know you're in love with him?

ALANA: I am not.

SANDY: It's so obvious! You hang on his every word, and get all—

ALANA: Nobody asked for your opinion! You don't know what you're talking about.

SANDY: I know you're making an ass of yourself!

ALANA: Hey, you wanna keep it down? If you keep shouting like that, we *will* get arrested.

SANDY: I wasn't shouting.

ALANA: Oh, would you just go! You don't want to be here, and I don't want you around if you're gonna be so judgmental.

SANDY: Alana,—

(MUTTON, a scruffy-looking man, slides into the scene.)

MUTTON: Tix. Tix. I got tix. Who wants 'em?

SANDY: What?

MUTTON: Tix, man. I got tix.

SANDY: *(To ALANA.)* Ticks?

ALANA: Tickets, Sandy.

MUTTON: You guys wanna see a show?

ALANA: Yeah, what've you got?

MUTTON: Well, lemme see. I got some quality *Godot* goin' down in Tribeca, a *Streetcar* over on the Bowery, or *Midsummer Night's Dream* right here in the park.

ALANA: How much for *Midsummer*?

MUTTON: Whoo-whee. Girl likes the hot stuff.

ALANA: Yeah, yeah. How much?

MUTTON: Well, it's gonna cost you. I mean, this is high profile stuff here. And Shakespeare to boot.

ALANA: Hey, quality's worth the price.

MUTTON: Right you are. Okay. *Midsummer*'s gonna set you back thirty a tick.

ALANA: Thirty?

SANDY: You've gotta be kidding!

MUTTON: Hey, if the price is too steep, I've got other shows. I got a lead on some cheap Neil Simon in Queens.

ALANA: No, no, I want *Midsummer*.

MUTTON: You sure?

ALANA: Yeah. Two tix.

MUTTON: Okay. You hang out here. I'll go pick a couple good ones outta my stash. *(MUTTON quickly slinks away.)*

ALANA: I need twenty bucks.

SANDY: What?

ALANA: I didn't think the tix would be so much. I need twenty bucks. *(Slight pause.)* Come on, Sandy. It'll be fun. Live a little.

(SANDY digs in his pockets and gives ALANA some money.)

SANDY: Okay.

ALANA: Thanks. You'll like it. Really. It's like nothing you've ever seen on TV.

SANDY: I'm just nervous. Where'd he go? Doesn't he have the tickets on him?

ALANA: Are you kidding? They don't carry the tix around. What if he's holding and he gets busted? He'd lose the whole stash. They hide them somewhere, and they only get them out when they're making a sale. Plus if we were Theatre Narcs

and we bought a couple of tix from him, that's just a misdemeanor. He'd be back on the street in a couple of hours. But if he was holding ten, twelve tix,… that's a felony.

SANDY: Something just doesn't feel right.

ALANA: Do you want your money back? I can go alone.

SANDY: Why won't you give me a chance?

ALANA: Sandy,… I really value you as a friend, but I just can't see us as a couple. We've got really different temperaments. I mean, like, right here. I love things like this, but you'd rather be on your couch watching a video. And that's fine, but it's not for me.

(MUTTON re-enters.)

MUTTON: Okay, I got your tix. You got the money?

ALANA: Right here.

(ALANA hands the money over to MUTTON, who pockets it, smiles and pulls out a badge, which he holds up.)

MUTTON: And you are busted.

ALANA: What?

SANDY: I knew it!!

(TINA, the cop, enters, gun drawn.)

TINA: Good catch, Mutt.

ALANA: Damn it!

MUTTON: You are under arrest for breaking article five, section four, of the state penal code, attempting to witness a live theatrical event.

SANDY: Officer, please. This is a first offense. We'll never do it again, I swear. Couldn't you let us off with a warning?

ALANA: Speak for yourself! I'll do it again! The theatre is a valid form of artistic expression. It doesn't hurt anyone!

(MUTTON turns on ALANA. His anger rises steadily as he talks, and he closes in on her.)

MUTTON: The theatre doesn't hurt anyone? How fucking naïve are you?! Families all across America are torn apart by the specter of the theatre everyday. Have you ever seen first hand what the theatre can do to a family? I've looked into the eyes of parents who were crushed when their children came home one day and said, "I want to be an actor." I've seen what happens to those actors when they found they couldn't make a living and turned to prostitution or waiting tables. Eventually they're forced to give up and become teachers. They fall into a depression and need years of psychotherapy. You think about the thousands of people whose lives have been destroyed by the dream of "the theatre!" And then you try to tell me that theatre is a victimless crime!!

(TINA takes hold of MUTTON's arm and pulls him back.)

TINA: Mutton, hey, take it easy. She's young.

MUTTON: Yeah, I know, I know. It just makes me crazy. I can't help thinking what fools these people are.

TINA: Well, they'll have some time to think about it in jail. You keep 'em here. I'll bring the van around.

(TINA exits. MUTTON takes out a pair of handcuffs and approaches ALANA.)

MUTTON: Turn around. Hands behind your back.

(SANDY suddenly pulls a small canister of pepper spray from his pocket and sprays MUTTON in the face. MUTTON immediately recoils, screaming in pain and holding his hands over his eyes.)

MUTTON: Aahh!!!

SANDY: Run!!

(SANDY grabs ALANA and pulls her back into the bushes. TINA races back in, gun drawn. MUTTON squints through his tears, looking in all directions.)

TINA: Mutton! You okay?

MUTTON: I will be. When I kick that guy's ass. Did you see which way they went?

TINA: That way, I think.

(TINA and MUTTON run off. After a moment, SANDY and ALANA emerge from the bushes.)

ALANA: Wow. That was… you were incredible.

SANDY: I couldn't let him arrest you.

ALANA: What were you doing with that pepper spray?

SANDY: I told you this park was dangerous. I never go outside without it.

ALANA: I just never thought you'd… that you would do something so dangerous. You're always so practical, reasonable.

SANDY: Well,… reason and love don't always mix.

ALANA: Yeah. *(Slight pause.)* I guess we should get out of here. Wanna go home and watch some TV?

SANDY: Hell, no. I've never felt so alive. Let's find that play!

(They run off, holding hands. Blackout.)

A MIDLIFE'S DREAM

Matthew Ethan Davis

CHARACTERS

OLIVIA
LIV
RICHARD
RICH

NOTE

This play is about a couple, RICH and LIV, in their mid-thirties, struggling to save their love, inspired by the memory of who they used to be, in their early twenties, as RICHARD and OLIVIA.

SETTING

Washington Square Park, night. Gorilla Repertory Company is performing *A Midsummer Night's Dream*.

TIME

The present.

Enter LIV. Enter OLIVIA. LIV looks at OLIVIA, remembering who she used to be. Enter RICHARD.

RICHARD: My love.

OLIVIA: My love.

RICHARD: The night…

OLIVIA: The night has flown away. The night…

RICHARD: Has lost its dream…

OLIVIA: Flown into the past…

RICHARD: Woken by your beauty…

OLIVIA: To long for a future…

RICHARD: Like a thousand moons, bursting into a starless night…

OLIVIA: Enveloping you. A night cloak, around your shoulders, galaxies dancing on the shoulders of my…

RICHARD: The darkest night, brightened by the hope of caressing…

OLIVIA: On the shoulders of my…

RICHARD: For eternity, you, my heart, my…

(Enter RICH.)

OLIVIA: Love.

RICHARD: Love.

OLIVIA: My love.

RICHARD: My love.

OLIVIA: They're running through forests of Shakespeare's loves.

RICHARD: It's a tribute. He. All is a tribute. To you.

RICH: *A Midsummer Night's Dream.* Again?

LIV: It's free. And remember...

RICH: If I'm not working, it's costing. Remember?

OLIVIA: It's a path, trodden barefoot into the poetry of your eyes. You wore the tie. My favorite tie.

RICHARD: It was a gift. Our first night.

OLIVIA: It spoke of your eyes.

RICHARD: You bought me a tie.

OLIVIA: So magic would follow you into the office.

RICHARD: Thoughts of you, permeate, like air, filling anyplace, any, everywhere.

LIV: And this is where you proposed to me. I thought it might be romantic.

RICH: It's free. Anyway.

LIV: Silly me.

RICH: You forgot.

LIV: Me?

OLIVIA: It arrived.

RICHARD: The news?

OLIVIA: The decision.

RICHARD: I'm here. No matter what.

OLIVIA: I'm in.

RICHARD: You're in.

OLIVIA: I don't have the money.

RICHARD: We'll find the money.

RICH: You forgot about...

LIV: The language. I thought... Imagine. Forget it. Shit. Forgot what? The play? The... ?

RICH: The meeting.

LIV: What meeting?

OLIVIA: We? We'll find the money? We?

RICHARD: It's a degree...

OLIVIA: I have a degree. I don't need another.

RICHARD: A degree of perspective. You don't have the money. Add me. We. We don't have the money. Two. More than one. More chance to find the money.

OLIVIA: You're proposing.

RICHARD: I'm proposing.

OLIVIA: To Shakespeare.

RICHARD: To you, actually.

RICH: What do you mean, what meeting? With the advisor. The financial advisor. I remembered. I remember. I remember all the time.

LIV: What good is going to some financial advisor going to do us? What is he going to tell us that we don't already know?

RICH: It's the middle...

LIV: That all the deferred loans are just building interest, recapitalizing every day...

RICH: We could try...

LIV: That no matter how much we pay out...

RICH: We could try to find…

LIV: It's not enough, we're completely deprived, our lives stolen right out from under us…

RICH: To find a way…

LIV: Because of all the goddamned debt repayments…

RICH: A way out.

LIV: For all the goddamned school loans and it's still not enough.

RICH: It's the middle of our lives…

LIV: The goddamned debt is growing right through the ground, tangling our every step, every day, as we walk, as we breath, as we try to soak up the sky…

RICH: It's the middle of our lives. Not the end.

OLIVIA: The cost. It's…

RICHARD: I'll borrow. I'll take out loans. Mortgage my future. I'll see you through.

OLIVIA: I don't…

RICHARD: Leave it to me. I'll handle it. I swear.

OLIVIA: But I…

RICHARD: I swear.

OLIVIA: Can you… ?

RICHARD: I swear.

OLIVIA: You do?

RICHARD: I do.

OLIVIA: I do.

LIV: You don't even touch me anymore. It's as if I'm another bill we can't pay that you just can't bring yourself to open. Happy marriage. Married to debt. I want out. I feel like a walking billboard everywhere I go, "I've Lost My Life. Brother can you spare $80,000."

RICH: Out of our marriage?

LIV: Out of my life. Whatever it takes.

RICH: If we had met with the advisor…

LIV: Fuck the advisor.

RICH: If we had met with him…

OLIVIA: Suddenly the future is sun-clouds of hope flying over a horizon.

RICHARD: You are my hope. You are my horizon.

LIV: Then, what? There would be hope? Or maybe he would tell me I should just go to a therapist who could put me on medication, or a spiritualist, who could tell me that if I was really connected to God and the reality of the universe trillions of years before man's footsteps ever imprinted the beaches, that all our debts would float into a context that would no longer unravel our lives?

RICH: That is an idea.

LIV: I've tried it. I closed my eyes and saw translucent angels forming from celestial embryos. I opened my eyes and I saw…

RICH: Me?

LIV: Our life. Surely, you of all people, I don't have to explain what that means.

OLIVIA: What does it mean?

RICHARD: Bonding our love? Our lives?

OLIVIA: What does it mean?

RICHARD: It means all meaning suddenly has new meaning.

RICH: I don't know what good it would do. Going to the advisor. I thought we'd try. I thought we'd try to save ourselves. I thought if we just showed up, if we hoped. I dressed up. I shined my shoes. I wore a tie. To try to overcome that dread that backs up my bloodstream. I was hoping to attract...

LIV: My eye?

RICH: Someone.

LIV: I'm someone.

RICH: Waiting. To see him. The advisor. I felt such a need. To be held...

RICHARD: Hold me.

LIV: By me?

RICHARD: Hold me.

RICH: Anyone but. It was as if everything in me cried out to be touched, to be held, to be held by someone who didn't know me. Know what we owe. What I dread. Someone who would only see... what they saw... not what you know.

LIV: Are you fucking someone?

RICH: No.

LIV: Do you want to?

RICH: All the time.

LIV: Then why don't you just get it the hell over with?

RICH: I tried.

LIV: I don't want to hear this.

RICH: I followed her home. Someone. An anyone. Someone I didn't know. I went to her apartment. All fragrances and seduction. She said anything I wanted, was mine. Any desire. Any fetish. Anything

but my name. I stood there, trembling in the center of my life.

LIV: It must have been fantastic.

RICH: It was like falling a thousand years down a canyon of loneliness. One touch. One kiss and everything I held sacred in my heart would have been knocked right out of its senses. You don't want me to tell you this?

LIV: I don't want you to tell me this.

RICH: You want to take back our promise of for better or for worse?

LIV: This is not what I bargained for when I married you.

RICH: Then what the hell did you bargain for?

LIV: I bargained for you.

RICH: This is me.

OLIVIA: This is the beginning.

RICHARD: The beginning.

LIV: Not like in the beginning.

RICH: The beginning.

OLIVIA: You'll take out loans?

RICHARD: Borrow. Charge. Whatever it takes.

OLIVIA: This is...

RICHARD: The beginning.

LIV: I bargained to have you. Not to cling desperately to you against the ferocious wind of your fantasies of other women, clinging for dear life out of desperation that if I let go for just a moment, that if my grasp loosens for even a thought, you will fly away in the storm of your obsessions. I can't live like this.

RICH: You think I can?

LIV: The middle of my life is not going to be this. Terrified of the next moment. Terrified of glancing away. Terrified of exhaling too fast. I won't.

RICH: You think I can?

LIV: If you're scared of losing me. You have. There. I'm lost. I'm gone. You're free. Run to her. Run to anyone. Give in to your compulsions. I'm no longer standing in your way. Run. Start the race. Go on. Build up a sweat. Exhaust yourself.

RICH: I'm exhausted already.

LIV: From wanting out?

RICH: From wanting you back.

LIV: I can't give you myself back. I'm lost.

RICH: Then take my hand.

LIV: It owes too much money.

RICH: Take my hand.

OLIVIA: In the end, who will we become?

RICHARD: Who we were in the beginning.

LIV: It's the middle of my life. If I run. If I just run away from you. Maybe I'll still be able to have a life. Only, I can't. When I breathe, when my heart moves, it's you, curled up inside me.

RICH: You were supposed to be there. I waited in that waiting room, waiting for you. I couldn't go in there without you. You have the figures. You know the numbers. You know the percentages. You know the interest rates. You know what we've transferred where to pay off what we borrowed to finance to untangle. I sat there. In the office.

LIV: All the time, you. Despite every-

thing. Despite myself. I can't stop my love for you. It overwhelms me.

RICH: In the office waiting room. Waiting for you. Like this. My shoes shined. My tie tied. And my insides falling like stones over a waterfall, crashing into rapids of panic and I couldn't move.

LIV: It's the middle...

RICH: My blood stopped. Finally backed all the way up. I couldn't stand up. I couldn't see. Without you in the room... Without you. There was no sense. Only darkness. For hours. For years. For lifetimes.

LIV: It's the middle of our lives...

OLIVIA: Our beginning.

RICH: Black. All around. Trembling for your hand, the touch of your hand. When all meaning rushes back in. I had to be here. Next to you, in the middle of my life, reverence staggering me when I least expect it.

RICHARD: Our beginning.

LIV: Not the end.

RICH: Even if it all is, is the waiting room, waiting for us, waiting for me, waiting for me patiently, eternally, if your hand is in mine, I can breath.

RICHARD: Take my hand.

LIV: Not the end.

RICH: Not the end.

OLIVIA: My love.

LIV: My love.

RICHARD: My love.

RICH: My love.

(RICH and LIV take each other's hands, as the lights fade to black.)

AMERICAN EYES

Jeni Mahoney

CHARACTERS

MAKA: Woman, twenties—speaks a few words of English.

SOSO: Man, thirties—speaks some broken English. A bore. He laughs like a donkey.

OBERON: Actor in *A Midsummer Night's Dream*, very sweaty. A fun guy.

EDITH: Thirties, interpreter. Bit of a geek. Also has an odd laugh.

VOICE OF BOTTOM: Performed by the same actor who plays OBERON.

NOTES

SOSO and MAKA speak a somewhat improvised foreign language (based loosely on Kartuli spoken in the Georgian Republic of the USSR—though the characters are not intended to be specificially Georgian—the important thing is that this is a language and not just random nonsense). EDITH interprets MAKA and SOSO's date for the audience with the help of a SOSO puppet and a MAKA puppet to signify who is talking. We only hear snatches of SOSO's and MAKA's dialogue because EDITH interprets quickly. EDITH is a professional—efficient and proud of her puppets and her work.

The park. EDITH enters, finds her designated spot and stands—ready to translate. Enter SOSO and MAKA on a first date. MAKA, eyes a-wonder, takes in the park. SOSO tries to impress MAKA, who isn't listening.

SOSO: Da parkshi olipari gargi da tsude—

(SOSO continues—we do not hear him.)

EDITH: *(Reveals the SOSO puppet from behind her back and bounces it as she translates in a "SOSO puppet voice.")* In the park you see all that is good and bad in America!

MAKA: *(In awe.)* Bicho, olipari zalian tevsi!

EDITH: *(Revealing the MAKA puppet, and using her "MAKA puppet voice.")* It is so colorful!

SOSO: Kho, kho, Damanjerri mesmis—

EDITH: *(As SOSO puppet.)* Yes, yes, believe me, I understand everything. You will find that America is very exciting.

(As MAKA puppet.) I am talking about the people. *They* are so many colors.

(As SOSO puppet.) Americans mix people as an artist mixes paint. But I am not interested in such mixing. You see, to become American is not in the skin or blood. The trick is in the eyes.

(SOSO searches for American eyes. He spots EDITH, who feels the glance and returns the look, uncomfortable with the attention. SOSO grabs EDITH and presents her to MAKA.)

SOSO: Ah-ha! Englishsuri—huh?

EDITH: *(As SOSO puppet, recovers and moves back to her space. The SOSO puppet points at EDITH.)* American. You can tell, right? But newcomers…

(SOSO searches the crowd with his finger, eventually his fingers lands on MAKA.)

EDITH: *(As SOSO puppet.)* …have eyes full of wonder. Americans do not see things so wonderful—like you.

(EDITH is disheartened by this suggestion. SOSO brushes his hand on MAKA's cheek.)

MAKA: *(Quickly changing the subject, she points in the distance. Trans: What's that?)* Rari?

SOSO: Ah, sabakabi—

EDITH: *(As SOSO puppet.)* It is a playground. For dogs! It is the most interesting thing—Americans keep dogs in their houses like a member of the family! They even have special food so as not to give the dog scraps, which would be an insult. Americans eat their own stinky leftovers.

SOSO: *(Laughs at this thought, a bizarre donkey laugh. Then turns suddenly serious.)* Damanjerri, gak bevri Englishsuri—

EDITH: *(As SOSO puppet.)* Believe me, I know these Americans… assholes. I have studied them so well that sometimes… sometimes I can have eyes like an American.

(SOSO does American eyes for MAKA. EDITH tries to see from her spot.)

SOSO: Vitsi?

(Trans: Do you see? MAKA studies him, then nods unimpressed.)

SOSO: Da kheme gak—

EDITH: *(As SOSO puppet.)* I have perfected American eyes. I have washed away the wonder and I am ready to work. I understand everything.

(SOSO puts an arm around MAKA.)

EDITH: Relax. We are having fun.

MAKA: To ar ginda…

EDITH: *(As MAKA puppet.)* But I am not ready to wash the wonder from my eyes. I am looking at these American eyes—

MAKA: *(Indicating EDITH's eyes, then SOSO's.)* Zan tsude chemehar.

EDITH: *(As MAKA puppet.)* —and I am sad. I don't want to *understand* everything. I want to *see* everything! I cannot believe all Americans have such old, dead eyes.

SOSO: *(Laughs his donkey laugh and pulls away shocked.)* Rari, ra ginda—ragori—

EDITH: *(As SOSO puppet.)* What? What are you thinking? Listen, I am smart, level-headed guy…

(Speaks directly to SOSO.) … ar ginda gargi didi bicho… *(Meaning: she doesn't want a boring guy.)*

SOSO: You want some excitement maybe too? *(Tries to look exciting.)* ahhhhh—to… cheme zalian tsuede… balashi… "coyote"—

EDITH: *(As SOSO puppet.)* But I am exciting also—adventurous like…

SOSO: Gizi Englisuri stuga.

EDITH: *(As SOSO puppet.)* Crazy American dog.

(SOSO makes a playful growling face. MAKA laughs, pleased with the results. SOSO shushes her. He makes a production of returning to his American eyes, MAKA is displeased. SOSO notes chess players in the distance—further proof of his personality.)

EDITH: *(As SOSO puppet.)* And look, there—playing chess? I am expert chess player. I am there all the time kicking people's ass. See these pants? I won thirty-six dollars yesterday and then I went to Gap and bought these pants—for you—for 32.99 plus 8% sales tax—that is 36.34—so I am even paying an extra 34 cents for you.

(As MAKA puppet.) Enough about your pants and your American eyes!

(SOSO agrees with a shrug.)

EDITH: *(To audience.)* He is so patient!

(As MAKA puppet.) —there is so much to see—like this guy—

(SOSO signals to MAKA that he is a drunk.)

EDITH: *(As MAKA puppet.)* —and this statue—who is he? And the lights! All those people... ? Flashlights? Is it dancing!?

(EDITH and SOSO look.)

EDITH: *(As SOSO puppet.)* Ah-ha! You are a lover of Theatre!

SOSO: Zan gargi Englisuri, Shakespeare—

EDITH: *(As SOSO puppet.)* the great... American... ? writer Shakespeare— *(Shrugs apologetically to audience.)* They say nothing is free in America—pay to come over the bridge, to park on the street, no-body gives you anything for free—except words. Words are always free—

(MAKA pulls SOSO toward the show; EDITH follows, at a safe distance. They watch for a few moments. MAKA points to actors in the distance.)

EDITH: *(As MAKA puppet.)* These are not having "American" eyes—look!

(As SOSO puppet.) They are actors, it is part of their performance.

(MAKA is enraptured, SOSO tries to be very serious. BOTTOM can be heard offstage.)

VOICE OF BOTTOM: *(Offstage.)* Methinks I have a great desire to a bottle of hay: good hay, sweet hay hath no fellow.

EDITH: *(As SOSO puppet, as SOSO whispers to MAKA.)* It's very serious stuff, Shakespeare, very great thinker.

(SOSO clearly has no idea what is being said, but listens and nods thoughtfully.)

VOICE OF BOTTOM: *(Offstage.)* I had rather have a handful or two of dried peas. But I pray you—

EDITH: *(As SOSO puppet, as SOSO whispers to MAKA.)* Such words are not easy to translate. It's like very old style English...

(MAKA looks to him eagerly for his translation.)

EDITH: *(As SOSO puppet.)* It is like about this woman and a... her donkey. They are... fighting this great enemy.

(As MAKA puppet.) Her donkey is falling to sleep.

(As SOSO puppet.) She is wanting him to rest before battle so he is strong.

(OBERON enters energetically and addresses SOSO familiarly, using him as a prop. SOSO responds with what he thinks is appropriate silent seriousness. MAKA waits intently for SOSO's translations.)

OBERON: "See'st thou this sweet sight?
Her dotage now I do begin to pity:
For meeting her of late behind the wood,
Seeking sweet savors for this hateful fool,
I did upbraid her, and fall out with her:"

EDITH: *(As SOSO puppet.)* He is saying he will kick this donkey's ass.

OBERON: "For she his hairy temples then had rounded
With coronet of fresh and fragrant flowers;
And that same dew which sometime on the buds
Was wont to swell,"

(SOSO suddenly seems to understand. EDITH translates his exciting revelation.)

EDITH: *(As SOSO puppet.)* Ah, Buds! He is wanting to have drinks with me later.

OBERON: "—like round and orient pearls, Stood now within the pretty flowerets' eyes,"

EDITH: *(As SOSO puppet.)* It is my eyes! He can see I am like American guy.

OBERON: Like tears that did their own disgrace bewail.

OBERON: "When I had, at my pleasure taunted her,
And she, in mild terms, had begged my patience."

(OBERON touches SOSO, who is offended.)

SOSO: Hey!

(OBERON pulls away from SOSO for a moment, speaking the next few lines to others.)

OBERON: Fucking sweaty piece of shit!

MAKA: Ra? *(Trans: What?)*

SOSO: Didi bicho de'damutwa, damanjerri to shene—!

EDITH: *(As SOSO puppet, doesn't want to translate, but tries.)* Um... gee. This guy? is... annoying?... person... um, maybe a homosexual person who is trying to make a... date... at... for me...

OBERON: *(Having returned to use SOSO as an example of a transformed scalp. But when he reaches his hand up SOSO swats it angrily away.)* "And gentle Puck, take this transformed scalp
From off the head of this Athenian swain:"

(SOSO grabs OBERON roughly. Oberon pulls his hands back quickly, trying to difuse the situation. SOSO doesn't let go.)

SOSO: I am not your girlfriend—!

(EDITH and MAKA try to pull SOSO away as OBERON tries to continue with his lines.)

MAKA: Soso! Ragari! *(Trans: Soso! What are you doing!)*

OBERON: "That he awaking when the other do,
May all to Athens repair;"

(OBERON is finally free, MAKA and EDITH hold SOSO.)

OBERON: "And think no more of this night's accidents,"

(SOSO attempts to break free and attack OBERON—he thinks he is being taunted. OBERON splashes SOSO in the face with "magic potion" and dashes offstage on his next line.)

OBERON: "But as a fierce vexation of a dream!"

(SOSO turns away covering his eyes. EDITH and MAKA, concerned, hover close. When SOSO looks up, it is EDITH he first sees.)

SOSO: Oh my God...

EDITH: Are you okay?

SOSO: You... you... are too beautiful

(EDITH looks for whom he might be referring to.)

EDITH: Maybe you should sit down.

SOSO: *(Grasping EDITH's puppeted hands with joy.)* And these dollies... on your hands... I lof these dollies.

EDITH: *(Flattered.)* You do?

(SOSO kisses the puppets.)

EDITH: They were my idea. I made them myself.

SOSO: You are remarkable voman.

EDITH: You don't think my eyes are too... American...?

SOSO: *(Looking deeply in her eyes.)* In your eyes I see... only... me.

EDITH: Really?!?

SOSO: I will buy you dinner. NO! It's not enough... champagne! NO! Peanut butter, soyburger dinner, whatever you like. You must let me or my heart will burst!

EDITH: Well, okay, if you think it will help...

(EDITH looks to MAKA who is relieved to free.)

MAKA: Sheme gak bicho sululi. *(Trans.: You take the nutcase.)*

EDITH: *(To audience.)* She says he's all mine!

(SOSO and EDITH exit.)

MAKA: *(To audience.)* Not. Exact. Translation. *(Watches the play.)*

OBERON: *(Returns, he is out of character.)* Listen, I'm sorry about... before... I—

MAKA: *(Struggling with the little English she has.)* Problem, no. Is... geezee... how you say? *(Makes the ears and sounds of a donkey.)*

OBERON: Asshole.

MAKA: Yes. Kho. *(Thinking she has learned the word donkey.)* Asshole. So... asshole goodbye.

OBERON: Good for you. You okay?

MAKA: Kho. I like much... this everyting.

OBERON: *(Holding out his hand.)* Well come on then, maybe I can make it up to you.

MAKA: Ra?

OBERON: I show you... everything.

MAKA: Everyting?

OBERON: Everything.

MAKA: *(Looks into his eyes.)* Good eyes. Wery much vonder.

OBERON: Thanks. I like your eyes too.

(She hesitates, though only for a moment, before grasping his hand firmly. They run off.)

Fate

Elizabeth Horsburgh

ELIZABETH HORSBURGH received a BFA in theatre from the Tisch School of the Arts in 1992 where she studied with The Atlantic Theatre Company. Her first play, *Escape Artists*, was produced by Monsterless Actors (Jennifer Costello and Micah Hollingworth, Artistic Directors/Producers) at the Sanford Meisner Theatre in 1996. *Ice Age* was produced by Theatrix (Helena Webb, Artistic Director/Producer) at The Kraine in 1997, and *Beautiful* was also produced by Theatrix at The Trilogy Theatre in 1998. Screaming Venus (Monica Sirignano, Artistic Director/Producer) produced a reading of *Under the Mosquito Net* at the Flatiron Theatre in 1999, and Reverie Productions (Colin Young, Artistic Director, Nina Waluschka, Producer) produced a reading of *Mommy and Daddy Are Doing Dirty Things* in the fall of 2000. Horsburgh is currently writing a new full-length play entitled *Big Bang*.

Fate was first produced by Screaming Venus (Monica Sirignano, Artistic Director) as part of its festival of one-act plays, *Kallisti*, on March 1, 2000, at the Camera Obscura Theatre, New York City, with the following cast and credits:

WOMAN .... Erin Walls
MAN .... Mick Hilgers

Directed by: Jan E. Murphy
Set design by: Daniel Jagendorf
Lighting design by: Elizabeth Greenman

Fate was subsequently produced at the New Georges Perform-A-Thon in the summer of 2000 and at the Manhattan Theatre Source Estrogenious 2000 festival in the fall of 2000. Both productions were directed by Jan E. Murphy and featured Erin Walls; Mick Hilgers appeared in the former production, and Ed Lane in the latter.

INTRODUCTORY NOTES

Although the audience never discovers the writer of the letter, the actors can make the decision themselves and the possibilities are infinite. When *Fate* was produced by Screaming Venus, the WOMAN started the scene by writing the letter on stage. I think it works better when the audience doesn't actually know who the writer is, but it was very effective for the actor to make that specific choice. The actors can also switch parts and have the MAN approach the WOMAN. In that case, the pronouns would need to be changed, and the last line, "You tramp," could be "You bastard" or "You beast." I personally like "You brute."

CHARACTERS

WOMAN
MAN

At rise: A busy street in New York City.

A WOMAN enters from stage left and sees a piece of paper on the ground. She stops and reads it for a few beats. A MAN enters from stage right, holding a roll of toilet paper.

WOMAN: Excuse me. By any chance, is this your letter?

(WOMAN shows him the letter.)

MAN: No.

(He tries to walk past her, but she stops him.)

WOMAN: I don't mean to bother you but are you sure this isn't yours? Don't worry, you don't have to be embarrassed.

MAN: It's not. Excuse me.

WOMAN: This letter isn't yours?

MAN: No. I have no idea what you're talking about.

WOMAN: *(Sadly.)* Oh. I apologize.

(MAN starts to walk away.)

WOMAN: I could have bet my life that it was. Oh, well…

(MAN stops and looks at WOMAN who pitifully reads the letter. He walks back.)

MAN: Can I see it?

(She nods, hands it to him, and he reads.)

MAN: That's… beautiful.

WOMAN: Isn't it?

MAN: The poor woman…

WOMAN: Woman? It was written by a man.

MAN: Are you sure?

WOMAN: I would say it's pretty masculine handwriting. All those strong lines…

MAN: But look at all those curves and squigglies and the language is so poetic… Well, whoever wrote it, it's so eloquent, and touching and tragic. A work of art. Can I read it again?

WOMAN: Sure. I read it a few times myself. I like the part that says he's not his one and only's one and only... *(Falters.)* Or something like that.

MAN: Here it is. Oh, how horrible. I just love it. It makes me want to die. *(Pause.)* Why did you think this was my letter?

WOMAN: I just knew.

(MAN stares at WOMAN in amazement.)

MAN: *(Whispering.)* Where did you find it?

WOMAN: Right outside that deli you just came from. I knew it must have been dropped only a few minutes ago 'cause no one had stepped on it and then I saw you go into the deli and something told me it was you.

MAN: Oh. That's so cool. I wish I did write it. Too bad.

(They smile at each other, nervously.)

WOMAN: It still is pretty cool. I, after all, did find the letter and I could have thought it belonged to someone else but I didn't. It was you.

MAN: *(Caught up.)* Sure. Okay.

WOMAN: And anyway, maybe the woman he gave it to...

MAN: Or the man she gave it to...

WOMAN: Yeah. Maybe he or she dropped it, threw it out even, and the writer of the letter never even walked down this street.

MAN: Oh, of course. The writer wouldn't have thrown it out. You were looking for the wrong person. If you took the trouble to write a letter like that, you wouldn't just drop it.

WOMAN: And judging from the sorrow and the passion this letter exudes, we can assume that the receiver didn't appreciate the tender emotions and sensitivity of the writer.

(They both look at the letter again and then back at each other.)

MAN: No... It's terrible.

WOMAN: A crime. A calamity. A catastrophe. A cacophony. No, not a cacophony.

MAN: The poor, poor... person. I just wish I could meet her, if it's a her. She's probably feeling lonely somewhere and I could make her feel better. I write poetry and I could show her some of my poems and I bet she writes poems, too, so she could show me some of hers and we'd bond for hours.

WOMAN: I write poetry.

MAN: You do? I'd love to see some. I really hope that wherever this person is that they meet someone who can appreciate their expressiveness and deep emotion and give them what they deserve.

WOMAN: I hope that wherever and whoever this person is that he or she will meet someone soon who will fill the hole this ungrateful and obviously blind person who rejected him or her left and he or she can unleash all their unbridled passion and lust to this new person.

MAN: I'm sure it wouldn't be too difficult for him or her to find another person who shares their excitement and desire and he or she can write more letters filled with joy and rapture and true love.

WOMAN: And really good sex.

MAN: That goes without saying.

WOMAN: I have a feeling this person will.

MAN: I know they will. And very soon.

WOMAN: Very soon. *(Beat.)* I'd love to see some of your poetry.

MAN: I have some from my last relationship. It was so sad. She was in London and I was here and it was such a drag but I wrote her all these poems about how lonely I was. And not just little short ones, either, but pages and pages of misery and heartache. It would be very courageous and intimate for me to show them to you.

WOMAN: I feel honored. I have a few of my poems memorized. I like to say them in my head at certain times of the day to inspire or revive me, kind of like a cup of hazelnut coffee. Or vanilla. Sometimes amaretto.

MAN: How fascinating.

WOMAN: Yes, it is. It would truly be a unique and powerful experience to share some of my most private poems with you.

MAN: I'm intrigued.

WOMAN: Most of them are about my last love. He broke my heart in a million places and then just as I glued them back together he came along and broke my heart again. You would think I would have learned after that but, "oh, no." After I had healed and moved on he swept me off my feet and then dumped me even worse than the first time. I have quite a lot of really exceptional poems as a result. I also have an ulcer.

MAN: How awful and painful and miserable and dreadful for you. But doesn't it make you feel ALIVE?

WOMAN: Oh, yes. I'm burning for him. Well, I'm pretty much over him but still burning a little. If he came to me now with renewed promises I'd take him back. Sure. Why not?

MAN: Of course you would! You LOVE him! Love is a powerful wind. It blows us one way and then the other.

WOMAN: Love is a hurricane! A cyclone! A tempest.

MAN: That's nice. You should make that the title of your next poem. "Love Is a Hurricane." I just got shivers.

WOMAN: Me, too.

MAN: I love getting shivers.

WOMAN: Me, too.

MAN: My latest girlfriend is such a disappointment. She seemed so exciting and romantic at first. She sent me roses and left little notes under my pillow and called me just to say, "I love you." All that good stuff. But now after one year no fights, no cold shoulders, no mysterious mood swings or disappearances. I'm bored to death. No room to wonder. No time to doubt. She's never mean to me. I can't remember even one time I ever wondered if she loved me. And I haven't written a new poem since we met. She's the cause of my creative undoing. My artistic drought.

WOMAN: The woman's a fool.

MAN: She's insane.

WOMAN: So, she leaves you no choice but to... *(Does something suggestive.)* spice it up yourself.

MAN: I've tried everything. Had several affairs. One with her best friend. Several with my ex's.

WOMAN: Oh, sure, the ex's. I know all about that.

MAN: I ignored her for a week, said things that hurt her, you know, hit below the belt, made fun of her mother, flirted with her boss, oh, and humiliated her in front of her friends, countless times.

WOMAN: She wouldn't know love if it bit her in the ass.

MAN: So, now you understand where I'm coming from. I need to be loved. I'm lonely for it. I must weep now.

(MAN tries to cry and then successfully wails. He tears at the toilet paper and wipes his nose. He puts his head on her shoulder, and she moves it to her chest.)

WOMAN: There, there. Oh, yes, there.

MAN: Nobody understands me but you. You're all I have in the whole world.

WOMAN: We must cling to the only love we've ever known. Or we shall drown in the sorrows of… of reality.

MAN: Oh, that's so good. Remember that.

WOMAN: I'll write it down. *(Takes out a small notebook and writes in it.)* I keep this notebook handy in order to preserve the momentary thoughts that I might want to review later. Very handy.

MAN: Don't ignore me!

WOMAN: Oh, forgive me!

(WOMAN embraces him wildly.)

MAN: I feel like I've known you all my life.

WOMAN: I know exactly what you mean.

MAN: I know you do.

WOMAN: I know you do, too.

MAN: I know you do, too.

WOMAN: And I know you do, too, as well.

MAN: Me too. Oh! I want to write you a love letter right now. I feel the words about to flow out of me and I must get them down.

WOMAN: Here's my notebook!

MAN: No! I must be at home next to my candles and incense. Come quick! To my abode! I'll write you one and then you'll write me and then we'll vow to never see each other again!

WOMAN: I'll read your letter every day and wonder where you are.

MAN: And I'll burn yours one night when I miss you too much to bear.

WOMAN: I'll see you in every man's face. Drink myself silly alone in my room. Try and feel the same way about every man I'm with and then one day…

MAN: One day you'll realize the pain is gone.

WOMAN: And I'll miss it. It had become so familiar. Like a part of me.

MAN: You know, I feel like I did write that letter. I wrote it to you and this is our last night together.

WOMAN: I knew you were him. I sensed it. In my soul.

MAN: *(Realizing.)* My God, you've been terrible to me. You dreadful, cruel woman! Love me!

(She pauses, enjoying it.)

WOMAN: Maybe.

MAN: We were made for each other. We complete each other. Make love to me. Here. On the street. In the cold. I don't care. I have nothing else.

WOMAN: Yes, on the street, in the dirt and the muck and the slime and the filth and how romantic, how disgusting, you're a pig, I adore you…

MAN: You tramp! I hate you!

(They kiss passionately and fall onto the street as lights fade to black.)

Velvet Ropes

Joshua Scher

JOSHUA SCHER was born and raised in Washington, D.C. He attended college at Brown University, where he received his BA in English literature with honors in creative writing. He first began his playwriting career while at Brown, under the tutelage of playwright Paula Vogel, and has subsequently worked under numerous other writers including Mac Wellman and Eric Overmeyer. Upon graduating, Scher immediately matriculated in the Yale School of Drama, where he is currently finishing up his last year in the MFA playwriting program. The Drama School has produced three of his works, *IS*, *felling giants*, and *Lullabye*. His plays have received productions and readings in New York City as well as in and around New England. For the past two years, Scher has also participated as a writer, actor, and mentor in the New Haven chapter of the 52nd Street Project. After attaining his MFA, Scher plans to move to New York and live and work in his duplex cardboard box in a condemned alley in Brooklyn.

Velvet Ropes was first produced by The Hangar Theatre (Mark Ramont, Artistic Director) on August 6, 1999, in Ithaca, New York, with the following cast and credits:

Everyone .... Brian Silaman
Everybody .... Keith Powell
Individual with Museum Headphones .... Brian Croty

Directed by: Matt August

The New York premiere of *Velvet Ropes* was on August 18, 2000, produced by The Drama League as part of the 2000 New York International Fringe Festival (John Clancy, Artistic Director; Elena K. Holy, Producing Director), with the following cast and credits:

Everyone .... Royden Mills
Everybody .... Jonathan Uffelman
Individual with Museum Headphones .... Doug Lockwood
The Museum.... Richard Kass, Allegra Libonatti, Doug Lockwood

Directed by: Matt August
Set designed by: Jill Beckman and Matt August
Sound by: Matt Urban
Costumes by: Matthew Schworer
Lightning by: Gwen Grossman
Stage Manager: Matt Urban
Publicity: David Gersten

AUTHOR'S NOTE

The most important element to grasp about *Velvet Ropes* is that it is indeed a comedy, one of vaudevillian proportions. I emphasize this only out of my sympathy for bad *Godot* productions all over that tend to forgo any semblance of the humor inherent in the text.

The real trick to this piece lies within specificity and ambiguity. The two are most definitely not mutually exclusive and exhaustive. The specificity is most obvious within the stage directions that describe moments such as "Proper art-observing posture" or "He begins. Stops. Begins again. Stops. Reconsiders. Etc." The importance of these descriptions is not the lengthening of time (indeed one could really make this play drag out ad nauseum), but rather to locate, lock down, and repeat a specific set of gestures immediately recognizable to all. It is a game. This attention to detail also comes in handy with the numerous scene breaks. Again it is an opportunity to designate and repeat within the same aesthetic. For instance, in both productions that I worked on, ragtime music was utilized not only as a transitional device, but also to tap into and bring out the aforementioned vaudevillian effect. This was a wondrous solution, and I suggest to all who produce this work to explore a musical score for the work.

In tandem with these gestural ideas is the theme of ambiguity centered around the inquiry as to what is and what is not real art in this world. A production is not responsible for clearing up these questions, but rather should delight in simply translating this ambiguity off the page and onto the stage.

> *"What stays in the museum is only the art-object, not valueless, but not the value of art. The art is what has happened to the viewer."*—Philip Leider, Art Critic

CHARACTERS

EVERYONE: EVERYBODY's companion
EVERYBODY: EVERYONE's companion
INDIVIDUAL WITH MUSEUM HEADPHONES: Self-explanatory

SETTING

A museum.

VARIATION 1
LEISURE TIME

In the dark.

EVERYONE: No, no. That's not funny.

EVERYBODY: What do you mean?

EVERYONE: That's just not funny.

EVERYBODY: I thought it was funny.

EVERYONE: Precisely.

EVERYBODY: Precisely.

(Lights are up by now, EVERYONE and EVERYBODY are standing center stage in a room full of nonexistent paintings.)

EVERYONE: Good we're agreed then.

EVERYBODY: Oh no we're not.

EVERYONE: We're not?

EVERYBODY: Not at all. I think.

EVERYONE: I find thinking to be pensive 98% of the time.

(INDIVIDUAL WITH MUSEUM HEADPHONES enters and walks downstage of them. He stands in front of a nonexistent painting in proper art-observing posture and observes the nonexistent painting.

(EVERYONE and EVERYBODY timidly hang back. They stealthily move slightly towards the INDIVIDUAL to get a better look and observe the individual from a distance.

(INDIVIDUAL WITH MUSEUM HEADPHONES pauses in observing the painting, listening to some interesting trivia about the piece and the artist. INDIVIDUAL WITH MUSEUM HEADPHONES says ooh [or ah] and nods, enlightened. Finished, INDIVIDUAL WITH MUSEUM HEADPHONES exits.

(EVERYONE and EVERYBODY rush up and stand in front of the nonexistent painting in proper art-observing posture, staring.)

EVERYONE: Hmm.

EVERYBODY: I know.

(They both lean in and squint at the picture.)

EVERYBODY: Hmm. There doesn't seem to be much going on here.

EVERYONE: No. No there doesn't.

EVERYBODY: Maybe the title will help.

EVERYONE: *(Reading.)* "System 3."

(Pause. They look closer at the painting.)

EVERYBODY: Not much help.

EVERYONE: No. Not much.

EVERYBODY: *(Standing back to get a better look.)* Who is the artist?

EVERYONE: *(Reading.)* Lordaun.

EVERYBODY: Oh. *(Pause.)* He's well known isn't he?

EVERYONE: I think I've heard of him.

EVERYBODY: I like it. Ready?

EVERYONE: Ready.

EVERYBODY: Next!

(They shift down to look at the next nonexistent painting.)

EVERYONE: Oh, come on! I could do that.

EVERYBODY: Ah, but you didn't.

EVERYONE: That's because I knew it was stupid.

(They look at it. Pause.)

EVERYBODY: What are you thinking?

EVERYONE: About how much this sold for. Ready?

EVERYBODY: Ready.

EVERYONE: Next!

(They shift down to look at the next nonexistent painting. EVERYBODY reads the title.)

EVERYBODY: Ooh. "Naked Woman on a Couch."

(They stare at it. They blink. Significant pause.)

EVERYONE: I think that's a breast right there.

EVERYBODY: *(Looking at where EVERYONE is looking. Gets excited.)* Oh yes, I think you're right. Right there, that is definitely a nipple.

(Pause.)

EVERYONE: Nice nipple.

EVERYBODY: Very nice. I've seen few as nice as this.

EVERYONE: Ready?

EVERYBODY: Wait, it's my turn.

EVERYONE: It is?

EVERYBODY: You went last time.

EVERYONE: *(Remembering.)* So I did. All right then. But hurry, the next one appears to be a nude as well.

EVERYBODY: Oh, alrighty. Have you noticed all the nudes are women?

EVERYONE: Men are too hairy when they're naked.

EVERYBODY: Ah. True, true. Ready?

EVERYONE: Ready.

EVERYBODY: Next!

(They shift down to look at the next nonexistent painting. Pause.)

EVERYBODY: *(Leaning back.)* She's kind of…

EVERYONE: Yes, yes she is.

EVERYBODY: What's the word…

EVERYONE: Fat.

EVERYBODY: Ah.

(Pause.)

EVERYONE and EVERYBODY: Next!

VARIATION 2
LET THE GAMES BEGIN

A basketball hoop stands, surrounded by velvet ropes. On the ground, a few feet in front of the hoop, sits a basketball. EVERYONE and EVERYBODY stand behind the ropes observing the artwork in proper art-observing posture. They stand there for some time switching positions trying to contemplate all the angles of it.

EVERYONE: Title?

EVERYBODY: *(Leaning over to read it off the ball.)* Nba. (Pronounced n{i}–bah with a silent i and p.)

EVERYONE: Nba. Huh. Nba.

(The two continue to repeat nba trying to locate the correct pronunciation, playing with each other. Eventually, the two stop horsing around, they are in public after all. As EVERYONE begins contemplating the art in proper art-observing posture, EVERYBODY kneels down and tries to reach out and grab the basketball. It is well out of reach. EVERYBODY keeps trying.)

EVERYONE: *(Realizing what EVERY-BODY is up to.)* Uh uh. Don't touch.

EVERYBODY: Why not?

EVERYONE: *(Indicating.)* Ropes. You must respect the velvet ropes.

VARIATION 3
EVERYONE'S A CRITIC

EVERYONE and EVERYBODY are staring at a nonexistent painting.

EVERYBODY: Kind of ehh.

(EVERYONE nods in agreement. EVERYONE reaches into his pocket and pulls out a remote control. He gestures with it as if to change the channel. It doesn't work. He tries again. Same response.)

EVERYBODY: Maybe it's a bad angle.

(EVERYONE begins waving it around and pressing the channel change button trying to get a better angle. It doesn't work.)

EVERYBODY: Shake it.

(EVERYONE shakes it as if there is one channel change left in the bottom. Nothing. He tries again. Nope. He hits it and tries again. Nothing. One more time. Nada.)

EVERYONE: Batteries must be dead.

EVERYBODY: Ready?

EVERYONE: Ready.

EVERYBODY: Next.

(They shift down to the next nonexistent painting.)

EVERYONE: You know, I just had an idea.

EVERYBODY: Oh, you shouldn't.

EVERYONE: I know, I know. But it just sort of happened. They should set up an art museum like a dry cleaners. Just hang all the paintings on one of those gigantic... things, that they hang the clothes on, and they push a button and all the clothes go around forever until they get to the one they want and they just push the button again. You could just stand there and push a button and all the art could sail by, stopping at any that interest you with just the push of a button. You wouldn't have to hardly move at all, just push a button.

EVERYBODY: I wouldn't get so tired.

EVERYONE: Precisely!

EVERYBODY: But what about the statues?

(Pause.)

EVERYONE: Hmm. *(He begins to answer, stops, ponders a moment, begins anew, halts.)* You're right. *(He sighs forlornly.)* Ah well, it was a nice thought.

EVERYBODY: Yes. I find thinking to be thought provoking 88% of the time. Ready?

EVERYONE: Ready.

EVERYBODY: Next!

(They shift down to look at the next nonexistent painting.)

EVERYONE: That's not a painting. That's just text. What's it say?

EVERYBODY: *(Leaning towards the painting.)* "Imagine an image of a vagina. A closeup. It is in black and white except for a drop of blood poised on a moistened pinnacle of pubic hair sloping downwards. Imagine the image. I know what you're thinking. Images like this should not be displayed in public places."

(EVERYBODY leans back to neutral. They consider. EVERYBODY begins to say something. Stops. Reconsiders. Begins again. Stops.)

EVERYBODY: Well I'm turned on.

EVERYONE: Next!

VARIATION 4
RULES

The basketball hoop stands center stage surrounded by velvet ropes. EVERYBODY has taken off his jacket (or shirt or jersey or sweater or hat) and is leaning over the velvet ropes swinging it at the basketball.

EVERYONE: Whip it, whip it! Come on, lean!

EVERYBODY: I'm trying, I'm trying. *(EVERYBODY relinquishes.)* It's no good.

(The two sit and contemplate.)

EVERYBODY: Well, now what?

EVERYONE: Now, now let's just think about this.

EVERYBODY: I find thinking to be preoccupying 73% of the time.

EVERYONE: I got it!

EVERYBODY: Exactly!

EVERYONE: *(Standing.)* Newton's... *(He doesn't know which of Newton's laws.)* One of Newton's laws.

EVERYBODY: *(Standing.)* I could go for one of his cookies.

EVERYONE: Quick give me your shoe.

(EVERYBODY does so.)

EVERYONE: For every action, there is an equal and opposite—

(EVERYONE throws the shoe at the ball. He misses. Motionless, they stare at it blinking.)

EVERYONE: Give me your other shoe.

(EVERYBODY hesitates.)

EVERYONE: Come on, come on.

EVERYBODY: Alright, but I don't see how scaring the ball—

EVERYONE: I'll hit it with the shoe and according to the law of consternation—

EVERYBODY: Concentration—

EVERYONE: Consecration—

EVERYBODY: Obligation—

EVERYONE: Conservation of moments—

EVERYBODY: Momentous—

EVERYONE: Mementos—

EVERYBODY: Mentos—

EVERYONE: Momentum the ball will move. *(EVERYONE throws the shoe and hits the ball, knocking it further away.)*

(Pause.)

EVERYBODY: Well it moved. Ah! Give me your shoe.

EVERYONE: You're joking.

EVERYBODY: No, no funny business. If force is F, and F equals $M. A.$, and $m. a.$ spells ma, and mom always knows how to fix things, then... I gave you mine!

EVERYONE: Oh for heaven's sake.

(EVERYONE gives EVERYBODY one of his shoes. EVERYBODY throws it at the ball. He misses.)

EVERYBODY: Don't ever say I don't have a healthy respect for tradition.

(EVERYBODY holds out his hand. EVERYONE grudgingly gives him his other shoe. EVERYBODY throws it and hits the ball, bouncing it off the back wall so that it rolls back towards them under the velvet ropes into the triumphant hands of EVERYBODY.)

EVERYBODY: The art of science.

EVERYONE: Are you sure we should be doing this?

EVERYBODY: No.

EVERYONE: Well, then now what?

(Pause. They ponder.)

EVERYBODY: Ah!

EVERYONE: What?

EVERYBODY: *(Trying to think.)* Shh!

EVERYONE: *(Whispering.)* What?

EVERYBODY: *(Still thinking.)* I'm thinking. It's on the tip of my brain.

EVERYONE: I find thinking gets you nowhere 61% of the time.

EVERYBODY: I got it.

EVERYONE: See I told you.

EVERYBODY: Are you so sure we shouldn't be doing this?

(EVERYONE deflates.)

VARIATION 5
SOMETIMES A CIGAR IS JUST A… WHAT THE HELL IS THAT!?

EVERYBODY is staring at a nonexistent painting. EVERYONE is covering up the title card with his hand.

EVERYONE: Well?

EVERYBODY: Three poles in winter.

(EVERYONE reads the title card.)

EVERYONE: Closest one yet. "Snow Field." What's your secret?

EVERYBODY: Clouds.

EVERYONE: I don't follow.

EVERYBODY: It's just like seeing the shapes in clouds. Ready?

EVERYONE: Ready.

EVERYBODY: Next!

(They shift down to look at the next nonexistent painting. EVERYBODY stands close to the painting while EVERYONE hangs back. EVERYBODY shifts places blocking EVERYONE's view. EVERYONE shifts to get a clear view. Unaware, EVERYBODY shifts again, again blocking EVERYONE. Again EVERYONE moves to see better. EVERYBODY shifts again. Frustrated, EVERYONE yanks EVERYBODY back and they stand side by side.)

EVERYBODY: It's… colorful.

EVERYONE: Yes. Quite… bright.

EVERYBODY: Hm.

EVERYONE: Mm.

EVERYBODY: Ready?

EVERYONE: Ready.

EVERYBODY: Next!

(They shift down to look at the next nonexistent painting. Pause.)

EVERYONE: Ooh, I've seen this one!

EVERYBODY: Really?

EVERYONE: Indeed.

EVERYBODY: Another exhibit?

EVERYONE: No.

EVERYBODY: An art book?

EVERYONE: No.

EVERYBODY: Well?

EVERYONE: I think a guest bathroom.

EVERYBODY: Oh. *(Looking again at the painting.)* Yes. It does sort of suggest a sensation of desiring to void myself.

EVERYONE: That's what I thought. Ready?

EVERYBODY: Ready.

EVERYONE: Next!

(They shift. EVERYBODY is standing stage right looking at one nonexistent painting. EVERYONE is standing stage left looking at another. They are perplexed. Pause.)

EVERYBODY: *(Reading the title.)* "Violin and Sheet Music."

EVERYONE: *(Reading the title.)* "Coffee and Newspaper."

EVERYBODY: Kind of boring titles.

EVERYONE: No not very creative. *(Referring to the painting.)* Kind of boxy.

EVERYBODY: Yes.

(The two casually shift to the other's respective nonexistent painting. They stare a moment and quickly shift back... and then back again.)

EVERYBODY: Are these...

EVERYONE: The same.

(They both read the title cards and then quickly switch places, rushing to read the other title card.)

EVERYBODY: Different titles.

EVERYONE: Different artists.

EVERYBODY: Different countries.

EVERYONE: And yet...

EVERYBODY: And yet...

EVERYONE and EVERYBODY: The same.

EVERYONE: How odd.

EVERYBODY: Ready?

EVERYONE: Ready.

EVERYBODY: Next!

(They shift down to look at the next nonexistent painting. Pause.)

EVERYONE: Ah, iconoclastic.

EVERYBODY: How do you mean?

EVERYONE: Well, all the, excessive utilization of... icons. Ready?

EVERYBODY: Ready.

EVERYONE: Next!

(They shift down to look at the next nonexistent painting. It is a portrait in profile. Pause. EVERYBODY looks at it and then looks off in a direction. He repeats this action.)

EVERYONE: Good looking fellow.

EVERYBODY: What's he looking at?

(EVERYONE approaches the painting and looks off in the same direction as if leaning in close to look out the periphery of a window.)

EVERYONE: Not sure.

EVERYBODY: Hmpf. He should've painted that.

EVERYONE: Artists.

EVERYBODY: I know. Ready?

EVERYONE: Ready.

EVERYBODY: Next!

(They shift down to look at the next nonexistent painting. Pause. A shiver runs through them both.)

EVERYONE: Eerie.

EVERYBODY: Haunting.

EVERYONE: Title?

EVERYBODY: *(Reading.)* "The Artist's Parents."

(They stare at it, hypnotized.)

EVERYONE: How about the next one?

EVERYBODY: Right behind you.

(They quickly shift down to look at the next nonexistent painting. Pause. They relax.)

EVERYBODY: Pretty.

EVERYONE: Yes.

EVERYBODY: *(Reading the title card.)* "Pink Iris." *(Pause.)* Now that's just lovely. Just a nice, big, pretty flower.

EVERYONE: You know from this angle, it kind of looks like a… Oh. Oh my.

EVERYBODY: What?

EVERYONE: Oh it's a, don't you see it?

EVERYBODY: *(Looking.)* Where?

EVERYONE: It's just… Oh.

(Quite embarrassed EVERYONE exits.)

EVERYBODY continues searching the painting.)

EVERYBODY: *(Calling after.)* Where? I don't see it. *(Exits following EVERYONE.)* Oh come on, what is it? At least give me a hint!

VARIATION 6
REFLECTIONS

The two are standing in front of a wall mirror in proper art-observing posture. They are motionless. They are transfixed.

EVERYONE: Disturbing.

EVERYBODY: Quite.

VARIATION 7
HEADS

EVERYONE and EVERYBODY stand in front of a sculpture. It is an upsidedown leafless tree in the middle of desert or plain perhaps.

EVERYONE: It is a mystery wrapped in an enigma.

EVERYBODY: The point of view is bleak, dark, disgusted.

EVERYONE: The style suggests a pungent fabulous.

EVERYBODY: It illuminates some notion of the acrid cartoon of the story of mankind.

EVERYONE: It is an uneventful, maundering, loquacious piece.

EVERYBODY: *(Furrowing his brow.)* I don't get it. Title.

EVERYONE: *(Reading.)* "Didi and Gogo by Brooks Atkinson."

(Pause.)

EVERYBODY: I still don't get it.

EVERYONE: Oh come on. That's an easy one.

(He waits for EVERYBODY to get it. Nothing.)

EVERYONE: Didi and Gogo, you know them.

(Pause. EVERYBODY appears to be getting it.)

EVERYBODY: Oh yeah, Didi and Gogo.

EVERYONE: They're the guys.

EVERYBODY: Yeah, *those* guys. *(Pause.)* What did they…

EVERYONE: They were always waiting… for Hamlet.

EVERYBODY: Oh yeah!

(Pause. They look at it for a while.)

EVERYONE: Maybe a new room.

EVERYBODY: *(Snaps his finger and points at EVERYONE.)* A new room.

VARIATION 8
FIELD LEFT

EVERYONE and EVERYBODY are staring at what they think is a nonexistent painting in proper art-observing posture. They stand there staring for a good half minute.

EVERYONE: Maybe the title will help.

(EVERYBODY leans over to read the title. He stands back up straight.)

EVERYBODY: No title card.

(EVERYONE and EVERYBODY continue to stare without moving for another twenty seconds.)

EVERYBODY: I think it's a window.

(At this point a large bird smacks into the window.)

EVERYONE: Brilliant.

VARIATION 9
DECONSTRUCTION

EVERYONE is standing a foot or two upstage of the spot from where EVERYBODY took his shot. The basketball is bouncing having just gone through the hoop. EVERYONE holds up his arms triumphantly.

EVERYBODY: No. No. That doesn't count.

EVERYONE: What are you talking about, that counts.

EVERYBODY: No, no. You jumped.

EVERYONE: So?

EVERYBODY: So! So! So, I didn't jump.

EVERYONE: That's not my fault.

EVERYBODY: But… No. No. You have to do what I said.

EVERYONE: I did do what you said. From this spot, right handed hook, no backboard.

EVERYBODY: No jumping!

EVERYONE: You didn't say no jumping.

EVERYBODY: *(Becoming increasingly infuriated.)* I don't have to say no jumping! It's implied, doofus! All I have to do is not jump and then no jumping may occur. I mean what kind of a pretext are we setting here? Aren't we working with some basic set of assumptions or do I have to list all exclusive possibilities, hm? Is that it? Before I take a shot I have to make sure to explicitly cover all conceivable bases? No jumping, no leaning, no lowering the hoop, no relying on the kindness of strangers, no employing the use of pyrotechnics.

EVERYONE: Couldn't hurt?

EVERYBODY: Couldn't... but... don't you... it would... Have you gone completely mad? Did you injure yourself jumping around like that? Did you pull something or bump that dense cranium of yours? I didn't say no using chickens. Does that mean chickens are fair game?

EVERYONE: Well game hens...

EVERYBODY: Or perhaps this is all my fault, hm. Perhaps instead I should have leapt all over the place— *(He begins jumping frantically around.)* Just bounce around to cover all my bases making sure to utilize any piece of poultry I can get my hands on. Or maybe I should shoot like a chicken might. *(Still jumping around he starts to mimic a chicken playing basketball.)* Does that seem about right? I mean is this... what you... had... in... What's so funny?

(EVERYBODY stops moving completely as EVERYONE has started laughing.)

EVERYONE: *(Laughing.)* Now that's funny.

EVERYBODY: *(Frantically looks for what was funny. Not finding it.)* What?

EVERYONE: *(Gesturing.)* That.

EVERYBODY: *(Mimicking the gesture.)* That's funny?

EVERYONE: Yup.

EVERYBODY: I said something funny?

EVERYONE: Yup.

EVERYBODY: But I didn't mean to.

EVERYONE: I know. That's why it was funny.

EVERYBODY: Is it because I used the word chicken? I'm never going to get this funny thing.

EVERYONE: *(Laughing again.)* There you go again.

(EVERYBODY stops moving. He glares at EVERYONE, which sends EVERYONE into hysterics. This infuriates EVERYBODY, but he tries to contain his anger. Finally EVERYONE stops laughing in order to catch his breath.)

EVERYBODY: I want you to explain this funny thing to me. Clearly. So I understand it this time.

EVERYONE: Funny? How do you want me to explain funny?

EVERYBODY: What makes something funny?

EVERYONE: Funny is funny.

EVERYBODY: How do you know when something is funny?

EVERYONE: People laugh.

EVERYBODY: But I laughed last time and you said it wasn't funny.

EVERYONE: No. It's not funny when you yourself laugh.

EVERYBODY: It's not?

EVERYONE: No.

EVERYBODY: So you can't laugh at yourself?

EVERYONE: Exactly.

EVERYBODY: So I can't find myself funny?

EVERYONE: When you find yourself funny, then you are no longer funny. You're pitiful.

EVERYBODY: I don't understand. Example.

(EVERYONE frowns at EVERYBODY for a moment. EVERYONE then begins to look around the room for an example. He finds one.)

EVERYONE: Ah! There. You see that.

(EVERYONE indicates a direction. EVERYBODY looks that way.)

EVERYBODY: What?

EVERYONE: Over that way.

EVERYBODY: What?

EVERYONE: There.

(EVERYONE indicates more emphatically in the same direction. EVERYBODY takes a step in that direction and squints.)

EVERYBODY: I don't…

(EVERYONE smashes EVERYBODY in the back of his head, throwing him forward.)

EVERYBODY: Ow!

EVERYONE: Did you see?

EVERYBODY: *(Rubbing his head.)* What did you do that for?

EVERYONE: You told me to.

EVERYBODY: I did no such thing.

EVERYONE: Indeed you did!

EVERYBODY: When?

EVERYONE: You asked for an example.

EVERYBODY: I asked for an example of funny.

EVERYONE: That was funny.

EVERYBODY: That was most certainly not funny.

EVERYONE: No, no it was.

EVERYBODY: I didn't laugh.

EVERYONE: Exactly.

(Pause. EVERYBODY considers. He stops and then advances upon EVERYONE.)

EVERYONE: Now don't get cross, I'm trying to help you. Do you think I am just doing all this to amuse myself? I'm not, I tell you. You asked for my help. And I am speaking quite honestly in telling you that, that, was funny.

(Pause.)

EVERYBODY: That hurt.

EVERYONE: Hurt you, but amused the onlooker. To me that was very funny.

EVERYBODY: So that made you laugh?

EVERYONE: Yes.

(Pause.)

EVERYBODY: So then, in this example, who was being funny, you or I?

EVERYONE: I.

EVERYBODY: But you can't laugh at your own joke and then be funny.

EVERYONE: But I was laughing at you.

EVERYBODY: Why?

EVERYONE: Because you were but the butt of the joke.

EVERYBODY: Oh. *(Pause. Advancing on EVERYONE.)* Maybe I should try telling the joke.

EVERYONE: Oh no you're not ready for such advanced funny.

EVERYBODY: I'm not?

EVERYONE: Not at all. To rush the levels would be quite disastrous. It's all in your timing. Plus you'd be trying to be funny and then it just wouldn't be funny.

EVERYBODY: Hmm. *(Pause.)* Have I been funny?

EVERYONE: Occasionally.

EVERYBODY: When I don't mean to be funny?

EVERYONE: Right.

EVERYBODY: When I don't realize I'm being funny?

EVERYONE: Now you've got it.

EVERYBODY: Because, I'm not trying to be funny.

EVERYONE: Mm hmm.

(Pause.)

EVERYBODY: So for me to be funny I've got to not try to do things that don't make me laugh?

EVERYONE: Yes.

EVERYBODY: But then aren't I still trying to be funny and thereby due to my efforts not being funny.

(EVERYONE tries to figure that one out.)

EVERYONE: No.

EVERYBODY: No?

EVERYONE: No. Because you're not aware of the funniness.

EVERYBODY: Oh. *(Pause.)* Funny is very passive aggressive.

(EVERYONE tries not to laugh.)

VARIATION 10
AN IMPORTANT LESSON

In another room full of nonexistent art they walk past an ashtray. Velvet ropes are set up in an inconspicuous manner. EVERYBODY throws a crumpled-up wrapper/piece of paper into the ashtray. EVERYONE smacks him.

EVERYBODY: Ow, that's getting old.

EVERYONE: Pick that up.

EVERYBODY: What are you talking about, I made it.

EVERYONE: That's not for trash.

EVERYBODY: I don't understand.

EVERYONE: *(Walking over and picking up the wrapper.)* That's an exhibit.

EVERYBODY: That's not art!

EVERYONE: Why not?

EVERYBODY: Utility.

EVERYONE: Hm?

EVERYBODY: It's useful. It has a use, a purpose. Art can't be useful.

(EVERYONE begins to answer, stops, pauses, begins again, stops. EVERYONE glares at EVERYBODY and confidently assumes proper art-observing posture. EVERYBODY grudgingly does likewise. Pause. They look at it.)

EVERYBODY: I like it. Realism.

(EVERYONE shakes his head patronizingly.)

VARIATION 11
H.O.R.

EVERYONE is standing on one leg. He places a hand over his eyes. With his other hand he lifts up the basketball.

EVERYONE: No backboard.

(He is about to shoot. EVERYBODY can't look, but glances periodically. EVERYONE shoots and makes the shot.)

EVERYBODY: Ah ha! My ball.

EVERYONE: What are you talking about, I made it.

EVERYBODY: You most certainly did not. You missed. My shot.

(He walks over, picks up the ball, and moves to a different spot to take a lead shot.)

EVERYONE: Over here. You have to shoot from over here. I made it.

EVERYBODY: No. I saw it.

EVERYONE: You saw it go in.

EVERYBODY: How would you know? Your eyes were covered. What, are you cheating?

EVERYONE: I heard it.

EVERYBODY: You heard it?

EVERYONE: I heard it out of the corner of my ear.

(Pause. EVERYBODY begins to answer. Stops. Reconsiders. Begins again. Stops. He raises his hand about to make a point. Stops. He walks over to where EVERYONE took the shot from. EVERYONE moves out of the way. EVERYBODY gestures, "Is this the right place?" EVERYONE nods. EVERY-BODY lifts the opposite leg that EVERY-ONE had raised.)

EVERYONE: Other leg.

EVERYBODY: Hmm?

EVERYONE: Other leg. Lift your other leg.

(Pause. EVERYBODY lifts his other leg. He places one of his hands over his eyes. He shoots. He misses. He raises his hands in triumph.)

EVERYBODY: That's right. Take your best shot. I'm unstoppable.

EVERYONE: You missed.

EVERYBODY: I missed?

EVERYONE: You missed.

EVERYBODY: I did not miss.

EVERYONE: Indeed you did.

EVERYBODY: How come when you shoot, it goes in, but when I shoot, it's a miss?

EVERYONE: *(He sighs.)* What are you now, a hor?

EVERYBODY: Why, how much you got?

EVERYONE: Your score. H-O-R.

EVERYBODY: Oh. Right. Ah, I'm not sure.

EVERYONE: Weren't you keeping track?

EVERYBODY: Weren't you?

EVERYONE: I haven't missed.

EVERYBODY: That's 'cause you cheat.

EVERYONE: *(Placing his hands on the ball which EVERYBODY is holding.)* Just give me the ball.

EVERYBODY: *(Pulling against EVERYONE's grasp.)* It's my shot.

EVERYONE: *(Pulling.)* No you missed it's mine.

EVERYBODY: *(Pulling.)* Right, you shot already so it's mine.

EVERYONE: *(Pulling.)* No according to the rules…

EVERYBODY: *(Overlapping; pulling.)* Oh now look who remembers the rules!

EVERYONE: Gimme!

EVERYBODY: Mine!

(They struggle [ad libbing] until the ball shoots out of both their grasps to far behind the velvet ropes. Pause.)

EVERYONE and EVERYBODY: Well now look what you did!

VARIATION 12
The Actor Is Not Important

EVERYBODY approaches the next artwork. It is a plant. When he steps within a foot of it, a sunlamp turns on directly over it. He steps back, it goes off. Pause. He steps forward again, the lamp turns on again. He steps back, it turns off. He plays this game for a few moments, until he simply stops, standing in front of it close enough so that the lamp is on.

EVERYBODY: This is fun.

EVERYONE: What are you doing?

EVERYBODY: Creating.

EVERYONE: Ah. It does look fun. What is it?

EVERYBODY: A plant.

EVERYONE: I can see that.

EVERYBODY: Oh. I'm sorry. A ficus I think.

EVERYONE: No, no. You're not getting me.

EVERYBODY: There is no need to get cross.

EVERYONE: I mean why is it here.

EVERYBODY: Oh. *(Pause.)* For us. Perhaps.

EVERYONE: Impossible.

EVERYBODY: Why? It is here, to be looked at presumably. We're here, looking at it. Therefore, transitive property, it is here for us.

EVERYONE: But who was to know we'd be here? We had no reason to believe we'd see this. We had no intention of finding it. So why would anyone put it here for us who aren't even supposed to be here?

EVERYBODY: Ah. Hmm. *(He begins to retort, stops, ponders, attempts a second time, stops.)* Good point. Still, it's quite nice.

EVERYONE: Oh yes.

EVERYBODY: I wonder.

EVERYONE: What?

EVERYBODY: Well, what section are we in?

EVERYONE: I don't follow.

EVERYBODY: If we know what section we're in then we'll know what we're looking at.

EVERYONE: Good thinking.

(EVERYONE begins searching through his museum brochure.)

EVERYBODY: Thank you. I find thinking causes melancholy in romantic poets 100% of the time.

EVERYONE: Ah. I got it. *(Pointing to his brochure.)* We're in the sculpture garden.

(Pause. They ponder the dilemma for a few moments. Baffled, EVERYBODY gives up thinking and makes a decision.)

EVERYBODY: Ah, so then it's a sculpture.

EVERYONE: Definitely.

(The two quickly assume proper art-observing posture.)

EVERYBODY: Looks like a plant though.

EVERYONE: Amazing isn't it. Post realism.

EVERYBODY: Truly. *(Pause.)* So then it is always different?

EVERYONE: Hmm?

EVERYBODY: The sculpture. It's never the same.

EVERYONE: Yes?

EVERYBODY: Changing and growing for every viewer.

EVERYONE: A powerful metaphor.

(Pause.)

EVERYBODY: Oh. Oh my.

EVERYONE: What?

EVERYBODY: I just thought of something.

EVERYONE: I thought we talked about that and where it leads.

EVERYBODY: Oh my.

EVERYONE: Well, out with it.

EVERYBODY: What if no one sees it?

EVERYONE: Hmm?

EVERYBODY: What if no one comes by?

EVERYONE: I still… hmm?

EVERYBODY: Then the growth lamp would never turn on.

EVERYONE: Oh. Yes, I suppose.

EVERYBODY: And it would…

EVERYONE: Yes. Oh my.

(Pause.)

EVERYBODY: Without an audience.

EVERYONE: The demise of art both figuratively and literally. Quite brilliant.

(Pause.)

EVERYBODY: I feel too guilty to move.

EVERYONE: But surely we must. We haven't finished our game.

EVERYBODY: Yes, I know. But how can I? *(Struggling with the idiom.)* I hold it's life in my, in my, well you know.

EVERYONE: Yes, I see your point. Hmm. Surely you are not responsible.

EVERYBODY: But I am. I am here. If I leave, then it—

EVERYONE: Yes. *(Pause. Ponders. A revelation.)* But that's not your fault.

EVERYBODY: How do you mean?

EVERYONE: Well, if you leave, you have done nothing more than move on. And that is all.

EVERYBODY: But if I leave then it will…

EVERYONE: It might.

EVERYBODY: It might?

EVERYONE: It might. And there is no responsibility within a possibility.

EVERYBODY: There isn't?

EVERYONE: How can there be?

EVERYBODY: Well, there's, hmm. I'm not sure.

EVERYONE: If you leave, someone else might come along, just as you have.

EVERYBODY: Ah. *(Pause.)* But what if they don't?

EVERYONE: Then they're to blame, not you.

EVERYBODY: Oh. But still it's my action.

EVERYONE: True. *(Pause. Ponders. Begins to answer, stops.)* But, the actor isn't important.

EVERYBODY: He isn't?

EVERYONE: No.

EVERYBODY: No?

EVERYONE: No, he's just a part of the circumstance.

EVERYBODY: I don't follow.

EVERYONE: Look, all you're doing is observing. Passing by. If you had never wandered this way, then nothing would be different. And you couldn't possibly be held responsible for something of which you have nothing to do with. Could you?

EVERYBODY: Indeed.

EVERYONE: So, then what does it matter that you happened to pass by? The situation is the same as it was when you knew nothing about it, except that now you know something. However, you are nothing more than a bystander, not a culprit.

EVERYBODY: Hunh?

EVERYONE: You are a participant and nothing more. You stumbled into a circumstance, accidentally.

(Pause.)

EVERYBODY: Well then who is to blame?

EVERYONE: No one.

EVERYBODY: No one? There must be someone.

EVERYONE: The circumstance.

EVERYBODY: Can you blame a circumstance?

EVERYONE: Well you can blame whoever constructed the circumstance.

EVERYBODY: Isn't that then someone?

EVERYONE: Look did you put the plant there?

EVERYBODY: No.

EVERYONE: Did you set up the growth light to only go on when someone stands there?

EVERYBODY: I wouldn't even know how to.

EVERYONE: Precisely. You are just an innocent bystander.

EVERYBODY: I am?

EVERYONE: Well you are standing by it.

EVERYBODY: So I am.

EVERYONE: Well then, there you go.

EVERYBODY: Here I go.

(EVERYONE and EVERYBODY walk away from the plant. The light makes a sound. The two turn around and look. Having been left on too long, the light explodes

and falls onto the plant igniting it. The two stare at it. It is drawn away rapidly into the flies. Pause.)

EVERYBODY: I'm thirsty.

VARIATION 13
ANOTHER IMPORTANT LESSON

EVERYONE and EVERYBODY have just entered. On the opposite side of the stage, a water fountain is brought in from the flies. It is placed in a manner conspicuously similar to the plant. The two turn and see it.

EVERYBODY: Oh thank God. I'm parched.

(He moves towards it. He stops and turns to EVERYONE.)

EVERYBODY: Is it all right to use it?

EVERYONE: Of course, why wouldn't it be?

EVERYBODY: It's not an installment?

EVERYONE: Hmm?

EVERYBODY: An installment. It's not an installment?

EVERYONE: *(Begins to answer. Stops. Reconsiders. Begins again. Stops reconsiders.)* I'm not getting you.

EVERYBODY: What do you mean you're not getting me? *(Gesturing ineffectively at the water fountain.)* An installment, an installment.

EVERYONE: Oh, oh. Do you mean an in-stal-la-tion?

(Pause.)

EVERYBODY: *(Begins to answer. Stops. Reconsiders.)* Same difference.

(EVERYONE scoffs.)

EVERYBODY: Well?

EVERYONE: *(Shaking his head disapprovingly.)* It's fine.

EVERYBODY: How do you tell the difference?

EVERYONE: Like you do with all important things. Velvet ropes.

EVERYBODY: Oh, right.

(EVERYBODY steps towards the water fountain to get a drink. When he comes within a foot of it, the fountain turns on and a flow of water jumps out dousing EVERYBODY. He steps back and it goes off.)

EVERYBODY: You know, I'm actually not that thirsty.

VARIATION 14
THE PROVERBIAL FART

EVERYONE and EVERYBODY are staring at a nonexistent painting in proper art-observing posture. They stand still for some moments. EVERYBODY makes a face.

EVERYBODY: That's, *(Inhales.)* that's, *(Inhales.)* that's disgusting.

EVERYONE: Hmm. I don't see it.

EVERYBODY: No.

EVERYONE: No?

EVERYBODY: That smell.

EVERYONE: Smell?

EVERYBODY: Yes, that smell. Can't you smell it?

EVERYONE: I don't smell anything.

EVERYBODY: Oh my God! *(Fights off the invisible smell.)* Oh. What? What is? Oh. In the name of all that is holy. Did you...

EVERYONE: I most certainly did not!

EVERYBODY: Well I didn't!

EVERYONE: I don't even know what you're talking about.

EVERYBODY: *(Backing as far away from EVERYONE as possible.)* You smell it. You can't stand there and tell me you don't smell it.

EVERYONE: I'm growing tired of this game.

EVERYBODY: This is no game man! This is, this is... Oh! *(Crouches down low to avoid the smell.)* Couldn't you have at least warned me?

EVERYONE: I didn't do it I tell you!

EVERYBODY: Well one of us did it!

EVERYONE: You know what they say, whoever smelt it... *(Smells it.)* Oh! Oh, that's, that's vile.

EVERYBODY: There. See. I told you. It smells like, like, like evil crawled up your butt and died.

EVERYONE: For the last time, it wasn't me!

EVERYBODY: You disgust me!

EVERYONE: I disgust you?

EVERYBODY: I'm glad we agree.

EVERYONE: *(Frustrated.)* Oh, oh. *(Smelling the fart yet again.)* Oh!

EVERYBODY: Are you sick or something?

EVERYONE: I have had just about enough of your antics. Now you own up to it or I'll—

EVERYBODY: Own up to it. Me? You're the one who f—

EVERYONE: That's it. That's it. I don't know if I'm more repulsed by the smell or by you.

EVERYBODY: You. You. You stink.

EVERYONE: I'm leaving. *(Walks off stage.)*

EVERYBODY: That's right. That's right, flee the scene of the crime. But you'll return. The culprit always... *(Smells the fart again.)* Augh.

(He runs off stage in the opposite direction of EVERYONE. Fifteen seconds pass. Another fifteen perhaps. The fart dissipates slightly.

(INDIVIDUAL WITH MUSEUM HEADPHONES enters, pauses, smells. It's awful. He subtly looks for the source of the smell. Anxious, INDIVIDUAL WITH MUSEUM HEADPHONES tries to observe the art. Something is said on the headphones and he inhales and nods enlightened.)

VARIATION 15
RE-ORIENTATION

Lights up. A row of three nonexistent paintings. EVERYBODY saunters on stage. He pauses and assesses the three paintings from a medium distance in proper art-observing posture, being sure to look them up and down quite thoroughly.

He then approaches the first of the three and reads the title card. He steps back and studies the painting as a pre-literate child would a menu in a restaurant.

He stands still a moment.

EVERYBODY: Next.

(He shifts down to look at the next nonexistent painting. He stands for a moment in

proper art-observing posture and takes it in. He leans over, reads the title card, and stands back up. He leans towards the painting observing it a little closer. Somewhat perplexed he turns towards his nonexistent companion.)

EVERYBODY: *(Trailing off…)* I don't get it…

(Pause. He straightens, turns back to painting, and assumes proper art-observing posture, recovering from the embarrassment, undaunted and thankful no one was around to witness it. He looks at the painting a few more moments.)

EVERYBODY: Next.

(He shifts down to the third nonexistent painting. He starts. He leans in, looks closely, and begins laughing. He stands back, definitely amused. He turns to his nonexistent companion again to share in the amusement, but stops, remembering.)

(He walks over to the doorway that he entered from and looks to see if EVERYONE is anywhere in sight. He's not.

(He walks across the room to the other doorway and looks to see if EVERYONE is anywhere in sight. He's not.

(He turns around and looks at the painting in proper art-observing posture. EVERYBODY tries to laugh. It's not the same. He turns away and wanders off stage forlornly.

VARIATION 16
TAKING HIM TO THE CLEANERS

EVERYONE is standing in front of a rather large frame that starts at the floor and is roughly 10x10. (Note: This is different from a nonexistent painting.) In the center is a button and above it a title card. EVERYONE walks up to the button and reads the title card.

EVERYONE: "Light Starch." Odd title. *(Referring to button.)* Push. This should be fun. Buttons are always fun.

(EVERYONE pushes the button and releases it. Large drycleaning machine sound.)

EVERYONE: Hey, it's like a dry…

(A long line of dry cleaning swings down and crashes into EVERYONE, knocking him over.

(Lying on the ground, covered with dry cleaning.)

EVERYONE: What a stupid idea.

VARIATION 17
PUNGENT FABULOUS

Lights up. In the center of the stage is a cushioned leather bench.

EVERYONE and EVERYBODY enter from opposite sides of the stage. They stop, seeing each other. The bench is between them. They look at the bench. They look at each other.

They both break into a sprint for the bench. They both leap onto the bench and struggle with each other to push the other off and take total control of the bench. The actors may ad lib a little here, as long as they promise not to use any expletives.

EVERYONE: Get off. Get off.

EVERYBODY: Mine. It's mine.

EVERYONE: I was here first.

EVERYBODY: You'll fart on it.

EVERYONE: *(Takes a self-righteous posture.)* I will not!

(In this moment of moral outrage, EVERYBODY succeeds in pushing a distracted EV-

ERYONE off the bench and onto the floor. EVERYBODY quickly sprawls out to take up as much of the entire bench as possible.

(A few moments pass. EVERYONE sits up on the floor and leans against the bench. EVERYBODY permits this. He looks at EVERYONE. He begins to say something. Stops. Reconsiders. Begins again. Stops.

(A hint of remorse sweeps in. EVERYBODY sits up. He moves down so that EVERYONE can fit on the bench too. He indicates to EVERYONE that it's quite alright if he would like to sit on the bench as well. EVERYONE gestures, "Are you sure?" EVERYBODY replies back in kind, "Of course I'm sure."

(EVERYONE gets up and sits on the bench. They both inhale deeply and sigh. A few moments pass.)

EVERYONE and EVERYBODY: I'm sorry about the fart.

(Pause of recognition. Pointing at each other.)

EVERYONE and EVERYBODY: You farted. I farted too. No wonder it stank.

(As if having solved a great problem, they both inhale deeply and sigh.)

EVERYBODY: Still, it was quite impressive.

EVERYONE: Quite.

EVERYBODY: Even as a joint venture.

EVERYONE: Oh, yes. The style suggested a pungent fabulous.

(Pause.)

EVERYBODY: I'm exhausted.

EVERYONE: Me too.

EVERYBODY: How long have we been

in here?

EVERYONE: *(Blowing out his lips.)* Well, for almost... well at least... for a good few... *(He stops. Looks up at the sun, but sees only the ceiling. He begins to answer. Stops. Reconsiders.)* For a while.

EVERYBODY: I tell you, I was drained after the first three paintings.

EVERYONE: I think if I look at another piece of artwork my eyes will shrivel like prunes.

EVERYBODY: If I have to walk through one more room, I will collapse.

EVERYONE: If I have to have a staring contest with one more self-portrait my head will implode.

EVERYBODY: There are a lot of those self-portraits.

EVERYONE: Apparently artists think quite highly of themselves.

EVERYBODY: I don't know why, not a single one of the self-portraits I've seen looks anything like me.

(Pause.)

EVERYBODY: Have we gotten our money's worth yet?

EVERYONE: One can never quantify the value of art. And we have yet to fully benefit from the required donation. I say about three more rooms.

EVERYBODY: I think we should just leave.

(They look around.)

EVERYONE: Easier said than done.

(Pause.)

EVERYBODY: Have you noticed that they kind of all look the same?

EVERYONE: I didn't want to say anything.

(*Pause.*)

EVERYBODY: I'm tired.

EVERYONE: You said it.

(*Pause.*)

EVERYBODY: You bored?

EVERYONE: Dreadfully so.

(*Pause. They sigh.*)

VARIATION 18
DE PROFUNDIS

EVERYONE is sitting at one end of the bench. EVERYBODY is lying down as best he can on the bench, asleep. EVERYONE sits there. EVERYBODY sleeps.

From stage left, the basketball slowly rolls across the stage in front of them. EVERYONE watches it go the whole way. The ball rolls off stage. EVERYONE looks after it. He stops. He contemplates. He turns to EVERYBODY and reaches over about to wake him. He stops. He reconsiders. EVERYONE continues to sit. EVERYBODY continues to sleep.

From stage right, the basketball slowly rolls across the stage in front of them. EVERYONE watches it go the whole way. The ball rolls off stage. EVERYONE looks after it. He stops. He contemplates. He turns to EVERYBODY and reaches over about to wake him. He stops. He reconsiders. EVERYONE continues to sit. EVERYBODY continues to sleep.

From stage left, the basketball small bounces across the stage in front of them. EVERYONE watches it go the whole way off stage. EVERYONE looks after it. He stops. He contemplates. He turns to EVERYBODY and reaches over about to wake him. He stops. He reconsiders. EVERYONE continues to sit. EVERYBODY continues to sleep.

From stage right, the basketball big bounces across the stage in front of them. EVERYONE watches it go the whole way off stage. EVERYONE looks after it. He stops. He contemplates. He turns to EVERYBODY and reaches over about to wake him. He stops. He reconsiders. EVERYONE continues to sit. EVERYBODY continues to sleep.

From stage left the basketball soars through the air directly over EVERYONE and EVERYBODY. It makes no bouncing sound off stage. I assume someone caught it.

Pause.

EVERYONE thinks about what just happened. EVERYONE becomes frightened and smacks EVERYBODY to wake him up.

EVERYBODY looks at EVERYONE and gets him to look offstage right. They await the ball. Nothing. EVERYONE begins to explain. Stops. Reconsiders. Figures it out. Begins again and proceeds to explain with tense gestures and noises. Stops. EVERYBODY doesn't get it. EVERYONE slouches in defeat.

VARIATION 19
WORD PLAY

EVERYONE and EVERYBODY are sitting on the bench with their backs against each other. They are each leaning back against the other.

EVERYBODY: Think of anything?

EVERYONE: No more thinking. It leads to catastrophe 33% of the time.

EVERYBODY: I've heard the only way to catch it early enough is with intro-spection.

EVERYONE: *(Painfully empathizing, rubbing his rear.)* Ooh.

EVERYBODY: I know.

EVERYONE: Oh no, I got something.

EVERYBODY: What?

EVERYONE: *(Seeing if it will pass.)* Shh.

EVERYBODY: *(Whispering.)* What?

EVERYONE: Shush. Oh no... *(Speaking a grandiose thought.)* If one cannot... Oh thank God, I lost it.

EVERYBODY: Close call.

EVERYONE: Who knows what will happen next time.

(Pause.)

EVERYBODY: Ooo!

EVERYONE: You got something?

EVERYBODY: I think so. What do I do?

EVERYONE: *(Beat. Makes a quick decision.)* Well, come on, let's hear it.

EVERYBODY: Alright. Ready? What do you call a guy with no arms and no legs hanging on a wall?

EVERYONE: Oh, come on. That's an old one.

EVERYBODY: No, no. It's a two parter. Come on. Come on.

EVERYONE: *(He sighs.)* Oh, alright.

EVERYBODY: What do you call a guy with no arms and no legs hanging on a wall?

EVERYONE: What?

EVERYBODY: Art.

(EVERYONE doesn't laugh.)

EVERYBODY: Right. What do you call his arms and legs?

EVERYONE: I don't know.

EVERYBODY: Pieces of Art.

(EVERYBODY exerts an enormous effort attempting not to laugh at his own joke. So he can be funny. Get it. It's an echo. From before...)

EVERYONE: That's repulsive.

EVERYBODY: Oh. Sorry.

(Pause.)

EVERYONE: You want to play the alphabet game?

EVERYBODY: Oh yes!

EVERYONE: Insults?

EVERYBODY: Of course. Cursing or no cursing?

EVERYONE: Only if necessary. You may go first.

EVERYBODY: Thank you. A, assmunch.

EVERYONE: Now was that necessary?

EVERYBODY: It was all I could think of.

EVERYONE: All you could think of.

EVERYBODY: Yes. All I could think of.

(EVERYONE gives EVERYBODY a stern look.)

EVERYONE: B, Buboes puss.

EVERYBODY: Ooo, good one.

EVERYONE: Thank you.

EVERYBODY: C, Crusty cu-

(EVERYONE gives EVERYBODY a very stern look and raises a finger.)

EVERYBODY: Cutthroat.

EVERYONE: D, Doofus.

EVERYBODY: That's one of mine.

EVERYONE: Oh. You're right, you did have your name on it.

EVERYBODY: E, Echinoderm.

EVERYONE: Echno... What's that?

EVERYBODY: Any of a phylum of marine animals, as starfishes or sea urchins, having similar body parts, as the arms of a starfish, arranged around a central axis and often having a calcium containing outer skeleton.

EVERYONE: That's not an insult!

EVERYBODY: Well, I wouldn't want to be one.

(Pause. EVERYONE considers and concurs.)

EVERYONE: Fart blossom.

EVERYBODY: *(Begins to protest. Stops. Reconsiders.)* Gigolo.

EVERYONE: That's with a J.

EVERYBODY: No it's not, it's with a G.

EVERYONE: No. You're wrong.

EVERYBODY: I am not.

(EVERYONE gives EVERYBODY a stern look.)

EVERYBODY: Fine. *(Directed at EVERYONE.)* Gap Kid.

EVERYONE: Haycock.

EVERYBODY: Is that an insult?

EVERYONE: Well it's got the word...

(EVERYBODY gives EVERYONE a very stern look and raises a finger.)

EVERYONE: Hay in it.

EVERYBODY: Alright. *(Pauses to think. Snaps his fingers in revelation.)* Idiot. Imbecile. Ignoramus.

EVERYONE: Okay.

EVERYBODY: Incubus.

EVERYONE: Alright.

EVERYBODY: Imp.

EVERYONE: Enough!

EVERYBODY: Incumbent.

EVERYONE: Good one. Gigolo.

EVERYBODY: *(Begins to object. Stops. Glares at EVERYONE.)* Kleptomaniac.

EVERYONE: *(Ignoring the insinuation.)* Labial juice.

EVERYBODY: Oh. Moron.

EVERYONE: Nincompoop.

EVERYBODY: Off-off-Broadway.

EVERYONE: *(Extremely offended. Begins to speak. Stops. Recovers composure. Ponders.)* What am I on?

EVERYBODY: L, m, n, o, p.

EVERYONE: P?

EVERYBODY: Oh!

EVERYONE: O or p?

EVERYBODY: Oh!

EVERYONE: Okay. Orifice.

EVERYBODY: No, pee!

EVERYONE: Oh, p…

EVERYBODY: No pee! I need to use a restroom.

EVERYONE: Oh gee… I see, pee. Are you ok? A bee! Why, didn't you go before?

EVERYBODY: Because I didn't need to before. Where's the closest?

EVERYONE: How should I know?

EVERYBODY: The map. You have the map.

EVERYONE: Oh. The map. Right. *(Pulls out the museum brochure. He looks at it. Taking his time…)* Ah. Here. Well. Let me see. This shouldn't be too difficult. Restroom, restroom. Ever wonder why it's called that? Right, sorry. Ok, the closest one… is in… ah. No that's not the closest. The closest one… is in… the West Wing. Which way is west?

EVERYBODY: That way. *(Points left.)*

EVERYONE: How do you know?

EVERYBODY: Because west is always left.

EVERYONE: West is always…

EVERYBODY: West is left. East is right. North, *(Points forward.)* south. *(Points behind them.)*

(Pause.)

EVERYONE: So left.

EVERYBODY: Right.

EVERYONE: Right?

EVERYBODY: *(Pointing left.)* West!

VARIATION 20
POP ART

Lights up. In the center of the stage stands a ceramic toilet. As far away as possible, possi-

bly upstage, stands a velvet rope. From off stage…

EVERYONE: I think I found it.

EVERYBODY: Where?

EVERYONE: Over here.

EVERYBODY: Where?

EVERYONE: Over here.

EVERYBODY: Thank God.

(EVERYONE and EVERYBODY walk on stage from different directions. As they walk onstage…)

EVERYONE: I told you I knew where I was going.

(The two stop short. They contemplate the object. This is too easy.)

EVERYONE: Hmm. I don't think it's—

EVERYBODY: I don't care.

(He takes a step towards the toilet unbuttoning his pants. When he gets within five feet of it, it automatically flushes. EVERYBODY retreats, EVERYONE assumes proper art-observing posture. At this point a large bird smacks into the urinal and ignites.)

EVERYBODY: I hate this place.

(EVERYBODY turns and looks at EVERYONE and quickly turns back assuming proper art-observing posture, thereby letting go of his unbuttoned pants which fall down.)

VARIATION 21
LINES

A basketball hoop stands, surrounded by velvet ropes. The ball is still far behind the ropes. EVERYONE and EVERYBODY stand staring.

EVERYBODY: We don't have any more shoes.

EVERYONE: No. No we don't.

(EVERYBODY begins pacing back and forth. EVERYONE tries jumping up and down to shake the ball loose. Perhaps EVERYBODY mouths, "No jumping.")

(EVERYBODY pauses. An epiphany.)

(EVERYBODY walks up and around towards a velvet rope closer to the ball. He takes one of the stanchions upon which the velvet rope hangs, picks it up, and moves it towards the hoop so that when he sets it down the basketball is now on the other side of the ropes and thereby no longer part of the piece. HA!)

(EVERYONE is horrified. EVERYONE begins to object. Stops. Reconsiders. Begins anew. Stops. Glares at EVERYBODY for a moment. EVERYONE then moves the stanchion at the other end of that rope and swings it around so that EVERYBODY is again blocked off from the ball by the rope. Ha ha! EVERYONE smirks triumphantly.)

(EVERYBODY quickly retaliates by taking up another stanchion and velvet rope and rearranging it so as to block EVERYONE from further interfering. EVERYONE retaliates in kind. The two leap into a frantic strategic movement of what from above might appear to be a demented fuzzy version of dots and lines.)

(After a moment or so, the two get caught up in the excitement of it and forget about the ball and hoop entirely and are swept away by the frenzy of form. They flip back and forth between cooperative formations and combative ones. [Possibly a series of tableaus here.])

(The halfway point of these formations should be a straight line of velvet ropes down the middle of stage and EVERYONE and EVERYBODY should be on opposite sides of the ropes. EVERYBODY moves towards the ropes.)

EVERYONE: You can't do that!

EVERYBODY: I most certainly can.

EVERYONE: No you're part of the piece now. The piece cannot change itself. Only the observer can change art once it's complete.

(EVERYONE quickly assumes proper art-observing posture and looks at EVERYBODY. EVERYBODY begins to respond. Stops. Ponders. Snaps his fingers. Nope, nope, it was nothing. EVERYBODY glares at EVERYONE. It hits him.)

EVERYBODY: You know from here it looks as if you, and not I, are part of the piece.

(EVERYBODY quickly assumes proper art-observing posture and looks at EVERYONE. EVERYONE begins to retort and stops. He stares at EVERYBODY. EVERYBODY leaps towards one of the stanchions. EVERYONE quickly leaps towards the stanchion at the other end of the velvet rope EVERYBODY is getting. They each pick up their respective ends and run in a circle so that EVERYBODY's end is now where EVERYONE's end was and vice versa, except now EVERYONE and EVERYBODY are on opposite sides of the rope.)

EVERYONE and EVERYBODY: *(Each pointing at the other.)* Aha!

(Each realizing the new reality gestures in frustration of having just been foiled and then quickly assumes proper art-observing posture.

(The game continues. New velvet rope formation upon new velvet rope formation. They move

faster and faster until ultimately they are both standing in the middle of the room, hands on their knees breathing quite heavily.

(The velvet ropes are arranged so they are blocking every exit of the room. The two regain their breath. They look around at the room and realize they are surrounded. They each look to the other for an explanation of what to do now.)

EVERYBODY: We could just move one of them again.

EVERYONE: Impossible.

EVERYBODY: Uh. Why?

EVERYONE: Because now we're both in the piece. Have you ever known an artwork to change itself?

(No answer.)

EVERYONE: Well, have you? Now we're never going to get out of here.

(The two look at the ground, upset. After some time EVERYBODY's eyes wander over and rest upon the basketball. He looks at it. He looks back at the ground. He looks at it. He looks back at the ground. He looks at EVERYONE. He looks at the ball.

(He nonchalantly saunters over to the ball. EVERYONE doesn't notice. EVERYBODY pretends to notice a piece of lint on his shoe and bends over to sweep it off. He picks up the ball. He stands there. EVERYONE sees him. EVERYBODY drops the ball. It bounces. EVERYBODY catches it.

(EVERYONE and EVERYBODY look at each other. EVERYBODY drops the ball again. It bounces. EVERYBODY catches it. EVERYONE and EVERYBODY look at each other. EVERYBODY starts to dribble. EVERYONE runs over and covers him.

VARIATION 22
SLIDING

EVERYONE and EVERYBODY enter from upstage. When they get to center stage all the lights go out.

EVERYONE: What did you do?

EVERYBODY: Me! I didn't do anything.

EVERYONE: Well, you're the one who has been doing everything.

EVERYBODY: Like what?

EVERYONE: You killed the plant.

EVERYBODY: I did not.

(A sound. A slide projection of EVERYONE and EVERYBODY in the museum [perhaps of them with the plant] is projected on the wall.)

EVERYBODY: Hey, that's us.

EVERYONE: No.

EVERYBODY: No. What do you mean no? That's my strong jaw line and your sagging—

EVERYONE: That is not us. That is an image of us.

(The slide changes to Magritte's painting of a pipe Ceci n'est pas une pipe. It quickly changes to another picture of EVERYONE and EVERYBODY. These pictures should all be of questionable moments in the play. This one is of EVERYONE when he made the basket with his eyes closed and EVERYBODY said he missed.)

EVERYBODY: There we are again. Oh.

EVERYONE: I knew I made it.

EVERYBODY: Trick photography.

(The slide changes again. It is upside down. It is a picture of them rearranging velvet ropes.)

EVERYONE: I don't remember that.

EVERYBODY: Pretty impressive though.

(The slide changes. A picture of the fart scene. No comment from either of them. They pretend not to notice. Another shot of the fart scene. Again they pretend not to see it. A third shot from the—)

EVERYONE and EVERYBODY: Alright already!

(The slide changes. It is a picture of the final tableau of EVERYONE and EVERYBODY.)

EVERYONE: I don't get it.

EVERYBODY: I don't like it.

(Lights out. Blackness. Silence. A picture of EVERYONE's face is projected onto EVERYBODY's face and vice versa.)

EVERYONE and EVERYBODY: Hey… You're…

(Pause. EVERYBODY leans over and smacks EVERYONE in the back of the head.)

EVERYONE: Ow. What was that for?

EVERYBODY: You're right. It is funnier when you tell the joke.

EVERYONE: *(Rubbing his head.)* I… I hate this place.

(Pause.)

EVERYBODY: You know, in this light, you are really quite attractive.

EVERYONE: You think so?

EVERYBODY: Oh, yes.

(Pause. Nothing changes. They wait.)

EVERYBODY: Well? Now what?

EVERYONE: Don't look at me, I don't even know why we came to this infernal place to begin with.

EVERYBODY: You were the one that made us!

EVERYONE: I did no such thing.

EVERYBODY: You most certainly did. You went off about our cultural betterment and such. Said it would enrich our lives. And there was nothing on TV.

EVERYONE: Oh please. I don't see how walking aimlessly around a vast neoclassic graveyard of products that suck the energy right out of you through your eyes could ever do anything more than…

(The lights come up and the slides disappear.)

EVERYONE: I'm sorry what was I saying?

EVERYBODY: Graveyard of produce.

EVERYONE: Oh yes. I mean it makes no sense. No sense at all.

EVERYBODY: What?

EVERYONE: Art.

EVERYBODY: That's what I've been saying.

EVERYONE: No, no, no. I mean why is it here?

EVERYBODY: To enrich our betterment.

EVERYONE: You're not following me.

EVERYBODY: Right you are!

EVERYONE: *(Takes a moment.)* Once an artwork is completed it goes one of two places, someone's living room or a museum.

EVERYBODY: Or the trash.

EVERYONE: Or the trash. Do you think that that is what an artist is shooting for during the process? The artist really wants this expression of inspiration to be the perfect centerpiece for a posh bourgeois living room or another martyr hung in a crowd of colorful victims sectioned off into specific rooms classified as movements arbitrarily constructed. I mean what does it mean to look upon a masterpiece after having already tried to take in eighty-four other masterpieces. It's blasphemous is what it is. As soon as they're finished they're nothing. They're dead.

(Pause.)

EVERYBODY: I don't know. I really liked the nudes.

EVERYONE: That's true, the nudes are rather fetching.

VARIATION 23
GIFT SHOP

Lights up, the basketball bounces across the stage and off. Some time passes. EVERYONE and EVERYBODY are heard offstage from the direction the ball came from.

EVERYBODY: Over here. Over here.

EVERYONE: Are you sure? Perhaps left. I'm feeling left.

EVERYBODY: No, no. They said east.

(Light shift. They enter the nonexistent gift shop and stop, dumbfounded, seeing the exit. Pause. Never taking their eyes off it...)

EVERYBODY: That's it.

EVERYONE: Yes. Apparently so. It just doesn't seem... real.

EVERYBODY: Too much art. That's why.

EVERYONE: *(Nodding and still looking at it.)* Yes. *(Pause.)* Tell me, which was your favorite?

EVERYBODY: Oh, well of course there's... I mean, the one with the woman who... and the room with all the... paintings. You know I can't really remember any of them.

EVERYONE: No. Nor can I. I remember them, just not individually.

(The two look around. EVERYBODY approaches a collection of nonexistent art posters hanging from a display rack and arranged like leafs of paper to turn through.)

EVERYBODY: Look at this.

(The two stand and turn through nonexistent poster after nonexistent poster. Stopping at one of the nudes they have seen.)

EVERYONE: Just like my idea.

EVERYBODY: *(Excited.)* The nude with the nipples. What's she doing here?

EVERYONE: I'm not altogether sure.

EVERYBODY: Do you think this is a mistake?

EVERYONE: Please. This is a museum. Everything has been aesthetically arranged according to an aesthetic principle by a team of anesthesiologists.

EVERYBODY: *(Thumbing through more and stopping again.)* Hey Dodo and Gigi!

EVERYONE: *(Flipping through.)* This, this is a masterpiece of masterpieces.

EVERYBODY: Ah. I don't follow.

(During the following monologue EVERYBODY begins to thumb through the nonexistent poster display and discovers price tags

on the pieces. Then noticing the basketball, the bird, and the plant each on a display pedestal, EVERYBODY rushes over to each one observing their price tags.)

EVERYONE: It's all things we've seen. It is the aggregate of all art. A statement that it is all the same. No one work more important than another. The unification of art into one sacred justification of democratic equality. A sensational finale of the play which is "Art" which ties up all the pieces in one dramatic swoop. For art cannot be without its audience. It's a rapid-fire exposure to inspiration. It's a comment on the act of viewing. It's a criticism of perusals.

EVERYBODY: It's a gift shop.

EVERYONE: It's a gift shop? How do you figure?

EVERYBODY: *(Referring to the pieces.)* These all have price tags.

EVERYONE: They're for sale?

EVERYBODY: Apparently so.

EVERYONE: Why would anyone want a photograph of a painting?

(Pause.)

EVERYBODY: Same reason they would want a painting that looks like a photograph.

EVERYONE: Oh, I love those!

EVERYBODY: Who doesn't?

EVERYONE: So neat and impressive.

EVERYBODY: If one loves paintings which look like photographs, which we all do, then the reflexive property insists that we must also adore photographs that look like paintings. *(Beat.)* Not to men-

tion that they're all nice and glossy. Much prettier than the rough texture of the originals.

EVERYONE: *(Quietly referring to the nude with the nipples poster.)* How much is the nude with the... *(Gestures, "Nipples.")*

EVERYBODY: *(Checking.)* Eighteen dollars and ninety-five cents.

EVERYONE: Quite reasonable for a nipple... Did I say nipple, I meant nipple. Damnit!

(EVERYONE begins to take the poster in order to purchase it.)'

EVERYBODY: And you can take it home with you.

EVERYONE: Then I wouldn't have to come to the museum to look at the artwork.

(The two start gathering posters and such that they want; the pace and excitement should escalate.)

EVERYONE: Why didn't we start here in the first place?

EVERYBODY: The wise consumer window shops before purchasing.

EVERYONE: Like a walk-in catalogue?

EVERYBODY: Or a sushi menu.

EVERYONE: Indeed.

(The two stop in mid-action as INDIVIDUAL WITH MUSEUM HEADPHONES enters without headphones, but carrying a bag full of souvenirs in one hand and a bird with the price tag on it in the other. EVERYONE and EVERYBODY watch the INDIVIDUAL enter and exit.

(Upon exiting, a bouncing ball is heard and the individual combusts. Singed clothes and

*random body parts [and possibly a cell phone]
fly back onstage. They stare after the INDI-
VIDUAL for some time and then each looks
at the floor somewhat confused.
Nonchalantly, but with a contained urgency,
the two begin to place the items they have
gathered back where they obtained them.*

EVERYBODY: I believe I left my shoes
in the ah… sculpture garden.

EVERYONE: Oh, I'll help you retrieve
them.

*(They both start walking back from where
they entered.)*

VARIATION 24
FRAME OF REFERENCE

*Surrounded by velvet ropes as in the previ-
ous basketball scene, "Lines," EVERYBODY
is holding the basketball. He's about to shoot.*

EVERYBODY: What's the score?

EVERYONE: You have a, a… well I'm
at… *(Sighs.)*

EVERYBODY: Well what are we going
to do?

EVERYONE: Start over?

EVERYBODY: No.

EVERYONE: We could just assign random letters?

*(EVERYBODY just looks at EVERYONE
in that are you kidding me way. Pause.)*

EVERYONE: Next shot in wins. Agreed?

EVERYBODY: *(Thinks about it.)* Agreed.

*(EVERYBODY takes a normal shooting
stance from a would-be free throw line. EV-
ERYBODY exhales. He bounces the ball
three times. He exhales. Bounces the ball three
times. He exhales. Bounces the ball three
times. He exhales. He begins to shoot, the
actors freeze. This is the final tableau, the
final work of art.)*

*(House lights up. There is no bow, no cur-
tain. [If the production uses stagehands, they
may take a bow.] EVERYONE and EVERY-
BODY do not move until the audience is
gone.)*

The Language of Kisses

Edmund De Santis

EDMUND DE SANTIS was born in Canton, Ohio. He earned a BA from Miami University in Oxford, Ohio. He moved to New York City when he was twenty-three, where he held various jobs, including buyer at Macy's, book publishing assistant, and photographic gallery assistant, before finally becoming an actor, which laid the foundation for his work as a playwright. De Santis later went to Hunter College and obtained a master's degree in theatre. In 1994, he became a founding member of The Harbor Theatre, a playwright-driven theatre company composed of writers, actors, and directors. De Santis has written many plays, eleven of which have been produced, including: *Thinking and Other Positions*, *Recensio*, *American Subway*, *buddies'n'stuff*, *Still Life With Noise*, *Blue Film*, *Bronzetime Soap-Op*, and *Ash Wednesday*. His play *Making Peter Pope* was produced by The Harbor Theatre in 1999, and appears in the New York Theatre Experience anthology *Plays and Playwrights for the New Millennium*. De Santis is a member of The Dramatists Guild. He currently resides in Greenwich Village in New York City.

The Language of Kisses was presented by the Harbor Theatre Company (Stuart Warmflash, Artistic Director) in a reading in March 2000 at the Grove Street Playhouse, New York City, with the following cast and credits:

Zan .... Donna Davis
Blue .... Vincent Sagona
Mara .... Carol Todd

Directed by: Laura Josepher

The author gratefully acknowledges the contribution and support of all members of The Harbor Theatre Company, where this play was developed.

Dedication:
To Christine "Dear" Joyce

"O lost, and by the wind grieved, ghost, come back again."
—*Thomas Wolfe,* Look Homeward, Angel

CHARACTERS

ZAN: Mid- to late forties or early fifties; a retired college instructor, an attractive, well-kept woman, without pretension, brooding, passionate.

BLUE: Somewhere in his twenties; a simple attractive guy; slightly retarded. A true naïf. Whenever he's unsure, he has a tic of ducking, as if someone is about to hit him on the head.

MARA: Zan's estranged daughter, early twenties; high-strung, headstrong; brash.

THE TIME

June.

THE PLACE

On a farm in Gideon, Ohio.

ACT ONE
SCENE ONE

Early June. The lights come up on the interior of a slightly ramshackle farmhouse, large and airy with old, worn furniture, fixtures and appliances. But the quality is homey, comfortable and clean. There is a kitchen, which breaks off into a living room area, with comfortable worn furniture, and in one corner a large desk with at least one drawer that locks, with stacks of papers, magazines, a manual typewriter. There are stacks of books all around the room, a bookcase which covers one entire wall overflowing with books. The air of this room is that of an academic. Along the back of the kitchen runs a screened-in porch off the kitchen door. The only things immediately visible outside are green trees. There is a door in the kitchen leading to a basement. And visible in the living room is the bottom of a set of stairs going to the second floor.

Van Morrison's "Sweet Thing" plays, first generally, then specifically from a radio near

ZAN's desk. ZAN is seated at her desk, writing at her typewriter. BLUE enters through the porch. He wears workclothes. ZAN doesn't hear him at first. He comes into the kitchen and looks at her for a long moment. She finally becomes aware of his presence, makes a small sound of surprise. They search each other's face. He walks slowly to the desk. She stands up to face him. Suddenly, they fall into an embrace and are kissing with great passion, as if an unmet urgency, which matches the song, has been unleashed. They speak to each other with their kisses, with their eyes. Their lovemaking is fierce, intense, and voracious. It peaks to moments of intensity, then gets suddenly gentle, with lips barely touching, before flaring up into heat again. He opens her blouse, she bites at him. She rips at his shirt and kisses his chest, pulling his shirt out of his pants. He lifts her skirt, pushing her onto the desk. He rubs between her legs. She cries out. She grinds herself forward, they stumble, laugh and fall to their knees on the floor, trying to mash their bod-

ies together. She rubs herself against him, inviting him. He pushes her back onto the floor, mounts her under her skirt. She suddenly pushes him onto the floor next to her, rolls onto him and mounts him. They are wild with pleasure. ZAN rises up and screams out.

Music stops. Blackout.

SCENE TWO

Late June. ZAN stands at her kitchen sink, trimming the ends of green beans. She wears a summer dress. She occasionally glances out the window in front of her, smiling to herself. In the background is the sound of a tractor off in the distance. It continues under the following. Suddenly, from the other side of the house ZAN hears the sound of a car approaching over gravel, followed by the sound of a car door opening and closing, and the car driving away. ZAN goes out to the porch and looks off. She comes back in the kitchen, paces madly for a moment, trying to compose herself. She goes back to the sink, almost hysterically starts to cut beans, slips and cuts her thumb with the paring knife. She quickly grabs a dishtowel and wraps her thumb. Moments later, a knock is heard offstage on the outside door of the porch. The door opens. MARA appears with a couple of bags and a knapsack. She gets almost to the door and sees her mother. She stops. They look at each other for a long moment. MARA enters the kitchen. ZAN wears a stupefied smile.

MARA: Say "I told you so." Say "take a powder." Say anything you want. Say something. I promise not to get mad.

(No response.)

MARA: Look at you. Haven't aged a bit. A little around the eyes. Like maybe I should talk. I have lines. In certain light. I look like shit, I know. Hair's a fright wig, huh? Boy, this humidity. I forgot. Say something.

(No response.)

MARA: I took a bus all the way. Believe it? Mistake. Toilet was dreadful. Stunk to high heaven. Stopped at the college first. Figured every summer you had one class. American Lit, Mondays and Wednesdays at nine to eleven and three to five. It meant the other days we'd go swimming at Helen's or to Aikens Lake with that ratty old picnic basket.

ZAN: I don't teach there anymore.

MARA: The secretary said. She wasn't very friendly. Did you quit?

ZAN: Yes.

MARA: So?

(MARA reaches out to touch ZAN, who casually pulls her arm away. ZAN goes to a kitchen cabinet to get a Band-aid.)

ZAN: Here you are!

MARA: You're so happy to see me, I can hardly stand it. Oh, you cut yourself.

ZAN: After all this time. After no word. Nothing. Not even a… Christmas card.

MARA: If I said sorry would it make a difference?

ZAN: Mara. It's bigger than you and me standing here right now. Not just "oh Mara's back, the one who left without a word, the one who stayed away for three years, the one who threw away chances and opportunities to try and find some star nonsense," don't get me started… Of course, I'm glad, you're alive, you're safe, you look healthy.

MARA: Thank you.

ZAN: But I'm over you.

MARA: I love you, too.

ZAN: Not like... in a bad way.

MARA: Oh. I'm relieved because I suddenly wanted to say you bitch I hate you, but I stopped myself. (*Turns away, looks around the house.*)

ZAN: Oh, Mara, let's not do that again.

MARA: Place looks great. Mmm. I love the smell of freshly painted rooms. (*Beat.*) It's not like I left you stranded or anything. You had friends. I'm sure Helen practically lives here. And little Bobby Passmore, you had him to help out, didn't you? Did he paint the house?

ZAN: Little Bobby Passmore died two years ago. He tried to race a train across the tracks on his motorcycle down at Old Bender Road. He was torn in half.

MARA: God. Sorry to hear that. He was so cute, too. I don't mean that disrespectfully, of course. You still swim in Helen's pool in the summer? I wouldn't mind going there later for a swim.

ZAN: Oh. No. (*Beat.*) You have bags.

MARA: I'm not going back to New York. I hate it there. I was hoping I could stay for a couple of days. Get the old bearings back, so to speak. But since you're over me and everything.

ZAN: Oh.

MARA: I noticed my swing is still on the tree.

ZAN: And your playhouse is still in the sycamore grove. How nostalgic, a trip down memory lane. Whew, glad that's over.

MARA: Come on, have a sense of humor, okay? I'm sorry it was shitty, I didn't call or write or send Christmas cards... I sent a postcard, didn't I?

ZAN: One postcard. So scribbled I couldn't read it. No return address or phone number.

MARA: I didn't know you cared so much.

ZAN: Was it a test to see how much I cared for you? I was a bad mother, I know it.

MARA: (*Turning away.*) Fuck off. Your pat answers.

ZAN: You fuck off! YOUR pat answers. Off to a great start, way to go Mara—!

MARA: So, can I stay?

ZAN: If you start acting up again, I don't think I can take it.

MARA: Are you really so mad that I left? I'm surprised you even noticed I was gone. All caught up in your big race for tenure and look, it turns out you quit anyhow!

ZAN: It's more complicated than that and don't ever blame it on my teaching, I gave you lots of time. You didn't want it. I'm sorry things didn't work out for you.

MARA: All right it's not fair of me. So, can I stay or not?

(*ZAN moves back to the sink and her beans.*)

MARA: No answer. Can I at least have something to drink, please? A glass of water?

ZAN: The glasses are still kept in the cupboard. Turn on the faucet, water.

MARA: Don't worry, I wouldn't expect you to wait on me hand and foot.

ZAN: Don't worry I wouldn't.

(*MARA gets a glass of water. Her body touches ZAN, who moves away.*)

MARA: It wouldn't kill you to be a little more cordial. You're not gonna get cooties if you touch me.

ZAN: Do you need to splash water every-where?

MARA: See? I needed a break from your constant nagging! Ma! I'm joking! Relax! *(Suddenly looks out the window.)* Ohmigod, look at all the sunflowers! You're planting corn and sunflowers and—I don't believe it! What's all that stuff?

ZAN: Vegetables. Corn. Sunflowers.

MARA: And… is that… like a gazebo?

ZAN: Yes it is well, a sort of. Gazebo.

MARA: I've only seen them in movies. Cool! *(Sits at the table, looks around.)* Wow. Little improvements everywhere! The place never looked this good when Dad was around! You must have a lot more free time now you don't teach anymore. I had a lot more free time the last couple of months. I stopped going to some of my temp jobs. To auditions. I stopped going to. Everything.

(No response.)

MARA: I had a nervous breakdown. On the #1 downtown. That's the subway.

(No response.)

MARA: I started having these. Episodes.

(No response.)

MARA: I thought people were following me.

(No response.)

MARA: I was attacked.

(ZAN stops what she's doing. She turns to MARA.)

MARA: I'm fine. I wasn't hurt. Physically. Or anything. It. It. It happened in the el-evator of my building. This guy, he lived

across the street. He was watching our apartment for a long time. Me. Us. He'd go to the roof. Spy down on us. We called the police lots of times. They could never catch him at it. I came home late one night from work. I was doing extra temp work, for the rent. One of my roommates moved out and left Sheri and me in the lurch. I came home and. There he was. Waiting. In the elevator. He whispers, "Pretty girl." But in this sleazy cartooney way— "Pretty Girrruulll"… He had this kitchen knife. He cut my bra open. I froze I swear I froze and you know, you think you've heard this a hundred times but you can't believe it's happening to you, you think oh God has this guy ever heard of Ban roll-on and you see the black sprouts of hair in his ears and nose and oh great the burrito I brought home from Burritoville's getting cold and I'm going to miss Seinfeld to-night and then it's over and… *(Rocks in her chair.)* He didn't. Penetrate me. He. Came on my shoe. *(Laughs, then gets teary.)* It was scary.

(ZAN puts her hand on MARA's shoulder.)

MARA: They couldn't convict him. Not enough evidence or something!

ZAN: Your shoe?

MARA: There's never enough evidence! You notice? If I was a man there'd be enough evidence, you bet there'd be. You know, if I was a man being stalked.

ZAN: *(Takes MARA's face in her hands.)* Mara. Did you stalk someone?

MARA: What!? *(Pulling away.)* No! I'm not lying! And I never stalked anybody when I was living here. That was—God, you'd believe anybody else before you'd believe me! You think I could make some-thing like that up? This guy was everywhere I went! I felt trapped! I didn't know where else to go. So can I crash here or not? I'm not going to beg you.

(The sound of the tractor sputters out.)

ZAN: Yes... ... you can stay.

MARA: Thank you. I'll start looking for an apartment in Mallory tomorrow I promise and a job. I don't expect you to support me. I could find something in an office. Or waitressing, I haven't done it in awhile. Just haveta get used to being treated like dirt again. This water's terrible. *(Refills her glass at the sink. She looks out the window.)* Who's that?

ZAN: Where?

MARA: On the tractor?

ZAN: The handy man.

MARA: Oh you have a handy man.

ZAN: The guy who. He's handy. He helps out. He built the... gazebo thing.

MARA: I figured you had somebody to . help out. He's so cute.

ZAN: He's not... cute. It's not high school.

MARA: Well from here he is. What's wrong with him?

ZAN: *(A little too quickly.)* There's nothing wrong with him. He's a great help. I don't know what I've done without him.

MARA: Ma, you have a crush on him, don't you?

ZAN: Mara... no, that's not... ... I know, I have an idea—why don't you go freshen up? I'm about to put out lunch for Blue, if you'd like I could make you a sandwich.

MARA: Blue?

ZAN: The handyman.

MARA: Blue?

ZAN: It's his name. Don't make a big deal out of it.

MARA: I won't. I'm starving. I would love a sandwich. Thank you. I'll run my bag up to my room and use the bathroom. I wanna look good for Blue.

ZAN: Oh.

MARA: You don't want me to look good for Blue?

ZAN: No, of course, I always want you to look your best but—

MARA: I'm just being playful. Don't tell me, he's gay!

ZAN: No, I meant—you'll have to sleep on the foldout couch in the addition while you're here, do you mind?

MARA: Why, do you and Helen have sewing circles up there now?

ZAN: It's Blue's room.

MARA: Blue's room? Oh, of course, how silly of me. "Blue's room." He lives here?

ZAN: *(With the slightest bit of an edge.)* What of it?

MARA: Why are you treating me so coldly, all I said was "does he live here?"

ZAN: Yes!

MARA: Does he pay rent?

ZAN: It's a special situation.

MARA: So he does the work and gets room and board in return and and...

ZAN: The place needs work. Constant maintenance. The land was going to waste.

MARA: But... it's... ... my... room.

ZAN: It was your room. It's Blue's home now, too. It's his room. I can't just take it away from him.

MARA: Then I'll sleep on the couch and use the washroom in the ADDITION! It's fine, it's more private anyhow. Though I don't see why Blue, if he's living here, isn't the one staying in the ADDITION! And p.s., the addition is the room Dad died in.

ZAN: Well there are no ghosts here.

MARA: I'll still have to come upstairs for a shower.

ZAN: You can use the shower in the basement, I had it fixed up nice down there.

MARA: With all those spiders! I hate that! I'll clean up after myself, don't worry, okay? I promise. Does Blue shower upstairs?

ZAN: Shower wherever you'd like.

MARA: You're right, what'm I thinking, I'm grateful you're even letting me stay. You're only my mother. I'll shower in the basement. I'll sleep in the basement if you want me to. You don't get any of my jokes, do you? I'll stay out of your hair. You'll see.

ZAN: I don't care what you think.

MARA: You're fucking him, that's it, isn't it, that's why you've been acting so weird!

ZAN: Could you do me a favor and not use language like that around Blue? It upsets him.

MARA: Excuse me, you're sleeping with him, aren't you?

ZAN: Go put your bag in the addition.

MARA: I'm out of line.

ZAN: I don't want you to say or do... anything... to... upset... him... he's extremely sensitive and—

MARA: What'm I going to say, what'm I going to do, don't worry, I won't even talk to him, okay, would you prefer I stay completely to myself because I can crawl into a cocoon for weeks at a stretch. I got good at it. Especially after I was...

ZAN: I didn't mean that, I only meant—

BLUE: *(From off.)* Zan. The choke on the tractor, it's—how do I put it how do I put it—

(BLUE enters the porch, shirtless. He uses his shirt to wipe the sweat off of his brow and his chest. He enters the kitchen, sees MARA; he becomes self-conscious and quickly puts on his sweat-covered shirt, backs out of the room onto the screened-in porch, head down.)

BLUE: —it's broke. Oh sorry. Uh.

ZAN: Come in, Blue. Come on, it's okay.

BLUE: I didn't know. There was company. Hi. I'll just. You have company. If it's the Avon lady I want some more of that men's aftershave. I like it. It's pungent. Unless you don't like it.

ZAN: Blue, this is Mara.

BLUE: Uh-oh that sounds serious. Should I fix the choke now? Or go downstairs and clean up. Should I stay down there awhile? I could work on the birdhouse. Zan?

ZAN: Mara's my daughter.

MARA: Hi Blue, nice to meet you. *(Extends her hand.)*

BLUE: *(Does a double take to ZAN and back.)* Oh! You! You're the! Daughter! The one who's. You went to be a movie star, right? Pleased to meet you.

ZAN: Mara's going to stay here for a few days.

MARA: I might even apply to the college. That should make you happy.

ZAN: I wish you wouldn't do that.

MARA: What, apply to the college?

ZAN: No. Anything for my happiness. Blue, mayonnaise or mustard?

BLUE: Depends what the lunch meat is.

ZAN: Turkey.

BLUE: Mustard, please. Thanks, Zan, most people don't ask and you get this sandwich with the totally wrong condiments. *(To MARA.)* Welcome. What's your name again?

MARA: Mara. I'm sure you heard all sorts of evil stories about me.

BLUE: Nah I don't think I did. Lemme think. Evil stories. About all the cats you blew up with firecrackers? Ooops, no, that was me. Nah, I never did that. Honest. Zan did you tell me evil stories about— what's your name again? Mara. How's that spelled. Like. M-e-

MARA: A.

BLUE: M-a-r-e——no, a!! I got it. No evil stories I can remember. She mentioned you that one time. That was it. Said you went off to be a star. How'd that pan out by the way? Sorry. That's personal. She said she burned all your pictures, so I wasn't sure what... ... you looked like. Ooooops. I'm about to put a lid on it.

(Awkward pause. ZAN puts a pitcher of lemonade on the table.)

BLUE: Zan's homemade lemonade.

MARA: Mom makes the best lemonade.

BLUE: I love it. I said it, she did it. I'm the living Tom Sawyer—right?—or some-

thing like that. No, that's wrong, right Zanny? It's that other story. And my dreams come true. That's all I mean. I could kiss you. Dum-de-dum-dum, time to head downstairs. See you soon. Mara. Right? *(Exits to the basement.)*

MARA: *(Waits a few seconds, then whispers.)* Is he... ?

ZAN: What?

MARA: Is he retarded?

ZAN: No! God, you're so...

MARA: I'm only asking!

ZAN: Blue's had rough times. He hasn't had time to catch up. He's—

MARA: —developmentally challenged then.

ZAN: Why don't you put your bags in the addition?

MARA: Could we not call it the addition? Could we call it the den or the family room that never was or something? It's just... it was added so long ago.

ZAN: Call it whatever you want.

MARA: 'Course family room sounds like a lie, doesn't it?

(ZAN ignores her, turns back to making lunch. MARA comes up behind her and puts her arms around her. ZAN stops and stiffens.)

ZAN: Excuse me, I have to get the mustard in the refrigerator. *(Extricates herself from MARA and goes to the refrigerator.)* Go, let me make lunch.

(MARA grabs her bags and exits. ZAN stands looking in the fridge, BLUE sneaks in behind her, puts his hands over her eyes.)

ZAN: Mara, I said—

BLUE: Not Mara!

(BLUE turns her around, begins kissing her neck, pushes her against the refrigerator. ZAN melts, wary of MARA. They whisper.)

BLUE: Talk to me Zanny Zan talk to me…

ZAN: Oh Blue—no—

BLUE: I told you I like your butt.

ZAN: No it's not my butt.

BLUE: I'm so sweaty.

ZAN: I know.

BLUE: I'm sorry.

ZAN: It's okay.

BLUE: Are you mad?

ZAN: No. *(Beat.)* I like it.

BLUE: I knew that.

ZAN: But maybe we shouldn't. While Mara's here. It's so unexpected.

(He kisses her several times swiftly on the lips, then kisses her fiercely for a moment, then pulls away. She becomes aroused. He's amused by that. He kisses her several times again, she kisses him back. They speak with their kisses. Sound of a door off. She pushes him away.)

ZAN: No! Not while she's—

BLUE: Then you'll be my secret love affair then.

(BLUE kisses her until she's fully aroused, lets her go, turns away, and exits.)

ZAN: Blue! *(Beat.)* Dear Blue. *(Feels a sudden ache of missing him.)*

(The lights fade on ZAN.)

SCENE THREE

Lunch. ZAN, BLUE, and MARA sit at the table, sandwiches and lunch things in front of them, potato salad, lemonade, cut-up radishes.

BLUE: I wanna go to New York someday. Didn't some famous guy get burned at the stake last year, uh no I'm thinking of another guy. Forget it. Zan, no room for pie!

ZAN: I don't know who you mean. Will you take that bag out to the compost when you're done?

BLUE: With delight, my lady. Yeah I don't know who I mean either, I coulda seen it on TV. Zan makes the best strawberry rhubarb pie.

MARA: Baking pies! You're a regular Mother Nature! Gardens and compost heaps and rosebushes!

BLUE: That compost heap is A-LIVE! P.U.! *(Laughs.)* Oh look these glasses are sweatin a blue streak, it's a scorcher, I think I'm gettin that heat rash again!

MARA: God, today would be a perfect day to go swim in Helen's pool.

ZAN: Use that Gold Bond I told you.

MARA: Maybe we should call her.

BLUE: *(To ZAN.)* You're always right. I keep forgettin the Gold Bond.

ZAN: Mara were you smoking pot in the addition?

BLUE: Dum-de-dum-dum.

MARA: Oh I hope you don't mind. Did you want a couple of hits?

BLUE: I do. Kidding! Not that I'm against it or anything.

MARA: *(Sees the way ZAN looks at her.)* Later, Blue. Well you know I get high. You've gotten high. I happen to know you have very liberal views about marijuana.

ZAN: Is it such a problem to go outside?

BLUE: I knew a pothead once. Pretty happy-go-lucky guy. That's bad, I guess. You a pothead?

MARA: No. I don't see why I have to go outside, that's all.

ZAN: Well then at least do it out on the porch, hm?

BLUE: Oh I know that Brooklyn Bridge! I wanna see that! You musta visited there a lot!

ZAN: Blue, we have to pick the rest of those cucumbers.

MARA: Not once. *(Holds up a radish.)* D'you grow this in the garden, too?

BLUE: Yep! And Zan tell her about the hyberd tomatoes out there too.

ZAN: The hybrids. I don't think Mara's interested in our garden.

MARA: I just asked you if radishes grew in your garden. *(To BLUE.)* See why I got stoned? We're on these different wavelengths—she's up here—"eeeeeeeeeeeeee"—and I'm down here "EEEEEEEEEEEEEEEE"—she's on ultra-high uptight frequency and I'm down here on lowkey frequency, get it—"eeeeeeeeEEEEEeeeeeeEEEEEE"? *(Laughs.)*

BLUE: *(Chews thoughtfully.)* I get it, I think. I know what I wanted to ask. In New York... did you live where the Jeffersons lived and I know they're characters on a TV show.

MARA: I think they were movin' on up to the East Side—I lived in a high rise on the Upper West Side—and you wouldn't believe how expensive it was. I had to live with two other—

ZAN: Mara, try the chicken salad.

MARA: —girls. It's okay, just cut me off. I don't have anything important to say. Is that dill? My favorite.

ZAN: Blue's, too. Sorry, I didn't mean to cut you off.

BLUE: No, my favorite is that yellow stuff remember? How expensive, a coupla hundred a month?

MARA: Are you kidding?

ZAN: Oh right, you like curry.

MARA: Shit, even sharing the rent, I ended about paying eight hundred a month.

BLUE: So that's like how much total three times... ... ...? *(Pretends to multiply it in his head.)*

MARA: Twenty-four hundred a month! And that's for a one bedroom.

BLUE: Holy mackerel, twenty-four hundred, that's a lot, right? Incredible!

ZAN: If you'd given him another minute he would've gotten it.

MARA: I didn't realize we were in school. Okay, Blue, you go stand at the board now and do problems, geez!

BLUE: I think she knows that, Zan. That much money so you can live in a box with lots of people on top of each other in boxes and boxes next to each other and like in this big box city! Man, that's a psych-out! I mean some people don't even make that in a year. You musta done pretty good as an actress, you did acting in New York, right?

MARA: Uh-huh.

BLUE: Well what did you act in?

MARA: I did a few scene showcases. I auditioned once for the Actor's Studio. That's where Brando studied.

BLUE: And you acted in movies?

MARA: Some.

BLUE: Well… what kind of movies?

MARA: Different ones.

BLUE: With Clint Eastwood?

MARA: No, like independent films.

BLUE: Oh like movies nobody sees, is that what she means that's why they're independent?

ZAN: Did I put too much dill in the chicken salad?

MARA: I did a soap opera once. No I think it's just the right amount.

BLUE: Daytime love and passion shows? Cool! You had love scenes, the whole bit?

MARA: Sure.

(ZAN looks at her.)

MARA: Actually, It was more like extra work. *(Winks at ZAN.)*

BLUE: Why'd you just wink at her?

MARA: No reason.

BLUE: All right, what's the big secret, you gotta tell me.

ZAN: Blue knows what a wink is, Mara.

MARA: So?

ZAN: So don't condescend to him.

MARA: I wunk at you for fun. I'm not condescending to Blue.

BLUE: I'm sittin right here, I'm not in the other room! Is it women or is it me?

MARA: I was thinking you're probably thinking oh Mara was a real failure as an actress.

ZAN: It never crossed my mind.

MARA: Let me tell you the acting profession is totally rigged. If you don't look a certain way like this Miss Perfect without a blemish with the perfect ass and boobs—

ZAN: It takes talent, too, though, doesn't it, at least a little?

MARA: Right and I have no talent therefore I could never make it, right?

ZAN: I was only saying. I only saw you act in high school plays.

MARA: And I was damn good in them!

ZAN: I guess you were good.

BLUE: See now you're gettin heavy on me or somethin here.

MARA: Oh Bluey, we're not getting heavy on you.

(MARA reaches across to BLUE. He flinches.)

BLUE: Uh-uh watch it, oh I thought you were gonna tickle me.

MARA: Uh-oh somebody's ticklish!

BLUE: Yeah and so another thing I wanted to ask you was did you ride that subway?

MARA: Uh-huh oh yeah almost everyday.

BLUE: Underground trains that's so cool—

MARA: Yeah underground with the rats and cockroaches everywhere—! It was so cool.

BLUE: Rats! Get outta here.

MARA: Thousands of em, millions! Yeah I swear, and you just look right down and there they are you see 'em all over the place, big fat rats. And I'm not only talking about the lawyers. Oh and I did a standup routine once. That's a joke.

BLUE: And cockroaches those are like those big bugs right?

MARA: Cadillacs. Gigantic brown hairy suckers big feelers moving around.

BLUE: Oh baby I feel real squiggly all over thinkin about it. And some fly don't they?

MARA: Some do. Most skitter. Like this. *(Skitters her hand quickly across the table.)* Skitter. Skitter skitter skitter. Fast like that and you—

(MARA skitters her hand towards BLUE, tickles him, gets him laughing.)

MARA: —no, really I swear they're like skittering all over and you're like trying to kill them and they skitter skitter and then you finally do and then they squish open—

BLUE: *(Is entertained and laughing.)* —stop I'm so ticklish——!

MARA: —I swear and all this gooey greeney yellowish stuff comes shooting out—and you have to squish these suckers really hard to kill em too—

BLUE: Eeuwwwwwww... ... gross! Stop——!

MARA: —and you have to go smash smash smash, I got so good at it, I could do it with my bare hands—

ZAN: All right... ... that's enough!

MARA: *(Winding down with the laughing.)* Whenever there was a bug in the apartment, it was Mara to the rescue. What's wrong... ... ... relax.

ZAN: Do we have to talk about it while we're eating?

MARA: Oh have some fun grim Grandma!

BLUE: *(Joining in the fun.)* Yeah, have some fun grim Grandma!

ZAN: What?

BLUE: *(Beat.)* Nuthin you know. I was playin.

ZAN: Oh.

MARA: I like your hair, by the way. It frames your face nicely. You decided to let it go naturally.

ZAN: Thanks.

BLUE: Zan I didn't say anything wrong, did I?

ZAN: No.

BLUE: Zan.

ZAN: No.

BLUE: Zan.

ZAN: What?

BLUE: You wanna go visit New York sometime? I wanna see that Statue Island Ferry.

ZAN: Blue.

BLUE: All right, Zan. But I didn't say anything wrong, did I?

MARA: Who needs New York when you have all this space, you can walk out that door and have space. And at night look up and actually see stars. Right, Mom?

ZAN: You said it.

BLUE: I like it here pretty much, too. *(Beat.)* Zan. No really, listen.

ZAN: What?

BLUE: You have. *(Points out some food on ZAN's chin.)*

ZAN: What? Did I get it?

BLUE: Here. *(Reaches out with his napkin and wipes it off.)*

(MARA looks at them. ZAN reflexively moves away from BLUE.)

ZAN: Anybody, more potato salad?

BLUE: No, thanks, Zan, I'm stuffed. I'll have my pie later. I better get this bag down to the compost, it's startin to rank up the joint.

(BLUE grabs a large garbage bag and exits off through the porch. He winks at ZAN and exits. ZAN gets up and starts clearing the table.)

ZAN: You don't have to do it now! *(Laughs, trying to avoid direct eye contact with MARA.)* Rank up the joint? Is that a phrase? I don't know, I've never heard that phrase…

MARA: Can we sit for a minute without you jumping up and acting like the maid? You afraid to be alone with me?

ZAN: Please don't say I'm afraid. I have things to do. I don't have time to sit around.

MARA: Okay you're not afraid. He's sweet.

ZAN: 'Cause I'm not. Afraid. Yes he is. Very helpful. I don't know what I'd do without him.

MARA: Yeah you mentioned… He's like a big kid.

ZAN: He's a man.

MARA: Well, he seems young. A young man. Crazy about you! Well tell me something, huh?

ZAN: What?

MARA: Well, uh what's he—what's he like in bed! No, wrong question, just kidding—I don't know—what made you quit teaching? Start with that.

ZAN: I got tired of it.

MARA: Just like that.

ZAN: Just like that.

MARA: Wow, you seemed to really love it when I was here.

ZAN: It was all a show.

MARA: Oh! A show! A good one! Coulda fooled me. Well what'm I saying, you did!

ZAN: Yes.

MARA: Yes. Well… what do you live on?

ZAN: What?

MARA: What? No, wrong question. *(Beat.)* What did Helen think of you quitting teaching?

ZAN: I'm not sure. *(Beat.)* I lease out the land. All that corn. It's not mine. I get income from that.

MARA: I get the sense you and Helen stopped talking to each other or something.

ZAN: Could we… could we just not… talk… about that.

MARA: What's the big deal?

ZAN: *(More insistent.)* I just don't want to talk about it, that's all.

MARA: Why are you acting so weird?

ZAN: Stop saying I'm acting weird. I hate talking to you when you're stoned.

MARA: You are, since I got here, like you're holding something back or I can't figure it out. I'm asking you a few simple questions about what's been going on with you—

(She reaches out to touch ZAN's arm, but ZAN pulls away.)

MARA: —and you act like I'm a leper! You can't even touch me.

ZAN: I don't like being interrogated, that's all.

MARA: I'm not interrogating you. Forget it.

ZAN: I don't expect you to tell me every detail of your experiences either.

MARA: Don't you even wanna know what happened with Johnny Ruvolo and me?

ZAN: No.

MARA: Fine, then.

ZAN: We don't have a lot in common anymore.

MARA: No I guess not. Maybe we never did.

ZAN: So this could be really difficult.

(BLUE enters the porch, stops and listens.)

MARA: A few days won't kill you.

ZAN: No, it's fine…

MARA: I won't get in your way I promise.

ZAN: No it's fine… *(Suddenly explodes.)* Just don't think you're going to ruin my life more than you already have, that's all! *(Turns away.)*

MARA: No, I wasn't planning on it, pardon me for living.

ZAN: I'm sorry. Look at me, I'm apologizing. Why don't you take a walk outside, look around?

MARA: All of a sudden I feel so… … … so… … … tired. I want to lie down now. Is that okay? Yeah. I think I will. Take a pill and sleep for a couple of days, just kidding, but you know what I mean, this sudden wave of… … … zzzzzzz… … …

ZAN: You know where the sheets are.

MARA: Yes. I know where the sheets are. Mom. Thanks for lunch. Thanks for everything. Oh hi Blue, how long you been standing there? Ever think about growing pot between that corn out there. Just kidding. But think about it. One or two plants. Perfect camouflage.

(MARA exits. BLUE moves to ZAN, she turns away, busies herself.)

BLUE: Hey okay?

ZAN: Hey okay!

BLUE: Mad at me?

ZAN: Not at all.

BLUE: You sure? Cause you know I'd never say anything to hurt you in a million years. In ten million years.

ZAN: I know. We're gonna read like we usually do, aren't we?

BLUE: I was hoping you'd say that.

ZAN: I mean read. Go out to the gazebo.

BLUE: Kiss?

ZAN: Meet me in the gazebo.

BLUE: All right. *(Looks at her for a long moment.)* Last chance for a kiss. Going going gone. *(As he starts to exit.)* Day'll come you'll wish you had that kiss…… !

(He is gone. ZAN stops what she's doing and looks out the window. The lights fade.)

SCENE FOUR

Lights come up to a small corner of a gazebo downstage. Foliage surrounds a wicker loveseat. A small pile of worn books. Lighting is late afternoon. ZAN and BLUE sit in the shade. BLUE reaches in his pocket, pulls out a pack of cigarettes, offers one to ZAN.

ZAN: Yeah right just what I need, to start smoking again.

BLUE: I quit. First thing tomorrow.

ZAN: You say every day.

BLUE: I don't smoke a lot.

ZAN: Enough.

BLUE: Times like now. After lunch. On the gaze bo. *(He pronounces it as two words: gaze bo. He rubs his fingers up her arm.)*

ZAN: A one track mind, you.

BLUE: I have other tracks. One track this very second that's all.

ZAN: Oh, and I know, I saw you smoking on the tractor today. I've never seen you do that.

BLUE: Uh-oh somebody has eyes for me, watchin me through the kitchen window?

ZAN: Speaking of which, that tractor's gonna end up costing way more than it's worth.

BLUE: You hate the taste, dontcha?

ZAN: What?

BLUE: When you kiss me. The taste of the cigarette.

ZAN: Your taste?

BLUE: *(Crushes out the cigarette.)* Mister Disgusto, right? I'll brush my teeth pronto. I'll use Listerine. Or Scope. If you prefer.

ZAN: If anything, I find it…

BLUE: What.

ZAN: … erotic. We should start.

BLUE: *(Moves closer to her.)* Okay.

ZAN: Reading.

BLUE: I wanna have the sweetest sweetest breath so you never stop kissing me.

ZAN: We didn't read yesterday, we have to stay in the habit.

BLUE: We'll read. Let's check my breath.

ZAN: No.

BLUE: Let's check.

ZAN: Not now.

BLUE: Check or I'll think I have bad breath and that's why you won't check.

ZAN: What?

(He grabs her and kisses her till she's aroused. He lets her go.)

BLUE: Pass?

ZAN: Pass.

BLUE: Feel how hard I am?

ZAN: No, it's okay.

(He grabs her, kisses her, she responds. He lets her go.)

BLUE: Feel it.

(ZAN feels him.)

BLUE: *(Tenderly.)* That's more like it.

(They sit for a moment. BLUE turns and looks at ZAN.)

ZAN: What?

BLUE: You're acting strange.

ZAN: I am?

BLUE: Pfff, yeah!

ZAN: Sorry. It's such a shock seeing Mara that's all.

BLUE: Yeah! That Mara! She's a card! Oh I get it, you're scared of Mara. She might see us. That's why we're not allowed to kiss.

ZAN: I'm not scared of Mara! I don't care what Mara thinks at all. Though I do think—

BLUE: Here it comes—

ZAN: Maybe it's better not to be so demonstrative around Mara.

BLUE: And that's bein what?

ZAN: All this kissing and hugging for one and the winks and the sly remarks.

BLUE: Sly remarks? Uh-huh, you're scared for Mara to know.

ZAN: To know what—

BLUE: That you could like somebody like me.

ZAN: Don't ever say I'm scared of Mara. I just think—

BLUE: You ashamed?

ZAN: No, how could you think I was ashamed?

BLUE: Somebody smart like you likin a retard. I heard her whisper to you about is he a retard.

ZAN: She was being insensitive—she doesn't know you.

BLUE: Can I ask you something? Why's she gonna ruin your life?

ZAN: What?

BLUE: Before, I heard you shriek—that's a word right?—don't think you're gonna ruin my life.

ZAN: Oh, Mara and I. You can tell we have our differences.

BLUE: Uh yeah. It's like I was in Bad Kitchen Day or somethin like I was time travelin or somethin.

ZAN: Bad what?

BLUE: Bad Kitchen Day. The day my Mom became somebody else. Somebody evil. Big head. With a bandana.

ZAN: I'm not like that.

BLUE: I didn't say… you were like that! I said I time traveled didn't I? When everything was dirty. Screaming filthy pigs dirty filthy pigs! Arms flying. Spit spitting everywhere. And clean everything out, the kitchen cabinets and underneath the sink and even the stove then the bathrooms, hands and knees scrubbing tile with the toothbrush, my fingers bloody then the bleach in the toilet good good now you know what it's like—

This big head machine screaming orders yelling you stupe can't you do anything right and then the world came to an end and that's Bad Kitchen Day.

ZAN: Oh Blue. I'm so sorry.

BLUE: I had enough Bad Kitchen Days that's all.

ZAN: When Mara's around I become I guess you'd say kind of hysterical. Inside, inside of me. She brings up. Stuff. Okay. I yell.

BLUE: Don't yell.

ZAN: Okay.

BLUE: No. Cause you have this whole yelling thing going on. Can I ask you one thing, though? Why do you hate her so much?

ZAN: I don't hate her.

BLUE: Oh. Then maybe you can help her. Like you helped me.

ZAN: Blue I can't help Mara.

BLUE: I'm only sayin. You helped me so good.

ZAN: She said she was only staying a couple of days. It's best not to get too worked up over Mara. She'll move on.

BLUE: I'm not worked up over Mara.

(He kisses her, cups her breast in his hand. ZAN pulls away.)

BLUE: What—aw—so I'm not gonna be allowed to do anything?

ZAN: Honey, while Mara's staying here— Blue?—I think we should even go back to the sleeping arrangements the way they were before.

BLUE: What, I can't sleep with you either? Why?

ZAN: No, I think you should go back to sleeping in her—your room. It's just till she leaves.

BLUE: Man, for somebody who doesn't care what Mara thinks, you sure are pretending a lot.

ZAN: Read! We have to be disciplined about it or we're never going to move ahead. *(Picks up the stack of books.)*

BLUE: Read read oh read what! I'm disciplined. It's too hot to read. *(Haltingly reads.)* "Da-vid Cop-per—field." I almost said cornfield. Charles Dickens. He's the guy that wrote that Christmas Scrooge story? It's a million pages! And it's in English English, right? *(Next book.)* "Catcher in the Ray"—

ZAN: Rye.

BLUE: —Rye I knew that. About baseball?

ZAN: No.

BLUE: Rye bread?

ZAN: No.

BLUE: I knew that. It sounds hard. *(Another book.)* "Look Homeward Angle."

ZAN: Angel.

BLUE: Angel. Science fiction?

ZAN: No.

BLUE: 'Bout angels?

ZAN: Not really. Sort of. Metaphorically. It's a coming of age story.

BLUE: It's pretty long, too. The print's so small. What about, you know.

ZAN: No, we've moved past nursery rhymes and fairy tales.

BLUE: They were way more fun. I found hard words in there. Plus I dig those pictures.

ZAN: I know, but you have to move on.

BLUE: Why? They're so much shorter. This book is so long it'll take me ten years to read it. Even though I do like the title and everything, it grows on ya, *Look Homeward... Angel.*

ZAN: If you hate it after the first few pages we'll stop.

BLUE: Sounds like a deal. And then we might do Winken Blinken. (He reads.) "Look Homeward Angel A Story of the Bu-u-u——"

ZAN: Buried.

BLUE: See? Already! Those little words! I thought "bury" was "berry" like in strawberry. It's a "u," why's it sound like a "e," course berry sounds like it should be spelled "b-A-r-y" anyhow I'm confused.

ZAN: I know it sounds just like berry I can't explain it, it's one of the quirks of our language.

BLUE: English is hard. I can do it. *(Reads.)* "A Story of the Buried Life. By Thomas Wolfey."

ZAN: Wolfe.

BLUE: Wolfe. *(Turns the page.)* Oh no it's one of those hard poetry books!

ZAN: No, relax, it's the epigraph.

BLUE: What's that?

ZAN: It sets the tone for the rest of the piece. It might even contain the theme.

BLUE: *(Teasing her in a highfalutin' tone.)* Oh, it sets the tone or the theme la-de-da! *(Reads on. Normal voice.)* "... a stone, a leaf, an un——found door; of a stone, a leaf, a door." *(Stops.)* Oh... ... heavy. What's it sposed to mean?

ZAN: Nothing. Maybe it's just an image. Keep reading.

BLUE: "And of all the for-got-ten faces. N-n-n—a-a-ked"—oooo—naked— there's sex in this book?

ZAN: Read.

BLUE: "—naked and alone we came into ex—ex—ex—"

ZAN: —exile.

BLUE: "—exile. In her dark 'womb' *(Pronounces it phonetically.)*—"

ZAN: "Womb."

BLUE: "Womb"? Looks like "womb" to me.

ZAN: Well it's womb.

BLUE: I'm just sayin, it's startin to make sense here why I never learned to read good.

ZAN: Well.

BLUE: Well what?

ZAN: Nothing. Read well. Plow on.

BLUE: "In her dark womb—" wait a minute does that mean what I think it does? And you just said plow on oh my God! Plow on in her dark womb! Ha! Get it!

ZAN: Read!

BLUE: "—we did not know our mother's face—from the prison of her flesh have we come into the unspeak—"

ZAN: —unspeakable—

BLUE: "—unspeakable and incom—"— oh forget it, this word's huge—

ZAN: "—incommunicable prison of this earth."

BLUE: "—the whatever prison of this earth!" *(Stops reading.)* Oh, man oh man! I like it. I'm not totally sure what the hell it means. But I think I gotta rush!

ZAN: We come from a place of peace and security into the chaos of being.

BLUE: Hey, Zanny!

(He brings his face close to hers. Smells her. He whispers in her ear.)

ZAN: Oh, honey, that's so sweet.

BLUE: I do. No foolin.

ZAN: Well I care a lot about you too.

BLUE: Say it.

ZAN: Blue, read.

BLUE: Say it!

ZAN: No.

BLUE: Well I love you. I know you do, too. Love me. You say it. Know when?

ZAN: I should go put a load of laundry in.

BLUE: When you're kissin me.

ZAN: If reading period's over, I have things I can be doing.

BLUE: Yeah, what things? You'd rather be in "messing-around-with-me" period. I'm sorry. But it's true. You know it. I know it. I want you. You want me. *(Hands her the book.)* Here. You read it. I love your voice. You have a lovely voice. It soothes me. It sends me. I get sent. I'll rub your shoulders. Huh? Sound like a deal? You like my big strong hands on your shoulders, she's melting look at those eyes. Read.

(BLUE begins massaging her shoulders.)

ZAN: *(Reads.)* "Which of us has known—" ohmigod Blue that feels so—

BLUE: Read!

ZAN: "—has known his brother? Which of us has looked into his father's heart?

Which of us has not remained forever prison-pent? Which of us— *(Lets out a loud moan.)* —is not forever a stranger and alone."

(He kisses the back of her neck.)

BLUE: I ain't alone…

ZAN: Blue…

BLUE: Read.

ZAN: "O waste of loss, in the hot mazes—"

BLUE: "—the hot mazes—"! —this is a dirty dirty book—

ZAN: "—lost, among bright stars—"

(He reaches down in front of her and rubs between her legs.)

ZAN: Blue.

BLUE: Read! Go back to the hot hot mazes—

ZAN: "—on this most weary unbright cinder—"

(He rubs her, she moans.)

ZAN: "—lost!" Oh! "Remembering speechlessly we seek the great forgotten language—"

BLUE: *(Down next to her, kissing her.)* — tell me, Mama, tell me—

ZAN: Blue no I can't—someone might be—watching—what if—

(He touches her. She moans. Her kisses tell him to continue.)

BLUE: Keep reading, don't stop sh sh don't stop… …

(He kneels in front of her, pulls up her dress. He puts his head between her legs. She sees stars.)

BLUE: Read!

(She cries out in wonder.)

BLUE: READ!

ZAN: *(Aroused nearly to tears.)* —uh uh "the great"—oh God—"—great forgotten language, the lost uh lane-end into heaven, a stone, a leaf, an—"—ohhhh Goddd—"an unfound door. Where! *(She cries out.)* When? O lost, and by the wind grieved, ghost"—oohhhhhhhhh Goooooddddddddd—"come back again—!"

(Blackout.)

SCENE FIVE

The next day. The lights come up to MARA sitting at ZAN's desk. She's wearing an extra large t-shirt, the one she wore sleeping. She's slowly paging through a magazine on the top of the desk. She puts it down. She picks up another magazine. It's a New Yorker. *She quickly scans through it, drops it back on the desk. She snoops around. She opens a drawer, looks in, moves a few items around, closes it. She sees a pile of papers, and picks them up and riffles through them. She opens another drawer, reaches in, finds a jar of candy, puts the jar back in the drawer and closes it. She sees the locked drawer and pulls at it. Nothing. She twirls a couple of times in the chair. She grabs a letter opener, and she tries to open the locked drawer with it. At the same time, BLUE enters the kitchen quietly and stands for a moment watching her.*

BLUE: Uh-oh desk's off limits ding ding ding ding ding—

MARA: Oh God you scared me. I woke up, everyone was gone.

BLUE: In case you wondered.

MARA: No, I used to keep some secret papers in this drawer, and I wondered if they were still in here. Like I have an insurance policy or something. I wanted to see what it was worth.

BLUE: I won't tell.

MARA: Thanks. No, it's okay, she said I could go in her desk. We share everything.

BLUE: Zan writes things.

MARA: Can't you tell how close we are?

BLUE: I still won't tell.

MARA: What does she write?

BLUE: Stuff on her typewriter.

MARA: What kind of stuff. Letters?

BLUE: I think stories. I'm not sure. But she's pretty serious about it.

MARA: Stories? Does she ever let you read them?

BLUE: Never ever. Her desk's super private, that's all.

MARA: God how long did I sleep?

BLUE: It's three o'clock.

MARA: A couple of hours? It feels like—

BLUE: The next day!

MARA: Oh! That makes more sense! Where'd Mom go?

BLUE: Hartville for groceries. She likes to go alone.

MARA: Why so far?

BLUE: Bargains. She says. Peanut butter's cheaper I think.

MARA: So here you are! You're really moved in up there!

BLUE: Home sweet home.

MARA: I went up and took a peek at my old room. That was a shock. I hardly recognized it. You sure are neat.

BLUE: Uh-oh, time for me to go back to work.

MARA: There's no sign of me left. My banners and my vintage Beatles poster. My Drama Club trophies. Do you know what happened to it?

BLUE: To what?

MARA: My CD player, it was practically brand new when I left. All my CDs.

BLUE: I didn't take it I swear.

MARA: And what'd you do with the Barbie and all the clothes, that's worth something today.

BLUE: Wait a minute... ... where? I'm confused.

MARA: In my old room! Your new room!

BLUE: It was bare when I came I swear I didn't take anything I didn't touch nothing don't blame me for that I didn't use it to buy drugs honest to God, I didn't, Mara, I swear don't get me in trouble for this.

MARA: Relax! I believe you! I was only teasing. It's the kind of thing Mom would do. Clean out the room. Find closure. She was always big on closure. By the way, has she ever mentioned anything about Helen? Or have you ever met Helen?

BLUE: I never—oh, oh—the woman behind the counter in the fertilizer store?

MARA: No, Mom's friend, Helen.

BLUE: I never met any Helen.

MARA: She's like Mom's best friend. She used to be. I'd love to know what happened.

BLUE: The Avon lady from Portsmouth?

MARA: No, not the Avon lady from Portsmouth!

BLUE: Cause the Avon lady from Portsmouth stopped sellin Avon cause of her breast cancer.

MARA: The whole situation is very weird.

BLUE: She lost her hair and wore wigs but she stopped coming around.

MARA: Why'd she quit teaching?

BLUE: Because she got cancer?

MARA: My Mom!

BLUE: I don't know about teaching or anything like that if Zan... no not since I knew her no. I gotta go. Zan said tell princess when she wakes up, there's a pasta uh pasta salad in the fridge. You should take it out to the gazebo, it's a awesome day.

MARA: Hey. *(Fishes a joint out of her bag.)*

BLUE: What?

MARA: Wanna smoke pot with me now?

BLUE: Nah it's the middle of the day and didn't you just get up? I gotta lot of work to do, I'd be workin slow. Probably crackin up a lot, too.

MARA: *(Lights the joint.)* That doesn't sound so bad. *(Holds it out to him.)*

BLUE: Plus I think Zan... mmmm... didn't she say she wanted you to do that on the porch?

MARA: Oh, you're so good! You're probably like the good kid she never had. Mom doesn't care if you smoke dope, does she? I mean, it's not like you're not OLD ENOUGH, right?

BLUE: Yeah... but nah I'll pass.

MARA: No biggie. You seem to know a lot about growing things, huh? And engines and stuff. And building gazebos, shit. I couldn't build a gazebo if my life depended on it.

BLUE: Sometimes, not always. I fix motors 'n 'stuff. The old Chevy truck out there I got that runnin.

MARA: That was my Dad's.

BLUE: Those are the keys hanging on that hook over there. You could drive it if you want, it won't go over forty-five maybe fifty-five possibly probably. Zan won't care.

MARA: Thanks. I'll possibly probably go for a ride later, see what's changed. Nothing stays the same. Except around here. Where were you before you came to live with my Mom?

BLUE: Different places. *(Ducks his head.)* Not as nice as this one.

MARA: Why'd you duck? I'm not gonna hit you.

BLUE: I didn't duck.

MARA: How'd you get this job?

BLUE: Uh. It's a like live-in work program.

MARA: Oh I get it. You were in prison or something?

BLUE: Ha! No I was never in prison. Oh man no I hope I never go to prison I hear they do stuff in prison. Oh.

MARA: So who set this up?

BLUE: I can't. Well. Say. Nobody really.

MARA: Mm that sounds mysterious.

BLUE: No, it's personal stuff you might not get.

MARA: I didn't mean to pry. Do you like living with my Mom?

BLUE: It hardly compares to anything else I've ever known.

MARA: Except the Anti-Christ screaming in your ears twenty-four hours a day. That's a joke.

BLUE: Oh I get it. She doesn't go to Church. But she's a good person. I learned more here so far than before. Zan teaches me to read.

MARA: You can't read?

BLUE: I can read! I don't read good. Slow at that. Comprehension. I got left behind. Stuff doesn't stay in my brain. Maybe my Mom dropped me on my head as a baby probably she got mad cause I wouldn't stop crying or something. Likely story.

MARA: Oh God, I hope not! What's Mom have you reading now?

BLUE: "Look Homeward Angels."

MARA: Thomas Wolfe. It sounds like her.

BLUE: Doors and leaves and stones or something. Some Eugene guy. There's a lotta talk. It's real heavy I don't get some of it. But I like it. It has some sex. I think.

MARA: I was in the play *Look Homeward, Angel* in high school.

BLUE: Oh yeah? Is that, what, you—you act in a play on stage, right? I saw a play once. I think.

MARA: Yeah. I played Laura.

BLUE: Who's that?

MARA: Laura's the older woman who comes to stay at the boardinghouse. Eugene falls for her.

BLUE: I don't think we got that far.

MARA: She rips his heart to shreds in the end and leaves him. And he grows up and leaves home. I probably shouldn't give away the ending. I was really good in that. But I'm past that I'm moving on with my life, listen to me, I'm becoming a living cliché. What else do you read?

BLUE: We do Winken and Blinken sometimes. For total fun. I like that.

MARA: What's that?

BLUE: A kid thing. A nursery rhyme it reminds me of something maybe my Mom but I don't remember too much. She was a real witch they say. But nice. *(Smiles.)* Your Mom makes learnin fun!

MARA: I'll bet she does. What else does she teach you?

BLUE: How to keep books and count like that you know in social situations. I was never too good at that either. Social situations.

MARA: You seem pretty good to me.

BLUE: I think I'll get my lemonade and go.

MARA: I drank all your lemonade before you came in.

BLUE: *(Ducks his head.)* It's okay. It's not all mine.

MARA: You ducked again.

BLUE: I'll drink water from the hose. It's cold and a little rubber taste won't kill me.

MARA: She likes you better than me. She likes everybody better than me! Always

did. She stopped making me lemonade long before I left for New York. We fought constantly about everything. Stupid stuff. It's the reason—I left—to escape, and Johnny Ruvolo the guy I was with at the time who she absolutely hated 'cause he didn't get straight A's, he was going there to play in a band which never went anywhere, the band or the relationship… And I wanted to try the whole acting thing. I thought. After almost three years. She'd be a little more—we could maybe come to some kind of—I don't know—I wanted her to transform—an understanding, maybe. Don't ask me why I even… but I do. She totally holds a grudge, can you tell?

BLUE: Oh, now… … no, she likes you!

MARA: Oh yeah, right! You don't know. She had me when she was young, like twenty or something. She never got over it. I think that's what she holds against me. Some stolen youth thing.

BLUE: I don't think—

MARA: And it's not like I asked to be born—

BLUE: Oh now, don't uh—

MARA: I NEVER ASKED TO BE BORN. *(Turns away, teary.)*

BLUE: *(Puts his hand on her shoulder, comforting.)* No now you shouldn't, you're goin and gettin all—oh, now you're not crying, are you?

MARA: Sometimes I wish I was never born at all.

BLUE: Don't say stuff like that.

MARA: God, I am a living cliché! *(Grabs his hand.)* I'm not crying. Don't freak out. Thanks. You're a nice guy. *(Turns and looks at him.)*

BLUE: Zan likes you. Besides, you're her real daughter she has to like you. Somewhere inside her. You're blood. You're probably in her will.

MARA: Do you like having sex with her?

BLUE: *(The change of thought stuns him. Ducking his head.)* Do I like—what?

MARA: I'm sorry, aren't you and my Mom sleeping together?

BLUE: NO! No we are not sleeping together and no what why would you—are you kidding!?

MARA: You're not?

BLUE: No! No. I never said I did! Did I?

MARA: No. But I assumed when I got here you and her were maybe—the way you were looking at her—you can tell me if you are. I'm not embarrassed by that sort of thing.

BLUE: No! No. I'm not. Zan is my friend. She helps me.

MARA: 'Cause some guys are into that.

BLUE: Zan is my friend. She helps me. Into what?

MARA: Older women.

BLUE: You mean—

MARA: A lotta guys think older women are—I don't know what—if it's a mother thing or what.

BLUE: I don't uh get it but no no I'm not. Into that. I don't. No. Ugh. No.

MARA: Forget it. I didn't mean to embarrass you.

BLUE: No. I'm not. Embarrassed. Uh.

MARA: I'm kinda glad.

BLUE: That's good. About what?

MARA: You're not, you know, with my Mom.

BLUE: You are? Oh, thanks, that's that's—nice!

MARA: If you were—sleeping with her—she'd be lucky.

BLUE: Okay then thanks for the info.

MARA: Blue, wait a minute, uh—I can't open this jar of jam, would you?

(She goes to the kitchen, gets the jar of jam, gives it to him, touches his arm. He turns away from her.)

MARA: I like talking to you, you know? Everybody's so jaded and stupid in New York. You're perspiring.

BLUE: It's hot, geez, I mean, you're not hot?

MARA: Yeah in this weather I wanna be naked all the time.

(She slips the t-shirt off of herself, wearing nothing but her panties. BLUE turns back to her and lets out a cry of surprise. Turns quickly around.)

MARA: I'm sorry, I didn't mean to scare you!

BLUE: No, I—you gotta warn a guy here!

MARA: Do you mind? It's so freeing. And cooler. Hey. Take your shirt off too.

BLUE: No, I'm fine, it's not the heat, it's the humidity.

MARA: In New York during the summer I was always naked in the apartment. Well not always.

BLUE: The news says this is the hottest summer in history I heard on the news.

MARA: A man living in the building across the street would look down on me from his roof without me seeing and then I would catch him. He'd call with his cell phone, I don't know how he got our number, and breathe into the phone and whisper like "Pretty Girrrrullllllll…" You could hear all the same street sounds as I could hear. Out the window. It was so weird.

BLUE: Hottest summer I remember.

MARA: I'd tease him, play with my breasts rub myself—

BLUE: Global warming, no lie.

MARA: My roommates and I would pretend to have simulated sex for him and watch him get off. I didn't really do that. Okay I did once.

BLUE: This is only the beginning, they say.

MARA: Blue.

BLUE: What?

MARA: Can I have the jam, please?

BLUE: Oh, right.

MARA: Look at me.

BLUE: Here. *(Hands her the jar, looks at her quickly, turns away.)* I should go.

MARA: I'm really attracted to you. Do you like my ti——… … … breasts?

BLUE: Uh. They're nice.   .

MARA: You can touch them if you want.

BLUE: *(Nods his head, shakes his head, nods his head, shakes his head.)* No.

MARA: I can tell. You want to.

BLUE: I probably shouldn't.

MARA: Feel. Here.

BLUE: No.

(MARA takes a fingerful of jam and puts it on her nipple.)

MARA: Blue.

BLUE: What.

MARA: Look.

BLUE: What.

MARA: It's something I did in a movie once. I thought it up. The director loved it said I was a genius. All right I admit it turned out to be this creepy soft-core porn thing, but—oh, it's not how it sounds. Come on, oh you're no fun. Now I just feel stupid. Look!

BLUE: I gotta go.

MARA: Then look first.

(He looks at her.)

MARA: Lick it off.

BLUE: I… …

MARA: Go ahead. You know you want to.

(She pulls him toward her. He moves in on her breast, he stops, conflicted. He holds, till she brusquely pulls his head to her breast. BLUE pulls away, his face smeared with jam. He panics, wipes his face with his sleeve.)

BLUE: OHMIGOD I'M SO SORRY I won't tell I swear, please don't get me in trouble I GOTTA GET OUTTA HERE!

MARA: I didn't mean to scare you! I just want you to know you can trust me. *(Puts the t-shirt back on.)*

BLUE: Oh I get it that's sign language for you can trust me okay! Got it! *(Looks at his wrist, but there is no watch. He backs up out of the room.)* Ooops, sorry, dum-de-dum-dum, out of time, gotta go. Have to pick up the daily mail, sometimes the mailman doesn't uh know which mailbox to put the mail in it's confusing I can't explain I could but it would take forever, see ya. Oh great, all sticky! Tell Zan. I don't know what. Tell Zan I'll see her... later. *(Exits onto the porch, stops, doesn't turn around.)* Ohmigod, don't tell her this! Bye!

MARA: Bye. I won't. Blue!

(He stops, doesn't turn around. Beat.)

MARA: Are you mad at me?

BLUE: No. I'm not mad at you.

(He exits. MARA goes to the fridge.)

MARA: *(To herself.)* No I shoulda said it more like "Blue, are you mad at me?"

(She gets her sandwich, takes out a pitcher of lemonade, pours herself a glass, takes it back to the desk. She takes a bite of the sandwich. She grabs a paperclip, bending it straight. She tries to use the paperclip to open the drawer. She moves it around a few times. Nothing. She stops and looks at the drawer, takes a bite of the sandwich, chews for a moment, then kicks the desk spitefully. She hears a click. She tries the drawer again. It opens. She reaches inside and pulls out the first folder she sees. She opens it and reads.)

MARA: "'The Language of Kisses'... ... by Vivian Hale... ... ...?"

(She becomes deeply absorbed. She takes the sandwich, the glass of lemonade and the folder off with her. The lights fade.)

ACT TWO
SCENE ONE

That night. ZAN is sitting at her desk, writing on her typewriter. She is completely concentrated, typing rapidly. She is listening to Arvo Pärt's "Te Deum" at high volume.

MARA enters quietly. She's been drinking. She stands behind ZAN, watching her type.

MARA: Where's my stuff?

ZAN: *(Whirls around, surprised.)* Oh Mara for crying out loud YOU SCARED ME you know how I hate anybody sneaking up on me like that! *(Turns the music off.)*

MARA: Sorry. I forgot. How absorbed you get, how otherworldly. Was that church music? It's pretty. What're you doing?

ZAN: Writing. Where's Blue, have you seen him?

MARA: Oh yes I'm fine, Mom, my day was a real hoot, and how're you?

ZAN: Where'd you go? Are you drunk?

MARA: I had a margarita. Or two. Or four or five. Around. I drove around. Stopped in a bar.

ZAN: I hope you weren't driving that old truck around drunk.

MARA: Well if I had five margaritas I guess I'm drunk... something about all that tequila. *(Hovering at the desk.)* What're you writing?

ZAN: Nothing. *(Pulls the sheet from the typewriter and crumples it.)*

MARA: Nothing. Stories! Where's my stuff?

ZAN: A story. What stuff are you talking about?

MARA: My stuff. The posters, my Dramatics Club trophies! The awards. I love all that shit. My yearbooks. Lookin' at that shit right now would really put me in touch. Brighten up my day. Night. Dusk. Whatever it is. Do a whole memory lane bit, tears and all. Oh. And the Barbie. A lot of people're stupid enough to pay lots of money for that kind of thing, we're talking thousands. You were smart to make me keep the original box, it increases the value, you're smart about that stuff practical money stuff why didn't that get passed on to me? I suck about money. You did keep it, right?

ZAN: All your high school mementos, your dolls and stuff, are in the basement. Take them, it's less junk down there.

(MARA opens the door leading to the basement, looks down.)

MARA: I still have nightmares about it. Spider central.

ZAN: Is that all you have nightmares about?

MARA: You! Being mean to me!

ZAN: I'm tired, I've had a long day.

MARA: What if I said I was going to move all my stuff back upstairs into my old room!

ZAN: I'd say, forget it!

MARA: Set it all up like it was originally! All cool and lifelike.

ZAN: I don't see this happening.

MARA: Put my acting award out and the plaques on the wall. My Best Thespian Award.

ZAN: I have an agreement with Blue!

MARA: Set up the CD player. Spend the whole day up in my room listening to CDs.

ZAN: I won't renege on our deal.

MARA: Yeah, what's this about, he's on some kind of work program, what is he an ex-con?

ZAN: Is that what he told you?

MARA: If he's the help—that's what work program means, right?—there's other rooms he could sleep in—the addition—or—I mean, maybe with you?

ZAN: You said you were only staying a couple days!

MARA: Mom, how many people know Blue lives here?

ZAN: What's that have to do with anything?

MARA: You travel far to buy groceries.

ZAN: I like the Amish market in Hartville.

MARA: So, is that what he's here for, some kind of work program?

ZAN: He showed up one night last fall in the barn, he was obviously frightened, hadn't eaten in days and he didn't even talk to me the first month—I could see he's had a rough life, he came from a nightmare childhood with a mother who had severe bipolar disorder. It impaired his ability to learn.

MARA: And this you know because—

ZAN: I can tell from the way he's described her. I've read case studies.

MARA: Oh so you're a psychologist now.

ZAN: Did Blue give you any indication where he went?

MARA: Why, is it time for you two to fuck or something? Sorry, that slipped. I know you are.

ZAN: That's why I didn't want to tell you about it. Him! Us! You don't know anything! About what we feel, how we are together. How Blue loves, how he taught me more about. Telling you, it sounds…

Trust. Foolish. I learned from HIM—to see the world with—God, this innocence this untainted magical I don't know. He's so damaged by the world so fragile, but still he sees light and joy. *(Goes to look out the window.)* It's way past supper and he never misses it! He left his tools sitting out, which isn't like him—I'm a little worried.

MARA: You sure have a funny way of showing it, so involved in your work. "Your work!" You always have work! Like some busy bee!

ZAN: I looked for three hours, I searched every inch of this property, drove around—I sat down to my work for two minutes, to write something down and—listen to me justifying myself. To you. Mara, did you say something to upset him?

MARA: Oh of course, devil daughter, what did I say, I don't know, I said there's lemonade in the fridge—I can see how upsetting that might be—he said there's pasta salad for me and then he left to pick up the mail or something. He said tell Zan I'll fuck her later I mean I'll see her later. I swear you have no sense of humor!

ZAN: Maybe because I don't find it funny! One thing I know, he takes off for hours when he's upset! And knowing you—

MARA: Where's he really from, some mental hospital!

ZAN: Not so loud, what if he comes around the corner!

MARA: *(Lights a joint.)* And don't say you know me, that's your charade, we don't know each other.

ZAN: Oh, Mara, you have to be joking! Haven't you had enough?

MARA: Party, party. So, Mom, what's the bit with Helen, really, I wanna know. Want some?

ZAN: I wish you'd go out to the porch.

MARA: I talked to her.

ZAN: Helen Turnbull? Did you hear me? Go out to the porch.

MARA: No, Helen of Troy, I traveled back in time! Yes Helen Turnbull!

ZAN: I don't see how you could possibly talk to Helen I heard she's in Italy on sabbatical. I said, the smoke bothers me!

MARA: She's back now 'cause I spoke to her on the phone today.

ZAN: *(Suddenly furious.)* Go out to the porch, this is still my house! YOU DON'T HEAR ME!

MARA: *(Moves out to the porch. They talk through the screen.)* Fine. I can play the hypocrite game.

ZAN: What hypocrite game, Mara, I don't like smoke in MY house in MY rooms on MY furniture!

MARA: Do you want to know what Helen said?

ZAN: You're determined to tell me!

MARA: We didn't actually speak. She kept hanging up. Except once before she hung up, she did say "I'm finished with you and your whole fucking family." So I went out there! To find out for myself. She held a gun on me! Screamed at me to get away! To get in my car and drive away! Pretty funny behavior for a woman I once referred to as Aunt Helen!

ZAN: We had a falling out. We didn't vote the same way about who was going to fill the spot of temporary department chairman at a faculty meeting and—

MARA: For that she shoots at me—? Maybe it was a warning shot, but still—!

ZAN: It was a silly disagreement, we didn't speak for a couple of days then it became weeks. It was one of those things—small at the time—but breaks two people up forever and—not a day goes by I don't miss her and her smiles and her wisdom. But we'll never be friends again. I'm sorry you had to find out that way.

(MARA puts out the joint, enters the kitchen and goes to the fridge.)

MARA: You are really good, I gotta say. God do you have any bottled water, I am parched.

ZAN: The water from the tap is fine. I quit teaching because it became all about politics. I had money left from your father's insurance. So—

MARA: My college money. Oops. The tap water tastes like metal.

ZAN: Your father's insurance money. I wanted to write. It's what I always wanted to do.

MARA: Did you buy any Coke at the store? *(Takes the pitcher of lemonade out of the refrigerator, pours a glass.)* Your lemonade's too sweet.

ZAN: Then don't drink it. Blue likes it sweet.

MARA: I didn't say I didn't like it, I said it's too sweet. What're you writing now?

ZAN: A short story… for myself, nothing really. I thought you said Blue came in for lemonade.

MARA: Maybe. I forget. Can I read it?

ZAN: No. Because he drinks almost the whole pitcher when he comes in for a drink and that pitcher's practically full.

MARA: Maybe he wasn't thirsty! He said he was drinking water from the hose. Why can't I read the story?

ZAN: I was only fooling around, trying to work something out on the page.

MARA: Why not say, it's none of your business!

ZAN: I don't show my work to just anyone. You know. I didn't mean…

MARA: I know what you meant. Have you been published?

ZAN: No, I write for myself.

MARA: Oh. What about Vivian Hale, has she?

ZAN: Who? What?

MARA: Has she been published?

ZAN: Uh I don't know, yes, I think I've heard of her, have you read her work?

MARA: I have now! "I think I've heard of her… … !"

(MARA pulls the folder out of her purse. It's folded in half. ZAN immediately recognizes and grabs for it. MARA lets her have it.)

ZAN: Mara, I swear to God, where'd you get that, give me that, how'd you get in my desk! You have no right. This isn't funny! You read this story YOU READ THIS STORY! *(Unlocks the drawer, puts the folder back in it, slams it.)*

MARA: Who's Vivian Hale?

ZAN: I use a pseudonym!

MARA: Why?

ZAN: I prefer the anonymity.

MARA: Where are you published?

(ZAN hands her the New Yorker *from the top of the desk.)*

MARA: The *New Yorker?*

ZAN: My agent says they're interested in seeing more of my work.

MARA: Your? Agent? They want to see more of Vivian Hale's work?

ZAN: Yes.

MARA: And if I open this *New Yorker,* there's going to be a story in here—*(She opens the* New Yorker, *scans the contents page.)* … … "What I've Said a Million Times Before" by Vivian Hale. *(Slams it shut.)* What about "Language of Kisses"!

ZAN: What about it?

MARA: Quite a story! Is that gonna run in the *New Yorker?*

ZAN: You shouldn't have read it, it's a first draft, I only wrote it last week! I'm not even sure I would ever have it published.

MARA: Is it… autobiographical? Parts of it are, right?

ZAN: The main character teaches in a small Midwestern college! That's where it begins and ends! I suppose the location is based on this area.

MARA: Oh I loved the scene at the mall— oh so many scenes I liked, I think you should turn it into a novel—but, the scene where the college professor sees the student she's just had sex with and his mother, how she ducks into the Limited. I laughed out loud. Especially at the part where she finds a skirt on sale and buys it. It reminded me so much of you. Well something you would do. Buying the skirt on sale, that is. Always at that sale rack. And the mother of the student the college

professor's just had sex with is her best friend. That little twist is really kind of… Reading it, you really felt the suspense of the best friend finding out about the college professor.

ZAN: I suppose the loss of friendship theme came out of my experience with Helen.

MARA: Oh, yeah, because the character of Ellen seemed so much like… Helen.

ZAN: I suppose—did she seem so much like Helen or more like your Auntie Vera?

MARA: Oh no definitely Helen. But the reason your characters had a falling out, when Helen—I mean, Ellen—finds out the college professor's been sleeping with her son—was he based on little Terry Turnbull?

ZAN: She only sleeps with him once. No that wasn't based on anyone.

MARA: That was a great scene! Maybe you could rework the opening a little bit, but I like the way the story's broken up in three parts and my favorite part's the last part where the enigmatic boy drifter comes into her life, hot stuff.

ZAN: He's a man, really.

MARA: Kiss kiss kiss. Redemption! It's almost pornographic. Almost!

ZAN: It's not literally about Blue! It's not literally about anyone! I am all the characters!

MARA: Has Blue read it?

ZAN: Of course not!

MARA: Who knows? He's already up to "Look Homeward Angels." Y'know, it's not like I don't get your attraction to Blue, he does have a certain hunky… I dunno.

ZAN: What? *(Grabs MARA suddenly.)* Mara, did you come on to Blue?

MARA: Oh right!

ZAN: You came onto him, didn't you, and he rebuffed you! That's what happened! The story of your sordid little life! Tell me the truth, you came onto him!

MARA: I set my standards a little higher, thank you. I don't go chasing retards.

(ZAN slaps her.)

MARA: Don't ever slap me again, get that? And my life isn't sordid! You should talk!

ZAN: What'd you do, bare your breasts the way you did with the boys in high school? You scared him, didn't you? And you have to put behind you the thing that rejects you! This fantasy you have about moving in, did you say something to him about his room?

MARA: My room!

ZAN: Whether he sleeps in my room or not—which is none of your business— it's still his room!

MARA: What if I told you your precious Blue pushed me up against that refrigerator and practically raped me, he rubbed jam all over my breasts, he went crazy licking it off, what would you say then?

ZAN: I know you! The lies. The convoluted stories. The drugs and alcohol. Look at you. You were never really attacked in New York were you.

MARA: "You were never attacked in New York, were you?" Like you know so much!

ZAN: Leave, Mara, go back to New York. Quickly.

MARA: I can't. I want my room back. And

I know how irrational it sounds, don't judge it, just go with it.

ZAN: I said it's out of the question.

MARA: Then tell me this! You think it's the wisest thing in the world, sleeping with him? Considering everything.

ZAN: Considering what?

MARA: How old is Blue anyway?

ZAN: He's old enough!

MARA: You think he's mature enough emotionally for a sexual relationship? With a woman so much older? Do you see my point? Maybe he should be with someone more… like him.

ZAN: A mature emotional life for having sex? Slightly oxymoronic coming from you!

MARA: We're talking about you now, not me! What could you possibly have in common with him he's not up to your intellectual standards.

ZAN: I help him to become more self-confident, I teach him, I understand him, he talks to me.

MARA: That's right, you kiss talk. *(Kisses the air.)*

ZAN: What did you say?

MARA: In the story the college professor's all in a tizzy kissing the enigmatic boy— excuse me—man drifter and he's in heaven and she's in heaven and he's ALL HARD and she's all wet 'cause they talk with their kisses or something like that.

ZAN: No, no—that's not so—that's a story! With Blue it's the things he says the little boy inside playing with me the miracle of that, touching so much innocence—

MARA: Spare me the fairy tale—

ZAN: Like I'm his—

MARA: LIKE YOU'RE HIS WHAT, HIS MOTHER!

ZAN: —his playmate—his friend—no, no, not his mother—!

MARA: I'm glad you finally decided to be somebody's mother!

ZAN: No, not his… no… … no… …

MARA: Who'd a figured you'd ever like them so young. Mom, wake up, if Blue isn't a boy, then, what is he? If you think you're setting some kind of moral or ethical example here, some act of rehabilitation by fucking him, you are sadly deluding yourself. Tell him to leave, don't you think?

ZAN: No!

MARA: For your own good. For his.

ZAN: I know what's for my own good and what's not!

MARA: You have to—whoosh, let him go—like in the saying, let the thing you love go, and if it doesn't come back hunt it down and shoot it, something like that. It's too bad you can't. Shoot somebody. I'm not talking about his age in years, I'm talking about his mental age but yeah his age age, too. You think he'd mind hauling those boxes or whatever from the basement?

ZAN: Go to bed, Mara.

MARA: It has to end some time, right? It's about sex. It can't go on forever. You look great now, but what's going to happen in ten, fifteen years? You have Grandma's neck, I don't wanna be around for that spectacle. Is he gonna wanna kiss Grandma's neck? I'm only being a realist

here. We all get old. What, is that tacky to say about Grandma's neck but you know it's true, you really have it in for me don't you—!

ZAN: Go to bed, Mara. Sleep it off!

MARA: Who knows, someday, you might even meet a man your own age you can fall for. (*Sits in the desk chair. Twirls around a couple of times.*) So it was like I died, huh? Y'know, the first part of the story, the college professor's daughter dies in a car wreck. Her grief over that. Great metaphor for moving to New York. Get it? New York? Car wreck? Get one of my jokes, at least!

ZAN: Everywhere you go there's a car wreck, Mara! *You* are a car wreck, Mara! What really happened in New York?

MARA: (*Starts twirling slowly in the chair and gradually speeds up.*) Y'know c'n I say one thing? In my defense. About that whole New York thing. I swear. That guy? That guy Roy? Suddenly I'm the big criminal. I'm the big stalker. That's all I'll say. I mean, Mara's always the fucked-up one, right, Mara's always the one that turns out to be the wrongdoer when things turn sour, she's the bad bad one, because she tries to be straight with everybody she meets. He was the one who invited me to his roof parties! Stupid goddamn yuppie parties. To look down to the place where he first saw me. Naked. He said keep the extra key! Standing in his kitchen blending daiquiris, didn't I hear him say, keep the extra key, like oh wow I was gonna spend the summer with him in the Hamptons! All of a sudden I'm being called a psycho—! Talk about psycho. That's all I'll say. He was the most beautiful man I ever saw. Not a hair on his chiseled torso. Called me his pretty girl. Talk about your stories! Maybe that's what you'd call it. "Pretty Girl." No. Call it something like "Lies! Deceit! Treachery! Videotape!" Who figured he ever kept that, I thought he taped over it. That slipped. Not too embarrassing. That's all I'll say. Wow, I'm getting really—this should be a ride at the amusement p—ohmigod Ma I think— *(Stops twirling and turns white.)* I'm gonna be si—!

(MARA runs off, sick. ZAN looks out the window. The lights fade.)

SCENE TWO

Several hours later. The light comes up to ZAN sleeping at the kitchen table. There's a small pile of boxes out on the porch near the door. BLUE stops on the porch, opens the top box, pulls out a Barbie box. He looks at it, puts it back. He comes into the kitchen. He goes over to ZAN and gets very close to her but doesn't touch her. He watches her sleep for a long moment, then he blows on her face.

ZAN: *(Waking, startled.)* ——noooo, get it off! Oh Blue! You're alive!

BLUE: Of course.

ZAN: I was dreaming.

BLUE: I see. Bad dream?

ZAN: I think. Somebody was putting something warm and furry on me but it wasn't a cat.

BLUE: Was it a mouse?

ZAN: No.

BLUE: I was blowing on you.

ZAN: Oh.

BLUE: *(Goes to kiss her.)* Kiss?

ZAN: No, wait. Give me a minute. My mouth is so…

BLUE: You waited up for me. You kept the porch light on. I knew you would.

ZAN: I wasn't really up. I was sleeping so deeply. I feel like I'm still sleeping.

BLUE: Wake up wake up it's a new day! Or at least it will be pretty soon.

ZAN: Shhh don't talk too loud, you'll wake her. Are you okay? I was worried.

BLUE: I'm fine.

ZAN: I thought maybe Mara… did she… hurt you?

BLUE: What could she do to hurt me? We talked some, that's all. What's the boxes on the porch?

ZAN: Her stuff. Where'd you go?

BLUE: I have my places.

ZAN: I guess so. I couldn't find you.

BLUE: You looked for me?

ZAN: Yes.

BLUE: I knew you would. It doesn't matter where I been. It's where I'm going.

ZAN: What're you talking about?

BLUE: Where we're going. *(Goes to her.)*

ZAN: We're not going anywhere till you eat. *(Goes to the stove for a covered plate of food.)*

BLUE: Listen to me, Zanny, I've been thinkin and thinkin and thinkin.

ZAN: Me too. Funny coincidence. Are you hungry?

BLUE: I don't get the coincidence.

ZAN: Nothing. I was thinking, too, that's all.

BLUE: Listen to me—

ZAN: I made cornbread. I opened the last jar of red raspberry jam you like.

BLUE: Zan! Forget food!

ZAN: Shh.

BLUE: Forget food. Food is not. I see the importance of it. But not now. I have something I have to—

ZAN: You can't go to bed on an empty stomach.

BLUE: Who said anything about goin to bed? Zanny... listen to me, don't move away from me, Zanny—! I'm asking you if you want to—come here—am I your man?

ZAN: My what, my man?

BLUE: Your man your man!

ZAN: Okay, shh. Yes, you're my man.

(He whispers in her ear.)

ZAN: *(Moves away.)* Oh honey you. Blue! That's so! Sweet—

BLUE: Don't give me the sweet stuff! You think I'm not serious!

ZAN: I think you're serious.

BLUE: I am! Now, listen to me! This is more than cornbread and fixing the truck and building the gazebo and cleanin out the basement and takin care of the garden.

ZAN: Shh. Blue I can't marry you, please don't ask me that.

BLUE: Why you're not married to somebody else I don't know about, are you?

ZAN: No.

BLUE: I mean, cause I knew you had a daughter and all but she like pops up outta nowhere and she's— geeeeez— Not that she's not nice. But she has some problems.

ZAN: Any woman would think it's an honor to be your wife. I'm so flattered you would even think of me that way—

BLUE: Don't talk down! What other way you think I been thinking of you?

ZAN: Blue, don't, it's not possible. Be realistic.

BLUE: Shut up. You didn't answer me. Answer straight. I didn't mean to say shut up.

ZAN: Blue, I'm old enough to be your... mother. Almost. That's what I mean realistic.

BLUE: Oh and what are you like thirty two or something?

(ZAN lets out a laugh.)

BLUE: Don't laugh at me.

ZAN: Honey, I'm not laughing at you. I'm closer to forty-two. Plus.

BLUE: Plus what? *(Starts to count on his fingers. Stops.)* Well I'm not gonna count it now. Big deal a couple years. See? Shows how damn good you look. I don't even see that in the picture, the way you and me feel about each other. *(Turns away from her.)* It always comes down to the retard thing.

ZAN: It has nothing to do with the retard thing, the retard thing's in your head!

BLUE: So there is a retard thing! Even if the retard thing's only in my head then it's a retard thing!

ZAN: Stop it! Turn and look at me right now, and look at me and when I say you are the most wonderful man I've ever known, look in my eyes and see I'm telling you the truth. I'm the luckiest person alive to have known you.

BLUE: Then marry me and you can know me forever. *(Moves in to be close to her.)*

ZAN: *(Moves away from him.)* No! Blue I don't even know if I believe in marriage. Listen, we have something special now, but these things pass, it's naïve to think it could go on like this forever—

BLUE: What's naïve?

ZAN: It means without guile.

BLUE: What's guile? Say it plain.

ZAN: Something you don't have.

BLUE: Then maybe I should have it, would you marry me then?

ZAN: It's part of life and growing up, passion dies.

BLUE: Fuck that I say! And you know I never use that word! The way you touch me!? You were the first, Zan. You are the one! Now, you look at me! I swear. The first I let in. I was scared. I'm still scared. Any second I'm thinkin. Wow. See. I. I. Ever since when I was little. I did a badsex thing. That's what she called it. My mom. One time we went up to Toledo to visit her brother, Uncle Jack. She was happy. She never went anywhere. We're goin on some bus. She's talkin to everybody. She sings "You Are My Sunshine" over and over which I hate. But I'm glad she's in a good mood cause I'd hate to see what would happen if she got in a bad mood on a bus. We get there and there's a cousin. Kathy. Big for her age. Let's get alone in my room, she says. She's got this toy or-

gan. With this cardboard to show colors. You follow the colors from the book. That's how you play songs. She tried to get me to play. Only I wasn't fast. She said you're an idiot you can't play it. Then she closes the door and starts to play. Soft first. Some song. Then louder. Crazier. Pounding. Not a song. Noise. I start jumpin around. She says, take your pants off. I did! My dinky's hard. It hurts even it's so hard. Stickin out. And Kathy's lookin at it. Poundin the keys harder yellin dance! makin sounds Indian whooping, I'm dancin around the room, my dinky's stickin out and it feels like it's getting harder and harder and… it's like I'm on the ceiling lookin down at myself, round and round… … and then… my Mom comes in. She says Kathy get out of the room. She says she'll kill me if she ever sees me doin that again. Takin my dinky out in front of Kathy! Don't I know it's a sin cousins can't have sex. And my dinky's still stickin out, it won't go down. And the madder she gets the more it sticks out! She says put your pants on. My pants won't go over my dinky, it's stuck and it gets harder and she smacks it, and it gets harder I don't know why. Next thing I know she grabs a ruler off Kathy's desk, she hits it, over and over, this'll make you soft, this'll wilt that weeney, and just then Uncle Jack runs in to save the day and I… cried. *(Beat.)* Man that hurt. The ruler had one of them metal edges. It was twisted. It stuck out. It got me. I had five stitches. That's what the scar is. Near my—see I told you someday I'd tell you how I got the scar near my dinky, well, I always called it a dinky, that's probably not the right word to use, but… *(Beat.)* When you touch me, when you touch my dinky, when you kiss me there, I—

(ZAN puts her hand over his mouth. He

tastes it. They kiss. Testing. Deep. They stop. They kiss more. Suddenly, the overhead light comes on in the kitchen, making the room look garish. MARA stands there, squinting, her hair standing on end and her mascara in rings around her eyes. ZAN and BLUE pull apart.)

MARA: *(Her head is pounding.)* What's all the noise? Oh, ain't this a sweet sight! What the hell time is it? Oh fuck my head is really— *(Opens a couple of cabinets, slams ones, cringes.)* Is there a goddamn aspirin anywhere, pound pound... *(Finds aspirin.)* You don't have one bottle of water anywhere in the house!? I don't suppose you have anything alcoholic. Somebody say something!

BLUE: Hi, Mara. How're you?

MARA: Hi, Blue. I have a hangover. How about you?

BLUE: No, I don't have a hangover.

MARA: *(Takes the aspirin.)* Is it morning yet? *(Sees the boxes on the porch.)* Ohmigod, my stuff! It is, isn't it? *(Goes to the top box, opens it.)* Look, the Barbie! You found her. *(Looks at it closer.)* Well, what's this, she wasn't put in storage very well, the box is smashed, all her clothes are covered in— what's that?—mildew! And a dead bug in here—euw! That brings the value down. Why're they all out here, why not put them near the stairs?

ZAN: Take a guess.

MARA: To air them out?

ZAN: I want you to take them when you leave.

MARA: I'm not leaving. I thought you said—

ZAN: You said. I didn't say anything. Go

back to New York, Mara, there's nothing for you here. Any illusion you have of creating some past existence, it's gone, those days are gone, nothing lasts and that's over.

MARA: Well, it's not acceptable.

ZAN: I don't care whether it's acceptable or not, it's the way it is.

MARA: All right. Look! When I said I can't go back. I meant. I had to leave New York. That's all I'll say.

BLUE: Dum-de-dum-dum.

ZAN: Is someone after you?

MARA: That left Auntie Vera's! Or here! Okay? I haven't got three cents to my name—

ZAN: Look, if it's a matter of money—

MARA: —and I want to take this right back where it started and choose the other path, whatever it is, I haven't found it exactly, but it's there and I need to listen to a few CDs and get high and I might be able to figure it out so, let's do this smoothly and no one will get hurt. It's my room anyhow, how many times do I have to say it! Blue did Mom tell you I'm moving back into my room? Maybe you can help me carry the boxes upstairs.

ZAN: Don't move, Blue.

MARA: It's time for you to go. Mom hates confrontation. That's why she can't come right out and say it.

ZAN: Make plans to leave.

MARA: It's her past, she's embarrassed. Come on, Blue, get your stuff. I'll drive you to the bus station and tell you all about it. There's always a bus leaving for somewhere. Mom will advance you a—I was going to say a week's pay, but in this case that would amount to a quickie fuck or something. Because to pretend it would be anything otherwise is a goddamn lie. And let's have as little lying as possible. By the way, I hope you use protection, it's a crazy disease-filled world out there and don't I know it, oops that slipped and I'm not even high!

BLUE: Zan's the one says when I go.

MARA: Oh, Zan's the one? Mom you have something to say?

ZAN: Come here my love and let me hold you in my arms? How's that, Mara?

BLUE: For your info, Zan and me're gettin married.

ZAN: No, Blue, don't——

MARA: Getting married! This is becoming surreal!

BLUE: Yeah, we're gettin married and there's nothing you or anybody can do to stop us, either accept it or not. But nothing says if we aren't married, you can't stay here, too, AS LONG AS EVERYBODY GETS ALONG!

ZAN: No, Blue.

MARA: Do you know anything about her?

BLUE: I know what I know, that's everything I need to know!

MARA: About her sexual proclivities?

ZAN: Mara, I'm warning you. Push me and I'll scream it out!

MARA: Scream what out, what're you talking about, what you did with what's his name?

BLUE: Let her talk, Zan, she's one to talk about sexual anything, who's gonna believe anything you say "Miss Take Your Shirt Off and Go Running Naked Around the House."

MARA: Oh poor baby, scared of a woman's tit! You liked it, though, didn't you?

BLUE: I ain't scared.

ZAN: (To MARA.) I knew it. You're a textbook case!

MARA: Oh, and what're you a textbook case of? Huh? Pedophilia? Are you going to tell him?

BLUE: Tell me what, you're actin like some TV gong show and it's makin me mad!

MARA: How your precious Zan likes having sex with young boys?

ZAN: (In a fury, threatening.) That's a filthy lie, Mara! Get your things get your things right now I mean it do you hear me, get your things and get out! Now!

(MARA exits suddenly, ZAN stands shaking with fury.)

ZAN: Blue, go out to the gazebo!

BLUE: Aw come on now, what's happening, Zan? I think I should stick around.

ZAN: I'm fine.

BLUE: Why're you upset about the young boys thing? I don't get it.

ZAN: It's Mara acting out. Forget it!

BLUE: What you mean like an actress like she was in New York?

ZAN: No. Blue, go out to the gazebo! This will end here and now.

BLUE: Look at you, you're shaking.

ZAN: She's leaving, don't worry, honey, I'm calming down now, I'm calm, see? She'll get her stuff, she'll be gone in a minute, everything'll be like it was! We'll forget she ever came, rest of the summer will be glorious! Go outside now, huh, wait for me out there?

BLUE: I dunno, Zan—

ZAN: Nothing bad will happen! Go on out there. I'm going to heat up your dinner for you and we'll have breakfast on the gazebo and—

(MARA comes back on with a Xerox of the story. She hands it to BLUE.)

MARA: Here, I made a copy of a story Mom wrote, read it, it's very enlightening——

(ZAN grabs the story, MARA tries to wrest it away from her.)

ZAN: You copied my story? Where do you get off doing something like that? Where are your bags, I want you gone, NOW or I'll call the police!

MARA: So dramatic! God! The police! Let me see how good a teacher you are! Let him read it!

ZAN: Let go of it.

(The pages tear, MARA takes her half and thrusts it at BLUE.)

MARA: Go ahead read it Blue. He's some big reader now!

ZAN: You've done it now, Mara!

(ZAN, in a rage, goes off. She can be heard moving around.)

BLUE: Zan, don't worry, I'm cool, I can't read this, the first word's "the," but past that I don't have any idea!

MARA: Sure, try it.

BLUE: *(Reading.)* "The Lang—" I don't wanna do this.

MARA: "The Language of Kisses," Blue! It's all about a college professor who sleeps with a student and gets charged with sexual abuse of a minor and is forced to quit her job.

BLUE: I'm not getting this. Is that supposed to be something somebody did or something? I don't wanna do this.

MARA: *(To ZAN, off.)* Sexual abuse memoirs are so literary these days. How many more students were there?

(ZAN comes on with an armful of MARA's clothes and goes to the porch.)

MARA: What're you doing with my clothes?

(ZAN throws the clothes out the door. MARA stomps her foot.)

MARA: Bring them in here right now!

(ZAN grabs the Barbie and walks to the outside door.)

BLUE: Zan, what's goin on here?

MARA: All right, you put that down!

ZAN: Blue. Go out to the gazebo!

BLUE: I don't think I should.

MARA: What're you doing with the goddamn Barbie!

ZAN: Goodbye, Mara.

(ZAN throws the Barbie out the door. MARA stomps her foot.)

MARA: Where'd you throw that? WHERE'D YOU THROW IT I ASKED YOU!

ZAN: In the barbecue.

MARA: I'm not moving an inch. Go get it out of there!

(ZAN takes two of the boxes from the porch and goes off.)

MARA: Where are you taking those boxes?

(ZAN re-enters.)

MARA: Bring those in here!

ZAN: "Language of Kisses" is a story about a woman! Who gets trapped in a loveless! sexless! marriage with a man, one of the nicest guys you'd ever meet, mind you, who has little drive and even less stamina and is rather spineless when it comes right down to it! All he does is sit around reading mystery books. But he is good looking! *(Grabs another two boxes and goes off again.)*

MARA: That's not what the story's about. Though, I have to say, it sounds awfully familiar. Tell him the real story. I said bring that STUFF in here! The woman's insane!

(ZAN re-enters.)

MARA: I'm not kidding bring those in here.

ZAN: And she marries him anyway because he brings home a good paycheck and has health insurance and she's pregnant and she doesn't want to give up her baby.

MARA: No the story's about a woman who has a thing for young boys—

ZAN: The woman has the baby. A girl. Mary. They call her Mary.

MARA: There's no Mary in this story.

ZAN: A month after the woman has the baby, Mary, she turns down a chance to study in London for a year. With a man she's admired all her life. At first she resents it, but she settles into it. She becomes a full-time mother. *(Picks up another box and goes off.)*

MARA: That's not the story, in the story the daughter dies in a car crash!

(The sound of a box crashing with breakables.)

MARA: I hope you're not breaking my stuff!

ZAN: And she likes it! Being a mother! She decides two years later to get pregnant again!

MARA: That's not how it goes! *(Looks in the box.)* Oh that's great, you broke the glass on the frame of my best thespian award! All right, that's enough! *(Picks the box up and brings it in the house and puts it near the stairs to the second floor. She continues to bring the boxes in.)*

ZAN: She manages to lure her husband away from Ellery Queen long enough to get herself pregnant!

MARA: Tell him the right one, the one with the car crash!

ZAN: And the woman does get pregnant and she has a baby, a boy—

MARA: The daughter dies in a car crash and the mother goes crazy with grief!

ZAN: And he's a beautiful boy!

MARA: She goes crazy with grief and plunges into the depths of lust!

ZAN: And they call him Harry.

MARA: She sleeps with one of her own students— the son of her best friend—!

ZAN: Not Harold.

MARA: There's no Harold in the story! Stop it!

ZAN: Not Harold, Harry, plain old Harry—

MARA: There's an enigmatic retarded guy later on, but his name's not Harry—

ZAN: —no, Harry's her bright baby, sharp as a tack and—

MARA: And?

ZAN: And beautiful.

MARA: And beautiful. It rings a bell, but which part of the story was it in? I don't remember a beautiful. Harry. And Harry was a?

ZAN: Baby boy—

MARA: Baby Harry?

ZAN: —and he brought nothing but joy and magic into the world. But the girl child, his sister, Mary, she's jealous of little Harry. She wants all the attention for herself—

MARA: This isn't the story I read—

ZAN: —she wants all her mother's and father's attention—

MARA: —there were no babies or jealous little girls—

ZAN: —she would act out, dirty herself, break things—

MARA: —you're making this up—

ZAN: —take off her clothes in public— she became a changed little girl overnight!

MARA: There's no baby Harry in the story!

ZAN: HE'S IN THE STORY NOW! And Mary resented baby Harry and hated baby Harry—

MARA: Blue, don't you listen! Cover your ears!

(ZAN takes two shoeboxes and thrusts them out the door. MARA covers her ears and begins to hum loudly. Suddenly, BLUE goes to the porch to stop ZAN.)

BLUE: Zanny, you're crazy here! STOP IT!

ZAN: Didn't I tell you to wait outside?

(ZAN pushes BLUE forcefully away, he shrinks against the wall.)

ZAN: *(To MARA.)* —and one day when she's alone with him—!

MARA: *(Taking her hands from her ears.)* Wait wait, who, when who's alone with who—!?

ZAN: The girl!

MARA: The girl Mary!

ZAN: When the girl Mary's alone with Harry, the boy, the beautiful baby boy—! The girl, Mary, finds the baby on the floor in his room.

MARA: This is starting to freak me out now, stop it!

ZAN: The baby fell out of his crib! His head hit the bureau! And the mother asked over and over, "Mary, do you know what happened, was the baby breathing"—but the little girl shrugged her shoulders—she didn't know—and the mother pressed her but the father believed Mary—in his eyes Mary could do no wrong—

(ZAN goes off for a moment. There is the sudden reflection of flames onto the porch. ZAN re-enters.)

MARA: Ohmigod the bitch is burning my stuff!

ZAN: No more Mara!

(MARA rushes to the sink to fill a bucket with water. ZAN stands behind her, goading.)

MARA: Hurry up, she's burning all my stuff—I smell lighter fluid! Blue, my stuff—!

(BLUE stays crouched against the wall.)

ZAN: But the mother knows the truth in her heart! in her heart she knows the truth and she asks the little girl over and over, Mary, did you hurt the baby, Mary, did you hit the baby's head?

MARA: *(Shakes ZAN off violently, hurling the water at her.)* No, no no no no no no no get away from me, you've flipped out, it's fucking cruel STOP SAYING THAT—

BLUE: *(Exploding.)* That's enough! Okay! That's enough no more God what's wrong with you people!

ZAN: —was it an accident, Mary, over and over, how did the baby fall out of the crib, Mary, why was the pillow on the floor, over and over, and all Mary can say is—

MARA: —what does she say, Mary, what's her answer—!

ZAN: "Dead baby Harry." That's all. "Dead baby Harry." The mother says, Mary did you hurt the baby—

MARA: Dead. Baby.

ZAN: Mary were you mad at the baby—

MARA: Harry… … no no no—prove it, show me proof!

(ZAN goes to a bookshelf. She goes to the exact book she is looking for without hesitation, pulls it out, opens it, and finds a photograph.)

ZAN: The mother says, Mary did you kill the baby! *(Thrusts the photo at MARA.)*

MARA: Nooooo! *(Looks at the photograph for a long moment.)* That's me. But who's the baby, who's that baby why have I never seen this before this is some kind of trick photography or it was a friend, someone's baby tell me…

ZAN: And the woman made herself forget. Destroyed all his things. Kept nothing. A few private photographs. Hidden in books no one ever read. It was mentioned less and less. And because she forgot or appeared to forget, because she couldn't forget, you don't just forget, but because it appeared to others that way… the people around her forgot. The girl, Mary, she forgot. And no one ever mentioned it again.

MARA: No.

ZAN: And the room they added on, Harry's room, they stopped calling it that and called it the addition.

MARA: No this can't be true. *(Begins to tremble, frightened, rubbing her hand over the photo.)*

ZAN: *(To both of them.)* That's the part I left out of "The Language of Kisses!" Now you see! Don't you!? *(Exits through the porch.)*

BLUE: What's wrong with you people!

(The lights fade on MARA fingering the photograph.)

SCENE THREE

8:13 a.m. the same morning, a few hours later. MARA sneaks around the corner and enters the kitchen sheepishly with her bags, practically empty and drooping. She still looks askew, but better. BLUE sits at the table, with a cup of coffee.

BLUE: Hi, Mara.

MARA: Oh she's not in here. Hi, Blue.

BLUE: Wanna cup of coffee? Not as good as Zan makes, but you won't die.

MARA: No, thanks. I'm taking off.

BLUE: Leavin without saying bye? That doesn't seem like such a brainy idea.

(MARA takes the photograph from the table.)

MARA: Oh yeah, she's likely to care. Killer killer girl, right? Who can blame her? Now it somehow all makes sense in a tragic odd fucked-up really kinda scary way. *(She starts to tremble. She pulls into herself, hugging her arms.)* Look at this I'm so freaked out. I gotta get outta here.

BLUE: Where you goin?

MARA: Auntie Vera's in Columbus. She's offered, so... I talked to her on the phone. She's a little nutso, has this wild obsession with Jackie O, dresses like her and acts like her and talks like her, she's a little strange and devotional, but she's got a big house in a really nice section and she means well. *(BLUE looks at her bags.)* Yeah. She didn't get everything, there's some underwear and a bra. A sweater. Not my favorite one. And all my toiletries. Hair dryer. Where is she?

BLUE: Out on the gaze-bo. She's in personal time mode. I usually listen when she's in that mode. I'm waitin to talk to her myself.

MARA: Man, you don't have any cigarettes, do you?

BLUE: I'm out. You didn't mean to do it. I counted. You were like three? When the thing happened. Is that right?

MARA: I'm racking my brains trying to come up with something, a clue an image. Like I get this reverberation, you know, like something you smelled a long time ago, know what I mean? And when you place the smell this whole scene like opens up. Know what's weird? I don't have any memories. Of early early kid stuff. When people say oh what's your first memory, some smartass always pops up and says "oh I remember climbing outta the womb!" Yeah right. Not me! My first memory's when I was eight and Rick Sutters put his finger inside me. And my second memory is when I was ten and I thought I was possessed by the devil!

BLUE: Oh. That musta been... hmmm interesting.

MARA: And then they pick up a bit after that. I mean how many people remember stuff from when they're three? Something so violent, hateful.

BLUE: I did crazy things when I was three. I bet. I don't remember either. See?

MARA: Blue?

BLUE: What?

MARA: If I did do something like that.

BLUE: Yeah?

MARA: God who knows what'll happen if I like faced it, shit, got help and found out I really was possessed by the devil or something.

BLUE: Help's probably a good thing, though. I don't know about the possessed by the devil part that's probably in your head.

MARA: I think it's pretty much over between me and you know who.

BLUE: Who? Oh, Zan? I think you should wait and see and talk to her first. You should definitely stay.

MARA: Blue. You're such an optimist. What the hell kind of name is that anyway? Naming you after a color.

BLUE: Oh sorry no my Mom said when I came out I was a blue baby so she called me what else da ta ta Blue. I had to have a heart operation or something. I'm okay now, though. She was always talkin about them hospital bills. Not pretty. How're you gettin to Columbus?

MARA: I was gonna take the truck. What do you think?

BLUE: Aw now see that's I don't know, it eats up oil like crazy and you can't go over fifty-five—

MARA: I think I can manage that, I'm not totally helpless despite all appearances to the contrary—

BLUE: And keep her below fifty-five? I dunno. You should ask Zan first.

MARA: Yeah, yeah, I don't speed. I don't! Listen, that thing yesterday when I took my top off. It was hot and I... I don't know... something comes over me.

BLUE: You get horny in certain social situations when it's hot and humid. I understand.

MARA: I guess. But you're really attractive, you know.

BLUE: Oh, gee... I'm not sure what to say to that...

MARA: Say thanks. I meant it as a compliment and that's what you're supposed to do when someone pays you a compliment—

BLUE: Thanks. Hey Zan. Mara just gave me a compliment.

(ZAN *suddenly enters, carrying some roses. She goes to the sink, putting the flowers in water. There's a long silence. MARA moves to the porch.*)

MARA: They say silence is louder than words, I think, isn't that what they say? Well, I'm gonna. Split. Can I have the picture? Of me and the baby? Oh and by the way, I'm taking the truck. Blue said it's okay as long as I give it lots of oil. And not go over what did you say—

BLUE: Zan?

MARA: Seventy-five or something? Just kidding, I know *fifty-five!* For what it's worth. I'm sorry.

ZAN: You can stay.

BLUE: Zanny, yes! It's an excellent idea!

MARA: You're kidding, right?

BLUE: I think she means it!

ZAN: I mean it. You can stay. I think we can—not that the road isn't fraught with difficulty—I was hoping we can meet on some common ground. I'd like to see if I can. I hope you would. Like to see if we can meet. On some common... are you listening to me.

MARA: Just like that. After everything.

BLUE: This is a good thing, Mara, don't blow it! Like one of those it was meant to be kind of things and then there it is bang right in front of you.

MARA: God, look at this! (*Looks at her trembling hands.*) I don't think I've ever trembled! I can't stop!

ZAN: I'll ask you to stay sober and clean up after yourself. Maybe get some kind of counseling. You'll do something. Get a job or go to school. And you can have your room back.

BLUE: Another excellent idea! Zan's hot today!

MARA: Yeah? I mean I wouldn't want to put Blue out or anything—what about Blue?

BLUE: Oh, listen, Mara, the room is yours, that's what I was gonna say to Zan—

ZAN: Blue will put his stuff in my room. And I mean it about staying sober.

MARA: What's the catch or switch or something I'm missing here because I'm waiting for you any second to say just kidding and that would probably freak me out not that I don't deserve it.

ZAN: I loved him more.

MARA: Who?

ZAN: Harry. The baby. More than you. Differently than you. I'm a mother, of course, my babies are special. I don't mean I didn't love you. But Harry he was—

(MARA starts to hyperventilate.)

ZAN: —he made me come alive and see life so differently and you understood that somehow—and he kicked the air so hard waiting for the day he could jump to his feet and join the world and he never got to and I... I blame myself for not seeing your pain, for loving him more. I drove you away from me.

MARA: *(Tries to squelch the emotion.)* Ohmigod! All I wanted—— *(Swallows it.)*

ZAN: Mara?

MARA: *(Choking on her words.)* —listen to me—

ZAN: Breathe.

MARA: —since I walked through that door— *(Can't say it.)* —all I wanted was for you—oh God I can't——

ZAN: *(Shakes MARA.)* Breathe Mara go on breathe!

MARA: —listen to me—!

BLUE: Mara you'll feel better if you say it.

MARA: I I I—can't I can't—

(MARA suddenly embraces ZAN, which takes her by surprise. She puts her arms around MARA. They embrace for a long moment. MARA rocks once with great pain. They pull apart. MARA, in a flurry, turns, grabs her bags and stands on the porch.)

MARA: I I I—can't talk— Ihavetogothankyouohmi—

ZAN: Mara!

MARA: —we'll see each other—again bye—

BLUE: Mara!

MARA: —Blue bye—

(MARA takes off. The sound of the truck starting.)

BLUE: I think you should stop her Zan. Zan?

ZAN: No, Blue, let her go!

(BLUE runs off.)

BLUE: *(From off.)* Mara, come on, wait a minute, come back, what're you doin—!

(The truck drives off. A moment later, BLUE enters.)

BLUE: I do not believe this she just got right in that truck and drove off, one minute everything's peachy keen and the next—it's the right thing for her to stay you have to call her at that Aunt Vera's place when she gets there and talk to her and work it out! For you two to get to know each other and get reacquainted and stuff man this sucks!

ZAN: Maybe it's best this way. Give her some time.

BLUE: Whatta you mean give her some time, there is no time, she needs your help now, did you see her she was practically a nervous wreck falling apart in fronta your very eyes—

ZAN: Give her time to think things over!

BLUE: She should be here now to be with you, say you'll call her at Aunt Vera's say that!

ZAN: Honey, what's the matter?

BLUE: Just say you're going to call her at Aunt Vera's say it! Honey!

ZAN: I'll call her at Vera's. I will. Are you okay?

BLUE: *(To himself.)* Bad news all around.

ZAN: What? Blue. Blue. Blue Moon. Put your things in my room—I meant that—Blue...

(ZAN goes to him. She kisses him. They look each other in the eyes. He turns away. She kisses him again. They look each other in the eyes. He turns away. She kisses him again, kissing him more insistently. He pulls away, cries out.)

ZAN: Blue what!

(He goes right for the basement door, opens it, reaches in and takes out a duffel bag with his things.)

ZAN: Oh! Why didn't you sneak out when I wasn't looking?

BLUE: I think I wanna take a break or something like that. I know it seems...

ZAN: Oh Blue.

BLUE: Take off for a week or two, that's all, you know so I can stand back and look at it and—

ZAN: A couple of hours ago you wanted to marry me.

BLUE: I can't marry you. I can't marry anybody. I can't.

ZAN: Blue I'm so sorry this whole thing spun completely out of control, I didn't want to subject you to any of it, that's why I told you—

BLUE: A bit of time by myself, you know, like how you like your alone time—

ZAN: I'm sorry it turned so ugly, ugly things like that exist between people that's the way the world is—I'm not perfect, I get mad I yell but not at you never at you again I swear! *(Moves close to him.)*

BLUE: Now see you're going and takin it all personal. I need space, too as a matter of fact I bet I need lots more space than you do—

(She starts kissing him. He pulls away.)

BLUE: —Zanny don't get somethin all started here I don't want to be rude, because I don't—

ZAN: Blue!

BLUE: I need to think is all. I'm only goin for a week or two!

ZAN: *(She is in shock.)* What about your tools!

BLUE: What tools? I don't have any tools.

ZAN: Your tools I bought them for you!

BLUE: I don't own tools. I don't want to own them. I can't own them. They belong to you, you paid for em. I don't want to own things. That's how people go crazy, owning things!

ZAN: I don't like you hitchhiking.

BLUE: I'm gonna go, okay? Zan, thank you, Zan, thank you for everything. I'll be back in a coupla weeks—

ZAN: No you won't I know it—

BLUE: I will—

(ZAN loses it, slapping at BLUE's chest.)

ZAN: I knew this couldn't last, this is life, not a story that's what this is—I knew you weren't for real I knew you—

(BLUE shields himself, ducks.)

ZAN: No no don't duck from me like that, don't duck from me Blue!

(ZAN takes his hand and puts it between her legs. BLUE tries to pull his hand away.)

ZAN: Blue touch me there please, touch me there Blue touch me there like you do please Blue don't leave me stranded here Blue don't pull away don't pull away!

(BLUE gets his hand free and moves away. ZAN turns to the kitchen table.)

ZAN: Great! Look at this you never ate your dinner from last night well this is no good now—!

(A silence.)

BLUE: Come on I don't wanna leave you like this! Mad at me.

ZAN: Then don't.

(BLUE picks up his duffel bag.)

ZAN: Will I be able to reach you, oh God this is happening so fast! Will you let me know where you are?

BLUE: When I get there.

ZAN: Blue, I'm not happy about this! Wait a minute, take this will you take this, you have to!

(She goes to a basket on the kitchen counter and takes out the copy of Look Homeward, Angel *and hands it to BLUE.)*

BLUE: I can't read "Look Homeward Angels" without you.

ZAN: You don't want to get behind in your reading. Try. Even a couple pages a day.

BLUE: No. When you say so long it means you'll see the person again, right?

ZAN: So long. Right.

BLUE: Then so long, Zanny Zanny.

(He kisses her lightly on the lips. She closes her eyes. He exits. ZAN opens her eyes, expecting to wake up from a dream. She lets out a cry. She rushes to the door. She wants to call out. She stops herself. She comes into the kitchen and she punches one of the cabinets. She walks into a chair and in a sudden rage, she kicks it across the room, maybe turns the table over. She looks around her, heaving. She goes to another kitchen chair and sits down, stunned, beginning to cry. She is racked for a moment, sobbing, then she suddenly laughs. The laughter builds and builds into a final scream of surrender. She sits staring ahead for a long moment, then finally gets up and turns off the outside porch light. She picks up the chair that she kicked. She stands at the side of her desk to scribble something down on a piece of paper.)

ZAN: He—was—a beautiful boy—

(She stops, steps away, thinks for a moment. She turns back to the desk and jots something else down. She shakes her head. She finds herself suddenly drawn to sitting and writing more. She nods her head, makes a sound of assent. She stares ahead of her for a long moment. It's almost as if she's a pianist looking at the piano before she begins to play the concerto. She picks up a sheet of paper, puts it in the typewriter and types a line. She looks at it. She smiles. She types another line. She reads it, she likes it, she types some more. She stops, reads it, becomes exhilarated and continues typing, until the world around her disappears. The room dissolves to one light on ZAN.

(Blackout.)

Word To Your Mama

Julia Lee Barclay

JULIA LEE BARCLAY was born in 1963 in Providence, Rhode Island, and grew up in New England. In 1986, she received her BA with high honors in theatre from Wesleyan University. She began directing plays in 1980 and writing plays in 1999, all in an attempt to unearth, in a modern context, the ritualistic and deeply spiritual roots of the theatre. In 1994, Barclay co-founded Monkey Wrench Theater and directed three plays by C.J. Hopkins, *Horse Country, screwmachine/eyecandy*, and *The Position*. While a resident artist at Mabou Mines, she directed extensive labs to create theatrical techniques for Monkey Wrench. As Monkey Wrench disbanded, she began a two-year collaborative project with three actors, Fred Backus, Renee Bucciarelli, and Chris Campbell, who presented this work, *Inside of a Shapeless Angel*, at The Present Company in New York. This work in turn led to an invitation to teach workshops at the Chisenhale Dance Space in London. Also at The Present Company, Barclay directed *Gorky's Wife* by Elena Penga. With Screaming Venus, she directed both productions of *Word To Your Mama*, as well as her short play *Cut Up*. She recently directed a reading of her newest play, *Rough Road*, for Jean Cocteau Repertory and is conducting experimental workshops at The Present Company. Barclay lives in New York City.

Word To Your Mama was first produced by Screaming Venus (Monica Sirignano, Artistic Director) as part of their festival of one-act plays, *Kallisti*, on March 1, 2000, at the Camera Obscura Theatre, New York City, with the following cast and credits:

Night Secretaries .... Nicole Higgins, Monica Sirignano, Kate Ward

Directed by: Julia Lee Barclay
Set Design: Daniel Jagendorf
Lighting Design: Elizabeth Greenman
Assistant Directors: Julie Blumenthal, Carolyn Raship
Stage Manager: Kimberly Justice

Word To Your Mama was subsequently produced by Screaming Venus as part of the 2000 New York International Fringe Festival (John Clancy, Artistic Director; Elena K. Holy, Producing Director). The cast and credits were as above, with the following exceptions:

Lighting Design: S. Ryan Schmidt
Assistant Director: Rachel Solomon

The author gratefully acknowledges the immense contribution and support of the members of Screaming Venus, where this play was developed, with a special thanks to the cast and her tireless assistant directors and stage manager.

Word To Your Mama is dedicated to Jani Mace, Robin Schmidt, and Darcy Seaver.

"All is water and the world is full of gods."—Thales

AUTHOR'S INTRODUCTION

Because *Word To Your Mama* is a text that needs to be directed onto the stage, meaning it is not a traditional play wherein there are characters, a given scenario, etc.; and because I have worked most of my life as a director in theater rather than as a writer, the editor and I felt it would be a good idea to give the reader an idea of how this piece was constructed. I hope in this opening essay to give the reader some sense of not only how *Word* looked, but also how one could approach it as a director as well.

To understand the *what* of the work, I believe the *why* is also important. What I have striven to do in theater is undermine the reality-grid of right now—meaning that which we say "that's the way it is" about, either publicly or privately, regarding, e.g., class/money, race/ethnicity, gender/sex, religion/God, nationalism/patriotism, etc.—through the creation of theatrical work that challenges these assumptions by, first, owning them as our own (not pawning them off on an "other" which somehow creates a world in which we live as victims), and, second, exploring the depths of our own assumptions/investments and investigating our own "desiring machines" (a concept of Gilles Deleuze and Felix Guattari's from their book *Anti-Oedipus*). The Deleuze/Guattari theory is that we all, to some extent, carry within us fascistic investments (meaning investments in a state of "being") and revolutionary investments (meaning investments in the process of "becoming"). Their desire was to enact a kind of radical psychology wherein our fascistic investments could be examined, owned, and somehow uprooted to bring about a social investment in something other than "being"—i.e., a static, repressive environment that rewards conformity and a certain kind of subservience to an other-centered order of things as they are. I believe their vision has to do with a more revolutionary social body—one in which the process of becoming itself is integral to living, and there is no need to impose a hegemonic force onto other living creatures (examples of this now and in the past: capital, Christianity and other Evangelical/missionary religions, slavery, women as property, man's dominion over/destruction of nature, psychology, "the Big Bang", etc.). This is an incredible reduction of everything they said, but serves as a (hopefully) useful starting point for understanding the root influence of my theatrical endeavors.

I have tried to do this by creating theatrical pieces that uproot the static nature of language, gesture, character, etc., in such a way as to bring about this process of becoming. If the work is successful, this "becoming" flows through our own bodies/souls/minds as players/writers/directors and thence into the bodies/minds/souls of the audience.

The concrete way I manifest these ideas in *Word To Your Mama* was first to break the text up into threes. I cast three actors to embody what is in a sense one consciousness. That consciousness itself I have broken down into a stream of consciousness (subjective), river of consciousness (social), and construction of consciousness (the zeitgeist—the rules of the social). In order to manifest this idea on stage, I broke the stage itself into three zones: one, the naturalistic zone, where the actors address the theatrical space as if they were in a fourth-wall theatrical production; two, the presentational zone, where the actors address the audience directly, as if in a Brecht play or a musical; and three, the communal zone, where the actors address what I call the "rules of the room" or the "grid," i.e., the forces that are creating the rules and expectations of the moment—theatrically, socially, spiritually, etc. I further broke these rules down into major areas, such as gender, class, religion, etc.

We then further created and broke down the actors' gestures into three discrete categories: idiosyncratic (personal); cliché (social—addressing gender, class, nationality, religion, and something I call the Blob, a concept that embodies the virtual Mall of America world we find ourselves in at the turn of the millennium); and transformative (ritual, addressing areas of experience that cannot be communicated in any other way; we created these gestures through a series of transformation exercises). In the end, we had a language of 140 gestures, including about five neutral stances. Throughout the course of rehearsals, the actors improvised to discover where they would be in the space and what gestures they would use. Through an excruciating process of notation carried out by my assistant director and stage manager, and tireless work by the actors, I was able to stage the entire piece based on these repeated improvisations. This was important to me, because the actors then owned the piece on a much more visceral level than if I had pre-staged it. This process also lent itself to far more physical complexity than could have been imagined by me alone in a room. The lines were also split up in this way, prior to the movement work. At the beginning of the rehearsal process for each production, the actors read through the script a few times without pre-assigned line breaks, with my assistant director(s) notating the results. After a few read-throughs, I compared all of the different versions and broke down the script accordingly. I have not noted the specific assignment of lines or gestures in this text because it is highly complex and also because I strongly feel that if someone else were to direct this piece, s/he should break up the lines and physical movements with the actors with whom s/he wanted to work. However, I have attempted to format the lines on the page in order to give the reader a feel for the rhythm of the piece as it played.

The other relevant "threes" that I worked with were three levels of "one mind as three voices": intellectual, emotional, spiritual, but in one body. One body means intimately related movement, and the effect is one organism. However, as the second production developed, I discovered that the less similar their movements were on the surface but the more connected their intentions were, the more they seemed like one organism manifesting in three distinct ways. We also worked with three levels of playing: presentational (the "big mask": obvious, i.e., a clear commentary on mask, not invested in that voice); naturalistic (the "tight mask": sneaky, i.e., a seeming investment in that voice); and ritualistic (the Self—with a capital "S"— larger Self, not simply ego/self, but instead communal/deeply personal, i.e., a confrontation with something about the nature of reality in the moment). The way in which language itself works on these three levels also shifts: the naturalistic lends itself to a literal interpretation of phrases, the presentational lends itself to a metaphoric interpretation, and the ritualistic lends itself to a more symbolic interpretation. This is important to keep in mind when reading the play: allow yourself to hear all of the possible resonances of each phrase and word. They can shift radically and are not fixed.

Having written all this, however, I wish to leave as a parting thought to whomever may read this play or want to direct it a note I gave to the three actors with whom I worked (and without whom this whole process would have been impossible):

The above are frameworks with which to start work. Resonators. Ideas. Not cages, but limits to work within and without. Other descriptions for the text: rants, ideas, dreams, thoughts, statements, beliefs, nightmares, realities, maps of an event into unknown/known territory. The event is up to you. Up to us. All of us on any given night, day, rehearsal, or performance.

*A large American flag hangs upstage. A small
table with three chairs sits in front of the
flag. On the periphery of the performance
space, in or near the audience, are three chairs.
The backs of these chairs face the audience.*

*Opening sequence: during the prologue to a
song such as Patti Smith's "Rock 'n Roll
Nigger," the three actors emerge from behind
the flag. They are Night Secretaries. They
are wearing secretary outfits with sneakers
and white socks. When the song's back-beat
begins in earnest, the Secretaries lift their
heads and shout "5, 6, 7, 8" and smile
broadly while doing an aerobics routine. The
central Secretary says at various times to "lift
your arms," "travel," and "take your pulse."
After awhile, one of the Secretaries stops the
song and routine by saying the first line.*

Wait.

Now.

A Man Can't Know What It's Like To Be
a true knight of faith.
Mother
is a witness.

That was such a nice letter to get.

No.

Wrong.

Revise schedule.

A good time to finish up old tasks.

Get sublet for Struggling Artist Magazine.

1962–1978

Someone's childhood.

Don't think about that.

Fear and Trembling.

I don't know if I'll be alive.

But, we're here.

Fish are good.

We've been here before.

Girls Meeting God on borrowed time.

What's going on here?

How did you Get here?

I am so glad you like my work.

Something which cannot be said—
So you say it anyway.

Experts say
we're losing focus.

The soul truth daily—
I pray all the time
I pray for Rain…

Two men sit looking at one another
one is "real" the other is made of plaster.

John Lennon with those sun glasses on,
arms folded, looking so inevitable.

You can live like the folks on the hill,
but first

two telephones
a candle
a skull
a blank box waiting to be filled
or put down
so another can raise himself up to
open the House.

We need help
in the Building.

I shall continue to want an impossible
lunch.

Please.

We haven't even eaten breakfast yet.

Any Surplus is Immoral.

You must learn how to
Begin plotting out the course
again with nothing.

only a giant goose with ribbons and neck-
laces being led on a leash by a man in robes
through a parade.

Reserved for the "Homeless."

Giant cockroaches scare me.

Mixed with the more open intense work
that is both so exhilarating and
(can be)
so draining.

We are more than a romantic figure:

The Persecution and Assassination of Miss
Besieged Sarajevo 1993
as performed by Doris Lessing.

There's nothing wrong with me.

There really isn't.

If I need to believe in God, He doesn't
exist, and if I don't need to believe in Him,
then He does.

Baudrillard.

The French.

Communists are all brainwashed.

Or, worse, post-structuralists.

Advertisements are meant to entertain.

I believe that god believes what I believe.

Isn't it incredible how little would get done if
all the secretaries in the world went on strike?

I was told by a lawyer for whom I was
working as a secretary that I wasn't "really
a secretary."

This was meant as a compliment.

We type endless letters about The Law.

These are very boring letters.

We are paid very little in comparison to
the lawyers who dictate these letters.

But we are paid more than the young
people who carry the files from one lawyer to another.

Therefore, we cannot complain.

No one who is not starving can complain.

This is The Law.

This is why Homeless People are so important to us.

Or "the homeless"… coalitions for life in
hell…

Nomads with carts.

No one.

Let's see the other names: drug addicts,
bums,
mental patients,
troublemakers,
creeps,
dangerous,
families,
the unfortunate,
the lazy,
the stupid,
the unlucky,
the "there but for the grace of God go I"
people,
alcoholics,
good for nothing,
Vietnam vets,
unwanted, abused,
set on fire,
left to die,
stabbed in a shelter,
allowed to rot,

smell bad,
look funny,
wish they were gone.

Why is he asking me for money?

Oh Christ, now he's blessing me.

Where do I go to get away from this but if
I move to suburbia my Son will be gunned
down by his Prozac-inhaling classmate
with a rifle…

Oh Lord Jesus… please help this Homeless because I can't…

What can I do?

What can I do?…

I'm not the Problem.

I don't even know how to Talk to Him!

He's not even a normal person!

There's Nothing wrong with me…

There's Nothing wrong with me…

Where are you going now?

Nice shoes…

What's for supper?

I'm famished.

Reality is banal and absurd, like how to
act mysterious.

Like how to smile as you kill.

I like fish.
Fish are good.

Tea?

12:30-3:30 on Sundays
building the Nation.

Revise script:
somebody's Patriotism.

The Childhood Theater
Presents
My Life During Wartime… with special
guest star… Loni Anderson.

John Lennon and Groucho Marx were on
a "new" Russian stamp.
Get it?
"Lennon and Marx."

The Revolution as Irony.

Quentin Tarantino is a winner.

Marx is a loser.

The Duma has voted to put the old statues back up in Russia.

Their Currency has collapsed.

What if we had sent a ballistic missile into
the USSR in 1980 when that computer
chip Malfunctioned and read a flock of
geese as incoming Soviet missiles?

Who cares? It didn't happen, did it?

What if we never thought kings were divine and that rich people were kings?

"There's something happenin' here…
what it is ain't exactly clear…"

Hasn't that been made into a commercial
yet?

Right.

Is there anything not for sale to Bill Gates?

Anything at all?

Let's listen intently and have a moment
of silence for anything that is not.

Secretaries…

slaves...
night help...
coffee.

I hate that noise.

Wait.

Now.

I too used to think I wasn't a "real secre-
tary."
I thought I was visiting.
I was a tourist in someone else's life.
I'm not anymore. I live here, too.
I think I'm welcome in the neighborhood.
I wish I wasn't so familiar.
I wish I could fly overhead and smile
knowingly and wisely down at the flock
of sheep below me.
But no. I've got my own set of tags now.
Branded for Life.

Please.

Never to forget.

This is good somehow.

For whom I'm not sure yet.

But, I'd give almost anything to see all the
Secretaries of the World unite and strike.

Because all hell would finally break loose,
and the chains of slavery between man
and woman would break
and the Furies of loss of patriarchal control would come roaring out of some pri-
mordial swamp and Kubrick's monolith
would reappear and bust out everyone's
eardrums
and we would Finally evolve into a better
species of human being...

These are our dreams as we nod off to
sleep...

Better fish or more art supplies?

Fish are good.

Have we met before?

I don't want to emotionally or spiritually
drain you.

Stop music.
Continue dance.

A Man Can't Know What It's Like to Be
Any Surplus.

Raise Boys and Girls Immoral,
the Same Way As Any Mother.

I am so glad you like my work.

Have you been fishing lately?

Are we all here?

Have you gone off for a little vacation?

Shiva Dial-Out Failure?

She was in the class of '86.
Supposed to be a leader by now...a world
leader...
Whatever happened to her anyway?

Train wreck? Bus explosion...

I heard she was macrobiotic and directing
Ionesco...
Isn't she a lesbian?
She used to be nicer than she is now...

What Did happen to her anyway?

No one really knows...too bad...so much
wasted potential.

Wrong.

You will never make art if you give in to
your potential.

Everybody's a bunch of liars.

Right.

Don't believe anything you hear.
Everyone's just a salesman.

Everyone'll sell you out and their own
Mother too.

It's Every Man For Himself, Son.

The Womb is Overrated.

Let's Get to Work.

Where do You want to go today?

We care about You... and your investments.

"We could be heroes, just for one day..."

We are Here for You.

We Like You.

You need to stop:
sneezing,
burping,
farting,
blowing your nose,
itching,
worrying,
having headaches,
being impotent,
being depressed,
using drugs,
smoking,
drinking,
calling in sick to work,
and looking over 25 years old.

We have drugs for you.

You can change.

There are No Rules.
There are No Limits.

Let's Get to work.

Work will set you free.

You are Free.

You have no zits.
No distinctive features.

No hair. No butt.
No breasts.

Just Perfect Abs.
Rock Hard Abs.
Abs to Die For.

Work
Will set you free.

I am so glad you like my Work.

Miss Sarajevo:
Building the Nation.

We will be looking into Structures,

Dictionaries,

Law Libraries,

Trademark Law,

Intellectual Property.

Revise script:
I'm So Glad You Like Our Work.

I don't know if I'll be alive.
Again
with nothing.

The big choice:
1962-1978

Again?

Reserved.
The same Way.

Wait.

Again?

What I can envision:

Flexible Spending.
401K...
hair spray...
lost puppies...
heartwarming stories...
Kwanzaa has been commercialized...

there's nowhere to go without a Sale.
Sale.
Sale.
Sale.

Who's for sale?
Who's Not for sale?
What's Your Price?
High or low?
Cheap whore expensive whore…
big car… little car…
golden parachute or shit sandwich?

I can't travel round these parts now with-
out wantin' to hurl… know what I mean
dip shit?
Hey that's pretty fuckin' funny… huh?
Hahahahahaha… Bang bang your dead.
Heh heh heh.
That's entertainment there motherfucker,
huh?!
Eat this!
Yeah, how's it taste motherfucker?!
What are ya, a Pussy??!!!

What's wrong with you?

What's wrong with us?

Any mother is immoral.

Haven't we been here Before?

No.

Yes.

NO.

I mention this, since we have discovered
that Phoebe has angel wings her mother
made.

Basically one wants to say something—
Instead, you change the channel to another static station:
Whatever truly is great is available equally
for all.

I shall continue
slouching towards Bethlehem…

Can I say that? Will I get sued?

How many lines of a poem constitute a
fraud?

How many words are instead a tribute?

Intellectual Property is a Big business.

Saving the world for Skittles in Kenya.

"We have reason to believe that the Trademark Office in Somalia is not operational
at this time."

I want to smoke a cigarette now because
I'm convinced this would be better if I
did so.

Am I ruining this?

My eyes don't work anymore.

My shoulder hurts.

About her plans for the future she replied:
"I don't know about that.
I don't know if I'll be alive."

Wait.

Stop.

A man types sitting on a wooden bench
with a window open to the Atlantic
Ocean.

Now.

I dreamt of enormous waves
crashing onto our cottage window.
I closed the open windows to keep the
ocean from sweeping us away.
Then I sat in the room and watched the
waves crash up against the glass.
I felt oddly secure under the circumstances.

Anything is possible.

Please.

It was in the dream.

Again.

In the dream, we were in a space ship—
in Zero Gravity.
I saw pictures from my past on video cam-
eras—a blurry stepfather on one screen—
a small child on another—
me, probably—
very colorful
but hazy.

And outside?

Outside the window, the planets were
Exploding, yellow, pink, orange, purple,
Red gasses forming a new universe.

Right before our eyes.

She said to me:
anything is possible.

She said: let's go there… instead.

She asked me:
Are you ready?

In the Movie a man sits in a wheelchair.
He has had a stroke and can barely speak,
but is watching coal miners being rescued
from a collapsed tunnel. As they emerge
from the mine alive, he whispers to his
son,

the deconstructionist,

God is here.

God is Here.

Again with nothing.

I saw—
Don't say it!

Don't say it! I saw God while I was waiting at a bus stop.

For a moment.

Blasted out of the universe,
like in the last scene of *2001*—
faster than the speed of anything—
I was shot up off the planet,
saw the stars and the rest of the universe
disappear rapidly behind me—
then I was outside of everything—
for a moment—
and I was shot back as quickly as I left.

My body never left the ground.

At the bus stop, a Mother was yelling at
her Son—a scene that usually disturbs me,
but didn't. It all had to happen that way.
I could see that.
Even as my thoughts said otherwise.

I don't like this part of the story.

And I got on the next bus.

No one,
not even the least,
needs another man's proposed plan.

Warning.

Where are you?

A fatal exception has occurred.

A child emerges in a dream; I try to hold
her, but then stop myself—I don't want
her to feel my hunger—afraid it will burn
her.

You have a baby, riddled with eczema.
You don't even know how to change her
diapers,
but your husband does.
You watch him to see how it's done.
It seems so simple.

Any surplus is immoral.

That was such a nice letter to get.

Thank you.

All is forgiven.

There is nothing wrong with you.

Whatever that hole is in you that you think you can drug or 12-step or talk away, you can't. It's part of you and always will be. It's what connects you to everyone else—that deep dark secret you think no one else can see or understand. It's not as deep and dark as it seems—it's not the void, it's not God—it's the shadow of your self-loathing. It's the bogey-man of the psyche. It's as thin as air—and as common. No one can fix you. Please don't let them try.

Now.

New York City.
New Jack City.
The Big Apple.

Where everyone wants to be famous and believes they will be—someday.

Except for those who dream of escape to islands, where they can sit on the sand enraptured by an eternally peaceful moment staring at the ocean. A kind of calm dreamed about in the midst of noisy chaos, coughing on the bus fumes walking to your job as a Secretary.

The night shift.

Blind ambition.

Taking you from day to day— tripping over the wreckage of generations of dreams of Money, a better world, better Art Supplies, a new Theater, a better Widget, a new Person, a Communist Utopia,

a stock market that never goes down, a child at Yale, the most brilliant book of the century, the Nobel Prize, the grace of God, the conversion of the masses, a nursery school that lets children play instead of teaching them seven languages, health insurance for everyone, a nose job to make you beautiful, being discovered, having a retrospective at the Whitney, eternal life, a statue in Central Park, a monument, life without end, a vision, a blinding vision, a better toaster, something that finally beats sliced bread—

an inevitable moment.

Transcendental existentialism... slouching towards immortality, waiting to be born.

We may want to start working twice a week.

There's Money in it.

Money from Home.

AT&T.

With good wishes.

From Friends and Family.

Walking to a place with no windows and no doors: a gated city.
They marched to this place in an orderly fashion.
All thinking they had heard something personal, something cosmic, something meant for them alone, when all it was was marching orders coming in at a high frequency...

Will we build it the same way again?

You always start off again with nothing.

A good time to finish up old tasks.

A good time to finish up old tasks.

A good time.

For a good time call…
Yourself.
Us.
Them.
Her.
Him.
The Government.

Call.
The Government.

See who answers.

Who's gonna answer?

I'm still here, you motherfuckers, I'm still
here!

Let's walk Away.

Get Off the bus.

De-train.

De-plane.

Disembark.

Go on Strike.

Let whoever wants to, go to work.
Cosmic scabs to be dealt with accordingly.

We've got Work of our own to do—
over here where anything is possible

Can you hear it?

The whistle of a distant train going somewhere Else?
Are you almost asleep in bed wondering
who those people are going off to another
place?

Are you a child waiting to be invited to
the party?
Waiting for Santa Claus
Or Jesus?
Waiting for redemption?
Or for presents?
Or for money to "come to you"?

Whose war are you fighting anyway?

Whose side are you on?

Do you even know there are sides?

Too many people live in Switzerland.

I'm going home now.

Going home to eat fish?

It's scary out here.

The true knight of faith.
She dances.

I've always wanted to Dance.

You have the ability to adapt to diverse
situations.
She is auditioning—has a script
before our eyes

There could be as many interpretations
as plans for her future.

Talk to actors.

Get sublet.

Begin plotting.

Call them first and ask if can leave scripts!

Day Worker
Needs Script

Basically what one meant when it comes to—
one always starts off again—

Wait.

Wrong.

Stop.

Remove paper jam. Now.

I am so glad you like my smile.

I am a Real Secretary.

Stop.

You have the ability.

Reserved for your Company.
With good wishes.

Let's go around again.

Let's see where this thing will take us.

Have you ever done something you wish you could take back? Prodded at that moment in time like a sore tooth—thinking, if only this and if only that. Wondering if it ever could have been otherwise and realizing, over and over again, to your horror, no—it couldn't. You are in fact "gonna carry that weight… a long time." Asking yourself continually, when can I lay it down? When do you know when it's time to lay it down? Whose decision is that, really? Isn't this the kind of thing someone's God should take care of? Where do I make the sacrifice? Who do you get absolution from? Who's in charge of the Redemption Business nowadays? And, then, the deafening silence of that goddamn one hand clapping. No one. Really. No One.

Your *self* has nothing to do with it.

Wait.

[today's date]

Wait.

How did we get here?

Where's the map?

Who's got the map?

Isn't there a map?

A way?

A course?

Shouldn't we ask someone for directions?

We could just be going around in circles.

Right.

Don't we have a drug for this?

I've never been here before. Have you?

Yes.

No.

YES.

"Let's dance…
Put on your red shoes and…"

Twirl around the May pole.

Does anyone do that anymore?
Twirl around a May pole?

May 1st:
May Day.
Mothers' Day.
Communist Workers' Day.
May Day. May Day.
SOS
Taken over.

Lost in translation.
Morse code.
Bombs dropping.
A past war.

Another war.
Someone else's war.
Not our war.

That's the war on TV. The TV war—the one in black and white.

The Real War.

Then there's the TV war in color with rock music.
The Bad War.

Then there's the war in green and black covered by Smart Bombs and CNN.
The Video Game War.

None of these are our wars.
These are
Television wars.
They are progressively smaller and smaller.
They are progressively more absurd.
They progress towards death of appetite.

Death of all life.

Not "just them."

We are not alone here.

We are going forward.

We are going forward whether we like it or not.

We're gonna party like it's…
Right now.

We are dying with "them."

There is no Them.

Just a lot of wars we consume.

None of which are Ours.

Our war, we are afraid, simply Cannot be televised.

There's no Money in it.

Do you think I should smile more?

Everybody's a bunch of liars.

Under the name of sympathy, which is—
Nothing but vanity.

I exhort therefore I am.

There's nothing wrong with me.

No?

No.

No, you must always fight your talent, or no real art will be made by you.

DeKooning said that according to a letter in *The New York Times*.

All the news that's fit to print.
Fit to print.
Fits in print.
Can print.
Will print.
Follow the money. Print will follow.

Money is speech.

Money Is Speech.

Wrong.

Right.

Now.

We declare these truths to be self-evident—
that all men can speak with cold, hard cash.
People are born,
and Cash renders them all equally for sale.

Are you worth three widgets or three million widgets?

How many widgets can fit in a Volkswagen?
How many Jews?
I mean clowns.

I mean… more flower less power…

I mean… more power less flower…

Working Assets.

Your Assets working for you.
We'll make the calls.
You just send us your Money and we'll
save a rain forest or something.
We'll drive our Volvos right to that damn
rain forest and save its ass.
Just watch us.
We'll get a cool theme song to go with us.
Something from Crosby Stills Nash and
Young to accompany us in our Volvos to
the rain forest with your Money to save
its ass—
handing out Ben & Jerry's ice cream pops
along the way...
Want a sticker?
Who do you want to save?
Do you have the T-shirt?
Michael Ovitz will give trumpets to poor
inner city kids in your name.
But we, we'll drive you in our Volvo that
you Paid for with your Stock Options, to
save that rain forest's ass...
hunh?
Is that something to write a song about or
what?

"Something's happening here... what it
is, is all too clear..."

Or we could just crash your Volvo right
into that tree over there
and see what happens.
See who lives, who dies—where we end
up—maybe walking around dazed and
confused through a desert of unspecified
origin.
Maybe the Sphinx emerges out of nowhere
and we have to solve a riddle or something
and we start all over again...
or Maybe something new.

According to the Experts, this isn't possible.

A witness confesses thereby that no one,
not even the least, needs another person's
sympathy, or is to be put down so another

Miss Besieged Sarajevo can raise herself up.

What about the tiara?

Nolle novum sub solum est. [Latin for "there
is nothing new under the sun"]

Please.

"Smile a little smile for me."

Have a nice day.

Secretaries of the Real, Unite.

Let's get to work.

ADM: Supermarket to the World.

Blue balloons flying up into the air with
words handwritten on parchment paper
tied to them.
Love.
Commitment.
Reunion.
Sympathy.

Little children smiling at their parents'
stock options.
They're Real People.
The Real People have stock in the stock
market.
They need to enhance their portfolios for
their Real Children.
Hurricane Mitch.
Wipes out all those Other People some-
where else.
Here, we have Stock Options.

We don't get killed in hurricanes.

We have not built our huts upon the sand.

Nothing bad happens to us.
Nothing happens to us.
We watch TV.
We Interact on the Internet.
We Buy Stuff.
We Sell Stuff.
We Buy and Sell electronic numbers.

We don't die.
We couldn't die if we wanted to.
We surf the Net.
We actually Surf a Net.
There's no water to dive into—
no water to drown in—
because there's a Net.

Close to the water—
seeing the water,
but Safe.

Maximum Security.

You'd think if people Knew that investing in the stock market killed other people, that they would stop. I mean, wouldn't you? I mean, doesn't it seem to you like every time we invest a dollar in the stock market or buy a product made in a sweatshop or by prison labor in China or Louisiana or Wherever that we are investing in Mutually Assured Destruction? I mean, first, "Market Forces" wipe out all those Other Poor Countries every couple of years to make sure they stay in line and give us their labor and stuff cheap. Then, most of us only see The Poor on TV, represented by Brown People usually, as they die in floods, earthquakes, wars, or trying to organize a union, overthrow a dictatorship or open the door to their own apartment in, say, the Bronx.

Warning.

Your program has performed an illegal operation.

And Finally, Here, where it's so Safe, a man on TV tells The Real People:
"You have to think of yourself as an optimistic product."

So, haven't we invested in our Own oppression?
If all we can be are proactive toasters with

Stock Options?

Is this what we really want?
Can you really say you are surprised by
Kip Kinkle,
Dylan Klebold,
Eric Harris, et al?

Drugged,
Wired,
Smart,
Armed and with the prospect of Toasterhood ahead of them?

I mean, what do you think?

Redistribute the wealth?
Start over?
What?

I don't know. I'm not seeing any Happy Meals here.

Warning.

Your program may automatically shut down and any unsaved may be lost.

"There's a man with a gun over there– telling me I got to beware..."

There's a lot of goodness in a bowl of cereal.

And in this lies the deep humanity in him.

Working Class Hero.

Any surplus is immoral.

Christmas Day.

"You can live like the folks on the hill, but first you must learn how to smile as you kill."

How to guard your deepest, most shameful secret.

The Redistribution of Wealth?

Christ on a Stick.

Christ on a Kite—

the resurrection, tied to a piece of twine—
a dumb show—
weirdly believed and worshipped, even
when the string is visible.

He's Flying for Christ's Sake.

How'd he get up there?

Let's check it out.

Let's send a Space Probe up there to see if
we can find him.

Let's raise boys and girls the same way.

Have a popsicle.

Eat meat.

Don't eat meat.

Drink milk.

Think Different.

Buy now. And Save.

Pay later.

No payments until we tell you there are.

Never pay.
Credit only.
In God we trust.
All others pay cash.

I'm with stupid.

"There must be some kinda way out of
here…"

Let's take a poll.

Wait.

Now?

This will end your Windows session.

Yes.

I can feel it,

Dave.
I can feel it.

Now.

It was so, like, real. Ya know? I was, like,
totally there. Totally. Especially when he
went, like, give away all your stuff, and I
was like, yeah, totally. And then he just,
like, left so we all went home and Dad
went, like, well, he's gone, so like let's have
dinner and watch that War on TV. And
so we were like O.K. And then I had a
dream that night that he was like there
and telling me, like, no really, give away
all your stuff and I went O.K. and got up
and told Dad and he's like yeah I had that
dream too, and so Now we're like totally
confused.

Dad's gone out on the Street with a Sign
telling everyone to give away all their stuff
and Mom's kinda upset, especially since
she just got the Whirlpool for Christmas
and I'm like still in school and the Cops
already arrested Dad once for causing a
disturbance and Mom doesn't know how
to make the mortgage payments, especially
since Dad sold all our Stock Options and
sent the money to Bangladesh or wherever, so, we're like screwed, but I think
Dad's like totally cool in a way.

So I like stopped eating, which will make
me lose weight anyway—even if it doesn't
bring That Guy back, and Dad's going to
give me a cardboard sign to wear and see
what happens. So, like, tell anyone if I die
O.K. 'cause I'm not really sure what I'm
doing, but I totally see this guy in my
dreams every night and so like, you want
my Physics books? I don't think I need
them anymore.

The Rapture.

The Apocalypse.

The Final Reckoning…

The Resurrection and The Light…

That's what we're here for?

Joy to the World.

I had a cross made of glow tape on my winter jacket when I was a kid. Other kids threw snow balls at me and made fun of the cross. I felt like a persecuted Christian from the days of old. I also felt like an idiot.

The Lord Has Come.

Now?

The Big Bang.

Are you Done Yet?

Are we There Yet?

Are you Finished?

Can we Go Now?

Can I quit my Job yet?

Have I been Terminated?

I have to pee, but I don't want to miss anything.

Call them first and ask if can leave scripts.

Borrowed time.

Silent contempt for maps.

Cut the word "peace" from any front page headline.

When a reporter asked, a Witness confesses thereby
There are Things to do before I die
And
if I die before I wake,
I pray the Lord my soul to take.

When she was ten years old she wrote:

"I have excepted Jesus with the help of my best friend. And my mother got fired (details later)."

The dishwasher meant freedom.

Who's going to help with the housework after the Second Coming?

Who's going to clean up The Unholy Mess?

Who's going to like my work?

No one seems to have thought this through.

Revise script.

We sat in his apartment.
He was dying.
He had said
"I don't want to leave you."
He was asleep.

I was looking out his 14th floor window
at a bright crisp October sky—
wind whipping through the trees.
The life of the Village noisily, relentlessly
moving forward on the street.
In that moment, I knew—
all that is important is that we are Here
Now.
Alive.

Venice is drowning in water—
the buildings seem like stone boats.
But Venice doesn't drown.
Instead,
it floats.

A woman with a tiara stands amidst rubble. She poses for a camera.

A Hindu god dances encased in a bronze circle.

On a postcard, John Lennon still stares out from behind his sunglasses in Central Park.

We're still here, motherfuckers.

We're still here.

Now,

What are we gonna do about it?

(BLACKOUT.)

REFERENCES/INSPIRATIONS/DEEP BACKGROUND

Laurie Anderson, Loni Anderson, Michael Bakunin, James Baldwin, Jean Baudrillard, Pina Bausch, Miss Besieged Sarajevo 1993 (Inela Nogic), David Bowie, Lee Breuer, William Burroughs/Brion Gysin, Joseph Chaikin, Coalition for the Homeless, John Coltrane, Crosby, Stills, Nash & Young, Miles Davis, Willem de Kooning, Gilles Deleuze & Felix Guattari, Bob Dylan, Archivio Filippi, Richard Foreman, fortune cookies, Fross Zelnick Lehrman & Zissu, P.C., Bill Gates, Girls Meeting God, Maxim Gorky, Matt Groening, Bob Gruen, *Harper's*, Eric Harris, Jimi Hendrix, Jenny Holtzer, C.J. Hopkins, *Inside of a Shapeless Angel*, Eugène Ionesco, Franz Kafka, Walter Kendrick, Jascha Kessler, Søren Kierkegaard, Kip Kinkle, Dylan Klebold, Jill Krementz, Stanley Kubrick, V.I. Lenin, John Lennon, Doris Lessing, Groucho Marx, Karl Marx, Phoebe Masterson-Eckart, Steve McQueen, Hans Namuth, *The New York Times*, *The New Yorker*, Michael Ovitz, Robert Rauschenberg, John Sayles, George Segal, Shiva, Peter Silverman, Patti Smith, Sophocles, Sowetan, Beth Tapper, Quentin Tarentino, Jean Veber, Peter Weiss, E.B. White, William B. Yeats; countless television & print advertisements; countless hours of television news; dreams, reveries, and the daily horrorshow/carnival/happy meal (and, finally, a crystal clear memory of the 1970s).

Cuban Operator Please...

Adrian Rodriguez

ADRIAN RODRIGUEZ was born in Weehawken, New Jersey, in 1972. He attended the University of Pennsylvania where he earned degrees in international relations and Latin American studies. He then won a Minority Academic Career Fellowship for graduate work in political science at Rutgers University. Rodriguez is one of the founders and current president of the Havana on the Hudson Project, a nonprofit organization that seeks to promote art and scholarship that explore the role of the Cuban diaspora in Cuba's past, present, and future. He has written numerous short stories and is currently working on a screenplay entitled *Teaching Sisyphus* and a new play called *Between the Devil and the Deep Blue Sea*. He works as a history teacher in the New Jersey public education system. *Cuban Operator Please...* is his first play.

Cuban Operator Please... was first produced by the Hudson Exploited Theater Company (Arian Blanco, Founding Member) on August 16, 2000, as part of the 2000 New York International Fringe Festival (John Clancy, Artistic Director; Elena K. Holy, Producing Director), with the following cast and credits:

Abel .... Omar Hernandez
Father .... José Antonio
Mother .... Mercy Valladares

Directed by: Arian Blanco
Production Manager: John C. Cunningham
Stage Manager: Ryan Strohmeier
Production Assistants: Gabriel Garcia and Harold Medford
Publicity: Mary Loredo

The author gratefully acknowledges the contribution and support of Scott Almond, Michael J. Beaver, Ramon Blanco, Tusnelda Blanco, Joe DiSanzo, David I. Maldonado, Eduardo Pena, Angel Rio, Jim Thalman, and Clint White.

Special thanks to my wife, Itandehui, and my brother, Andres.

This play is dedicated to my father.

A NOTE FROM THE PLAYWRIGHT

Cuban Operator Please... is my first play. It is very personal. The souls of loved ones float across the stage and speak their minds. What you see is what *I* see, what *I* know. The characters speak the only way I can imagine them speaking, the only way I could ever have them speak. As such, the play is unapologetically bilingual. However, it is not just a bilingual play for a bilingual audience. The spatial distance that separates Cuban families and that is the condition of exile similarly reflects the emotional distance that separates many sons from their fathers. If you listen closely even foreign tongues may become intelligible. Indeed, sharing a language makes communication easier but even that is often not enough.

Escribí esta obra en nombre de todos los que hemos nacido en el exilio para que nuestros padres y abuelos sepan que *sí* escuchamos y *sí* entendimos. Pero tambien la escribí para que nuestros padres y abuelos sepan que el amor que sentimos por nuestra familia lucha diariamente con el dolor del exilio, con la distancia que nos separa de una tierra que nos llama. Algunos ya son americanos y otros seguimos siendo cubanos pero todos somos incompletos. En fin, aparte de ser un regalo de una generacion a otra, esta obra es un intento a sentirme mas completo.

SCENE 1

Union City, New Jersey, 2000. A small, modest apartment. Dark. Upstage right is a small dining room table with four chairs. An old rotary telephone is mounted on the wall. Downstage center is an old sofa and a rocking chair. In front of the sofa is a coffee table covered with books and newspapers. In fact, there are books in piles all around the room. An end table which doesn't match is found to the right of the sofa. On it are a gaudy glass ashtray, a cheap modern telephone, and an answering machine. Upstage center is an old television set with a rug lying in front. The front door of the apartment is stage left. Next to the entrance is a coat rack.

Action begins with the sound of keys jiggling. Lights on stage go from dark to dim. A young man, ABEL, enters stage left. He is approximately thirty years of age and is wearing a wool overcoat that is clearly too big for him, a scarf, a pair of gloves, and boots. He is unshaven, and a bright orange sticker on his coat reads "VISITOR."

He is obviously coming in from the cold. He stomps his feet as if to remove snow, nonchalantly drops the keys on the floor, takes off his gloves and also drops them on the floor, walks to the sofa, and lays down without undressing. After a few seconds, ABEL sits up and takes out a pack of cigarettes from his coat pocket. He takes out a cigarette but his hand trembles too much to light it. He tosses the pack on the coffee table, takes a deep breath, and puts his head in his hands. Pause.

ABEL: I can't do this. I can't do this. Ten years being the strong one. Ten years ignoring the fact that he was getting older. Ten years making jokes and philosophizing about death. "The only democratic thing in the world is death." Ha, ha. (*Long pause.*) I'm really not afraid of death… at least not my own. Others? I'm not so sure. It seems to me that other people's deaths are far more problematic than one's own, especially when mourning is required. I never met my grandfathers because they both died in Cuba before I was born. I've seen pictures, I've heard stories, but I've never been able to get emotional about them. I've conjured up images of what they must have looked like laughing, eating, talking, but nothing. No smiles come to me. No tears. Nothing. Sometimes I think that I'd like to see pictures of the corpses. Not toe-tag, autopsy corpses like on television—those look anonymous— but in a coffin serene-looking corpses. Perhaps this would help me deal adequately with never having known them or what seems even worse—not being able to mourn them.

(*Telephone rings. ABEL looks over at the telephone, tries to light cigarette again while waiting for the answering machine to answer.*)

ANSWERING MACHINE: (*ABEL's nonchalant voice.*) Leave a message. Thanks.

BROTHER: (*Voice heard through answering machine.*) Abel pick up. Pick up the phone. Why did you leave? (*Pause.*) You *always* leave… Well, anyway, Dad's not doing good. It could be soon. Do you hear me? I know you hear me. It's going to be soon. (*Long pause.*) God, I hate it when you don't answer the fucking phone.

(*Phone is slammed.*)

ABEL: (*Under his breath.*) Fuck you too.

(*Pause. Pointing at answering machine.*) My brother, he cries. People die, he gets sad, he cries. (*Disgusted.*) He must be well adjusted. It's surprising considering how much I tortured him when we were children. If you're a boy and you cry, well, you're a pussy. However, when you're a man and you cry then… then you're sensitive… you're in touch with your inner child… shit like that. I… I never cry. A person needs to feel a certain "nearness" to the events around them in order to respond with tears. I feel only distance. My whole family has died far away. Far away in time and space. Every death I've had to deal with has always been at a distance.

(*ABEL walks over to the coat rack and removes his scarf and his coat and places them on the coat rack. While he is doing this, from stage right, FATHER enters wearing dark pants and a white dress shirt. Completely unacknowledged, he sits on the rocking chair next to the sofa. ABEL sits down again and unties his boots.*)

ABEL: I never chose to be distant. I inherited distance. I was born into distance. My father left behind his entire family in 1968. First wife. Three children. Mother. Father. Brothers. Sisters. All of them. He boarded a plane in Havana and arrived in Miami forty-five minutes later. His wife and children didn't want to leave. He *had* to. Cuba was… *is* hell. He was leaving hell behind. Romantic leftists would like to think otherwise, but they're wrong. There was nowhere to hide. At work, in the bus, in the street where you lived, in the bathroom, in your soup. Nowhere to hide. So he left. He applied for a visa to leave the country and after suffering physical intimidation, public humiliation, and forced labor in the sugar fields, he was permitted to leave the country. So he hopped on a plane in Havana, scared out of his fucking mind, not letting go of the armrests or opening his eyes until he was in Miami. He got off the plane and retrieved his bag. He was then given a winter coat at least four sizes too large by Goodwill, got on a bus and headed north putting even more time and space between Cuba and himself. He didn't sleep for the twenty-hour ride and finally got off the bus in Union City, New Jersey, wearing his enormous winter coat, stepping into a humid ninety-eight degree July morning. *(ABEL tries to sleep.)*

FATHER: Abél siempre lo veía todo, analizaba todo. Siempre supo que yo era medio cobardón. Desde chiquito lo sabía. Sus ojitos me reclamaban, me retaban. Yo trataba de nunca verle los ojos. Al final no se a que le tenía miedo si yo me quería ir. Mejor dicho, me tenía que ir. *(Stands up and walks right down to edge of stage.)* Pero lo que nunca entendió Abél es que en Cuba si no tenías miedo estabas jodido. Eso es lo que quería el gobierno, que todos vivieran asustados. Por el miedo fué que pude dejarlos a todos. El miedo fue el que me llevó a pedir la salida. El miedo me subió al avión. *(Pause.)* Gracias a esa cobardía que siempre me sacó a cara Abél, pude llegar a los Estados Unidos. Abél veía muchas cosas pero no entendía todo. Aún no lo entiende. El miedo me permitió sobrevivir. Esa emoción bochornosa, regalo de un gobierno asesino, me salvó, aunque fuera aquí, a tres mil millas de todo lo que era mío.

(FATHER walks back and sits in the chair once again. After unsuccessfully trying to get to sleep, ABEL grabs his pack of cigarettes off of the coffee table and successfully lights one. He takes three strong drags of the cigarette and then places it in the ashtray. He gazes up at the ceiling and takes a deep breath. ABEL then walks over to several piles of books upstage right. He searches through several stacks and finally pulls out a photo album. He sits on the floor, places the album in front of him and opens it.)

ABEL: We always laughed when my father told us this story. He told us that all he could think about was how enormous the American who donated the coat must have been. "Ese abrigo tiene que haber sido del americano mas grande del mundo." He wasn't funny very often so I could never forget his face when he told this story. Most of the time he was serious. Not sad or even angry, just serious. Even in pictures. My mother told me that it was the winter that made him so serious. He really hated the cold. I can remember him leaving at five o'clock in the morning, while it was still dark out. He would wear long underwear under his slacks. He would put on a raggedy thermal sweatshirt with a zipper in front because he hated having to put a shirt on over his head arguing that it was oppressive. Then, finally, his enormous coat and a pair of snow gloves. He would grab a bag that looked like a doctor's bag, put on his hat tight over his head and go out into the cold. He never talked in the mornings. The wind and snow outside were a brutal reminder of how much distance he had put between his past and his present. Many people have told me that my father was a different man in Cuba. He drank beer and ate out. He'd hit on women and laugh often. But the snow... the snow erased those feelings in my father. *(Pause.)* It really used to snow back then. From October to March, there was snow all the time. This must have been particularly offensive to a Cuban. In Cuba the weather was great all the time. Here it snowed all the time. It killed him slowly.

(*Pause.*) I loved it. The snow made everything clean and white. It made the streets look quiet. It made me feel at home. I couldn't understand how far away home really was. Every adult I knew would constantly remind me that we were all exiles. Exiled in a cold, foreign place. Far away from Cuba, from palm trees, from the sun, from the beaches, from our families. *I* thought my whole family was here. (*Pause.*) I'd watch the snow fall at the window, watch it turn dark outside, and wait for my father to come trudging home through the snow after work. I wanted to see him laugh and smile as he approached the house, make a snowball and throw it at the window where I was waiting so we could laugh together. But that never happened. He walked slowly with his head down, protecting it from the wind. The door would open, he'd put his bag down, take off his hat, sit down, I'd sit on his lap, and we'd be quiet. He never talked in the evenings either. It was dark and cold and distant. We were in exile.

(*ABEL sits and looks through photo album slowly. FATHER stands up and walks behind ABEL, looking over his shoulder at the photo album.*)

FATHER: Todos los días que salía a trabajar en esa oscuridad y en ese frío lo que quería era pegarme un tiro. No hay nada mas triste, mas duro, que dejar la seguridad y el calor de tu casa para pasar frío y trabajo. En Cuba uno trabajaba tranquilamente. Uno saludaba a todo el mundo en el camino. ¿Cómo estás fulano? ¿Cómo estás fulana? Tomaba café seis ó siete veces antes de llegar al trabajo. Pero aquí no. Aquí uno tranca la puerta cuando se va, baja la cabeza y no piensa en nada hasta que llegara a la casa otra vez. Eso si, nunca me quejé. Uno nunca puede quejarse del trabajo porque el trabajo es lo que deja uno comer. Pero ese frío coño, ese frío no me dejaba vivír. Las nevadas tapaban todo, hacían desaparecer todo. Luego se ensuciaba y era como si un volcán se hubiera cagado sobre el pueblo. La nieve solo es bonita en fotografías porque a las fotos no les importan las consecuencias... el peso de esa nieve en mis hombros. ¡Que va! Pero para Abél todo era fotografías. Un mundo de fotografías que el inventaba, dibujaba en su mente. Y cuando uno no se comportaba como los personajes que el había imaginado en su fotografía nos juzgaba con esos ojos y después se iba lejos de aquí en sus pensamientos. Se sentaba en mis piernas pero yo se que el no estaba cerca.

(*FATHER returns to the rocking chair. ABEL stands and walks downstage.*)

ABEL: (*Frustrated.*) I only wanted him to tell me that it was cold, that he hated it. That he wanted to see, to feel, the sun near him again. That he missed his family. That we were all an accident. That this wasn't how it was supposed to be. That he had another life, a better life. (*Pause.*) But he never talked. (*Slowly.*) He never fucking complained. I *know* he hated it all, but he'd never say it. He was too far away from it all.

(*ABEL looks down and flips through the pages of the photo album. Lights fade to black.*)

SCENE 2

Union City, New Jersey, 1977. Same set. MOTHER is in the kitchen sitting at the table speaking on the telephone to FATHER. ABEL is sitting in front of the television wearing a red baseball cap. He is transformed into a six-year-old child.

MOTHER: (*Speaking into the telephone,*

distressed.) Te digo que no se. Déjame preguntarle otra vez. (*To ABEL, loudly.*) ¡Abél! Dime otra vez lo que te dijeron.

ABEL: (*Bored, without looking away from TV.*) Collect call from Cuba.

MOTHER: (*Increasingly annoyed.*) ¿Y qué mas?

ABEL: Nada mas.

MÓTHER: ¡Abél que esto es importante! (*Pause.*) ¿Qué mas te dijo la operadora?

ABEL: Que era René. Creo que era tío René.

MOTHER: (*Angrily.*) ¿Y porqué no dijiste que si ?

ABEL: (*Defiantly.*) Because you weren't here.

MOTHER: (*To telephone.*) Dice que era René. ¿Que habrá pasado? (*Pause.*) Cálmate Ramón. Voy a tratar de comunicarme. (*Pause.*) Yo te llamo. (*Hangs up telephone. To ABEL, loudly.*) ¡Tu papá te va a matár!

ABEL: ¡No! Déjame hablar con papi.

MOTHER: Ya colgó.

ABEL: Llámalo otra vez.

MOTHER: Déjalo que el está trabajando.

ABEL: Yo siempre hablo con el a la hora del lunch. Llámalo.

MOTHER: Que no te dije.

ABEL: El quiere hablar conmigo.

MOTHER: Habla con el cuando llegue del trabajo.

ABEL: Va estar cansado. El habla conmigo por teléfono todos los días. El me deja oír las máquinas. El me va a llevar a trabajar con el un día para que yo pueda ver las máquinas.

MOTHER: ¿Y para qué tu quieres ver las máquinas? ¿Ya quieres ir a trabajar? ¿Te quieres poner viejo como tu papá?

ABEL: Llámalo.

MOTHER: Lo llamamos cuando hable con tu tío en Cuba.

ABEL: Pero...

MOTHER: ¡Ya! Ni una palabra mas que voy a llamar a Cuba.

(*Lights fade on kitchen. ABEL stands up, removes his cap and walks downstage.*)

ABEL: Placing a call to Cuba was a major event, a monumental undertaking. My father never called himself so my mother had to muster up all of her strength and all of her English words and call. The problem was that there were very few telephone lines open to Cuba and the ones that were available were so poor that you could hardly understand a word that was being said on the other line. So when your call finally went through a shouting match began where few words were intelligible and one hung up never really knowing whether or not the other side heard a thing you said. Cold war politics and third world infrastructure conspired to keep families distant.

(*Lights fade on ABEL and focus on MOTHER in the kitchen speaking into the telephone.*)

MOTHER: (*With heavy Spanish accent.*) Cuban operator please. (*Pause.*) Ocupado. Que novedad. (*Dials again. With heavy Spanish accent.*) Cuban operator please. (*Pause.*) Ocupado. (*Dials again. With heavy Spanish accent, increasingly agitated.*) Cuban operator please. (*Pause.*) Coño. Voy a pasarme toda la tarde en esto. (*Dials again.*

With heavy Spanish accent, increasingly agitated.) Cuban operator please. (*Pause.*) Ocupado. (*Dials again. With heavy Spanish accent, increasingly agitated.*) Cuban operator please. (*Pause.*) Dios por favor... Por favor. (*Dials again. With heavy Spanish accent, increasingly agitated.*) Cuban operator please.

(*Pause. Lights fade to black.*)

SCENE 3

ABEL is asleep on the sofa. His hand is outstretched holding the photo album that is resting on the coffee table.

ABEL: (*Awakens suddenly from a nightmare.*) No! (*Sits up confused.*) Nightmares. Fucking hell. How unbelievably predictable. I haven't had a nightmare since I was eight years old. Dad's in the hospital and I have a nightmare. Perhaps I should call Juan's therapist. (*Pause.*) Right. (*Sarcastically.*) If I start being afraid of the dark again I'll think about it.

(*ABEL opens the photo album again and begins flipping through the pages as if looking for a specific picture. After a few seconds he closes it. He lights another cigarette and begins smoking it. He walks to several piles of books looking for another photo album. He moves to another stack of books and finds the photo album he is looking for. He picks up the photo album and begins flipping through the pages.*)

ABEL: (*Slowly.*) So much snow. Snow in all of the pictures. (*Pause.*) He hated the winter because it wouldn't let him forget the man he was and it reminded him of how far away that man was from him. The snow that piled up in great heaps outside our door, which fascinated me to no end, made us both feel the distance of exile. It separated him from everything that had

made him happy in the past and it separated me from him.

(*FATHER, now wearing a black tie, enters from stage right and sits in rocking chair unacknowledged. ABEL continues.*)

ABEL: Two days after arriving on that bus he was working at a purse factory in West New York. It was on the corner of 59th and Jackson and just about every Cuban who arrived in the late sixties, at one time or another, worked at this factory. So many Cubans worked there that in Cuban circles it became popularly known as "La Escuelita," the little school. What did it teach? It taught you to work hard and shut up. My godfather had a purse handle stapled to his hand by a malfunctioning machine. He said nothing fearing that he might be fired, finished his shift, three more hours, and then wore the handle to the emergency room. He almost lost two fingers on his left hand and snuck out of the hospital at five thirty in the morning so as not to be late for work. My father only worked there for a few weeks. He soon began working for an embroidery factory. Embroideries were the biggest industry in the area. It was established in Hudson County in the 1940s by German Jews. By the 1960s Hudson County was the embroidery capital of the world. Jewish owners, American capital, Italian union men, Cuban workers. My father worked at the Schiffli Brothers Art Embroidery factory on 54th and Adams making patches for Warner Brothers, the military, and the counterculture. He *hated* patches. They reminded him of Castro's soldiers. They reminded him of those commie homosexual drug-abusing hippies he saw on the streets on the way to work. But what really pissed him off, what really drove him out of his mind was the Road

Runner. Do you know how many colors go into a tiny Road Runner patch? Twenty-seven. A nightmare for embroidery workers who would be forced to spend days on end respooling thirty-foot embroidery machines every four minutes. Beep-beep.

(ABEL sits back in sofa and looks through the photo album. FATHER begins to speak from rocking chair.)

FATHER: Yo llamaba a Abél todos los días a las doce en punto. Contestaba su madre e imediatamente Abél empezaba a gritar para que le pasaran el teléfono. Le encantaba oír las máquinas de la fábrica. Me preguntaba que que hacía, que si ya venía para la casa, que si le traía algo, que cuando lo iba a llevar a trabajar. En fin era la misma conversación todos los días. Pero nunca le fallé. Lo llamaba todos los días. A veces hasta le traía regalitos del trabajo. Hilos colorados y amarillos que sobraban. Boberías. Pero el los guardaba como tesoros. Si le regalábamos juguetes no les hacía caso. Uno nunca sabía lo que le iba a gustar a Abél. Me parece que lo único que le interesaba era coleccionar atenciones pequeñas. Cosas cotidianas sin valor. Un día le llevé una cajita verde y blanca adonde venían las agujas de las máquinas y estuvo horas mirándola, abriéndola y cerrándola. Despues de tres ó cuatro horas me dijo que se podían oír las máquinas de la fábrica cuando abría la caja. Abél durmió años con esa cajita.

(The telephone rings. FATHER looks at ABEL waiting for him to answer the phone. ABEL waits for the answering machine to pick up. The ringing becomes more and more difficult for him to ignore.)

ANSWERING MACHINE: *(ABEL's nonchalant voice.)* Leave a message. Thanks.

BROTHER: Pick up the phone. *(Angry.)* Pick up the phone. Godammit pick up the fucking phone. *(Pause.)* I just talked to the doctor. He told me to call you. It's now or never asshole. He could die any minute now. Do you think hiding in the apartment is going to make things easier? Sometimes I think you don't give a shit. You're a fucking alien. It's now or never. Do you understand?

(ABEL stares at the answering machine for some time.)

ABEL: I'm a fucking alien. I'm an alien because I can't perform on cue. I know what I'm supposed to do. I even know what I'm supposed to feel. There are images in my head of me throwing on my coat and rushing to the hospital to embrace my father one last time and tell him that I had wronged him and that I loved him... but... I... won't. I can't. Should I do it so Juan doesn't think I'm a fucking alien? So my mother will be proud? So they can for one moment feel that everything was and is okay? So they can feel like a loving little family? The fact of the matter is that *they* are... a loving little family. Holidays. Barbecues. Children. It bothers them that I'm not happy... like them. *They* think I'm sad. But they don't get it. I'm not *sad*. I'm not depressed. I'm not anything. I'm just like my father. *(Continues to look through the photo album in a more determined fashion.)* What did he love? What did my father love? I'm not saying he was a bad father who never cared for us. On the contrary, on certain occasions he was that great father we all fantasize about. Through enormous sacrifice Christmas morning was always filled with gifts that I know he really couldn't afford. When I was ill he rushed home from work and held me for as long as I needed. At those precise moments when I needed him the most he was there. But he was always *just* there. He never behaved tenderly or even got excited about anything. He worked at the embroidery factory for twenty-seven years doing the *same exact* job. He was a shuttler. That's all. He never demanded a raise or a promotion. He never looked for another job. Nothing. He was just there.

(*FATHER speaks abruptly. ABEL ignores him and returns to the sofa to look through the photo album.*)

FATHER: (*Enraged.*) ¡Que carajo querías?!? Sin inglés, sin conocidos que te ayuden. ¿Tu crees que me gustaba ese trabajo? Ese *chan chan chan* de las máquinas doce horas diarias. *Chan chan chan.* ¿Querías que llegara a la casa feliz, sonriente? Pues no. No lo podía hacer. Ese trabajo, ese frío… era una… era una… una anestesia. El trabajo nos dió seguro. Nos dió comida. Pero a mi… para mi… era una sentencia de muerte. Asi que si no lo entiendes el problema es tuyo. Yo me sacrifiqué para todos. Para que Juan tuviera postalitas. Para que tu tuvienes ras libros. *Yo* me sacrifiqué. ¿Y para que? ¿Para que?

(*Long pause. ABEL finds a picture of his father in a baseball uniform and takes it out of the book. He throws the photo album on the floor.*)

ABEL: (*Very peacefully.*) This is my favorite picture of my father. It's a picture of him in a baseball uniform with some of his teammates. Only one thing made him look like the man that was so far away. Baseball. (*Pause.*) He loved baseball.

(*FATHER walks over to sofa and looks at picture held by ABEL and smiles. He continues looking at the picture for a few seconds while ABEL speaks and then he returns to his rocking chair.*)

ABEL: The man in the picture, the man my father used to be before having to abandon everything, was known as "El Americano," the American. He must be sixteen years old in this picture. Starting pitcher of the Estrellas de Collante, a semi-professional team financed by the private hospital at Collante. The man is this picture was a semi-professional baseball player. He looks proud, smug, cocky, confident. He once told me that his team had traveled to a local town named Fomento for a game. He was going to pitch since it was an important game and he was the best pitcher on the squad. Before the game they were invited to have breakfast at a local restaurant and as he was eating he noticed a group of young women asking one of his teammates who El Americano was. They wanted to see the famous pitcher who overpowed his opponents with speed. When he was pointed out one of the young women remarked surprised: ¿Aquél flaco es el Americano? That skinny guy over there is the "American"? Utter disbelief. That 105-pound sixteen-year-old boy with enormous ears was expected to go to the majors to play with the Americans? Yes he was, and he pitched a shut-out game that afternoon to prove it. He would soon be in Havana playing with the Americans. I could see it in his eyes.

(*ABEL goes for another cigarette, but there are none left. He places the pack of cigarettes back on the coffee table with a trembling hand. He composes himself and continues speaking.*)

ABEL: He tried to teach us to play baseball but Juan and I were just no good. He even bought us uniforms once. A red one for Juan and a blue one for me. He took us to the park in our uniforms to teach us how to play but Juan couldn't hit and I couldn't catch. My mother even brought a camera. It was embarrassing. I never really wanted to play baseball again but I did wear the uniform as often as I could. I'd sit on the floor next to my father and watch the games on TV but I'd be bored by the third inning. So bored. What I could listen to were the stories of baseball in Cuba... the epics I'd call them. They *were* epics you know. Cuban baseball players were heroes for me. And not just on the ballfield either. A guy named Sabourin not only started one of the earliest teams but also fought in the War of Independence. Battlefield exploits aside, it was the *ballfield* legends that were the best. "El Diamante Negro," the Black Diamond, Mendez was a pitcher in the tens and twenties in Cuba who consistently beat Major League teams who came to play winter baseball in Cuba. Cristobal Torriente was another player who gained hero status in Cuba by hitting three home runs against a team that included the legendary Babe Ruth, who didn't even make it to first base during the game. Let's see... There were four teams in the national professional league when my father was growing up. The Lions of Habana, the Scorpions of Almendares, the Tigers of Marianao, and the Elephants of Cienfuegos. Although all of the teams were extremely competitive, it was the Habana-Almendares rivalry that captured most of the attention. In the championship series of 1947, Habana played against Almendares. Each team was managed by a legend. Both had been stars not only in Cuba but also in the Major Leagues. Alfonso Luque, an extremely ill-tempered man who everyone suspected of playing with a gun in his jersey, managed Almendares while Miguel Angel Gonzalez managed Habana. The season was decided in the last three games of the series with Almendares winning the championship after Max Lanier pitched two winning games in seventy-two hours. An astonishing feat. (*Pause.*) Baseball was heroic in Cuba and my father was going to be one of those heroes. Owners of sugar mill teams, club teams, even the military wanted my father to play for them. (*Pause.*) But my father never got the chance to complete astonishing feats. His mother, my grandmother, thought it would be dangerous for him to leave Trinidad... It was too dangerous to travel to Havana. Too dangerous to play far away from home.

(*ABEL lays down on the sofa and places the picture over his eyes and forehead. FATHER stands up.*)

FATHER: Martín "El Maestro" Dihigo, Pedro "Perico" Formental, Manuel "Cocaína" García, Lázaro "El Príncipe de Belén" Salazar, Santos "El Canguro" Amaro, Roberto "El Gigante del Central Senado" Ortiz, John "Bemba de Cuchara" Lloyd, Conrado "El Guajiro de Laberinto" Marrero, Roberto "El Tarzán" Estalella, Lorenzo "Chiquitín" Cabrera, Agapito "El Triple Feo" Mayor, Eustaquio "Bombín" Pedroso, Alejandro "El Caballero" Oms (*Long pause. Sadly.*) Ramón "El Americano" Fernandez. (*Pause.*) Coño, como quería jugar pelota.

(*ABEL removes picture from face.*)

ABEL: After retiring from thirty grueling years in an embroidery factory my father watched four baseball games every day. Professional, minor league, college, Mexican, Japanese, baseball all day. My parents have no money and since my father's retirement they've lived on my mother's $15,000 a year salary. Nonetheless, seventy-five dollars a month went for cable television so dad could watch his baseball games. My dad wasn't selfish and my mother was anything but irresponsible with money. We hoped that watching those games on television would keep him alive.

(Lights fade to black.)

SCENE 4

MOTHER sits at kitchen table sewing. MOTHER holds the telephone between her ear and her shoulder.

MOTHER: ¿Nada de noticias? *(Pause.)* Yo tampoco. He estado tratando de pegarme pero todas las lineas están ocupadas. Tu sabes como es esto. *(Pause.)* Ramón sospecha lo peór. *(Pause.)* Si sabes algo me llamas. *(Pause.)* Bye.

MOTHER hangs up telephone behind her. ABEL wearing his red cap walks to the kitchen and stands at the doorway.

ABEL: ¿Qué pasa mami?

MOTHER: Nada mi cielo.

ABEL: ¿Que dice papi?

MOTHER: Papi esta trabajando. *(Pause.)* Abél, mi hijo, vete para la sala que yo tengo que trabajar. *(Pause.)* No pasa nada.

(ABEL leaves kitchen. MOTHER picks up phone again but does not dial.)

MOTHER: Me preocupo mucho por Abél. Pasa todo el tiempo hablando solo. Conversando con si mismo. No inventa amiguitos, ni grita. Solo habla. Habla con nosotros también. Mucho. No es antisocial. Tiene amigos. Juega todos los deportes. Pero me parece que prefiere estár solo todo el tiempo. *(Ironically.)* Es igualito a su padre. *(Dials operator. With heavy Spanish accent.)* Cuban operator please. *(Pause.)* Sigue ocupado. *(Hangs up tele-*

phone and begins to dial again but stops.) Cada vez que llaman de Cuba me pongo nerviosa. Sí, porque el teléfono es para transmitir información importante... mas cuando las cosas son asi. A cada rato llaman para unos cumpleaños o el día de las madres pero hoy... hoy no cumple año nadie. Hoy es un día normal así que si suena el teléfono y es de Cuba es porque hay tragedia. Tragedia. Hasta el sonido del teléfono es diferente. Hasta ese mensajito que las lines están busy tiene voz trágica. Y yo la mensajera de las tragedias. Y Abél... Abél es el intérprete de las tragedias. Se las explica solito. Como fué la tragedia. Quien estaba presente. Todo. Sin lágrimas. Sin gritos. *(Continues dialing. With heavy Spanish accent.)* Cuban operator please. *(Pause.)* ¡Por Dios! Esto es una locura. *(Hangs up telephone and dials again. With heavy Spanish accent and increasingly agitated.)* Cuban operator please. *(Pause.)* ¡Qué tortura es esto virgencita! *(Hangs up telephone and dials again. With heavy Spanish accent and increasingly agitated.)* Cuban operator please. *(Long pause.)* ¿Que?! *(Pause.)* ¿El teléfono? Un minuto. *(Looks at a tattered phone book.)* Trinidad. Siete, Siete, Tres, Séis, Uno. *(Pause.)* *(Louder.)* Trinidad. Siete, Siete, Tres, Séis, Uno. *(Pause.)* *(Screaming, almost frantically.)* Trinidad. Siete, Siete, Tres, Séis, Uno! *(Long pause.)* *(Screaming.)* Es Rosa. Ramón está trabajando. ¿Que pasó? *(Pause.)* *(A bit impatiently.)* Los niños estan bien René. ¿Que pasó? *(Pause.)* Se murió la viejita? *(Pause.)* ¿Ayer por la mañana? *(Long pause.)* ¿Cuándo la entierran? *(Pause.)* *(Disbelief.)* ¿Ya la enterraron? *(Quietly to herself.)* Ramón se muere. *(Pause.)* Nada, nada. *(Crying, mutters.)* Adiós. *(Hangs up telephone but does not release receiver. Cries.)*

ABEL: Que pasa Mami?

MOTHER: Se murió tu abuelita.

ABEL: Cuál?

MOTHER: La mamá de tu papá.

ABEL: ¿La que no dejó que Papi jugara pelota?

MOTHER: (*With tears in her eyes and forced smile.*) Si papito. Esa misma. Papi esta al llegar. No le vayas a decir nada.

ABEL: ¿Porqué no?

MOTHER: Porque se va a poner muy triste tu papá.

ABEL: El nunca se pone triste.

MOTHER: No empiezes Abél. No le digas nada.

ABEL: ¿Tu crées que va a llorar? (*Pause.*) Si el llora yo creo que voy a llorar también.

MOTHER: (*Frustrated.*) Abél no vayas a decirle nada.

(*Lights fade to black.*)

SCENE 5

ABEL is laying on the sofa with the picture over his eyes and forehead. As he begins speaking, he sits up.

ABEL: Se murió tu mama. Just like that. The moment he walked through the door I told him. Your mother died. I waited for his reaction but there was none. I followed him as he took his hat and coat off, as he put his bag down, as he sat down. No reaction. I sat on his lap as if it were any other day. He didn't speak. I didn't speak. I felt ashamed...

(*ABEL stands up and begins to pace frantically. FATHER enters from stage right carrying a dark suit jacket and is startled by ABEL. He quickly realizes what ABEL is talking about.*)

ABEL: I felt ashamed for him. Didn't he love her? Wasn't this the worst possible news? He should have raced to the telephone. He should have broken down crying and screaming. He should have grabbed me by the hand, picked up his bag and hat and gotten on the same bus that brought him here... that brought *us* here. He should've taken us *home*. To Cuba. To where he was a man. To where we could smile and cry and scream. To where there was no snow or embroidery factories. To where it was never dark. To where people felt pain *and* happiness... He should have taken us home to meet our grandfathers and great grandfathers. To sit on their laps and to watch them die. (*Knocks everything off the coffee table. Proceeds to sit on top of it as if it were a raft.*) We could have taken a raft just like the millions who risk their lives to work and die in Miami. We would have floated back home to Cuba to die together. To die like we were supposed to. To mourn like we were supposed to.

(*ABEL lays back on the coffee table, head in hands. FATHER walks to the coffee table, kneels down next to it and reaches to touch ABEL but he stops. He stands up and looks sadly at ABEL.*)

FATHER: (*Quietly.*) O tal vez para vivír. Si Abél, para vivír. Trata de vivír, mi hijo.

(*After a brief pause the telephone rings. ABEL ignores it. While the phone rings FATHER puts on his suit jacket and places a white rose on the suit jacket's lapel.*)

ANSWERING MACHINE: (*ABEL's nonchalant voice.*) Leave a message. (*Pause.*) Thanks.

BROTHER: Abel. Answer the phone. Abel! (*A pause followed by a sob.*) Abel, he's dead. Papi se murió. (*Furiously.*) Why don't you pick up the fucking phone ?! He's dead!

(Sound of phone being slammed down is heard. FATHER walks over to coat rack and takes ABEL's coat. FATHER looks once again at ABEL and walks out stage left. ABEL sits up on the coffee table, faces the audience, and after a long pause talks directly to them.)

ABEL: In 1996 the Atlanta Braves played the New York Yankees in the World Series. Knowing that my father was a Red Sox fanatic and that as such he would have to root against the Yankees, I asked him who he wanted to win. He quickly responded: Atlanta, of course. But now I had him, for in Cuban exile conspiracy circles Ted Turner, the owner of the Braves, was a Communist. So I asked him how it was possible that he could root for the Atlanta Braves, an obviously Communist organization. And without hesitating for a second he responded: That's true, but the only thing I hate more than Communists, are Yankees. When I was a kid I hated baseball because I thought it was too Cuban. As an adult I hate baseball, because it's too American. Now I just miss my father and I wish I could cry about it.

APPENDIX
ENGLISH TRANSLATION

The following are direct translations of all of the Spanish portions of the play. All English lines are omitted. The translation should help non-Spanish speakers begin to understand the Father. However, the translation loses much of the rhythm and nuances of the original Spanish. As such, the play should always be performed in the bilingual format.

Scene 1

FATHER: Abel always saw everything, analyzed everything. He always knew that I was a bit of a coward. Ever since he was a little kid he knew it. His little eyes chided me, they challenged me. I tried to never look into his eyes. Ultimately, I don't know what I was afraid of, I wanted to leave. Better yet, I had to leave. *(Stands up and walks right down to edge of stage.)* What Abel failed to understand was that in Cuba if you weren't afraid you were screwed. That's what the government wanted, that everybody live in fear. It was fear that permitted me to leave them all. Fear moved me to request permission to leave. Fear carried me on to the airplane. *(Pause.)* Thanks to the fear that Abel always used to humiliate me, I was able to reach the United States. Abel saw many things but he didn't understand everything. He still doesn't understand. Fear allowed me to survive. That humiliating emotion, the gift of a murderous government... saved me. Even if it is here, three thousand miles away from everything that ever belonged to me.

FATHER: Every morning that I left for work in that darkness and in that cold, what I really wanted to do was put a bullet in my head. There is nothing sadder or harder than leaving the security and the heat of your home to suffer harsh cold and hard work. In Cuba one worked calmly. You greeted everybody on the way to work. You drank cafe six or seven times before ever even getting to work. But not here. Here, you lock the door, you lower your head, and you don't think about a single thing until you get home again. Nonetheless, I never complained. One should never complain about work because work is what allows us to eat. But that damned cold, that cold wouldn't let me live. The snow covered everything, made everything disappear. Then it would get dirty and it was as if a volcano had shit over the entire town. The snow is pretty only in pictures because pictures don't care about consequences, the weight of that snow on my shoulders. But for Abel, everything was pictures. A world of pictures that he invented, drew in his mind. And when one didn't behave like the characters he had imagined in his pictures, he would judge us with those eyes. And then he'd go far away from here in his thoughts. He would sit on my lap but I know he was nowhere near me.

Scene 2

MOTHER: *(Speaking into the telephone, distressed.)* I told you I don't know. Let me ask him again. *(To ABEL, loudly.)* Abel! Tell me again what they said!

MOTHER: *(Increasingly annoyed.)* What else?

MOTHER: Abel this is important! *(Pause.)* What else did the operator tell you?

ABEL: That it was René. I think it was Uncle René.

MOTHER: *(Angrily.)* Why didn't you accept the charges?

MOTHER: *(To telephone.)* He says it was Rene. What could have happened? *(Pause.)* I'll try calling him. *(Pause.)* I'll call you back. *(Hangs up telephone. To ABEL, loudly.)* Your father's going to kill you.

ABEL: No! Let me talk to Dad.

MOTHER: He hung up already.

ABEL: Call him again.

MOTHER: Leave him alone. He's working.

ABEL: I always talk to him at lunch. Call him.

MOTHER: I said no.

ABEL: He wants to talk to me.

MOTHER: Talk to him when he gets home from work.

ABEL: He's going to be tired. He talks to me on the phone everyday. He's going to take me to work with him one day so I can see the machines.

MOTHER: And why do you want to see the machines? Do you want to start working already? Do you want to get old like your father?

ABEL: Call him.

MOTHER: We'll call him after I talk to your uncle in Cuba.

ABEL: But. . .

MOTHER: Stop. Not another word. I have to call Cuba.

MOTHER: *(With heavy Spanish accent.)* Cuban operator, please. *(Pause.)* Busy. What a novelty. *(Dials again. With heavy Spanish accent.)* Cuban operator, please. *(Pause.)* Busy. *(Dials again. With heavy Spanish accent, increasingly agitated.)* Cuban operator, please. *(Pause.)* Damnit. I'm going to spend all afternoon on this. *(Dials again. With heavy Spanish accent, increasingly agitated.)* Cuban operator. please. *(Pause.)* Busy. *(Dials again. With heavy Spanish accent, increasingly agitated.)* Cuban operator, please. *(Pause.)* Please God, please. *(Dials again. With heavy Spanish accent, increasingly agitated.)* Cuban operator, please.

Scene 3

FATHER: I called Abel everyday at twelve on the dot. His mother would answer and Abel would immediately begin to scream demanding that she pass him the telephone. He loved to hear the machines at the factory. He would ask me what I was doing, if I was coming home yet, if I was going to bring him something, when I was going to bring him to work with me. In short, it was the same conversation every day. But I never failed him. I called him every day. Sometimes I would bring him gifts from work. Red and yellow yarn that was left over. Insignificant things. But he would guard them like treasure. If we gave him toys he ignored them. One never knew what Abel was going to like. It seems to me that the only thing that interested him was collecting tiny mementoes of af-. fection. Quotidian things with no real value. One day I brought him a little green and white box where the needles for the machines at work were stored, and he spent hours looking at it, opening it and closing it. After three or four hours he told me that he could hear the machines from the factory when he opened the box. Abel slept many years with that box.

FATHER: *(Enraged.)* What the hell did you want? No English. No friends or acquaintances to help. Do you think that I liked that job? The roar, roar, roar of the machines twelve hours a day? Roar, roar,

roar. Did you want me to get home happy, smiling? Well no. I couldn't do it. That job, the cold... it was... it was an anesthetic. The job gave us security. It gave us food. But for me... for me it was a death sentence. So if you can't understand that, then that's your problem. I sacrificed myself for all of you. So that Juan could have baseball cards. So that you could have books. I sacrificed myself and for what? For what?

FATHER: Martín "the Master" Dihigo, Pedro "the Parakeet" Formental, Manuel "Cocaine" García, Lázaro "the Prince of Belén" Salazar, Santos "the Kangaroo" Amaro, Roberto "the Giant of Central Senado" Ortiz, John "Spoon Lips" Lloyd, Conrado "the Hick of Laberinto" Marrero, Roberto "Tarzan" Estalella, Lorenzo "the Midget" Cabrera, Agapito "the Triple Ugly" Mayor, Eustaquio "the Bobbin" Pedroso, Alejandro "the Gentleman" Oms *(Long pause. Sadly.)* Ramon "the American" Fernandez. *(Pause.)* Damn, I really wanted to play baseball.

Scene 4

MOTHER: No news? *(Pause.)* Me neither. I've been trying to get a hold of him but all the lines to Cuba are busy. You know how this is. *(Pause.)* Ramon expects the worst. *(Pause.)* If you hear something call me. *(Pause.)* Bye.

ABEL: What's wrong mommy?

MOTHER: Nothing my angel.

ABEL: What did Dad say?

MOTHER: Your father is working. *(Pause.)* Abel, why don't you go to the living room so I can get some work done. *(Pause.)* Nothing's wrong.

MOTHER: I worry a lot about Abel. He spends all of his time talking to himself. He doesn't invent friends or scream. He just talks. He talks to us too. A lot. He's not antisocial. He has friends. He plays sports. But it seems to me that he prefers to be alone all of the time. *(Ironically.)* He's just like his father. *(Dials operator. With heavy Spanish accent.)* Cuban operator, please. *(Pause.)* Still busy. *(Hangs up telephone and begins to dial again but stops.)* Every time we get a call from Cuba I get nervous. Yes, because the telephone is used to transmit important information... and even more so when things are like this. Every once in a while they'll call for a birthday or Mother's Day but today... today is nobody's birthday. Today is a normal day so if the phone rings and it's from Cuba it's because a tragedy has occurred. Tragedy. Even the ring of the phone is different. Even that little message saying that all lines to Cuba are busy sounds tragic. And me, I'm the messenger of tragedies. And Abel, Abel is the interpreter of tragedies. He explains them all by himself. How it occurred, who was present, everything. Without tears. Without screams. *(Continues dialing. With heavy Spanish accent.)* Cuban operator please. *(Pause.)* This is crazy. *(Hangs up telephone and dials again. With heavy Spanish accent and increasingly agitated.)* Cuban operator please. *(Pause.)* Mother of God, this is torture. *(Hangs up telephone and dials again. With heavy Spanish accent and increasingly agitated.)* Cuban operator please. *(Long pause.)* What? *(Pause.)* The number? One minute. *(Looks at a tattered phone book.)* Trinidad. 7-7-3-6-1. *(Pause. Louder.)* Trinidad. 7-7-3-6-1. *(Pause. Screaming, almost frantically.)* Trinidad. 7-7-3-6-1. *(Long pause. Screaming.)* It's Rosa. *(Pause.)* Ramon is working. What happened? *(Pause. A bit impatiently.)* The kids are okay

Rene. What happened? *(Pause.)* She died? *(Pause.)* Yesterday morning? *(Long pause.)* When do they bury her? *(Pause. Disbelief.)* They've already buried her? *(Quietly to herself.)* Ramon will die. *(Pause.)* Nothing, nothing. *(Crying, mutters.)* Goodbye.

ABEL: What's wrong, mommy?

MOTHER: Your grandmother died.

ABEL: Which one?

MOTHER: Your father's mother.

ABEL: The one that wouldn't let dad play baseball?

MOTHER: Yes, honey. That's the one. Dad's about to arrive. Don't say anything to him.

ABEL: Why not?

MOTHER: Because your father's going to be very sad.

ABEL: He never gets sad.

MOTHER: Abel don't start. Don't say anything.

ABEL: Do you think he's going to cry? *(Pause.)* If he cries I think I'll cry too.

MOTHER: *(Frustrated.)* Abel don't say anything to your father.

Scene 5

FATHER: Or perhaps to live. Yes Abel, try to live. Try to live, my son.

The Elephant Man –
The Musical

Jeff Hylton and Tim Werenko

JEFF HYLTON (co-author, book and music, lyrics) and TIM WERENKO (co-author, book) both graduated from New York University. In addition to *The Elephant Man – The Musical*, which is now in its second year of performances in New York's West Village, they have collaborated on the upcoming film *My Favorite Things (aka The Boob Movie)*, the screenplays *Ackerman Hill* and *Memoirs of a Doorman*, the musical comedy *Joyce!!! (as in DeWitt!!!)*, and, with composer Georgia Stitt, on the new musical *Watertown*. Werenko is the author of the serious novel *Onkeeton Ghosts* and Hylton is the author of the silly novel *Hahrper & The Thing*. Hylton also wrote the children's musical *Galileo's Telescope* with Sean McCourt. Hylton lives in Brooklyn, New York, with his lovely wife Christa. Werenko lives in New Jersey with his beautiful wife Gwen, their son Alexander Boon, four cats, one large dog, and a parrot named C-Squared.

The Elephant Man – The Musical was first produced in its present form by Captain Rancid, LLP, on September 7, 1999, at Upstairs At Rose's Turn, New York City, with the following cast and credits:

John Merrick .... D.P. Duffy
Dr. Lipscomb .... Kenneth Dine
Jessica Curvey .... Jennifer Morris
Horace Augsquatch/Presby Raincoat .... Jeff Hylton

Designed and directed by: James Riggs
Costumes by: Shawneen Rowe
Musical direction by: Anne Holland
Musical arrangements by: Georgia Stitt and Sean McCourt
Technical director: Collette Black

A substantially different version of *The Elephant Man – The Musical* was produced at New York University in 1990, and at HERE, New York City in 1996.

The authors wish to acknowledge the contributions of the following persons to these developmental productions: D.P. Duffy, Kenneth Dine, Erick Pinnick, Scott Stanley, Christa Hylton, David Autry, Janet Dunn, Kelly Main, Toby S. Pruett, Karma Tiffany, Georgia Stitt, Mark Wade, Ted Koch, Sean McCourt, Jeff Zeidman, Shawneen Rowe, Tracy Metro (née Weitzman), Debbi Christie, Jason Sinopoli, Frank Coleman, Hope Leopold, Anne Holland, James Riggs, Jonathan Teel, Randi Behrenfeld, Jodi Bliss Harris, Rebecca Strom, Sarah Lassez, Marc Mahoney, David Josefsberg, Michael Warwick, Jennifer Roup, and Jennifer Goss.

Music for *The Elephant Man – The Musical* by Paul Jones and Jeff Hylton may be obtained by contacting Jeff Hylton, 485 Court St. #4R, Brooklyn, NY 11231; 718-694-9546 (voice); jeff@elephantmansings.com (e-mail).

The Elephant Man – The Musical is dedicated with tons of fleshy love to Neeney and Danny.

PRODUCTION NOTES

The Rose's Turn production was played by a cast of four on a tiny stage with nothing in the way of a set except an upstage curtain, behind which there was room to hide one actor. All props were large, colorful (almost cartoon-like) versions of the required objects. This bare-bones approach has proved to work very well. Of course, higher production values would work as well. (We'd do more if we could.) I would suggest that however the physical aspects of the production are approached, wit should be a key ingredient.

As printed here, the show runs somewhere around seventy minutes. A slightly expanded version exists, which features one additional song and a chorus of freaks among other embellishments that round the show up to a full-length evening.

ABOUT JOHN'S DEFORMITY

Under no circumstances should the actor playing John not wear deformed gear. Director/designer James Riggs built a perfectly appropriate headpiece for Merrick. He attached such disparate bric-a-brac as a small plunger, half a football, half a soccer ball, toy cars and helicopters, a Boba Fett action figure, a couple of troll dolls, and other stuff the rest of us have yet to identify to a large rugby helmet. He then painted the whole thing fleshy-pink—making the ordinary objects almost impossible to identify, yet still strangely familiar. The idea is that it is strangely funny, strangely confusing to the eye—and, most importantly, impossible to ignore or get used to.

CHARACTERS

JOHN MERRICK: The "Elephant Man"
DR. JAMES LIPSCOMB: A failing physician and romantic novelist
HORACE P. AUGSQUATCH: The cruel overseer of a freak show
JESSICA CURVEY: A young woman with a problem
PRESBY RAINCOAT: A kind, influential producer
GRACIELLE*: A director
SCOTT*: A producer
BOB*: An intense, incomprehensible choreographer

*These characters appear only in the film/video of John's audition. (Note: HORACE and PRESBY are played by the same actor.)

TIME

The present

LIST OF SCENES AND MUSICAL NUMBERS

SCENE 1. A freak show, London
    Opening ("The Elephant Man") .... COMPANY
    "My Dream" .... JOHN MERRICK

SCENE 2. Dr. Lipscomb's home, London
    "Moby" .... DR. LIPSCOMB
    "*Il Pepe Rivoltante* (The Penis Aria)" .... JESSICA
    "I Was That Man" .... DR. LIPSCOMB

SCENE 3. A freak show, London

SCENE 4. Dr. Lipscomb's home, London
    "Mother"* .... JOHN MERRICK

SCENE 5. A lecture hall, London
    "A Significant Lecture" ... DR. LIPSCOMB, JOHN MERRICK

SCENE 6. A theatre, then a street, London
    "Paleface Must Die" .... JOHN MERRICK
    "Animal"** .... JOHN MERRICK

SCENE 7. Dr. Lipscomb's home, London
    "I Was That Man" Reprise .... DR. LIPSCOMB
    "Ever'body Wants Their Life to Be a Musical" .... PRESBY

SCENE 8. Various locations, London, and New York
    "The Scene That's a Song" .... JOHN MERRICK,
                           DR. LIPSCOMB, JESSICA, PRESBY

SCENE 9. Dr. Lipscomb's home, London
    "Destiny" .... JESSICA
    "My Dream" Reprise .... JOHN MERRICK,
                           DR. LIPSCOMB, JESSICA

SCENE 10. A Broadway theatre, New York
    "A Tear 4 Corey Feldman" (incorporating
    "Ballad of Pakky Derm," "Cows," and "Pakky
    Derm, Superstar") .... COMPANY
    "Meaty!" .... JOHN MERRICK, JESSICA

SCENE 11. An awards ceremony, New York
    Closing ("The Elephant Man") .... COMPANY

*Music by Jason Sinopoli.
**Music by Rick Siegel.

SCENE 1

A freak show. There is a sign that reads "Horace P. Augsquatch's Cooperative Cornucopia of Incredible Genetic Aberrations. Home of the Terrible Elephant Man." A SLIGHTLY DISTORTED VOICE echoes hauntingly through the space.

SLIGHTLY DISTORTED VOICE: But sometimes I think my head is so big because it is so full of my dream!

(HORACE leads DR. LIPSCOMB and JESSICA through the audience starting at the entrance and working towards the stage. As HORACE leads the way through the space, he ad libs about the patrons in the audience as if they are the freaks the others have paid to see.)

HORACE: Ladies and gentlemen—Don't be shy. Keep movin'. Look at it. You know you know you wanna. Go on—look at 'em. They's terrible—They's disturbin'—And what about that one over there? Revolting—Shocking!!—And they're all appearing daily and nightly here at Horace P. Augsquatch's Cooperative Cornucopia of Incredible Genetic Aberrations, 69 Feces Street, DoubleSouth Ballsex. In no way affiliated I am legally required to add with Horace G. Augsquatch's haberdashery and sucky-sucky palace at 65 Feces Street.

DR. LIPSCOMB: Now see here, my good man. Haven't you got any more substantial genetic anomalies than these?

JESSICA: He's a doctor, you know. Something of a freak specialist.

HORACE: *(Points out one man in the audience.)* Look at that! That's not enough of a horrible aberration of nature for you?

DR LIPSCOMB: Quite frankly, that's just a show queen. Freakish, to be sure—but far too common in these parts to have any real scientific value. I am interested in specimens with… whose… wrong body-stuff—discombobulates… a really—lot…

JESSICA: He's also a writer.

DR. LIPSCOMB: Yes, well—romantic novels mostly. With a pathological bent. And lots of humping…

HORACE: Oh, you wait. I've got a freaky freak that'll shrivel your sac. *(To JESSICA.)* But are you sure you can take it, dumplin'?

(The actors step onto the stage, where there is a weathered curtain which is obviously hiding something.)

JESSICA: I'll have you know I have two doctorates of my own.

HORACE: I can see that. Ph-double D's. Eh, gov'nur. Right? Right—right? Right? Right? Her giddy flapjacks, right? Eh? Right?

(HORACE and DR. LIPSCOMB share a moment of enthusiastic appreciation of JESSICA's hooters. As the moment fades, HORACE remembers what he had been about to do.)

HORACE: Oh, yeah. The sac-shriveler. May I present to you—Doctors. The Terrible Elephant Man!!!

(He pulls the curtain aside, revealing JOHN MERRICK sitting in his filthy, small cage. JOHN looks at them and sweetly, casually, smiles at them.)

JOHN MERRICK: Hi. How's everybody doing today?

(DR. LIPSCOMB and JESSICA both turn away from him—JESSICA screams, DR. LIPSCOMB coughs into his handkerchief. HORACE chuckles at their reaction. The opening vamp sneaks in. Suddenly the three

of them break character and turn to the au-
dience—and sing with intense gravity.)

HORACE, DR. LIPSCOMB, JESSICA:
(Variously.)

He's not your average deformity.
He's like nothing you ever did see.
He is talented and he is good.
He knows what he wants but he's sad,
    trapped, and misunderstood.
John Merrick.
His name is John Merrick.
His head is too large, as you might have
    guessed.
His body is really quite far from the
    best.
But if you looked into his one good
    eye,
You'd realize that he's a special guy!
They call him
The Elephant Man.
The Elephant Man.
John Merrick.
His name is John Merrick.

DR. LIPSCOMB:

Could this be the man to re-ignite my
    career?

HORACE:

He can't ignite nothing but terror and
    fear.

COMPANY:

His depression increases with each
    frightened scream.
He would die in his cell, if it weren't
    for his dream.
The Elephant Man.
The Elephant Man.
John Merrick.
His name is John Merrick.

His anger is growing,
But change-winds are blowing.
Might fate be bestowing
The chance to get going?

One opportune showing
Could make things start flowing
And stop him from throwing
His whole life away.

JESSICA:

This man, he has a mission
To reach the position
Of total fruition.
He has the ambition,
Despite his condition,
To get what he's wishin',
To follow his dream.

COMPANY:

To follow his dream.
The Elephant Man.
The Elephant Man.
John Merrick.
Se llamo Juan Merrick.

MEN:

This story we tell of a soul in the dark.

WOMAN:

Attempting escape from a world cruel
    and stark.

ALL:

Must end with success,
Far away from the strife.
He must be afforded the chance to let
    him have a life.
Be not just
The Elephant Man.
The Elephant Man.
Be maybe
The Elephant King...
The Elephant God...
His name is
John Merrick. God.
John Merrick. God.

*(The three of them return to character, and
precisely at the moment just before the song.
JESSICA and LIPSCOMB pull themselves
together as HORACE looks on and chuckles.)*

HORACE: I warned you.

DR. LIPSCOMB: Dear GOD! I've never seen anything like it!

JESSICA: I wish I could say the same.

DR. LIPSCOMB: Tell me—does he understand his situation? Those words he spoke, was he communicating, or just mimicking sounds? Can he feel emotion? God, but he makes me wish I weren't already deeply entrenched in study of the tortoise with the pink fuzzy shell. Still, would you ever consider releasing him into medical custody?

HORACE: Are you rich?

DR. LIPSCOMB: Yes. I mean no.

HORACE: *(Leers at JESSICA.)* Huh? I might be willing to discuss an equitable trade: Flesh for flesh.

JESSICA: My IQ is 169.

HORACE: I bet it is. Eh? Right? Right? Right? I tell you what, let me give Doctor Perky-Boobies here my card. *(He digs deep down inside his pants and finally pulls forth his business card.)* That's my, uh—home number there. And you feel free to call me any time you want to discuss the Elephant Man. Or, you know—anything else. Like us having sex together. *(He closes in on JESSICA, going through a series of horrifically obscene gestures.)*

DR. LIPSCOMB: You're a little lanky for my tastes, but you do have rather an attractive musk about you.

JESSICA: Can we please leave now?

DR. LIPSCOMB: What? Oh, certainly, dear.

(They exit.)

DR. LIPSCOMB: *(As he exits, muttering.)* I tell you in all my days I have never seen anything like that poor disgusting creature...

HORACE: Remember... Call anytime*!* Oh, she wants me.

(JOHN peeks cautiously out from behind the curtain. HORACE sees him. Still pleased by his flirtation, he gives JOHN a half-hearted tongue-lashing.)

HORACE: What the bloody F. was that? "How's ev'rybody doin??!" You do three things: You cower in the corner. You whimper and drool. Cower, whimper, drool. Is that so hard? My bloody wife can do it, and she's only eleven years old. I wasn't jokin'—I will sell you to that loopy butcher... Cower, whimper, dr— *(Checks his watch.)* Blimey, it's time for "Blue's Clues."

(He skips offstage with incredible enthusiasm. The lights fade away, except for a light on JOHN's cage; he looks up from his cowering crouch.)

JOHN MERRICK:
Another day in the cage
Another sunrise in the past
My anger is hard to assuage.
How long is this hell going to last?
I did not ask to be this way.
I did not want to bear this face.
I hate him more than I can say—
This thing that was born in my place.
Oh, why?
Whatever did I do?
Oh, why
Am I constantly put through
This disgraceful, agonizing life?
When all I want is to...

(As JOHN sings the rest of the song, his cage rises and he is free for this moment—to sing and dance; to be himself.)

JOHN MERRICK:

Sing, and dance, and act my way
Into a real live Broadway show.
There's no question where I'll stray,
New York is where I've got to go.
I know that I've got what it takes
To take the Great White Way by storm.
No way that I could make mistakes
With all this poise and grace and form.

I've crouched in back and watched the
    cast.
I know what performers are.
I know fame is fleeting and fast.
Who says what makes a star?
But picture me all decked out and for-
    mal.
They'll laugh.
They'll smile.
And think me normal
In a Broadway dancin' show.
Like Momma taught me.
A real live Broadway show!
Yeah!

*(After the song, JOHN's cage descends upon
him once again. He looks around, remembering the truth of his situation. He cowers
in the corner.)*

SCENE 2

*Open on JESSICA and LIPSCOMB in
LIPSCOMB's rooms.*

DR. LIPSCOMB: Jessica, dear. After all
this time together, do you… do you—love
me, would you say?

JESSICA: Yes, of course, doctor. Like an
embarrassing uncle. You know that.

DR. LIPSCOMB: Now, do you love me
like a good, sweet embarrassing uncle; or
do you love me like my Uncle Beatrice
loved me? *(He suavely unzips his fly.)*

JESSICA: Doctor, what are you doing?

(He takes a step toward her, she counters.)

JESSICA: Doctor—you know very well
that this is… that I've never…

DR. LIPSCOMB: I understand, sweet
darling. You're afraid. But, trust me,—
there is absolutely nothing to be frightened of…

*(During the song, he strips to his boxer shorts
and becomes so enthusiastic that he is shaking his nasty business in the audience's faces.
JESSICA watches with a look of mild terror
on her face.)*

DR. LIPSCOMB:

Don't be scared of Moby.
Moby is your friend.
Don't be scared of Moby.
Can't you comprehend?

He is here to please you.
Make you grin.
Make you smile.
You know he wouldn't tease you.
Just tell him when.
He's got style.

Don't be scared of Moby.
Moby is your pal.
Don't be scared of Moby.
He knows you're my gal.

He can give you pleasure
You cannot conceive.
He's my greatest treasure.
He'll make you believe.

(He dramatically rips his t-shirt off of his body.)

You can't be complete without him.
It isn't just some nasty thrill.
God's grace meant this to be.
There's a space in you that he's meant
    to fill.

He is here to free you.
Make you his,
Make him yours.
Who on earth will see you?
As it is,
We're indoors.

Don't be scared of Moby.
Horses ran, doves flew.
Don't be scared of Moby.
He loves you.

(He walks toward JESSICA. Apparently, she meets Moby, for she is both horrified and furious. She stomps upstage and pulls out a large placard on which is written "DAYS SINCE THE DOCTOR HAS MADE A PASS AT ME" and under that "09." She rips off the "9," which leaves the board reading "00.")

JESSICA: Damn you, James. I've worked my whole life to make something out of myself—and not one of you filthy men has ever given a monkey's foreskin who I was inside this tight, hot body!! You had a journey—playwright wanna-be, doctor, manslaughter, shit-lucky acquittal, romantic novelist, laughingstock freak-hound. I've tried for a journey—but to filthy men like you I'm nothing but an object. For sex. A sex object, if you will. And, heaven knows, I've never ever been able to... I'm not happy. What about my needs, Jim?

DR. LIPSCOMB: Well, I think being ridden hard and put up wet would be an incredibly fulfilling place to start.

JESSICA: *(Takes a few steps toward him, stops.)* No. Dammit, no! *(Deliberately.)* I'm going to go find myself! *(Birds are heard chirping sweetly as she steps downstage to sing, in the style of an aria from a grand opera.)*

JESSICA:
I had always hoped my life
Would be a pure and beautiful thing.

I would grow to be a wife,
I'd be a pure and beautiful thing...
Then Sister Ruth detailed
The things which lovers do.
My train of hopes derailed.
God, it repulsed me through and
    through.

Yes, as I grew,
I learned the truth.
My childhood flew.
Goodbye to youth.
Hello, forsooth,
Per Ruth,
Pursuits uncouth.
I met the boys.
Felt butterflies.
I kept my poise,
I shut my eyes.
But twixt their thighs
There lies
That rank surprise...

Il pepe rivoltante.
I mean, come on, who would want a
Mouthful of... ick.
Il pepe disgustoso.
They're all awful and oh, so
Screamingly sick.
Viemo con la paiera del pepe.
I live in terrible fear of the prick.

(Lights out on her, up on the DOCTOR.)

DR. LIPSCOMB:
Once upon a time there was a scientist and a physician.
He occupied a quite respected medical position.
His clientele, oh, so impressive. He gave the Queen examinations.
He was a healer held most holy.
Then came those mixed-up vaccinations.
And in like twelve minutes time went from a hero to a lowly... Lowly...
What am I now?

(Spoken.) The tortoise with the pink fuzzy shell??

> I was that man.
> That man was me.
> But now I'm merely
> What you see.
> Down on my luck.
> Murdering words.
> And here I'm stuck
> My life sucks turds.

> Where are my friends?
> Where is my wife?
> What is this lonely
> Not quite a life?

> I once was great,
> As they think they are.
> But then, of course, fate
> Said "You've gone too far."

> All I've known since then is mass unfelt
>   humiliation.
> I sit and write my books and plan my
>   reconciliation.
> What I need to find is
> Something new,
> Unforeseen.
> What I have in mind is
> Some way to
> Vent my spleen.

> Oh, they laugh at the very notion of me.
> They'll never unbend, take me seriously.
> All those pious, conceited, heretical men.
> Oh, those "Try us accreted all-medi-
>   cal" men
> Who refuse to even condescend.
> To acknowledge my existence.

(Spoken.) What a bunch of pricks.

(An invisible chorus backs him up, repeat-ing the syllable "loo." He finds the card HORACE gave them—a lightbulb can al-most be seen going on above his head.)

> I've found a case
> Like they've never known.
> Something astounding.
> Dramatic in tone.
> I made my name.
> I beat the test.
> Put then to shame.
> But I'm still the best.
> Yes, I was that man.
> That man was me.
> I *am* that man!

(The lights fade as he revels in newfound determination.)

SCENE 3

The freak show. DR. LIPSCOMB is here; he looks about nervously. HORACE appears from the shadows behind him.

HORACE: Well, pluck my pubes. I knew you'd be back. So—have you come for the Elephant Man, or for the sex?

(DR. LIPSCOMB checks his watch, shrugs. He and HORACE retire to the shadows to-gether.)

SCENE 4

Back in DR. LIPSCOMB's flat. DR. LIPSCOMB enters, reeling with post-hump fluster.

DR. LIPSCOMB: *(To audience.)* Doctor's log: James no middle name Lipscomb. Ph.D. M.D. Doctor. Last ditch career sal-vage effort 4 Q B strike 78G. The El-ephant Man. First Entry. Bought from one Horace P. Augsquatch—standard lowlife DoubleSouth Ballsex freak show owner.

(JESSICA, wearing a priest's collar, escorts JOHN, with a sack over his head [burlap is best], into the room. JOHN is hesitant to enter, but after a few attempts, JESSICA

succeeds in leading him to his seat near LIPSCOMB'S desk.)

DR. LIPSCOMB: *(To JOHN.)* Now then. I'll need to ask you a few questions, if you don't mind. Good. *(He refers to a small index card.)* Now then, your name is If-You-Don't-Stop-Calling-Mr.-Timberlake's-Suite-We'll-Be-Forced-To-Call-The Authorities?

JOHN MERRICK: No.

(LIPSCOMB is just realizing he read the wrong card—and quickly pulls out the correct card.)

DR. LIPSCOMB: No. Your name is John Merrick.

JOHN MERRICK: Actually—Joseph Carey Merrick, but all my imaginary friends and admirers call me… John.

DR. LIPSCOMB: Fascinating.

JOHN MERRICK: Well, where is my cage?

DR. LIPSCOMB: Just down in the dungeon. Oh, you'll love it. It's pure titanium, just like on the space shuttle. It even has an automatic "hose down" feature: three times a day on a timer.

JESSICA: Why don't we give him the spare room just beyond mine?

JOHN MERRICK: Room?

JESSICA: Room.

DR. LIPSCOMB: Room?!

JESSICA: Room.

JOHN MERRICK: Room!!

DR. LIPSCOMB: Fine, if you'd rather. There's no bidet, but we make do regardless. That was a dooky-pun.

JOHN MERRICK: My own room?

JESSICA: Yes, of course.

JOHN MERRICK: I think I'm gonna like it here.

DR. LIPSCOMB: *(To audience.)* As time has passed,

(Pause. They look around a bit, finally concurring on when enough time has passed. Also during the pause, JESSICA accidentally squeezes a bit of JOHN's head, which sends a significant spray of unidentifiable liquid across stage from one of the sacs on JOHN's head.)

DR. LIPSCOMB: He has warmed under the caring glow of my reassuring demeanor. Within the bounds of our newly established trusting relationship, he began to answer questions. Mother: one Catherine Virginia Merrick—apparently a dancer… a fact the subject seems exceedingly proud of. One sister, given up for adoption at birth. No father to speak of.

(LIPSCOMB crosses JOHN and kicks him in the knee to test his reflexes. In retaliation for the kick, JOHN whacks LIPSCOMB in the gut. LIPSCOMB crosses back to continue addressing the audience.)

DR. LIPSCOMB: After some of the most extensive examinations I have ever performed, I feel that I am on the verge of a major breakthrough. Note: Jessica is continuing with her nursely duties despite the fact that she is on a personal *odd*-esy to find herself. *(To JESSICA.)* Jess… Sister Curvey—I have some crap to check on at the university—Could you see that Captain Rancid here is taken care of? There's a good girl. Later, chunky chum. *(He exits.)*

JESSICA: *(Calls after him.)* Just don't be too long. My coven meets at four, and I still have three cats to kill.

(JOHN and JESSICA look around the room, in awkward silence. They make eye contact.)

JOHN MERRICK: Sister.

JESSICA: Mr. Merrick. And please—call me Jessica—I'm, uh, not ordained. It's just an experiment, this, really. Oh, we got that latest book you asked for.

(She hands him a book: "Charles Nelson Reilly—On Acting.")

JOHN MERRICK: Thank you. Thank you, Jessica. But you needn't call me Mr. Merrick—you can call me, you know, Captain Rancid, or Cottage-Cheese Boy—like the doctor. I don't mind. I understand.

JESSICA: I would never think to call you such a thing. Your name is John Merrick.

JOHN MERRICK: Yes. It is. No one's really used it before. It almost makes it sound as if I'm not just a freak.

JESSICA: Mr. Merrick! I never want to hear that word again. You are a kind and a unique man. There is no shame whatsoever in being genetically challenged.

JOHN MERRICK: Can it really be that I'll never again be forced to cower in the corner and whimper and drool—show after show until I hear the screams of children and Episcopalians in my sleep. I'll never again have to perform agonizing rhythmic gymnastic routines with strips of my own dangling flesh. God,—God: I'll never be put on degrading display ever, ever again!!

JESSICA: No Mr. Merrick! No. I swear you shall not.

DR. LIPSCOMB: *(Re-enters, excited.)* Oh, Jess, Meat Sack, wonderful news! The hall has been officially retained, and the invitations go out tonight! All the best medi-cal minds in London are sure to turn out to get a good head-to-toe gawk at you in all your gory. God, I am so aroused!!

(He exits again. JESSICA looks at JOHN sympathetically—JOHN is obviously hurt by this speech. A tender moment passes between JESSICA and JOHN. Then JESSICA exits. JOHN looks after her, then tries to look through his new book. Beat. He looks around cautiously, then pulls a tattered old volume of show tunes from a secret place. He flips to a page.)

JOHN MERRICK:
Grey skies are gonna clear up.
Put on a hap—…

(He flips to another page.)

Oh, what a beautiful morn—…

(He closes the book and clutches it to his man-bosom.)

Mother.
Where did you go?
Why did you leave me?
Mother.
Want you to know
How much I love you.

Mother,
I'll make you so proud.
If they must laugh,
Let them laugh.
I don't mind.
If they must stare,
Let them stare
'Til they're blind.
So unaware of who they see.
Mother, we'll show them.
Mother.
I wish you could see.
I wish you could see.
I wish I could be
Me.
Just me.

(Beat. JOHN pulls out that indispensable acting text, "William Shatner—To the Actor." He is carefully absorbing every nuance of every concept, taking time to gesture, etc. Throughout the next, he is executing Shatneresque exercises, poses, pauses, etc. LIPSCOMB enters.)

DR. LIPSCOMB: Morning, Sir Hideous. How goes it?

JOHN MERRICK: Fine, thank you. And yourself?

DR. LIPSCOMB: Oh, Blimp Noggin. Just you wait.

JOHN MERRICK: (À la Shatner.) Henry Higgins. Just—You—Wait.

DR. LIPSCOMB: I have run across a journal written by a Doctor, uh, what was it? Theves? Treves? Teves? Oh, well, no matter. It was about a case something like yours. Proved extremely helpful... Oh, but I won't bore you with that. The fact is that the big and important lecture takes place tomorrow as scheduled. All the finest physicians in Her Majesty's Curing Corps will be there. Oh, Vomit-Face. Thank you so much. I could never have done it without you.

JOHN MERRICK: No. You couldn't.

DR. LIPSCOMB: Oh—life is so good! Are there any more books you would like to read right now?

JOHN MERRICK: Not right now, thank you.

DR. LIPSCOMB: Theatre magazines. With pictures of dancers like your mother, perhaps?

JOHN MERRICK: (His best Shatner, incorporating the Doctor's previous enthusiastic gestures.) I am *not* looking for pictures of my mother. Believe what you like. She was a dancer.

DR. LIPSCOMB: I'm sorry, Flesh-ball. I do believe you. I...

JOHN MERRICK: "Lecture." "Research." "Diagnosis." Poking; prodding; parading me in front of a bunch of snobby gawkers. Never "treatment." Never "cure."

DR. LIPSCOMB: I never said...

JOHN MERRICK: (His best best Shatner.) Can you make me normal, Jim?

DR. LIPSCOMB: No. Yours is a genetic disorder, started when your mother fucked an elephant. There is no way to alter its effects. I'm sorry.

JOHN MERRICK: Fix your career, though, can't it? So it's back to work for both of us. No matter who's in the audience, I'm nothing but a freak in a freak show.

DR. LIPSCOMB: Hey—Vomit-Face...

JOHN MERRICK: And will you stop calling me all those terrible things. My name is John!!

DR. LIPSCOMB: But, those are just little affectionate nicknames. Like you calling me Complete Bisexual Slut, and Crabs-a-poppin'.

JOHN MERRICK: I've never done that, Doctor.

DR. LIPSCOMB: Oh. You know, I think you're right. Dreadfully sorry, there, Jello Fellow—John. Listen. You just say the word and the lecture is canceled. I've come to think of you as a friend. Truly, Feta-Head... John, I am not going to exploit you without your permission.

JOHN MERRICK: I'm sorry, Jim. I shouldn't have said all that. I just didn't sleep well last night.

DR. LIPSCOMB: Bad dreams?

JOHN MERRICK: Nothing like that. Just sick of sitting.

DR. LIPSCOMB: Sitting?

JOHN MERRICK: Yes. The cumbersome, disproportionate nature of my head makes it utterly impossible to slumber in a substantially reclined position.

DR. LIPSCOMB: Nature of your head?

JOHN MERRICK: Yes. It's rather… large. And deformed. If you look at it.

DR. LIPSCOMB: *(Looks carefully.)* Well, I'll be a Nipsey Russell! I should probably make a note of this. Note: Subject has big head. My, we certainly were waxing serious there, weren't we? Any more of that and you'd have to start building a model of Saint Phillip's.

JOHN MERRICK: The church? Why would I want to do that?

DR. LIPSCOMB: I'm not sure. The requirements of true drama, I suppose.

(JESSICA enters dressed as a Hare Krishna, shaved head, etc.)

JESSICA: Would you like to make a donation? The cost of one lovely flower can bring a brethren soul to a plane of harmonic consciousness as yet unattained.

DR. LIPSCOMB: Charming, Jess. You happy?

JESSICA: *(Spying the Shatner book, she launches into a passable imitation of Scotty.)* No. Dammit, Jim. You've got to give me more time.

DR. LIPSCOMB: *(Tries his hand at Shatner.)* That's not good enough, Ms. Curvey. *(JOHN nods approval at*

LIPSCOMB's effort.) John—you don't have to do this if you don't want to. The lecture is at ten o'clock tomorrow. I'll be there. I hope you will, too. *(He goes.)*

SCENE 5

A lecture hall somewhere in London. DR. LIPSCOMB, notes in hand, paces nervously. Beat. Then JOHN's voice is heard from behind the curtain, which now serves to conceal LIPSCOMB's remarkable specimen (JOHN).

JOHN MERRICK: *(Offstage.)* Well, when are we going to get this show on the road?

DR. LIPSCOMB: Oh, John. You came!!

JOHN MERRICK: *(Offstage.)* No. But I am here. That was a spunky pun.

DR. LIPSCOMB: Very well then. Your attention, please, gentlemen. Gentlemen.

> Distinguished members of the medical profession,
> Welcome. I'll commence, on my discretion.

(Spoken.) Aaaah!

> I see the purpose of my lecture
> Has got you all a'wondering.
> You can cease your blind conjecture,
> You'll see I'm done with blundering.
> I've an amazing and intricate case
> That shall restore me to my place.
> To achieve my objective,
> I'll change your perspective
> Of me and my former disgrace.
>
> I've found a man with
> Significance.
> Oh, significance.
> Astounding and resonant, new and
>   elating

Significance.
I'm pounding your hesitant view by
    instating
Significance.
Surrounding his resident putrid inflat-
    ing,
I'm founding a precedent through
    demonstrating
Significance.

His symptoms
Are
Alarming.
They
Are fearful
And
Disarming.
But
He's cheerful
And
He's charming.
Have a heart.

The truth is,
It's
Distressing.
In
His skin, some
Strange
Out-pressing.
There
Has been some
Co-
Alescing.
I've a chart.

*(LIPSCOMB presents his "chart" of
JOHN—which is a stick figure with a
lumpy head—drawn in magic marker on
the palm of the DOCTOR's left hand.)*

(Spoken.) Now,

You'll notice the numerous
Growths that are tumorous
Over and thither and thence.
As he's become older,

The mass on the shoulder
Has started to wither, and hence,
We gather he's healthy,
Or, rather, he's wealthy
In terms of expendable skin.
His head has expanded
So much, it's demanded
The spine be unbendable.

(To JOHN.) Grin!

(JOHN sticks his head out, grinning.)

DR. LIPSCOMB:
    The fleshy deposit
    Has grown so, what was it?
    The left arm is virtually rot.
    So out of proportion,
    This human distortion.
    What nature should nurture, he's not!
    Frenetic discord or
    Genetic disorder,
    I don't wish to cause you distress.
    Though my facts would be ample,
    I've brought an example.
    Here. In a state of undress.

*(He draws the curtain. JOHN is exposed,
in all his gory. He is wearing only something
that could best be described as a diaper.)*

DR. LIPSCOMB: *(Spoken.)* You're
speechless, aren't you? Because

    He's significant.

JOHN MERRICK:
    I'm significant.
DR. LIPSCOMB:
    He's significant.

JOHN MERRICK:
    I'm significant.

DR. LIPSCOMB:
    Deformity fated to ratify science.

DR. LIPSCOMB, JOHN MERRICK:
    Enormity stated begat my compliance.

Significant.

JOHN MERRICK:
He said
I was significant.

DR. LIPSCOMB:
You're significant.
His elbows…

JOHN MERRICK:
My elbows…

DR. LIPSCOMB:
Unmatching.

JOHN MERRICK:
Unmatching.

DR. LIPSCOMB:
His face is…

JOHN MERRICK:
My face is…

DR. LIPSCOMB:
Dispatching.

JOHN MERRICK:
Dispatching?

DR. LIPSCOMB:
These cases…

JOHN MERRICK:
These places…

DR. LIPSCOMB:
Aren't catching.

JOHN MERRICK:
Need scratching.

DR. LIPSCOMB:
Never fear.

JOHN MERRICK:
Here and here.

DR. LIPSCOMB:
Beneath, though…

JOHN MERRICK:
Beneath, though…

DR. LIPSCOMB:
His torsos,

JOHN MERRICK:
My… torsos,

DR. LIPSCOMB:
His cancer…

JOHN MERRICK:
A dancer…

DR. LIPSCOMB:
No more shows.

JOHN MERRICK:
Once more shows.

DR. LIPSCOMB:
The answer?

JOHN MERRICK:
Entrancer…

DR. LIPSCOMB:
The floor knows,

JOHN MERRICK:
At floor shows.

DR. LIPSCOMB:
Lend an ear!

JOHN MERRICK:
Dreams are dear.

DR. LIPSCOMB:
He's important.

JOHN MERRICK:
At least I'm important.

DR. LIPSCOMB:
So important.

JOHN MERRICK:
Here I'm important.

DR. LIPSCOMB:
> The ramifications defy mere enlist'ry,
> Important.
> And damn if there's patients in my
>   queerish hist'ry
> Important.
> Like he's important.

JOHN MERRICK:
> I'm significant.

DR. LIPSCOMB:
> You're significant.
> Although you're indignant
> And he is malignant,
> I've found a precise diagnosis.
> His problem, I've called,
> What has got you appalled,
> Is acute neurofibromatosis.
> Yes, acute neurofibromatosis.
> Acute neurofibro-
> Acute neurofibro-
> Acute neurofibromatosis.

JOHN MERRICK:
> Acute neurofib-
> Acute neurofib-
> Acute neurofibromatosis.

DR. LIPSCOMB:
> Acute neuro-
> 'Cute neuro-
> 'Cute neuro-
> 'Cute neuro-
> 'Cute neuro-
> 'Cute neuro-
> 'Cute neurofibromatosis.

JOHN MERRICK:
> Oh, fibro-
> Oh, fibro-
> Oh, fibro-
> Oh, fibro-
> Oh, fibro-
> Oh, fibro-
> Oh, fabulous fibromatosis.

DR. LIPSCOMB:
> Moses supposes that fibromatosis
> Engrosses all those as
> Exposed.

JOHN MERRICK:
> If Moses exposes my fibromatosis
> And shows us,
> He'll go unopposed.

DR. LIPSCOMB:
> Acute neurofibro-
> Acute neurofibro-
> Oh, beauteous fibromatosis.

BOTH:
> Acute neurofibro-
> Acute neurofibro-
> A cutey with fibromatosis.
> Acute neurofibromatosis.
> Acute neurofibromatosis.
> Acute-
> Acute-
> Acute-
> Acute neurofibromatosis-
> Matosis!

DR. LIPSCOMB: And that was a complete run-thru. Then I shall open the floor for questions, and that will have been that. Jess, are you sure there's no one out in the hall?

JESSICA: Not a soul.

DR. LIPSCOMB: Well, you know what they say about men of medicine.

JESSICA: No. What?

DR. LIPSCOMB: Their weighty thoughts often impede punctuality.

JESSICA: Really? I've never heard that before.

DR. LIPSCOMB: You travel in different circles.

JESSICA: I travel in a wiggly line. You travel in circles.

JOHN MERRICK: Why don't you just reschedule?

DR. LIPSCOMB: No!! They might come back this time. They must.

JOHN MERRICK: This time? How many of these lectures have you given?

DR. LIPSCOMB: Sixteen.

JESSICA: Seventeen.

DR. LIPSCOMB: Seventeen?

JESSICA: Little Jimmy Six-Toes.

DR. LIPSCOMB: Oh, yes. Seventeen. They actually came to the first five or so. Then attendance dwindled a bit. I always assumed it was because I was presenting ideas so revolutionary that they dared not think of them.

JOHN MERRICK: That was probably it.

DR. LIPSCOMB: No matter. I'll just go home and toss off a sexed-up fictionalization of John's inspiring story. That is, after all, what I do.

JESSICA: Can't you see the cover: like, Fabio all illustrated with his rippling massive chest, and rippling massive head?

JOHN MERRICK: I loved "The Insatiable Intern," by the way.

JESSICA: No, "The Urologist From Uranus" is still my favorite.

DR. LIPSCOMB: God, look at me. I made a fortune writing medical-themed romantic novels! It's so humiliating. I might as well face it: I am not a doctor!!

JOHN MERRICK: Jim, don't say that.

Of course you're a doctor. You've got one of those dangly things.

JESSICA: A penis!

JOHN MERRICK: A stethoscope. Jim, you give everything to follow your dream. That's the most noble and courageous thing any person can do.

DR. LIPSCOMB: But there comes a point, John, where it turns into the stupidest. You know what my problem is? I'm insignificant. (He exits. JOHN starts to follow him, JESSICA stops him.)

JOHN MERRICK: Isn't there something I can do?

JESSICA: John, you've endured so much already. He has to walk his own path. We all must find our own paths. For instance, I'm off to have my ass pierced. Bye, John.

JOHN MERRICK: But what should I do?

JESSICA: Do what you want to do.

(She exits. JOHN looks around the empty auditorium thoughtfully. Beat. He pulls out a copy of "London Backstage." He then pulls a pen from somewhere amidst the folds of skin on his head, and begins circling auditions. The lights fall.)

SCENE 6

The following scene is actually a short video—filmed at various locations—and edited to show the scope of JOHN's humiliation and rejection throughout the town—from theatre to theatre to theatre. The video is shown while the actor playing JOHN MERRICK changes out of his diaper. [The scene can also consist only of voice-overs and sound cues played during a blackout.]

JOHN, wearing his sack on his head, waits his turn, and is finally shown in to an audition studio with a rehearsal PIANIST and table manned by foul-looking auditors.

JOHN MERRICK: Good afternoon. Thank you for seeing me. My name... is John Merrick.

SCOTT: *(Screams—he always screams...)* 'Scuse me, are you aware you have a sack on your damn head?!!

GRACIELLE: Scotty-potty, calm down. Is just his way to stand out. I say we let him sing.

SCOTT: O-damn-kay!

JOHN MERRICK: Thank you. Again, I am John Merrick. And I'll be doing a piece from the musical "Little Big Horn." Ahem. *(To PIANIST.)*

> Eagle must fly.
> Sun must move through sky.
> And Paleface have to die.
> Yes, Paleface must motherfucking die.

GRACIELLE: I think he is fantastica. Let's see him move. Bob!

(BOB demonstrates an insanely difficult and strange dance combination. JOHN does it perfectly.)

BOB: Ready?

> 1-2-3-4-5-6-7-8...
> Limp, Limp, Swivel, Hitch,
> Limp, Hop, Curve, Flick,
> Prance, Prance, Prance, Duck,
> Over, Under, In, Out,
> Limp, Limp, Drop, Roll,
> Clap, Clap, Cross, Lick,
> Crawl, Crawl, Crawl, Kick,
> Crawl, Crawl, Drip, Freeze.
> Okay now, just you.
> Ready?
> 1-2-3-4-5-6-7-8...

(JOHN does the strenuously absurd dance impeccably.)

SCOTT: Good, damn good!! You're so damn good!!!!

GRACIELLE: He would be a brilliant Conrad Birdie the Second.

JOHN MERRICK: They like me. They really like me. Who the hell are they?

GRACIELLE: Come, we must see the face of such talent.

(JOHN removes his sack. BOB screams and runs away.)

SCOTT: *(Offstage.)* Oh, my damn God!!

GRACIELLE: *(Offstage.)* My bowels, they are unlocking!!

SCOTT: *(Offstage.)* Get out! Get damn out!!

GRACIELLE: *(Offstage.)* You sucked anyway!

(JOHN looks around in dismay, then flees the room. The following echoing, haunting voices tear through the dark.)

VARIOUS VOICES:

Audition? There ain't no part for a whale in our show!

A stuffed whale, Barnaby!

(Cruel laughter.)

(Screams.)

Get out of my theatre. *Now!*

You can have all the money. Just don't hurt us.

Who could tell if he could act anyway, with all that... skin!?

Away with you!

You know, a couple of subtle tucks and a nose job, and maybe… Shut up!!

Mom always said, "Don't play ball in the house!"

Get away.

No… no… no… no…

(The DISTORTED VOICE returns.)

SLIGHTLY DISTORTED VOICE: But sometimes I think my head is so big because it is so full of their screams!!

(JOHN runs from the torrent of rejection. He stops onstage, exhausted and furious.)

JOHN MERRICK: I am not an animal! I'm an actor!!!

> Everyone sees an animal
> When they look towards me.
> Great! Let them see an animal.
> If that's what they think that I am—
> Then that's what I'll be.
>
> Run away from me.
> Get away from me.
> From the horrible, terrible, Elephant Man.
> That deplorable, stareable, less than a man.
> From that sight.
> What a fright!
>
> Oh, the animal.
> Look, the animal.
> Feed the animal.
> Me, the animal.
> The baby looked odd.
> The baby looked odd.
> The baby looked odd…

(Spoken.) Go on—

> Pick a creature with some horrid shape,
> Some monstrous thing.

> I'll be ev'ry beast you wanna see.
> And I'll tap dance and sing!
> Brilliant animal.
>
> I'm a tiger. I'm a bear.
> Sir, what would you like to see?
> Oh, a lion? No, I'm sorry.
> But, I wasn't born free.
> Funny animal.
>
> I'm at home within my cage.
> The doorless cell of my skin.
> It's my license to menagerie,
> My dramatic chagrin.
>
> The monster has no place.
> The monster has a face
> Like no other.
> The bold, tragic tale
> Says the monster must fail
> Like his mother,
> That dreams die within.
> That life can't begin.
> My hubris is bigger and better than anyone's I've ever heard.
> There should be a word.
>
> So write a movie. Write a play.
> If I'm a yarn, why not spin it?
> Yes, you could write your touching play.
> But you wouldn't cast me in it.
> Not an animal.
> I'm an animal.
> Just an animal.
> Free the animal.
>
> So look at me. Laugh at me. Have your fun.
> Your reaction's understood.
> But before everything has been said and been done,
> You'll look because I'm good.
> Thus spake an animal!

(Blackout.)

SCENE 7

DR. LIPSCOMB enters his flat, moping. He paces, somehow not realizing that PRESBY RAINCOAT is dogging his every step—walking directly behind the DOCTOR, and studying the back of his head with bizarre curiosity. LIPSCOMB even exits into the restroom. Beat, then a flush is heard, and LIPSCOMB re-enters—PRESBY still millimeters behind him—The DOCTOR still unaware of this fact. He makes his way downstage, and opens his left hand—revealing that the "chart" has been sloppily crossed out.

DR. LIPSCOMB: Well, Jim. Good show.

Who was that man?
Where…

(PRESBY leans into LIPSCOMB's neck, taking a loud whiff of his man-musk. It is only now that LIPSCOMB notices PRESBY. He steps to the side, fully revealing PRESBY for the first time—smoking jacket, lavender scarf [with matching toenails] and all.)

DR. LIPSCOMB: Can I help you? How did you get into my home?

PRESBY: I'm astonishingly wealthy.

DR. LIPSCOMB: Ah—who are you?

PRESBY: The Elephant Man, aye?

DR. LIPSCOMB: Yes. But how did you know?

PRESBY: *(He pulls out several scripts and starts tossing them at LIPSCOMB.)* In "Waiting On Nodot," why does Nodot never arrive? *(Toss.)* In "A Trolley Called 'I Want You,'" why does Vivian have to be institutionalized and why does Marlon scream? *(Toss.)* Oh, look. A musical. *(Sings.)* "Butte, Montana, where the wind comes sweeping down the plains." *(Toss.)*

DR. LIPSCOMB: My God, man— these… these are my plays. Where on Earth did you get these?

PRESBY: I have an extensive network of spies, Dr. Lipscomb. You once wrote some fabulous stuff. Not like the clit-twiddling dreck you churn out now.

DR. LIPSCOMB: But what does all this mean?

PRESBY: It means that you and I are going to make your John Merrick a star.

DR. LIPSCOMB: Huh?

PRESBY: I am Presby Raincoat. Yes— THE Presby Raincoat—producer for the theatre… *(Clears his throat.)*

DR. LIPSCOMB: My God—what can you want with me?

PRESBY: Don't interrupt me. Ever. *(Really clears his throat.)* You see, James…

Once in ev'ry very great while,
Given theatrical laws of averages and
    fortunes,
A musical that's striking rare is written.
What is it can make the world smile?
Why it's tunes and tunes and tunes and
    tunes and more tunes.
A musical that leaves the masses smitten.
And they always come from Britain.

'Twill make you laugh,
'Twill make you cry,
And ever after, till you die
It will be part of you,
Deep in the heart of you.
It somehow changes you.
It rearranges you.

And will you grieve,
As you leave?
So distraught
Your life's not

A musical? Oh, sure.
But you'll sing laud
To your God—
That you bought
My big thought-
Ful souvenir brochure…

So you can relive,
And relive
This gift I give,
And I give.
Give, give, give, give, give, give.
Live, live, live, live, live, live.

I have been fortunate enough to have produced the last four hundred and thirteen
of these musicals. And, I believe that you
are the man who should—nay, must—
write the next. For John to star in.

DR. LIPSCOMB: But, Mr. Raincoat, I
can't. It's been twenty years since I've written a play…

PRESBY: Sh! You will. Because I am going to share with you what I've found. And
I have found the very secret… to life…
itself! Do you want to know? Do you really want to know?

Ever'body wants…
Ever'body wants…
Ever'body wants their life to be a mu-
    sical…
'Cause music'll
Take away the sting
Of any nasty thing
That might be happening…
If just please only you could sing
A soulful, happy ballad…
Forget your doleful, crappy, pallid,
    humdrum life.

Oh, ever'body wants…
Ever'body wants…
Ever'body wants their life to be a mu-
    sical…

'Cause music'll
Wistfully caress
The centers of your stress
With waves of happiness…
Hep hip-hop, hopeful happi—yes!
A solid, driving number
Could ease your squalid, striving, cum-
    bersome, dumb life.

Even mis'rable people singing
Are happier than happy people talking.
See 'da mis'rable people singing:
They're doing senseless in-place walking.
'Cause they have to move their feet
To the music's moving beat.
Your life may be dung,
Ah, but dung when it's sung
Is a multi-million dollar treat!

Oh, abject misery
If it's in a major key
Is such a sight to see…
Good great big God, I'm glad I'm me!

*(DR. LIPSCOMB is by now completely
swept away.)*

DR. LIPSCOMB:
    Ever'body wants…

PRESBY: Yes.

DR. LIPSCOMB:
    Ever'body needs…

PRESBY: Yes!

DR. LIPSCOMB:
    Ever'body craves

PRESBY: YES!!!!

PRESBY and DR. LIPSCOMB:
    Life to be a musical!
    With music al-
    Luring and divine.
    Come join a chorus line.
    You'll sparkle, sing, and shine.

PRESBY:
They all so wish their life was mine…

PRESBY and DR. LIPSCOMB:
Producing joy and rapture.
Just try it: You sing, boy and capture
some plum life.

Write a show that is mesmerizing…
Write a show that could not be lusher.

PRESBY:
Hey. Hey look at me organizing
The next big Raincoat gusher!
Yes, your life is pink balloons
When your life is full of tunes.
Sure, your boy is a freak,
But the freak doesn't speak,
The sorry sack of skin, he croons!!

Just write me something true
And emotional and new.
And make it hummable, be-do!!
Then, sir, you'll soon be stoked you're
you!!!

DR. LIPSCOMB:
Oh, ever'body wants…
Ever'body wants…

PRESBY:
Pippin and *Gypsy* and *Porgy and Bess.*
Carousel, Carnival, Carrie and *Chess.*
Cabaret, Camelot, Candide and *Mame.*
Follies and *Funny Girl, Forum* and
Fame.
On Your Toes and *Anything Goes* and
Smokey Joe's and *Fanny.*
I Do! I Do! and *Two By Two* and *Crazy
For You* and *Annie.*
Phantom and *Can-Can* and *Grease* and
Les Miz.
Passion and *Purlie, Penzance* and *The
Wiz.*
Chicago, She Loves Me, Show Boat and
State Fair.
Dreamgirls and *Dolly, Legs Diamond*

and *Hair.*
Dames At Sea and *The Apple Tree* and
Do Re Mi and *Whoopee.*
*No, No, Nanette, Yes, Yes, Yvette, Me And
Juliet* and *Snoopy.*
On The Town and *Wonderful Town* and
New Girl In Town, Evita.
Irene and *Jennie, Roberta, Sweet Char-
ity, Rosalie, Drood, Rio Rita.*
*Kiss Me, Kate, Strike Up The Band,
They're Playing Our Song, Lend An
Ear.*
*Follow The Girls, Into The Woods, No
Strings, Wish You Were Here!*
Rent and *Big* and *Nine* and *Cats,*
and *Cats* and *Cats* and *Cats* and that's

What ever'body wants…
Ever'body wants…

PRESBY and LIPSCOMB:
Ever'body wants their life to be a musical!!!

PRESBY: Well, James — whattaya say?

DR. LIPSCOMB: Yes!!.

PRESBY: Fabulous.

*(LIPSCOMB and PRESBY back awk-
wardly away from the intimate pose they
struck at the end of the song—LIPSCOMB
in PRESBY's arms, held aloft and with his
legs firmly wrapped around PRESBY's mid-
section. There are a few beats in which they
manage to miss seeing the other's longing
gaze—then they exit separately—awk-
wardly.)*

SCENE 8

*JOHN wanders down the street, slowly. JES-
SICA, now in male drag—a business suit—
calls to him.*

JESSICA: John!! There you are! The Doctor told me you hadn't been back to the

flat since the lecture. Are you all right? You look terrible. I mean—even for you. I mean...

JOHN MERRICK: Jessica, darling — you're very sweet, but why don't you just leave me alone. I know you don't want to be here. I think I'll just go home to the freak show.

JESSICA: You most certainly will not. You're the first real male friend I've ever had. You're the first guy who cared about the real me. Who never even so much as glanced at my full, buoyant breasts.

(As she mentions various parts of herself, she manages to emphasize them through her suit— and JOHN seems to see them for the first time. And he is totally transfixed by them—just gapes at her body for the rest of her speech.)

JESSICA: My round, soft-yet-tight ass. My amazingly shapely legs; my perfect and perfectly singular features; and my full, buoyant breasts again. You saw me for the person I could become. The person I so wanted to be. I can't describe to you what it means to have had my potential so respected by another human being.

JOHN MERRICK: *(Hasn't heard a word.)* They are incredibly full and buoyant, aren't they.

JESSICA: *(Follows his vacant leer.)* Oh, God—John. Not you, too. Filthy men. Filthy, filthy men!!

(JESSICA rushes off, leaving JOHN alone and upset... very upset. This song takes place in various locations in London, as JOHN and JESSICA, separately, roam aimlessly, and DR. LIPSCOMB works on his play. We also see PRESBY.)

JOHN MERRICK:
And now I'm all alone again.

JESSICA:
Myself.

JOHN MERRICK:
She is so lovely...

JESSICA:
So, what am I?

JOHN MERRICK:
Hot snatch like that will never let
Me...
Put it in 'em

JESSICA:
I am on my own.

JOHN MERRICK:
I want to die.

BOTH:
I wish I were less miserable than I am.
My dreams are done.

DR. LIPSCOMB:
Act one, scene one.

JOHN MERRICK:
I wander through the streets of London.
I ponder all I wanted to do
With my life.
Turned away again, I feel undone.
Another hell I must slog through.

JESSICA:
What to do?

DR. LIPSCOMB:
Act one, scene two.

JESSICA:
I'm passing by these places I've frequented.
The phases I've been prone to explore
Here of late.
My passions were misled and delinquented.
Someone tell me what is the score.

JOHN MERRICK:
Nevermore.

DR. LIPSCOMB:
Act two, scene four.
I must do some research
Down at the record store.

(He exits. PRESBY appears.)

PRESBY:
The lonely mogul on his throne.
Must be the
Only mogul so alone.
Just me, the
Broadway king.
Rich and clever.
I do my Broadway thing
But I never
Get the guy.

JESSICA:
Who am I?

PRESBY:
I really just wonder why.

JESSICA:
Who am I?

PRESBY:
Then I just eat and cry.

JESSICA:
What have I done with my life so far?

PRESBY:
Dammit, Madonna has
Been to my house.

JESSICA:
I once was a person, and not bizarre.

PRESBY:
Maybe this means that I'm straight…

JESSICA:
Guide me, fate!

PRESBY:
I'm not straight…

JESSICA:
I can't wait…

(LIPSCOMB enters with a stack of albums.)

DR. LIPSCOMB:
Goodness but my play is great…

(JOHN approaches the old freak show. There is a sign that says "Please Welcome Back: The Rhinoceros Guy.")

JOHN MERRICK:
Disgraced at the bottom.
Disgraced at the top.
Disgraced at auditions.
This has got to stop.

(LIPSCOMB pulls out an old Shaun Cassidy album.)

DR. LIPSCOMB:
Da doo, run, run, run.
Da doo, run, run.

(Spoken.) Perfect!

JOHN MERRICK:
Why must I want it?
And why must I need?
Why am I dreaming?
Can't I concede?

(Now, LIPSCOMB has found a Sweeney Todd *album.)*

DR. LIPSCOMB: I remember the first time I had a little priest—

(LIPSCOMB also visibly browses through a copy of Michael Jackson's Off the Wall, *a Loverboy album, the cast recording of "State Fair 2: Harry's Revenge," and many others.)*

JOHN MERRICK:
I might as well proceed.
To where?

PRESBY:
The lonely mogul.

JOHN MERRICK:
Do I care?

PRESBY:
The only mogul.

DR. LIPSCOMB:
The songs do come along very nicely.

JOHN MERRICK:
I look for a job at a club
Downtown.

DR. LIPSCOMB:
They're catchy, and they're crafted precisely.

JOHN MERRICK:
The bouncer tries to give me the rub.
Off to a pub.

JESSICA:
My whole life is nothing.
My whole life is rot.
Always sought a journey,
Always, where I got
Was not
What
I wanted.
Everything done,
Nothing done well.
These blasted confusions.
I want to excel.
But hell.
I fell.

*(Fantastic sleazy go-go music fills the space.
She rips off her suit jacket—quite stylishly.
She looks down at it in her hands. She rips
off her tie—even more stylishly. She seems
swept away—and proceeds to, quite expertly
and sexily, strip…)*

Now, *that* I can do.
Hey! I can do that!

(Spoken.) I can do this!

Feminists of the world forgive me, but—
I want to do this! I'll not fight the stares
of men anymore—It's my destiny!!!

(She runs off.)

DR. LIPSCOMB: *(Perusing script.)*

It just needs a bit of excitement.
A bit or a person to flesh
It out.
To push it past any indictment.
A feature to render it fresh.
Something that's spec… ial.

*(JESSICA enters the room, does her strip
routine. LIPSCOMB does not look at her.)*

JESSICA: Jim, Jim! I found it. Something
I can really do. Look, look! Look!

DR. LIPSCOMB: *(Without looking.)* Very
nice, Jessica. Now go away.

*(JESSICA stops stripping and leaves, de-
jected. DR. LIPSCOMB looks very slowly
towards the spot where JESSICA was just
dancing.)*

DR. LIPSCOMB: Yes! *(He starts writing
again.)*

JOHN MERRICK:
There's one thing that's nice in the city.
Whatever you look like, they'll let
You drink.
And now in the glass, I am pretty.
Why bother being upset?

SLIGHTLY DISTORTED VOICE: But
sometimes I think my head is so big because it is so full of Jim Beam.

JOHN MERRICK:
Yet.

JESSICA:
Guess that was no big deal.

Stupid to think it was real.
Why bother being upset?

DR. LIPSCOMB:
I'm done with all that's vital.
Now, I just must find a title.

JESSICA:
I thought that it was worth a bet.
I'll forget...

PRESBY: *(Tragically holds aloft a Pringles can.)*
What the fuck?

JOHN MERRICK:
I'll forget...

JOHN MERRICK and JESSICA:
The past.
And look to a future at best suicidal.

(DR. LIPSCOMB has pulled out a Jesus
Christ Superstar *album briefly.)*

DR. LIPSCOMB:
That's it! It's finished.

JESSICA:
I'm finished.

PRESBY:
I'm horny.

JOHN MERRICK:
I'm finished.

PRESBY:
Oh, blast.
I haven't been laid since I banged Billy
Idol.
I hate my life.

JOHN and JESSICA:
Forget my life...

PRESBY:
The lonely mogul.

JESSICA:
The genius stripper.

JOHN MERRICK:
The shit-faced monster.

DR. LIPSCOMB:
The happy playwright.

ALL:
Something...

JOHN and JESSICA:
Is over and

PRESBY:
Has got to be

JOHN, JESSICA, and PRESBY:
Done.

DR. LIPSCOMB:
Has just begun.

*(He reveals the cover of his script, and its
title: "PAKKY DERM, SUPERSTAR." He
gives the script a big smooch, exits excitedly
with it.)*

SCENE 9

*DR. LIPSCOMB's rooms. JOHN sits alone
on the sofa, moping. JESSICA enters slowly,
in her old, normal clothes. She looks at
JOHN, then sits beside him, assuming a
similarly slumped position.*

JOHN MERRICK: Seen the doctor?

JESSICA: No. He's probably out giving a
rectal exam to the Rhinoceros Guy.

JOHN MERRICK: I have decided that I
don't like my life. My life sucks.

JESSICA: Hermano. My life sucks big
green obsequious Machiavellian donkey
turds.

JOHN MERRICK: Well put. Thank you,
Jessica.

JESSICA: For what?

JOHN MERRICK: You, I think, are the only person ever who has always treated me as a human being. That means a very lot to me. And I'd be a big, disgustingly deformed liar if I said it isn't made all the sweeter by the fact that you are a smart and exciting and devastatingly beautiful woman. Inside and out. So, thank you.

JESSICA: What did you say?

JOHN MERRICK: You, I think, are the only person ever who has always treated me as a human being. That means a very lot to me. And I'd be a big, disgustingly deformed liar if I said it isn't made all the sweeter by the fact that you are a smart and exciting and devastatingly beautiful woman. Inside and out. So, thank you.

(She turns and looks at him, stares at him—long and deep. Birds chirp sweetly as she steps downstage.)

JESSICA: You're welcome.

> Well shut my mouth, and
> Stop my heart, and
> Open my eyes.
> So this is how the
> Feelings start, hey
> What a surprise.
> My heart is pounding, my
> Pulse is racing, a-
> Quiver my thighs…
> It's nice, astounding, I
> Feel I'm facing my
> Fear of what lies
> Behind their flies.
> But he's not like other guys…

> I'm quaking, I'm glowing, I'm warmed.
> He's caring and gentle, malformed.
> Just watch him sit and brood.
> My God—I'm in the mood!

> My fear is gone, I've
> Found my place and
> That place is fine.
> I mean, come on, next
> To his face, his
> Dick must look divine.
> And said dick will soon be mine.

(She dives on him. They drop to the floor behind some bit of furniture and start to go at it. After another bit, LIPSCOMB enters, ecstatic. He does not even appear to notice what they are doing.)

DR. LIPSCOMB: John! Jess! I'm so glad you're back. I've the most incredible news!

JOHN MERRICK: This had better be good.

JESSICA: This had better be very, very good.

DR. LIPSCOMB: John, have you ever heard of a Presby Raincoat?

JOHN MERRICK: Of course—Duh! He produced "Aardvarks," "The Slightly Deformed Man Who Liked Music And Had Inexplicable Powers," "Miss Beirut," "Remembrance Of Things Past"…

JESSICA: Isn't that the musical it takes all week to see?

JOHN MERRICK: Yes. Six nights and an afternoon. I have the recording, if you'd like…

DR. LIPSCOMB: John, how would you like to go to New York?

JOHN MERRICK: New York, New York?

JESSICA: A crap of a town.

DR. LIPSCOMB: Presby Raincoat heard about those clandestine auditions of yours and he asked me to write a Broadway musical for you to star in. Presby, of course, loves it, and is going to produce it. Soon!

JOHN MERRICK: On Broadway?

DR. LIPSCOMB: Yes. It's the story of your life!! Well, I've taken a few liberties, of course, but—

JOHN MERRICK:
Can I sing?

DR. LIPSCOMB:
You can sing.

JOHN MERRICK:
Can I dance?

DR. LIPSCOMB:
You will dance.

JOHN MERRICK:
Will I act?

DR. LIPSCOMB:
You can act
In your own real Broadway show.

JOHN MERRICK:
In my own real Broadway…
When do…

DR. LIPSCOMB:
Pack your bags.

JOHN MERRICK:
We leave?

DR. LIPSCOMB:
We leave today.

BOTH:
New York City is where we are going to go.

DR. LIPSCOMB:
Say goodbye to a life that is bleak.
Jessie, grab your strippin' shoes.

(JESSICA strikes a jubilant, ambitious pose.)

Because, my dears, by the end of the week,
You will both have lost those blues.

JOHN MERRICK:
Like momma taught me.

I've crouched in back and watched the cast.
I know what performers are.

DR. LIPSCOMB:
And although fame is fleeting, you'll last.
John, you'll stay a star.

JESSICA:
I picture you, all decked out and formal—

DR. LIPSCOMB:
They'll laugh.

JESSICA:
They'll smile.

JOHN MERRICK:
And I will be normal.

ALL THREE:
In a Broadway dancin'-
We're gonna do it.
A Broadway, Broadway show.
Yeah!

(Lights out.)

SCENE 10

They are now in New York to rehearse for JOHN's show. After the lights fade on the previous scene, and throughout Scene 10, we are exposed to a headspinning montage of images (or as close thereto as the budget will allow) which augment the live action of the scene (e.g., sounds of set construction and rehearsals). Varying stages of publicity announcements are seen, leading to the marquis for the show, PAKKY DERM, SUPERSTAR. There is also the cover for "The Pulchritudinous Producer" by J. Lipscomb. JOHN's Playgirl *spread, television ads, and interviews. PRESBY is at the back of the house with a megaphone and a Slim Jim. We are instantly in a rehearsal. The cast grabs scripts and scrambles around onstage to find their marks. The music shifts to a driving vamp, landing on song sound bites as they come up.*

PRESBY:
Show business!!

(Spoken.) You delicious whores!

This is show business!!

(Spoken.) What is this? Answer me!!!

JOHN MERRICK, JESSICA, and DR. LIPSCOMB:
It's show business!!

PRESBY: Yes!! And rehearsals start now! So, the overture overtures and there's fog and there's fog and there's an excruciating abomination terrifying passersby. That's you, John, love. And then there is the opening number!

JOHN MERRICK, JESSICA, and DR. LIPSCOMB: *(Variously reading from the scripts.)*
Come hear the yarn of Pakky Derm.
With looks so foul that he'd make you squirm.
He lurked the sewers of Londontown.
All lonely and frightened, but craving renown.
Determined, six-foot fleshy worm
Was Pakky Derm,
Reluctant freakish messiah
Fling your jowls wide, Pakky!

PRESBY: I've got chills. And yes, they *are* multiplying. No, wait. I'm sorry—it was just gas. Now if you'll all just do it much better from now on then we just might have an opening—

DR. LIPSCOMB: While we're stopped—uh—The part of the Doctor: is it gonna be Mandy Patinkin or *(Crosses his fingers in fierce hope.)* Donny Most?

JOHN: *(Over.)* Lord Raincoat, about the water ballet… I get sort of an all-over-body shrinkage. Like as if I was an enormous cockandballs.

JESSICA: *(Over.)* Should I really not take my clothes off until Act Two?

PRESBY: You adorable worrywarts! And you don't even know yet that I just fired the new director. But what is this?

JOHN MERRICK, JESSICA, and DR. LIPSCOMB:
It's show business.

PRESBY: And what you need to remember is that

Show business
Is a lot like mad science!
In that you cobble together necrotic tissue into a passable façade, and then you put that best face forward and hope the audience doesn't notice the electrodes on your neck.

(Spoken.) Is that clear? Of course it is. Okay opening over and we're moving through the freak show towards the reveal. And we'll stand in for Horace and the doctor.

(The cast hits the pose of the reveal of JOHN in the Freak Show. JESSICA and DR. LIPSCOMB scream.)

PRESBY: John, I'm sorry, but you're just not disgusting enough. I'm not going to be happy unless I'm gagging. *(PRESBY looks around as if daring anyone to make a blow-job joke.)*

JOHN: I'll work on it.

(He steps down right and works on being grosser as the scene goes on.)

PRESBY: It's all I can ask. All right, my loving pimples. We'll pick up here tomorrow. James, if I may have a jiffy.

(The others exit. PRESBY addresses LIPSCOMB.)

PRESBY: You know I love your work and this show is a masterpiece but what I need you to do is to expand the emotional lives of the characters. Can you get your brain around that?

LIPSCOMB: What does that mean? Because it sounds like it doesn't mean anything.

PRESBY: It's very simple, James. What did I teach you?

LIPSCOMB:
    Show business
    Is a lot like Chinese water torture.
    You choose your points quite carefully
    Then you hone them and refine them
    And then drip drip drip drip drip drip
        drip drip drip drip drip them onto
        the people's foreheads.
    Of course hopefully you stop before
        they go insane.

PRESBY: Precisely! Now you go write like the dirty bitch you are.

(DR. LIPSCOMB starts offstage, then turns back to PRESBY positively coyly. Then he exits.)

JESSICA: *(Entering.)* Lord Raincoat! Mr. Patinkin refuses to come out of his dressing room until Mr. Lane comes out of his dressing room. And Mr. Lane refuses to come out of his dressing room until the soft serve machine is installed.

PRESBY: Good great big God!! What are we trying to do here today, my tootsie pops?

ALL:
    Show business!

PRESBY: And what's it like?

ALL:
    It's a lot like mad science!
    And a lot like Chinese water torture.

PRESBY: And scene doctor's office if you please.

JOHN MERRICK: Lord Raincoat—I know this isn't strictly a dramatization of my life. But the part in this scene where I cure the doctor's problem by touching it to my head—I can't heal people with my head—with hemorrhoids or otherwise. Is it realistic to act like I can? What if people don't buy it? What if it offends Scientologists?

PRESBY: John. This is Broadway. There's no room here for your small-time doubts. This is the big time. And what else is this?

JOHN MERRICK:
    It's show business!

PRESBY: You're damn right—and what did I show you?

JOHN MERRICK:
    Show business
    Is a lot like diddling ponies!

PRESBY: Yes! Now, do we need to go back to the stables?

JOHN MERRICK: No. I remember. I remember! *(Shatner out the wazoo.)* I—will—heal—those—'roids!!!

(PRESBY exits, leaving JESSICA and JOHN alone onstage. JOHN kind of nods toward the area upstage of the curtain. JESSICA pulls a condom that would accommodate a small tree from her pocket, and rushes behind the curtain with JOHN. Beat. PRESBY re-enters.)

PRESBY: Good morning, saddletramps! Audition Scene, if you please my sweet festering lepers. And with technical. Full tech today!!

(Lights up on JOHN with his burlap sack, down center. He is auditioning.)

JOHN MERRICK: Thank you for seeing me. My name is Pakky Derm and I'll be doing a piece from "Les Barnyard Miserables." Ahem...

> Cows
> In your multitude.
> Scarce to be counted
> Dotting the hillside
> With lo-ing and pies...

(Over the last portion of JOHN's rendition of "Cows," JESSICA, PRESBY, and LIPSCOMB converse in the wings.)

DR. LIPSCOMB: John is truly fantastic, isn't he?

JESSICA: You ought to have him up in ya.

PRESBY: Um—don't we you have a finale to rewrite, Jimmy-poo?

JOHN MERRICK: *(Breaking character.)* We're changing the finale? Again?! We start previews in less than a week!

PRESBY: Call me silly—but I just thought it might be nice to have a finale that doesn't suck.

DR. LIPSCOMB: I can't write! It's too hard! I need a diet Mountain Dew. Can I get a diet Mountain Dew?

PRESBY: James!!! All of you!! What is this and what's it like?!

JOHN MERRICK, JESSICA, and DR. LIPSCOMB:
> It's show business!!
> And it's a lot like mad science!

> And a lot like Chinese water torture.
> And a lot like diddling ponies!

PRESBY:
> And a lot like juggling orphans!!!
> And an awful lot like waltzing with a
>   moose!

PRESBY: James. Write. My. Finale.

(Beat. LIPSCOMB pulls PRESBY to him and kisses him with great force, then runs off, quill in hand. JOHN keeps practicing looking nasty.)

PRESBY: I could feel his little tentpole.

(JESSICA is left alone backstage with PRESBY, who listens to her next speech with tragic understanding and humiliated identification.)

JESSICA: You know, sometimes love is right in front of you and all you have to do is open your eyes. But then again sometimes it isn't, and you die lonely and sad and with your useless crank permanently stained bright orange from the countless hours of eating Cheetos and beatin' it to Lifetime Original Movies.

LIPSCOMB: *(Rushing in, breathless.)* I have it!! I have the ending!!!! It doesn't suck! It doesn't suck at all!!

PRESBY: I love you!!!

JESSICA: I'm pregnant.

PRESBY: Well, there's our sequel.

> Oh, this is show business

(Spoken.) And what do you need to remember, my darling waterslides, to make tomorrow night's opening the most important thing that ever happened?

ALL:
> Show business

Is a lot like mad science!
And a lot like Chinese water torture.
And a lot like diddling ponies!
And a lot like juggling orphans!!!
And an awful lot like waltzing with a
moose!!

PRESBY:
And a lot like Corey Feldman

ALL:
Yes, a lot like Corey Feldman.
Corey Feldman!
Corey Feldman!!

PRESBY: I may cry. *(Steps directly down-stage and into a spotlight.)* Ladies and gentlemen, welcome to the Broadway premiere of "PAKKY DERM, SUPERSTAR!!" We must remind you that pregnant women and persons with heart conditions are urged not to look directly at Mr. Merrick. You'll find sickness bags underneath your seat. Now please, sit back and enjoy "PAKKY DERM, SUPERSTAR!!"

(Blackout. The music of the overture of "PAKKY DERM, SUPERSTAR" is heard. It is blatantly stolen from other famous over-tures, beginning identically to Gypsy's *over-ture, and incorporating bits from* Jesus Christ Superstar, Sweeney Todd, *and others. It fades into a spurt of fast forward sounds, which stop at the following sound montage of overlapping voice-over lines.)*

VOICE 1: Award-winning musical actor and white-hot-pop-star-of-the-moment Pakky Derm swept the Grammys last night as his debut album "Feel My Neck" walked away with every conceivable award…

VOICE 2: *(Overlapping.)* Singer/Mystic Pakky Derm took time out from his Middle Eastern concert tour to hammer out a lasting peace between Israel and Palestine. PLO leaders and Israeli officials are reported at this very moment to be frolicking hand-in-hand in the streets of Jerusalem, singing "We Go Together" from the musical *Grease*…

VOICE 3: *(Overlapping.)* Pakky Derm met with the Pope today for nine hours…

VOICE 4: *(Overlapping.)* Spiritual icon Pakky Derm took top honors at last night's Academy Awards…

VOICE 5: *(Overlapping.)* The Nobel Prize for Peace was announced today, and its recipient surprised no one…

VOICE 6: *(Overlapping.)* On the eve of his so-called "Farewell Concert" in Central Park, the debate rages on as to whether or not Senator Pakky Derm is in fact the reincarnation of Jesus Christ…

(Countless lighters flick on and off from the blackness during this chorus.)

VOICE-OVER CHORUS:
Pakky Derm
Superstar.
We all believe you will take us far.
Pakky Derm
Superstar.
Please be our king, be our lord and czar.
Pakky Derm…
Pakky Derm…
Pakky Derm…

ONE VOICE: Oh, my gosh—it's him. It's Pakky Derm!!!

(Sounds of unbridled adoration and adulation come from all corners of the space.)

ANOTHER VOICE: Master Derm, please enlighten us. How did you get to be so rich, wise, good, famous, and just cool?

(Lights up on JOHN in a horrifically gawdy outfit, ready for "Meaty." He is flanked by a horrifically sexed-up JESSICA.)

JOHN MERRICK: *(Spoken.)* Well let me tell you something, my children.

> When I was a boy,
> They called me a freak.
> But now I enjoy
> Ah-bein' unique.
> God gave me this face.
> God gave me this bod.
> God gave me this grace.
> Now I'll give you God.
>
> You got to be meaty, boy, if you want
>   to find some peace
> You got to be meaty, boy, if you want
>   to know release.
> You got to be meaty, boy, if you want
>   your pain to cease.
> I was nowhere, nothing, nada.
> 'Til God showed me what a
> Special gift I've got. Ah!
> With a couple of pounds of extra skin,
> The pearly gates part—you walk right
>   in.
> If you're meaty, boy.
> If you're meaty, boy.
> And I'm meaty, boy.
> I'm meaty, boy.
> Tell your parents, boy.
> Throw some money, boy.
> I'm meaty, boy.
> I'm meaty, boy.
> People go crazy.
> Folks get un-lazy
> And minds get hazy

(The name "PAKKY" appears in lights all over the back wall as he finishes the song.)

> For meat!
> For meat!
> For meat!

> For meat!
> For meat!!!!

(The lights go down. We hear thunderous applause.)

SCENE 11

There is massive applause. Lights come up to reveal JOHN, LIPSCOMB, PRESBY, and JESSICA on the stage of some big awards show (the "Toe-Knee" Awards). They each hold an award statue (the coveted "Toe-Knee" Award). They all smile proudly.

JOHN MERRICK: I just have to say again, that I owe it all to James Lipscomb. I wouldn't be here without him.

SLIGHTLY DISTORTED VOICE: But sometimes I think my head is so big, because it is so full of whipped cream.

JOHN MERRICK: Can't anybody hear that but me??

DR. LIPSCOMB: And I owe all this to John. He helped me realize my oldest dream. And, of course, Presbylicious.

(He takes PRESBY's hand, they gaze at one another lovingly.)

JESSICA: I have to thank both of you, but I also want to thank my mother. My real mother. I've never told you this before, but I'm adopted, and my natural mother, Catherine, was a dancer. I owe my talent to her.

(On hearing this news, JOHN and DR. LIPSCOMB look at each other warily. They soon reject the prospect.)

JOHN MERRICK and DR. LIPSCOMB: Nahhh.

(PRESBY is handed some telegrams.)

PRESBY: Oh, look, gang. *(He hands them out.)* Well, who are they from?

JESSICA: It's from the guy who pierced my ass—Simone!

DR. LIPSCOMB: It's… it's from Justin Timberlake.

JOHN MERRICK: *(Ecstatic beyond words.)* It's from Tommy Tune!!!!!!

(Everyone looks at JOHN with unchecked rapture.)

> I had the aspiration
> To reach a new station,
> That of a sensation.

HORACE:
> With his odd formation.

DR. LIPSCOMB:
> He caused fascination.

JESSICA:
> And with our relation,

JOHN MERRICK:
> I found all my dreams.

COMPANY:
> He found all his dreams.
> And gave us our dreams.
>
> Into the light from out of the dark.
> Flash in the pan, or a fluke, or a lark?
> The astounding success means his
>   quest is complete,
> For he's chosen the reason they stare
>   as he walks down the street.
> He's the Elephant Man.
> The Elephant Man.
> John Merrick.
> John Merrick.

(The COMPANY, singing with ever-increasing, almost to the point of erotic, fervor.)

> Elephant, elephant, elephant, elephant,
> Elephant, elephant, elephant, elephant,
> Elephant, elephant, elephant, elephant,
> Elephant, elephant, elephant, elephant,
> Elephant, elephant, elephant, elephant,
> Elephant, elephant, elephant, elephant,
> Elephant.
> Elephant.
> Elephant.

(JOHN gets carried away, breaks out singing. The expressions of the rest of the cast betray that this is not a rehearsed moment.)

JOHN MERRICK:
> I'm the Elephant Man.

(When this incredibly indulgent and lengthy display is finished, PRESBY walks offstage in disgust. JESSICA and LIPSCOMB attempt to carry on.)

COMPANY:
> Elephant! Elephant! Elephant! Elephant!
> Elephant!
> Elephant

(Pause. PRESBY'S voice comes from somewhere backstage.)

PRESBY: *(Offstage.)* That asshole!!!

(JOHN glances over at the COMPANY, who sing tenuously.)

> Man!!!

(Satisfied, JOHN resumes his triumphant pose.

(End.)

House of Trash

Trav S.D.

TRAV S.D. (Travis Stewart) has been writing and performing his own work for the theatre and its subsidiary arts since childhood. His professional career began as a stand-up comedian in nightclubs when he was fifteen; in 1985, he was named the Funniest Man in Rhode Island. He studied writing, directing, and acting at Trinity Repertory Conservatory in Providence, Rhode Island, and film at New York University's Tisch School of the Arts. Since 1996, he has been director of the company Mountebanks, which produces The American Vaudeville Theatre as well as Trav S.D.'s plays and performance pieces, which have been presented at HERE, Surf Reality, Todo Con Nada, The Present Company, Solo Arts, Dixon Place, the Bowery Ballroom, the Knitting Factory, and many others. Trav S.D.'s theatre criticism has appeared in The *Village Voice*, *American Theatre*, *Reason*, *Backstage*, and on the Internet on nytheatre.com.

House of Trash has never been presented in its entirety. It was first produced in a truncated version by Trav S.D. and Mountebanks on January 21, 2000, at HERE, New York City, with the following cast and credits:

Preacher Bob .... Chris Cantwell
Ma .... Tony Koplin
Toby .... Corey Einbinder
Hayseed .... James Sturtevant
Phyllis .... Gilda Konrad
Joanie .... Rev Jen Miller
Rupert/Claude .... Bill Hargett
Ray .... Jim Melloan
Babe .... Loren Kidd

Directed by: Trav S.D.
Associate Director: Scott Stiffler
Lighting Designer: Ian Hill
Sound Design: Arthur Schlenger
Props/Sets/Costumes: Allison and Jessica Ward
Fight Choreography: Mary Briggs

A second production, also of a truncated version of the play, was presented by Trav S.D. and Mountebanks on August 16, 2000 at Surf Reality, as part of the 2000 New York International Fringe Festival (John Clancy, Artistic Director; Elena K. Holy, Producing Director), with the following cast and credits:

Preacher Bob .... Trav S.D.
Ma .... Gilda Konrad
Toby .... Jon Weichsel
Hayseed/Pubert .... Hank Flynn
Angel .... Rev Jen Miller
Ray .... Robert Pinnock
Babe .... Loren Kidd
Claude .... Jim Castelleiro

Directed by: Trav S.D.
Musical Director: Beau Mansfield
Sound Design: Arthur Schlenger

Music for *House of Trash* by Trav S.D. may be obtained by contacting Travis Stewart, 650 Leonard Street, 3rd Floor, Brooklyn, NY 11222.

CHARACTERS
(in order of appearance)

JESUS H. CHRIST: Messiah

PREACHER BOB MAGGOT: Garbageman moonlighting as a
 Baptist preacher

ANGEL: Manson family member and alien abductee

PUBERT: Glue-sniffing metal-head teen

TOBY: Alienated skin-head teen in love with his teacher

HAYSEED: Farmer in love with a goat

MA: Toothless tobacco-chewing hag

RAY: First trucker in the U.S.A. with a gorilla companion

CLAUDE: Gorilla

BABE: Ray's long-suffering, neglected, and abused wife

SCENES

PROLOGUE: The Theatre

ACT ONE

    SCENE ONE: Baptist Church

    SCENE TWO: Hayloft over Preacher Bob's barn

    SCENE THREE: Hayseed's Field

    SCENE FOUR: Ma's TV Room

ACT TWO

    SCENE ONE: Toby's bedroom

    SCENE TWO: Bob's yard

    SCENE THREE: Ray and Babe's house

    SCENE FOUR: Hayloft over Bob's barn

ACT THREE

    SCENE ONE: Babe's bedroom

    SCENE TWO: Ma's TV room

    SCENE THREE: Hospital room

    SCENE FOUR: Toby's bedroom

    SCENE FIVE: Ma's TV room

ACT FOUR

    SCENE ONE: Street

    SCENE TWO: Hayseed's Field

    SCENE THREE: Hayloft over Bob's barn

    SCENE FOUR: Basement of parish house

ACT FIVE

    SCENE ONE: Bob's house

    SCENE TWO: Town dump

    SCENE THREE: Hayloft over Bob's barn

    SCENE FOUR: The Theatre

EPILOGUE: Church

SONGS

"Gates of Gehenna"
"Goat Song"
"Haunted House"
"I Like to Drive My Truck"
"Red Meat"
"Deer Caught in the Headlights"
"White Trash"

AUTHOR'S NOTE

The Trash of the play's title does not refer to "poor white trash," a designation I despise, however glibly and callously it is thrown around by upper class people of all races (from which are drawn—not coincidentally—the nation's supply of critics). It is instead the result of a metaphysical and political struggle to make sense of man's eternal and current predicament: he is an idealistic creature who is made out of pretty poor stuff. His dreams, badly realized, become horrible jokes; at his best he is only a heartbeat away from some animal act. My exploitation of poor white folk in this instance is less akin to Jerry Springer's than to Jeff Foxworthy's: the latter, at least, has the wisdom to know that he's no better a person than anyone else.

SET NOTE

A unit set will serve the entire play—perhaps a triptych of flats containing a collage of front pages from the *National Enquirer*, the *Sun*, and *Weekly World News*. Around the fringes, in the manner of folk painter Howard Finster, is scrawled text: "Goat-song = Tragidy," "God aint ded," and "Look, won't ye at Leviticus 16: 5-10." Where furniture is called for, it should have a salvaged quality: broken wooden kitchen chairs with cracked paint and the like. Two items backstage will loom over the proceedings: (1) a video screen, the largest that can be found or afforded, and (2) an American flag, made of painted cardboard.

PROLOGUE

Enter JESUS.

JESUS: Hello. I'm Jesus H. Christ, the author of this tragedy and a great many others. You know, in my over 2000 years in the salvation industry, I've consorted with a great many characters you might say were at the bottom of the barrel. In fact, some of my best friends have been thieves, prostitutes, and, yes, even tax collectors, although you're not likely to hear some of my more vociferous followers advertising that fact anytime soon. But that's neither hither nor thither. I'm here tonight after a long retirement from the theatre because the play you are about to see is completely vulgar and I wanted you to be sure that it bears my stamp of approval. You know this word? Vulgar? You just think you do. The Romans, no friends of mine, used this word to mean "common" and they meant no aspersion. St. Jerome used the Latin root for his Vulgate—a Bible for the common man. Time was when to know that someone was vulgar (that is to say, common) was to know that he would possess certain virtues: that he would be plainspoken, i.e., truthful; and disinclined to set himself above his brother: egalitarian. "Love thy neighbor": a vulgar thought from a common man: me. And if a man ever loses these virtues—if he ever ceases to be vulgar in this way—well, as one of our great vulgar actors Mr. T. in his role as B.A. Barrabas said: "I pity the fool." One last thing: this play is made out of recycled materials. The plot is loosely based on a Roman play by Terence, *The Self-Tormentor.* However the author has had the temerity to throw in his own two cents as well, so there may be considerable deterioration in quality in comparison with the original masterpiece and the work may deviate wildly from the intentions of its original author. But, then, this is also true of the Bible. And now: *House of Trash.* Enjoy!

ACT ONE
SCENE ONE

A Baptist church. Enter PREACHER BOB, a large middle-aged man with graying temples, a dark black moustache, and a thick, furry unibrow. He wears dirty white coveralls with a crucifix painted over the right front breast. He also has on work gloves and work boots.

BOB stands at a pulpit, on the front of which is a crucified teddy bear. The teddy bear is worn and mud-splattered, as though it had spent a considerable amount of time affixed to the front bumper of a truck.

BOB: Now, I been kickin' this around some,
Turnin' it over in my mind,
Mulling it over, so to speak…
Ponderin' it, studyin' it…
And I come to a conclusion.
And the conclusion I come to is this:
MAN.
I say, "Man."
A man, Everyman, mankind, call it what
    you will…
You take that man and you look at him,
And you'll see that a man,
Born on this earth by the Good Grace of
    God,
is kinda like A NEW BUILT HOUSE.
Sounds funny, don't it? But it's true.
You build yourself a new house.
It's a well-made thing:
Corners are square, joints are tight, roof
    and beams is solid
And everybody says that's Jim Dandy.
That architect, that carpenter, they did a
    bang-up job.

"Sold! I'll take it! Where do I sign?"
Time passes:
Along come a man
to take possession of this great, new, beautiful virgin house.
A laze-about bumstead who warms the sofa cushions all day
whilst his mangy pups run feral, flea-covered and foul mouthed
about the grounds
like hyperactive Hun children
and commence the long, slow process of depreciation.
I seen it happen. You have, too.
Perfectly good house at the outset, uncared for.
You know what that's about.
Shingles start falling off after awhile, paint peels. Porch sags, roof leaks, lawn gets to be a foot high, and old cars start collecting in the back yard.
Chump who owns the place, he's in watchin' TV.
That AIN'T THE BUILDER'S FAULT.
I'll say it again, brothers and sisters. It ain't the fault of the builder.
A little care here and there, a little upkeep
and that house'd be good as new for quite some time.
But for the want of a small amount of industry
this here house in question is gonna collapse.
See what I'm gettin' at here?
Parents are the builders of children.
They lay the foundation, they raise the roof,
the whole thing is a sort of a monument to their own vanity really.
I know pride's a sin but it's an easy one to forgive in this case.
Children are a worthwhile project.
And then... and then.
Look at me. I was a kid once.

Folks raised me right.
Sent me to church, put me to work, taught me the value of a dollar,
Help old ladies cross the street.
But then I came a man, and they cut me loose.
And, folks, I'm here to testify it was like a dam bust.
I went out and started discoverin'
the liquor and the fast women and the bar-rooms
and pretty soon that ole house of mine started to look a shambles.
The beams is rotted through with termites
tumble-down timbers
and the bricks is a-fallin' off the chimbley.
It makes me very sad to think
Of what I was, and what I am.
And, you know, I look at this country and I see the same thing, you know.
A sturdy and functional pine cabin
built to take anything you care to name,
blizzards, hurricanes, Indians, grizzly bears,
anything, that is, except rot from within
and that's what we got, people.
Each man his own Babylon,
200 million Sodoms and Gommorahs.
You search your wormy heart and you'll know it's true.
The City on a Hill,
The Land of the Free and the Home of the Brave,
Has become a vast rubbish heap.
and we don't need no carpenter no more.
We need a garbageman.

(Music up.)

The trashman in his own small way is Christ-like. He takes it upon himself to wallow amongst the foulest and most objectionable byproducts of our civilization. The physical evidence of all his missteps, liquor bottles, all the junk he reads, the cast-off correspondence and confessions of his illicit dallyings with the lizard. Why's he do it? In the pages of the Old Testament we read about a spot outside the Holy City of Jerusalem called Gehenna where the children of Israel sent their trash to be burned. That means that in that Holy City in them Holier than Holy times they must have had someone like me. Since times immemorial the chosen folks have leaned on a garbageman moonlighting as a holy man. You're lookin' at the first one of the new millennium.

BOB:

> Ever since the world began, there's always been a
> Whole lotta trouble 'bout a woman and a man.
> I been workin' by the Gates of Gehenna,
> Dumpin' out the ashes from the garbage can
> of God—Might sound odd
> I might sound like a jerk,
> But I love my work, saving souls.
> Now, Moses went to Sinai and he brought back the ten-a
> Commandments on the tablets which he threw like a fool.
> I been workin' by the Gates of Gehenna,
> gatherin' up the remnants of the Golden Rule.
> Righting wrongs—Singin' songs
> To God's great glory,
> It's the same old story, saving souls.
> Armageddon's coming and I'm gonna be ready,
> Ready as a man can be.
> I said a prayer to Jesus and I'll never forget he,
> Promised me a place at jubilee! Lucky me!
> Now, Daniel wasn't worried when he went in the den o'

> Lions and the angels didn't let him down.
> I been workin' by the Gates of Gehenna,
> totin' all the garbage of this doubtful town,
> far away, Judgment Day
> This is the Jeremiad
> Of the Dad from Glad, saving souls.

SCENE TWO

Hayloft over BOB's barn. PUBERT and ANGEL are sitting around, passing a joint back and forth. ANGEL is dressed head to toe in black Goth clothes. She wears lots of big rings and has a lot of patches on her jacket—pentagrams, skulls, etc. She wears severe black lipstick, nail polish, and eye makeup. Her face is powdered. PUBERT wears ripped jeans, work boots, flannel shirt, leather jacket. These are all too big and seem to hang off his body. He always wears a ridiculous amount of heavy chains, which make tons of noise when he walks around. He sports a mullet and wears a John Deere cap. He is as thin as a skeleton and has the same unibrow that Bob has.

Music: The Doors: "Soft Parade" title track. (Note: Let Jim do his preaching bit in the black, let the music start and fade the black up on "A place for me to hide.")

ANGEL: I can't wait to get back on my hog, man. It's been way too fuckin' long. It's a Harley. You know? A Harley? It's at my mom's farm, man. I hope it's alright. I covered it up with garbage bags just before I went in the joint.

PUBERT: Does your mother live nearby?

ANGEL: I'm... uh... not at liberty to say.

PUBERT: Come on. Why not?

ANGEL: I guess I can tell you this much. You ever hear of… the Manson family?

PUBERT: Sure. Hasn't everybody?

(ANGEL nods broadly, as if to convey information.)

PUBERT: No way. Your mom's one of the Mansons? Which one is she, man?

ANGEL: I can't tell you. Her identity's been a secret all this time. If someone found about her activities, Charlie could get in more trouble.

PUBERT: Whoa. "Charlie." Hey, that shit's fucked up. Charles Manson fuckin' killed people, man.

ANGEL: *(Peevishly lights a cigarette, looks away.)* All right. Pubert.

PUBERT: What? What?

ANGEL: You know so much, right?

PUBERT: Yeah, well I know enough. That shit was wrong. They fuckin' offed people with knives, man. I tell ya, it's sick.

ANGEL: Yeah. Were you there?

PUBERT: No.

ANGEL: So how do you know?

PUBERT: What do you mean? How does anybody know? Everybody… they found 'em guilty! The cops…

ANGEL: Oh, yeah. The cops. The cops! Need I say more?

PUBERT: What about that movie, where he stops that guy's watch with his mind, man?

ANGEL: Wow. You know, if you believe shit like that, you and I are headed for trouble.

PUBERT: Why would they put it out there if it weren't true?

ANGEL: Who puts out the movies, Pubert? Huh?

PUBERT: I don't know… Hollywood.

ANGEL: Yeah—Hollywood! The fucking Trilateral Commission, okay? So you have the CIA, the FBI, the National Security Agency, and the Mafia, okay, in this very intricate web of power, okay? They're the ones who put that story out there. They're the ones who tell you everything you think. How about that? Every thing you think. And you don't even know it. You're getting these subliminal messages, you know, "Buy Coca Cola," and you're made to think it's original with your own mind. But it's not. Where are the bodies of all those space aliens, man? *(Violently stabs her forefinger into her temple.)* Think about it!

PUBERT: What fuckin' space aliens?

ANGEL: Did I tell you about my abduction?

PUBERT: Who'd you abduct?

ANGEL: No, dudes, I was the abductee… and the culprits, let's just say they weren't from mother earth.

(Lights down except for a spot on Angel, who steps downstage to deliver her mini-soliloquy. Crickets chirp to set the scene.)

ANGEL: I met them cats out in the desert. Looked like FBI agents. Said their saucer was down. Just like in the books. Before I know it, this ray comes shooting out, and I'm unconscious. I wake up. And I'm on this table, and one of the guys is on top of me, putting it in me.

(Lights back to normal on PUBERT's line. ANGEL returns to his space.)

PUBERT: You had sex with an alien?

ANGEL: Yeah. I think he fertilized my ovum. The next thing I know one of the aliens is giving me, like, an abortion.

PUBERT: A space abortion.

ANGEL: Then this guy gave me this green lollipop to eat. It was good! Tasted like chicken. Then we went past Pluto. The guy showed me out the window. He showed me the moon of Pluto—Charon. I never heard of it before. When I got back, I looked it up, and there it was, so I know it really happened.

PUBERT: Whoa! what's it called?

ANGEL: Charon.

PUBERT: Whoa. Whoa, right?

ANGEL: That's what I'm sayin.' *(Sniffing some glue.)*

PUBERT: Hey, don't bogart that shit. Spread the wealth.

(Enter TOBY. TOBY is a bald, wild-eyed teenager in paramilitary clothes. He, too has the same unibrow. He is soft-spoken and shy, but the intensity and intelligence in his eyes speak volumes. He would like to murder everyone in the entire world.)

TOBY: Hey, Pubert. Whatchu doing out here?

PUBERT: Oh, hey Uncle Toby. This is my Uncle Toby. He's younger than me but he's still my uncle. We're hiding out from my dad. But don't tell nobody, okay?

TOBY: I dunno. Yer pa's awful worried about you.

PUBERT: No, he ain't. He might be upset, but if he is, it ain't on account of me. It's on account of that goat of his that's been sick. Bobo. I HATE THAT FUCKIN' GOAT!!!!

SCENE THREE

Sound of goat and small bell in the black.

Lights up on HAYSEED'S farm. HAYSEED is stringing some barbed wire on a fence post. He is a handsome man, of ruddy complexion, who wears a flannel shirt, khaki coat and trousers, paint-stained army boots, and a John Deere cap. He too sports the family unibrow. It should be clear from the outset that this is a man without a thought in his head but whatever work he happens to be doing at the time. As he works, he is approached from the other side of the fence by PREACHER BOB. HAYSEED does not cease working during the following scene.

BOB: "Something there is that doesn't love a wall." Robert Frost said that. You ever heard of Robert Frost?

HAYSEED: Interviews… people… on TV…

BOB: H'm… Nope, that's David Frost. Robert Frost was a poet. Spoke at President Kennedy's inauguration years ago.

HAYSEED: Didn't see it.

BOB: 35th President of the United States.

HAYSEED: Jack Frost.

BOB: No. Robert Frost. There is no Jack Frost.

HAYSEED: There ain't?

BOB: No.

HAYSEED: Then how come they say "Quicker'n you can say 'Jack Frost'"?

BOB: That's Jack Robinson.

HAYSEED: They let a baseball player speak at the President's inaug'ral?

BOB: What baseball player?

HAYSEED: Jackie Robinson!

BOB: No. Forget it.

HAYSEED: *(Pause.)* Roger Wilco!

BOB: "A rose by any other name would smell as sweet." That's Shakespeare.

HAYSEED: Yut.

BOB: "A rose is a rose is a rose." That's Gertrude Stein. I bet you're wondering how I know all this.

HAYSEED: Yut.

BOB: A book of quotations fell out of a dumpster while we were emptying it into the truck the other day. I've been reading bits and pieces in the bathroom whenever I take a shit.

HAYSEED: More power to ya.

BOB: "Knowledge is power." Who said that?

HAYSEED: Don't know. Who?

BOB: I don't know, either. I was asking you! *(Pause.)* I'm talkin' trash and I know it. Found it in the trash and I'm talkin' trash. Don't pay it no mind. *(Pause.)* See, uh, thing is, me and your Ma is kinda worried about this thing with Pubert, Hayseed. Seems to have gotcha all wound up.

HAYSEED: Yut.

BOB: We know he's been missing. Wanna tell me what's goin' on?

HAYSEED: Don't know.

BOB: Well, somebody knows. You been working out here day and night. Gonna give yourself a heart attack, you keep it up. You hear?

HAYSEED: Bobo's got goat leukemia. Dr. Roy give him a month to live. Said his hair's just gonna keep coming out. Soon he won't be able to "bah" and I'll have to spoon feed him and wipe the pus off his beard.

BOB: Well, if he's all that sick, he don't need any barbed wire. *(Pause.)* I wasn't going to bring this up, but you're spending entirely too much time out here with this goat. People are beginning to talk. Dammit, Hayseed, Bobo's a goat and a goat is a goat but Pubert's your own flesh and blood and I can just see that's what's eatin' ya. You wanna get it off yer chest? Now, I'm just a garbageman moonlighting as a Baptist preacher, but I got two perfectly good ears and more'n my share of horse sense so if you're in a pickle, spill it, and we'll see if we can't jerry-rig some kinda Rube Goldberg device to make things back to hunky.

HAYSEED: Well, it's kinder like this…

> I got a kid, he makes me tense.
> Hey, nanny, nanny, no.
> I close the gate, he jumps the fence.
> Hey, nanny, nanny, no.
>
> Hey, nanny, nanny, nanny.
> Hey, nanny, nanny, no.
> Hey, nanny, nanny, nanny.
> Hey, nanny, nanny, no.
>
> We butt heads from dawn to dusk.
> Hey, nanny, nanny, no.
> Get so angry I could bust.
> Hey, nanny, nanny, no.
>
> Hey, nanny, nanny, nanny.
> Hey, nanny, nanny, no.
> Hey, nanny, nanny, nanny.
> Hey, nanny, nanny, no.
>
> I slave over pots and pans.
> Hey, nanny, nanny, no.

But he only eats tin cans.
Hey, nanny, nanny, no.

Hey, nanny, nanny, nanny.
Hey, nanny, nanny, no.
Hey, nanny, nanny, nanny.
Hey, nanny, nanny, no.

That damn kid, he makes me swoon.
Hey, nanny, nanny, no.
He'll lose his footing one day soon.
Hey, nanny, nanny, no.

BOB: Don't you fret. We'll help you straighten out Pubert.

HAYSEED: I was talkin' about Bobo.

SCENE FOUR

TV room. TV screen—a horrible succession of images and sounds, a sort of compendium of the most horrible bits from slasher movies; Nazi documentaries; the worst, most foulmouthed dialogue, etc. Must be so extreme as to be comical, and it would be best if the bits are obscure—recognition of the bits would be too distracting.

MA, a toothless hillbilly woman with a bit of white beard and the family unibrow sits watching TV. There is something primitive, almost Neanderthal about her face. She wears a cotton dress made out of patches, a shawl, and house-slippers. Her hair is scraggly and gray, with a couple of bobby pins shoved in as her maximum gesture of femininity. She periodically spits tobacco into a coffee can she is holding.

BOB: How do you watch that stuff, Ma?

MA: It's easy.

BOB: Shesh. Tsk. My favorite movie is *Shane*. How come they don't make 'em like that no more?

MA: It's just somethin' to have on to pass the time.

BOB: Why don't you plant flowers or somethin' useful?

MA: Flowers smell like piss. What are you in here for anyway? I can't follow the story.

BOB: Story?! Well if you can peel yerself away from that demolition derby I'll tell ya a story that'll put milk back in yer paps.

MA: Better be good.

BOB: Hayseed's Pubert done run off with some painty-faced harlot from the Satan cult.

MA: Satan cult? Now how do you know that?

BOB: Hayseed found 'em neckin' and smokin' pot up at the college when he went up to buy fertilizer. Got so ticked off he hauled off and whupped Pube, and Pube stole off with this floozy. Twenty-five-year older, she is. Said she's one of these Goths like on *20/20* and a dead ringer for Marilyn Manson. Tattooed from head to toe like a Feejee cannibal, with an earring on her lip, and pentygrams like polka dots on a clown's overcoat.

MA: Pentygrams, eh?

BOB: Five-pointed emblem of the Satanic cult people. Steal children from kindergartens, rape 'em, and then erase their memory so they think nothin' ever happened. For all I know it happened to me. (*Shudders.*) Diabolical! Hayseed ain't liftin' a finger to save that boy's soul. He's up to his elbows in that goat of his. You'd think he'd pull his hand out his ass for two seconds and listen to the word of God. Communication. That's what it is. That's what I'm always telling the families down at the parish. You don't have trust in a family. Something's gone bust. Pubert may have felt he had something he needed to talk about, but he felt he couldn't bring it up, he couldn't discuss it with his father. So he went off and did his own dirty thing anyway. See what I mean? Communication.

MA: Why don't you tell that to Hayseed?

BOB: No, I couldn't do that.

MA: Once again you're barking up the wrong tree, Bob Maggot.

(Spooky music and wind sound comes up.)

MA: *(Gazing into space.)* Sure as I'm settin' here Pubert's dead and in a gutter some place, his dead eyes starin' face down in a muddy tire track.

BOB: Now just how do you know that?

MA: The TV.

BOB: It was on TV?

MA: There was a disturbance in the reception. A woman feels these things. He's crossed over into the spirit world.

BOB: Ma, I said it before and I'll say it again. You're touched in the head.

ACT TWO
SCENE ONE

TOBY's room. TOBY is bouncing a tennis ball against the wall. Knock at door.

MA: *(Off.)* Toby, what's bangin' in there?

TOBY: I'm bouncin' a tennis ball.

MA: *(Off.)* Open this door!

(TOBY opens the door. MA enters, plucking a chicken.)

MA: What'd I tell you about lyin'?

TOBY: What?

MA: That was the headboard of your bed bangin' against the wall there.

TOBY: No it wasn't!

MA: Don't LIE to me—

TOBY: Look at my bed! My bed's all made up!

MA: I know every time you tell a lie. I see two "L"s in your eyes.

TOBY: Ma, Ma, watch. Listen.

(TOBY throws the tennis ball against the wall once and catches it.)

TOBY: See?

MA: *(Pause.)* You must think I'm a complete idiot. I grew up with eight brothers. I know what jerkin' off sounds like!

TOBY: Ma, I gotta tell you something.

MA: You better tell me you're sorry.

TOBY: For what?

MA: Look, you've never given me an ounce of trouble in all your sixteen years. If you're gonna start now…

TOBY: Ma, Pubert's not dead.

MA: What did you say?

TOBY: Pubert's not a ghost. He's out in the barn. He's got a girlfriend up—

MA: Of all the low-down, sneaky, no-account ways to do.

TOBY: The two of them were up there having sex and smoking pot.

MA: I don't believe it.

TOBY: I think she's one of the Manson family.

MA: I never heard anything so disgusting in all my life.

TOBY: Yeah, it was pretty disgusting.

MA: Imagine telling me a lie like that just to get yourself off the hook. You ought to be ashamed of yourself! *(Begins hitting him with the chicken about the shoulders.)* Trashing the good name of the deceased!

TOBY: Pubert's not dead!

MA: *(Still hitting him.)* Lyin' to me about haints!

TOBY: There are no such things as ghosts!

MA: *(Still hitting him.)* Jerking off all hours of the day!

TOBY: I don't jerk off!

MA: *(One final swat.)* And lying about that! You'd best get your mind right. I'm tellin' your father and you just better hope he ain't wearin' the belt with the lone star buckle. You goddamn weirdo! Sick, perverted faggot! *(Starts to go, then comes back.)* And clean up this room! It looks like a pigsty! *(Exits.)*

TOBY: And you'd know about sties, wouldn't you? Ignorant old bearded sow. I'd like to carve her ears back for her. Close to the skull. Then see what she thought about the state of my room, with a hole running blood on each side of her head. My room. MY room! A mess, yes... littered with books and pamphlets and papers an unlettered heifer like herself could never hope to understand with her third grade education and her lifetime membership in the Flat Earth Society. The width, the depth and breadth of her ignorance would form a maw so titanic it could swallow the whole solar system—a solar system which she doesn't even believe exists! If the universe is this roomful of light, and people's brains are these identical keyholes—how is it that some let a shaft of light pass through and others eclipse it? What is the unseen obstruction? Brains look the same, weigh the same, have the same number of folds, yet some mystery antic of nature would produce in one the greater portion of sentience and leave the other retarded. And there is no rhyme or reason, no combination of ingredients that will produce new intellect in uniformity. Men are not Mendel's peas which can be bred with certainty. Idiots! Imbeciles! Phrenological freaks and pious pinheads! Mongoloids, monsters, the scum, the dross, the dregs. Mankind is the only species that would keep them alive at the general expense. We feed them, clothe them, give them vaccines. And all the while, all the while, they scorn us, laugh at us, belittle our learning and call us freaks. But I say to you that it is you who are the freaks, you who are the aberrations, who are trapped in the bodies of men but not endowed with a man's faculty to reason. You jokes, you puppets, you weak-kneed and watery-eyed animals in the clothing of men. Someone invented the loom for those clothes you put on. You, who don't even know what a loom is! The question is, why? In the world of beasts, the runt gets the last meat on the carcass, sickens and dies. The beast man keeps his cerebral runts alive—nurtures them, fattens them—makes them king! Loves them and lives with them. Calls them father, mother, brother! And much to his cost. For they procreate, they populate the earth, poison the atmosphere with their flatulence. This limp strain of longhaired ape would strangle the planet and produce nothing to sustain it except more filthy unwashed, undifferentiated hordes of upright locusts. Taking us down with them. We who have carried them on our backs for thirty centuries. The time has come to withdraw that which we have so graciously decided to share with the human race: the wheel, fire, the printing press, rockets to the moon. Those who would live in our company from now must pass a simple intelligence test. And if you don't pass, you shall be cast out, as in the allegory of Eden. Let them spurn us and laugh at our books and slide rules while they shiver naked in the snow, wild-eyed with hunger at the International Concentration Camp at Antarctica! Let them see if they can invent fire a second time, these hicks and morons and societal leeches. They'll see just how funny the man in the horn-rimmed spectacles is. They'll realize to their cost that they need us, but it will be too late. We shall bale their corpses into bricks and build a ziggurat in their memory that will dwarf the highest city skyscraper!

SCENE TWO

Music: Perverted version of "The Andy Griffith Show" theme.

Immediately after. TOBY is now outside. Enter PREACHER BOB with a shotgun. He wears a hunting cap, reflecting aviator shades, and t-shirt that says something like "I'm Not a Hunter, I'm a Wildlife Population Control Specialist." He holds the gun down, but it is roughly pointing at TOBY.

BOB: Toby, I'd like to have a word with you.

TOBY: *(Eying the gun apprehensively.)* Uh, hi, Dad.

BOB: Toby, I've just been talking to your mother.

TOBY: You have?

BOB: I have. And I must say she told me some things I'm not too pleased about.

TOBY: She did?

BOB: She did. You know what I'm talking about?

TOBY: I think I probably do. Yes, sir.

BOB: You know what it says in Leviticus about doin' that?

TOBY: I didn't do it.

BOB: You know the eighth commandment, right? Thou shalt not bear false witness—?

TOBY: I'm telling the truth.

BOB: You don't have to lie. We all know everybody does it. I'm just telling you not to do it. You're body's a temple, Tobias. Don't defile it. You've been pollutin' your... temple. What do you think I should do about it?

TOBY: I honestly don't know, sir, since I keep telling you—

BOB: You don't? You have any ideas?

TOBY: No, sir.

BOB: You don't. Toby, I always say let the punishment fit the crime. You see this gun?

TOBY: *(Gulps.)* That gun?

BOB: Yes.

TOBY: Yes, I see that gun.

BOB: Know what it's for?

TOBY: Uh, I'm not sure.

BOB: Well, you'll know soon enough.

(Cocks the gun. Long pause.)

BOB: Son, it's for you.

TOBY: Me?

BOB: That's right. I was waiting for the right time to give it to you. I didn't think it arrived yet, but from the sound of what your mother tells me, I think you need a hobby. A good, clean hobby, if you catch my drift. I don't want to get into the details with you. You know what it is you been up to. Just know that from now on, if you feel the need to shoot your load, this is the gun you do it with. You get me?

TOBY: Uh, I don't think I'm comfortable with the idea of firearms.

BOB: Don't be ridiculous! Of course you are! It's in your blood, son. Every man in this family from the time guns come to merry ole England had hisself one of these and knew how to fire it off.

TOBY: Yeah, but you said killing is wrong.

BOB: I didn't say kill anyone with it, did I? It's for sport!

TOBY: Sport? How do you use a gun for sport?

BOB: You kill rabbits with it. Now son, this here is a thirty aught six and don't you worry about a thing. I'll teach you everything a young man needs to know about cleaning, loading, carrying, aiming, and shooting.

TOBY: Aiming and shooting.

BOB: It's okay to be squeamish. I was at first, too, but then I was only eight years old. My dad had me brace myself against a beam in the barn before I fired. Broke my shoulder, but I loved every minute of it.

TOBY: Dad, I really think this is a bad idea.

BOB: Oh, you do, do you? Huh. You think this is a bad idea. Well, you know what? You don't have no say in it, mister. You're gonna learn to fire off this gun and you're gonna keep it and you're gonna like it. You know why? Because it's gonna grow on ya. No one likes guns at first blush, boy! They're what you might call an acquired taste! But they're also a necessary evil. 'Course, we don't need to get food with 'em anymore, and there ain't any more Indians or Mexicans or anything. But a well-regulated militia being necessary to the security of a free state, the right of the people to keep and bear arms shall not be infringed.

TOBY: What's that mean?

BOB: It means that gun may be necessary some day to protect yourself from, oh, I don't know... the Federal Government...

TOBY: The government? But you're always talking to me about patriotism. "My country, right or wrong," you said.

BOB: I am, that's right. I firmly believe that. You should do whatever the government tells you to do.

TOBY: But you want to shoot at government agents.

BOB: That's right.

TOBY: How come?

BOB: I hate 'em. I don't believe the government ought to interfere in people's business.

TOBY: *(Pause. Dryly.)* I'm a little confused.

BOB: Try not to think about it. I haven't thought it completely through myself. There remains one unambiguous and universal employment for domestic firearms, however. Puttin' holes in criminals.

We live on the modern frontier, Tobias, with our own modern day Jesse Jameses roamin' free to terrorize decent, law-abidin' citzens. Your nephew Pubert's one of 'em.

TOBY: A law-abiding citizen?

BOB: Aw, you're funnin' me now. You know as well as I do your nephew Pubert's a unregenerate criminal-type on a one-way path to jail, the electric chair, and hell. Jesse James reincarnated in a Budweiser t-shirt.

TOBY: Then you don't think he's a ghost?

BOB: A ghost! Toby, I love and respect your mother, but she's a complete crack-pot whose opinion ain't worth the mud pigs flop in. First and foremost, there's no such thing as ghosts.

TOBY: I'm relieved to hear you say that.

BOB: Sure! Everybody knows that when you die, you turn into an angel!

TOBY: Oh. Pa, I got something to tell you. I know where Pubert is. He's in the old hayloft in our barn. Some woman's with him. They been there since this last night.

BOB: Over our barn? Why didn't you say something, boy? His pa's worried sick.

(TOBY opens his mouth to talk—)

BOB: Well, you told me now. That's the important thing. Well, he's got the gall bringing that woman over here, that's all I can say. His twenty-five-year-old concu-bine, so they can have their roll in the hay over to grandpa's place. Hey? Like this is the "Sex Motel." House of a preacher? They're out there fornicating like a couple of half-baked jackrabbits. Say! What'd you let 'em do a thing like that for, anyhow? Lettin' the two of them fornicate out there

like a couple of half-baked jackrabbits?

(TOBY opens his mouth to talk—)

BOB: Strong arm ya, did they? Knowin' Pubert, he probably pulled a knife on ya. Sure. Big knife. Six-inch Bowie knife. he got a knife like that. I give it to him for Christmas. He do that to ya?

(TOBY opens his mouth to talk—)

BOB: Lord forgive that boy. Lord forgive that monstrous, wild boy. Imagine a thing like that. Usin' a knife like that on his own uncle. A six-inch Bowie knife that's for huntin' and fishin' and a-scrapin' rust off the tractor to commit violence against his own kin. He'll answer for that, I can tell ya. He was drinkin', I suppose.

(TOBY opens his mouth to talk—)

BOB: Oh, I can see the whole thing, in living color. Drunk on Wild Turkey. So blind drunk he can hardly stand. High on that coke, too. The two of them. Out of their minds, insensible—reckless. So much so that they stop off at Grandpa's, one door over from Hayseed's farm so they can go for a roll in the hay, so doped up they can't hardly stand. That hayloft air— I know it. It's like another drug itself. Thick, sweet, hot, moist. Goes right to the head. Sure, I remember. Your eyes get watery and irritated up there. Your nos-trils get greedy for it, open right up wide. Skin gets all flush, excited. And it's hot up there in that hayloft! Hundred and five degrees. You work up a sweat not doin' nothin'. Just standin' there. Just standin' there not doin' nothin'. Just talkin'. Talkin' about nothin'. So you're not doin' noth-ing, just standin' there not doin' nothing' and ya ain't talkin' about nothing. Just nothin'. That's all yer talkin' about. Nothin'! It's a game you play, the two of ya. Neither one's thinkin' about the words. Just waitin' to see how it'll happen. Who'll hop on who. Heart's just thumpin', man. Like there's a little guy bangin' on the inside of your chest, yellin' "Let me out!" And the two of you, you're drunk on Wild Turkey, so you just gotta kinda stumble into her, and the two of you, you just go, tumblin' gentle into the hay, laughing and kissin' them whiskey-flavored kisses. That's how it happens. Bury your face in her sweaty neck there, and just kinda sloppily slidin' your mouth up and down from her ear to her shoulder. Just like eatin' watermelon. Once you get down on that shoulder, boy, why it's only a matter of time afore she unbuttons her damn shirt herself. You don't have to do a thing, don't have to think about a thing. Your body does the whole trick itself. Your mind don't have to move a muscle. Soon her jeans are slidin' down them sweaty slim legs, boy. By God, she's a woman, boy! WHHOOOOEEEEE! YEAH! Lookee thar! Hell! She don't have to tell you twice. When you're eighteen, there ain't no amount of whiskey gonna make Johnny fall down. So you git on in there and ya, ya DO YER BIDNESS! YES, SIR!!!

(In his excitement, BOB fires the shotgun off in the air. There is a startled pause as the report from the rifle fades to silence.)

BOB: *(A little embarrassed.)* I'd better get out there and put a stop to this thing before them two kids give me a heart attack! Here, hold this.

(BOB hands the gun to TOBY and heads offstage.)

TOBY: Do you think I could be the heroic type, dad? I want to do good. I want to be a great man, a great scientist, a great hero. Does that mean I'm still a baby?

When I was little, you used to sing to me when no one was around. Remember? That rich, bashful bass whispering to me. You sang "Ole Black Joe" and "The Wabash Cannonball" and "Boil That Cabbage Down." "Short'nin' Bread." "Froggy Went A-Courtin'" or maybe that was a dream. I dreamed you played the banjo to me one night, and I woke up crying. I dreamed you tried to strangle me and I woke up crying that time, too. What I want to know is, what's it gonna be?

> I live in a Haunted House. I live in a funeral home.
> Peeling paint upon the walls. Dust around this family's bones.
> Haunted House. Haunted House.
> We don't get good food to eat. We don't have nice clothes to wear.
> It's the ugliest house on the street. No one comes to visit us there.
> This Haunted House, Haunted House.
> Take me to the luscious land of the living—I deserve it.
> I'm too young for the eulogies they're giving. I haven't earned it.
> Deep within my attic room, you might hear me pace the floor.
> I'm sick of living in a tomb. I can't take it anymore.
> This Haunted House, Haunted House.
> I live in a Haunted House, I live in a trailer park.
> Black velvet painting on the walls, and a dashboard Jesus that glows in the dark,
> Haunted House, Haunted House.

SCENE THREE

RAY and BABE's house. RAY, a bit of a dude, is teasing CLAUDE, his gorilla, with a beer.

Ray wears snazzy Western duds: ten-gallon hat, pointed cowboy boots, open collar Western shirt, leather vest, jeans, and a belt with an enormous decorative buckle. He's in his early forties. Has a beard and a beer gut.

RAY: Come on, Claude. Come on. Come get the Michelob.

(CLAUDE takes the beer and starts to drink.)

RAY: *(Laughs.)* You hot shit!

(Enter BABE, smoking a cigarette. She is wearing provocative lingerie, but is a little disheveled—slightly drunk. She, too, is in her early forties. A former beauty, time has been cruel to her.)

BABE: I don't know who's the bigger animal, you or him. I told you I didn't want that gorilla in the house.

RAY: It's my house. I'll bring whoever I want in.

BABE: Look: I pay half the bills and you are gone ninety percent of the time. I think I'm entitled not to have a gorilla in my own goddamn house! Someday I'm liable to up and sell that thing when you're not looking. Then you'll know I mean business.

RAY: You do, and I'll break every bone in your goddamn body. You understand? Huh? Don't you listen to her, Claude baby. She's just an old stinker, that's all.

BABE: Let's go, Clyde.

RAY: It's "Claude." How many times I gotta tell ya, it's Claude, after the late great truckin' actor Claude Atkins! Can't you get that through your head?!

BABE: Yeah, I'm sorry. I must be ignorant or something. I'm not up on all these trucker movies.

RAY: *(Rolling his eyes.)* It's a TV show, Babe! "B.J. and the Bear." Where were you during the great truckin' heyday of the mid- to late seventies?

BABE: Going to college, Ray. I suppose that makes me an idiot, too.

RAY: *(Holding up his hands, as if to say "You said it, I didn't.")* Hey…

BABE: That was some show, I guess, where a truck driver had a gorilla.

RAY: It was a chimp.

BABE: And Clint Eastwood was the truck driver.

RAY: No, no! Goddamn it, Babe, you just do this to piss me off! Clint Eastwood was in the *Every Which Way But Loose* movies!

BABE: And he had a gorilla.

RAY: He had an ourang-atang! I have a gorilla!

BABE: *(Sarcastically.)* Oh, you do?

RAY: Yes! I'm the first truck driver in the country with a gorilla companion. Claude Atkins had a chimp, Clint Eastwood had an ourang-atang, but I'm the first truck driver in the whole goddamn country with a gorilla! Doesn't that mean anything to you?

BABE: Oh, yes, shit loads. I got a husband who can't get it up, but gives valentines and bottles of Michelob to one of the great apes.

RAY: He is great. He is. You're just making fun of him, I know. It's just like a woman to downgrade a man's accomplishments.

BABE: So you're a pioneer, is that it?

RAY: You're damn straight. And one day, somebody's gonna see that, and write me up in the history books.

BABE: So that's what American history's come down to. It's a sad commentary, Ray. Populate a continent. Put a man on the moon. First trucker with his own gorilla.

RAY: You knew what you were getting into when you married me.

BABE: Wait: Ray, let me just… say this, so there'll be no confusion about it in the future. Never, for an instant, for a second, for a millisecond, for a nanosecond, in my wildest dreams, when I stood at that altar in Las Vegas did I picture a gorilla, a gorilla shitting up my living room fifteen years down the line!

RAY: What are you saying? You saying you made a mistake?

BABE: I'm not saying anything, Ray. Not a thing.

RAY: Good. We'll be out of here soon enough. Me and Claude have a load of cigarettes in the rig we got to get to Wilmington by tomorrow afternoon.

BABE: "Keep your eyes on the road, and your hands upon the wheel." *(Exits.)*

RAY: Yeah, you'd like me to jack-knife, wouldn't ya? Women, Claude. You're lucky, you don't have to deal with 'em. They're shaky machines, at best. Step on the breaks—ya don't stop. Step on the gas, ya got no idea how much acceleration you're gonna get. They're always breaking down. And they need a tune-up once a month. That woman can laugh at me, all she wants—but she'll never be to me as sweet, as fine, and out-and-out dependable as an eighteen wheeler.

> Pounding through the night, hammer to the floor,
> I've never ever been in love, with my big rig more—than now.

> Holy Jesus, Joseph, Mary, Tom, Dick, and Harry—Holy Cow.
> I like to drive my truck, hucketa, hucketa, hucketa, huck.
> I like to drive my truck, hucketa, hucketa, hucketa, huck.
> I must admit I'm stuck on the diesel engine's roar.
> My truck is my good buddy, and that's a big ten four.
> Freewheelin' down the freeway, on each of eighteen wheels,
> And I got lots of leeway to do whatever feels—real and right.
> Like drivin', drinkin', getting stinkin' drunk and drivin' through the night.
> I like to drive my truck, hucketa, hucketa, hucketa, huck.
> I like to drive my truck, hucketa, hucketa, hucketa, huck.
> I can't believe my luck, no, I could not ask for more.
> My truck is my good buddy, and that's a big ten four.
> I got me a gorilla, he rides in all my cabs.
> I helped him join the Teamsters, he helps me beat up scabs—lawdy lawd.
> Yes, we have no bananas—Just kiddin', Claude.
> I like to drive my truck, hucketa, hucketa, hucketa, huck.
> I like to drive my truck, hucketa, hucketa, hucketa, huck.
> I don't give a fuck about no hussy or no whore.
> My truck is my good buddy, and that's a big ten four.

(The doorbell rings.)

RAY: I'll get it, Claude.

(RAY opens the door. It is TOBY, with books.)

RAY: Yeah?

TOBY: I'm here to see Mrs. LeBlanc.

RAY: Yeah? Well, I'm Mr. LeBlanc. *(Points to CLAUDE.)* That's Mrs. LeBlanc! *(Pause.)* No, I'm just funnin' ya. That there's a gorilla.

TOBY: No kiddin'? Housepet?

RAY: Truckpet.

TOBY: Is he housebroken?

RAY: Truckbroken.

TOBY: I can see where keeping a gorilla in your truck forces you to re-invent the language.

RAY: You want a beer?

TOBY: I'm sixteen.

RAY: I'm sorry, I haven't got any vodka.

TOBY: That's all right. Say, if you don't mind, I'm here to see Mrs. LeBlanc.

RAY: That's right. Who may I say is calling?

TOBY: I'm Tobias Maggot. Your wife's been tutoring me in the gifted student program.

RAY: What's that mean, retarded, something like that?

TOBY: Something like that.

RAY: *(Sizing him up.)* No... no... you ain't retarded. I don't believe you're one bit retarded.

TOBY: Well... give me time.

RAY: So you're bright, then.

TOBY: So bright my mama calls me "sonny."

RAY: I'll go get Mrs. LeBlanc.

TOBY: Thank you.

(Exit RAY. TOBY eyes CLAUDE warily. CLAUDE, curious, moves slightly toward him. TOBY backs cautiously away. CLAUDE moves closer. TOBY puts a sofa between himself and CLAUDE. CLAUDE grabs a book and starts to play with it. He sits down and starts to read. TOBY watches in awe. Enter RAY and BABE.)

BABE: Toby! Oh, Toby, I'm sorry he left you in here with the ape. Ray, how could you do that?

RAY: *(To BABE, with triumph.)* Look! He's readin'! I told you Claude's got talent! You just have to draw him out!

BABE: I'd like to draw his ass out the front door.

RAY: *(Waving her away with his hand.)* Ah!

(RAY gives BABE a peck on the cheek.)

RAY: We're goin'. See you in a couple of days.

BABE: I'll keep a light burning in the window.

RAY: Oh, don't bother your head about no light. Just set this kid on the window-sill. He's so bright his ma calls him "sonny." Come on, Claude.

(Exit RAY and CLAUDE. BABE and TOBY stand there while the sound of the rig disappears in the distance. Pause.)

TOBY: Your husband, he's...

BABE: An asshole.

TOBY: Well, uh... I just don't get...

BABE: How we came to be married?

TOBY: Yeah.

BABE: It's a long story. I have always had serious reservations about my husband Ray, from the moment I laid eyes on him. Yet, when we were younger, he possessed one beguiling feature which, when employed to its best advantage, would occasionally fill me with a rapture that could be relied upon to blot out every ugly, beastly quality the brute possessed. In short, he was prodigiously endowed, and blessed with a fiery animal spirit. Late at night, he would mount me like the mechanical bull at Gilley's, grab a handful of my hair and stick his willy through a hole in his ripped jeans into my grateful and waiting pudenda. Then he'd ram it upstairs repeatedly 'til I'd swear to sweet Jesus he'd cleave me in twain. Up and down, up and down, the bed'd be bouncing like a Puerto Rican low-rider. And Dad'd yell up, "What are you kids doing' up there?" And I'd say, "Watchin' 'Hee Haw,' dad!" And he'd say, "Well, it ain't that funny." He was a stupid son-of-a-bitch. And, man, those were my Saturday nights for a while, all through high school. Ray brought me to heights of ecstasy in my teenage years I never thought it possible for a human being to achieve. I married him for those moments.

TOBY: And now?

BABE: Poor thing just kinda swings there like Dumbo's trunk.

TOBY: I think you deserve better than that.

BABE: Like what?

TOBY: Like, I dunno. Somebody new. Someone whose body's not riddled with liver spots, whose chest doesn't rattle when he breathes, whose nerves haven't been shot through drugs and drink. A man who can read the warning label on a bottle of Drano and do simple sums without frowning. Someone who's not a disgusting swine unfit to wash the shit out of your underwear like Ray is. *(Steps into spotlight.)* You need a man… a boy, really… perhaps the only person you can really talk to in this whole town. Someone who tried to understand your grown-up problems from his limited vantage point at your feet. Someone who's sat in the front row just so he wouldn't have to squint to stare at you. Who's learned more from the husky warm buzz of your voice and flutter of your eyelids than all textbook assignments put together. Who's traced the contour of your neck, the base of your jaw, your slender shoulders again and again until he memorized you, could do a sculpture of you. Who would only bring you flowers but he knows that they're mere piss to your perfume. Who would learn to play the harp for you if you decided you liked music. Who would powder the ground before you as you walked with the pulverized bones of royalty. Who would exterminate the world at your whim. Who would raze holy temples to make you a home. Who would club baby harp seals to make you a coat. Who hates the world, hates everything, but loves you, adores you, needs you and everything you stand for, everything you represent. Who would die for you, KILL for you. Someone like… like… that.

BABE: *(Pause.)* You have a rich fantasy life, Toby. There's nobody out there like that… is there?

SCENE FOUR

Hayloft. PUBERT and ANGEL are getting it on. Enter BOB, carrying a bible and wearing lots of stars and bars regalia. He watches

them for a bit. Then there is the sound of
gunfire from outside. The kids jump apart.

BOB: (Diplomatically—or nervously—
looks away as the two pull up their pants.)
That's Toby! You follow your uncle's example, Pube, and you can't go far wrong,
you know. Got himself a hobby. Hobbies
are the important thing. Some people go
fishing, I tell people how to run their lives
based on the wisdom in a very old book.
Why don't you kids take a moment now
and join your old grandpa as we peruse a
few helpful passages?

PUBERT: No, sir. don't wanna.

BOB: "Don't wanna." I guess you just
wanna worship Satan.

ANGEL: What makes you say that?

BOB: Oh, I don't know. Them pentagrams mostly.

ANGEL: It's just a shape, man.

BOB: No such thing, sister. It's a powerful symbol of evil. People should be careful who wear such things on their clothes.
(Realizes he is covered in Confederate signs,
then shakes it off.)

  I won't tell you how to run your life,
      sir.
  But I really must convince you life is
      sweet.
  Otherwise the whole thing has no pur-
      pose
  Otherwise we're piles of red meat,
  Piles of red meat, piles of meat.
  I don't say you gotta go to Jesus.
  Nothing quite so pat or quite so neat.
  All I say is do good unto others
  Or brother you're a pile of red meat.
  Pile of red meat, pile of red meat.
  When you die, what's there left of you?
  A lump of bone and gristle and inani-

  mate sinew.
  When you die, who's got control of
      you?
  Where is the soul of you? Where is
      the soul of you?
  I don't say you always got to smile.
  Or shake the hand of every man you
      meet
  But we're only here for such a little
      while
  Why spend it as a pile of red meat?
  Pile of read meat, pile of red meat.
  When you die, what's there left of you?
  A lump of bone and gristle and inani-
      mate sinew.
  When you die, who's got control of
      you?
  Where is the soul of you? Where is
      the soul of you?
  I don't say you always got to smile.
  Or pat the back of everyone you meet
  But we're only here for such a little
      while
  Why spend it as a pile of red meat?
  Pile of read meat, pile of red meat.

ACT THREE
SCENE ONE

BABE's bedroom. BABE and SOMEBODY
are sleeping in the bed. It is after dark. A sweep
of headlights across the wall and the sound
of a rig pulling in. A door opens and shuts.
RAY enters the room and flips on the light.

RAY: So!

(BABE bolts up, fearful. Pause. CLAUDE
sits up.)

RAY: (Shocked.) Claude!

(CLAUDE jumps out the window. RAY
starts to creep toward BABE menacingly.)

RAY: You done read your last book, college.

(BABE stands up on the bed. She backs up as he approaches. Aaron Copland's "Fanfare for the Common Man" and sound effects from a wrestling match come up. A series of alternating blackouts and tableaux wherein BABE and RAY are engaged in various wrestling holds, culminating in RAY's pinning of BABE.)

SCENE TWO

MA watching pro wrestling—sound effect segue from previous scene. Enter BOB.

BOB: Ma, I—

MA: Goddamn it, Bob, right in the middle of wrasslin'!

BOB: Sorry.

(BOB bows out. Fade out.

(Fade in, the TV is on something else—the same violent programming from previous scene. BOB re-enters.)

BOB: Ma, I think it's time we sent Pubert home.

MA: Still say he's alive, huh? Still have that theory?

BOB: What do you mean? I just seen him out in the barn.

MA: Ectoplasm…

BOB: Ma, I mean it, one more time and it's back to the state farm.

MA: *(Relenting.)* It would be just like that demon-seed to FAKE bein' a haint to cast doubt on my skills as a psychic.

BOB: The Lord hates a conjurer, ma.

MA: Is that what you come in to say?

BOB: Pubert oughtta be back with Hayseed.

MA: Then put the fear of God into him.

BOB: I tried that, but everybody just got confused.

MA: Then put the fear of man into him.

BOB: What are you jabberin' about?

MA: Spook him. Give him the willys. Show him how it really is in the world. Wolves! Hire someone to come after him, stalk him like a deer. He'll be back to his pa in no time, shakin' in his boots. He'll shit his drawers!

BOB: *(Considering it.)* That don't seem the most straightforward way to me.

MA: You asked me and there's your answer. This here's a cure that'll stick. If it's done right it'll keep him down on the farm the rest of his life.

BOB: H'm, there's a troubled man over at the parish who sorta owes me a favor. He might do something like this. Still… I don't know. I tell ya, Ma, I used to know what right was. I did. Nowadays I don't even know how to spell it. You take that "Rite-Aid." You tellin' me that that $300,000 a year head o' that company don't know how to spell "r-i-g-h-t?" Or am I losin' my mind?

MA: You can't make a silk purse out of a rat's ass.

BOB: You're a font of folk wisdom, Ma.

(Sound bite: Tom Joad's "I'll be there" speech from The Grapes of Wrath.*)*

SCENE THREE

Hospital room. In the bed is a PERSON covered head to toe in bandages. TOBY sits beside this person.

TOBY: It's me.

(The PERSON in the bed groans. It is clearly the voice of a man, not MRS. LEBLANC.)

TOBY: Don't try to talk, Mrs.LeBlanc.

(PERSON groans.)

TOBY: I have a lot of hate. Where it comes from, I don't know. I feel like a pit bull must sometimes, black, blind with rage, the gorge rising in my throat and bitter bile churning through my breast like some turgid, toxic maelstrom. I have no idea what I am capable of in these Mr. Hyde moments.

(PERSON groans, as if for the nurse.)

TOBY: I want to perform decapitations, immolations. A kitten bites me and I want to dash its head against the wall. It's just how God made me, I guess. And NOW. That fatty bastard, that pasty-fleshed, ignorant TICK does this to you, to YOU... his WIFE, his own wife who he's sworn to love, honor, and cherish—

(PERSON groans, as if to protest that he's got the wrong room.)

TOBY: Hush, hush, let me finish. For a kinder, gentler, sweeter angel never walked the earth. And so I begin to contemplate... my revenge.

(PERSON groans.)

TOBY: Don't worry. I'm in control now. But I got a hair trigger temper see, and all I need is one thing, ONE THING to set me off. And I just hope he does. I just hope we cross paths some time soon. 'Cause my daddy got me this gun, see? And he's been teaching me to use it, Mrs. LeBlanc—

(PERSON groans.)

TOBY: Babe. And if it happens, I know

you'll be right there with me and I'll be doing it for both of us.

(PERSON groans.)

TOBY: Babe.

(TOBY exits. Pause. Enter a NURSE.)

NURSE: Okay, Mr. Rodriguez, time to change your dressings.

(PERSON groans.)

SCENE FOUR

TOBY's bedroom. TOBY sits on his bed cleaning his rifle, ramming a long brush in and out of the barrel. Enter PREACHER BOB.

BOB: Hey there. Doin' your homework. That's good to see.

TOBY: Dad, I need to talk to you.

BOB: Don't worry about a thing, Toby. I think we got this dang deal with Pubert puzzled out. We got us a game plan. Before he can holler "uncle" he'll be dreaming of home and mother.

TOBY: It's not about Pubert.

BOB: Not about Pubert?

TOBY: It's about me.

BOB: Well, Land of Goshen, Toby, is that all you can think about is yourself?

TOBY: It's something I did.

BOB: Well, you don't need to brag on yourself, Tobe, we already know you're terrific.

TOBY: You see, one of my teachers—

BOB: Goddamn it, Toby, if you try and flaunt your brains in my face one more time I'll pop you one in the goddamn mouth!

TOBY: Yes, sir.

BOB: That's why families are breaking up in this country, Tobe. It's people puttin' their own needs ahead of those that love them. If you got out and mixed with people instead of hibernatin' in yer room all the time, you'd get some sense of that. *(Exits.)*

SCENE FIVE

TV room. MA is watching TV. TOBY enters, unseen by her.

TV ANNOUNCER ONE: Ghosts, spirit manifestations, poltergeists. Could these phenomena be real? We talked to eminent parapsychologist Dr. Sylvia Cauley at the University of Edmonton.

TV VOICE TWO (WOMAN): When you look at these phenomena objectively you begin to get this sense there's something there, that there's some force or energy at work that empirical science hasn't yet found a way to measure.

TOBY: Ma.

TV VOICE TWO (WOMAN): We've conducted many thousands of interviews with people—normal, healthy adults, everyday people—

TOBY: Ma?

TV VOICE TWO (WOMAN):Many of them convinced, mind you CONVINCED, that they've experienced a paranormal phenomenon.

TOBY: Ma?

TV VOICE TWO (WOMAN): Many of them expressed the feeling that there was someone right there in the room with them, yet, when they turned to look, there was no one with them at all.

ACT FOUR
SCENE ONE

Enter MAN.

MAN: Hey, aren't you Preacher Bob Maggot?

BOB: Yes, sir. What can I do for ya?

MAN: Well, you can start by pickin' up my garbage. It's been pilin' up for a week and a damn half.

BOB: I apologize, brother. I got a lot on my mind.

MAN: Uh huh. And I got a lot on my lawn. If you can't be on time, I'll get someone else to do it.

BOB: There is no one else. I'm the only game in town, mister. I'll pick up your trash for you. But just now I'm about the Lord's business.

MAN: If you don't pick up my trash you won't have MY business.

BOB: Well, I'll be goddamned.

SCENE TWO

HAYSEED working on his fence. Enter BOB, still fuming from the previous scene.

BOB: They're awful unjust to the poor white man in this country, Hayseed. It's the last socially acceptable prejudice. We're the butt of scorn of every other American faction and called names you wouldn't call the dog that ate your baby. Cracker, redneck, peckerwood, slackjaw, yokel, white trash— Trash! As though a man were a potato peel, a candy wrapper, a cigar butt. Trash, refuse, garbage, waste, waste! Spilled sperm, bottom feeders, cannon fodder. My people come over to this country 300 years ago as indentured servants—practically slaves—and since then we've been share-croppers, miners, factory workers, gas station attendants and groundskeepers, the people who clean the pools and ring up the groceries. I come that close to paying the black man's dues in this country and still they're all railroaded into thinking I'm capable of oppressing anybody. It's like blaming Tom Joad for the sins of Henry Ford. You gotta have power to oppress somebody! Ted Turner and Ted Kennedy, all the pretty privileged Teds, are slapping each other's knees red over that one. Couple of fat cats buffalo the people into thinking they're saints and make me out to be a rodeo clown. Now Roseanne's our Aunt Jemima and Jeff Foxworthy's our Uncle Tom. Somewhere, somehow, someone's probably laughing at me right now. But I haul your garbage. Your garbage. A hair away from wiping your ass without a glove. You oughtta give me a medal for that. Instead that just makes you all the more contemptuous of me, as though I deserve it somehow. I oughtta burn your house down for that. Instead, I seek to practice Christian forgiveness, becoming the butt of your jokes for yet another reason. Everybody's whipping boy. Everybody's scapegoat. And that's all anyone knows about a scapegoat. Is kill the scapegoat. Kill the scapegoat.

HAYSEED: What's that?

BOB: The sacrificial lamb to appease an angry God, boy. Cut your losses and buy a little more time. Abraham, a knife and his first-born son. God says you do it and you do it. But sometimes it ain't God that tells ya, just your own craven needs of the moment. Smoke and mirrors. Ya wanna shield yourself from consequences so you kill a scapegoat.

HAYSEED: *(Automatically.)* Kill the scapegoat.

SCENE THREE

Hayloft. PUBERT is sleeping. Enter AN-GEL with a primitive headdress made out of a goat's horns and hide.

ANGEL: Hey, Pube. Pube. Check out the cool headdress I made for our confabulation with the Dark Master.

PUBERT: *(Horrified.)* That's… that's Bobo—!

ANGEL: It was. Now it's a headdress.

PUBERT: That's savage. You're wearing his skin. You know, it's like *Silence of the Lambs* or something.

ANGEL: Uh, people have been wearing goatskin for like a million years, Pubert.

PUBERT: Yeah, but I know that goat.

ANGEL: Yeah, and you hate him right? You said you want to kill him.

PUBERT: What did you do?

ANGEL: I thought you were in 4-H! I clubbed him, bled him, and skinned him. Out in the woods. The women in my family have been doing it for ages. It's like Ma always said: stabbin' a motherfucker ain't nothin' but a thing. It stops moving after awhile and the knife just slides in and out just like you were fuckin' a mannequin.

PUBERT: Whoa. My dad's gonna freak.

ANGEL: Let him freak. Let him freak-a-deak. Bring on the whole freakadoidal package. Listen, dudes, I had me a li'l revelation. You know that place where the brethren brought me? Charon? get a piece of this: I found out that Charon and Pluto are the Greek lord of the underworld and his fuckin' hellhound. How about that?

PUBERT: So?

ANGEL: So? I think they were transmitting me a message in space code.

PUBERT: Like what?

ANGEL: Like who they REALLY ARE. Like yeah. Like I read this book once where Satan and his fallen angels came to earth like a long time ago and left like 10,000-year-old batteries and archaeologists found 'em, man. They found 'em. You know? And this is where this shit comes from!

PUBERT: What shit?

ANGEL: The pentagram.

PUBERT: I don't getcha.

ANGEL: What if I told you *(Points to pentagram on her jacket.)* that it's a LANDING PAD. Them cats are coming down again and this is their sign that they're gonna do it. We're about to head into the evolutionary order above human just like it says on page forty-three of the Bible.

PUBERT: Sounds like Yogi's Space Ark!

ANGEL: Hey, fuck that! That's a cartoon! Yer head's full of farts, man. Do I look like a cartoon?

PUBERT: Yeah, Grape Ape.

ANGEL: You'll get yours, fuckin' dude. First of all, Grape Ape is like 50 feet tall. Come down to the real world for a change. Come back to us, Pubert, come back to us. Now here's what we gotta do: We just connect the dots and it forms a sort of cosmic radio antenna based on the vibrations of our spirituality. We enact a ritual and it takes us on an astral journey. And it works. Especially if we sniff glue.

PUBERT: Yeah, where's that glue?

SCENE FOUR

Parish. RAY sits at a table, knitting. Enter BOB:

BOB: Howdy. I was hopin' I'd find you here.

RAY: Ain't got nowhere else to go. Mighty nice of you, lettin' me hole up in the parish house.

BOB: I believe in giving a man a second chance.

RAY: Second chance, hell. A man has a disagreement with his own wife in his own home and you'd think the sky had fallen in. What is it anybody's business? You know? I'll work it out on my w—with my wife later. But, no. Big Brother's got to get involved. A man pulls up to his own house, there's sirens and lights flashing, somebody starts reading you your rights. Well, before I knew it, my fist come down on that man's nose and I was makin' my way through the town sewer. It don't seem right, do it?

BOB: Never hit a woman, Ray. You'll never hear the end of it… *(Pause.)* You uh wanna tell me what happened?

RAY: Well, it was like this…

> I done the Texas two step on her face.
> And I broke every beer mug in the place.
> Yeah they'll know she is my woman when they see that six-inch scar.
> I'm just a deer caught in the headlights of her car.
> I sealed her high school yearbook up with tar.
> And I burned every picture of her pa.
> Scalped her with a tommyhawk and told her she's my squaw.

I'm just a deer caught in the headlights
    of her car.
These women make me helpless, swear
    to God.
All they do is make me lose my head.
And when my head is severed from
    my bod-y.
They make me lose my knuckle skin
    instead.
Her nose is broke, I think I broke her
    arm.
I wanna tell the whole world, I never
    meant no harm
Now the sirens are behind me and I
    don't guess I'll get far.
I'm just a deer caught in the headlights
    of her car.
Oh these women.

BOB: How come ya done all that, Ray?

RAY: I found her in bed with a Congolese
gorilla!

BOB: Is that a fact? How'd she hook up
with one of them people?

RAY: *(About to cry.)* He was my friend…

BOB: *(Nods knowingly.)* It's an old story.

RAY: See, the whole thing is, I can't get to
my truck. They put a squad car on my
damn truck. Damn deputy's watching the
thing twenty-four hours a day. I can't make
my living without that truck. Can't even
keep myself in beer money or prescriptions.

BOB: As long as you stay sober, that's the
important thing. Can't let you drink here.
Them's the rules.

RAY: This knittin' ain't helpin' much.

BOB: The trick is to buy the yarn from
the factory outlet where it's new. That way
the dye's fresh, and you can sniff it. It eases
the withdrawal.

RAY: Yeah?

BOB: Sure. Worked when I kicked.

RAY: No kiddin'. You were a drunk, too, eh?

BOB: Used to was. but I haven't had a
beer in… I can't think when.

RAY: Well, if you can do it, I can do it.

BOB: That's the spirits. *(Pause.)* 'Course,
if a beer fell in my mouth now, I wouldn't
spit it out.

RAY: No?

BOB: No. In fact… you know, Earl our
handyman is off for today. I don't think
anybody'd be the wiser if we wanted to
pop open a couple.

RAY: Yeah?

BOB: If we wanted to.

RAY: Really? You sure it's okay?

BOB: Well, I'm the preacher here, ain't I?
I guess it's okay if I say it is.

RAY: Sure, sure, whatever you say.

BOB: You'll find two sixes of Coors Light
in that cooler over there.

RAY: What'll you drink?

*(The two men laugh. RAY gets the beers.
The two drink.)*

RAY: Preacher Bob. You done so much
for me. I don't know how I can begin to
repay you.

BOB: Well, Ray, see, that's what I come
here to talk to you about.

RAY: Yeah?

BOB: Ordinarily when we bail troubled
people out such as yourself here at the
parish, we ask 'em to work it off somehow.

RAY: You ain't gonna make me do garbage detail?

BOB: No, no, nothing like that. No, no. Though I think that's a service every man should have to perform at one time or another, just to see what it's like. It ain't near as bad as people make it out. You wind up with a lotta free stuff!

RAY: I can imagine.

BOB: No, I have a special job for you. I need someone who ain't known much hereabouts to do me a service. I figured since you're on the road all the time, most of the people in town won't know your face.

RAY: Well, the cops will. What do you want me to do, rob a bank?

BOB: No, it's sort of an acting job. You won't have to go near the cops.

RAY: Say, what kind of a preacher are you, anyway?

BOB: I'm a garbageman moonlighting as a Baptist preacher. And I do the Lord's work in mysterious ways. Are you interested?

RAY: I ain't heard the job yet.

BOB: Here's what I want you to do.

(BOB whispers to RAY. Sitcom transition music.)

ACT FIVE
SCENE ONE

BOB's house. Enter PUBERT, eating a sandwich. Enter BOB.

BOB: Hey, Pubert. Whatcha eatin'?

PUBERT: Frog sandwich.

BOB: I beg your pardon?

PUBERT: Frog sandwich.

BOB: Mind telling me where you got a frog sandwich?

PUBERT: Grandma give it to me.

BOB: (Snatches the sandwich away from PUBERT.) How many times have I told you never to eat anything your granny makes unless someone's watchin' her the whole time? She's goin' through the change.

(BOB looks around for a place to put the sandwich. In desperation, he places it in his shirt pocket.)

BOB: Now then. I was wonderin' if you wouldn't mind doin' a job of work for me, by way of paying your board.

PUBERT: Sure.

BOB: Good, good. Now, then. You see this… table we got the telephone settin' on here?

PUBERT: Yes.

BOB: Well, this table has got one leg shorter'n the others and I don't like the way it wobbles. I wonder if you couldn't rig up some little somethin'… uh… folded piece of cardboard or a block o' wood, or something, to kinda shore it up a bit on that side.

PUBERT: Is that it?

BOB: What's the matter? Not glamorous enough for ya?

PUBERT: Well, it isn't much of a chore.

BOB: Let's see now… what time is it? (Looks at his watch.) About five minutes to seven. How long you think that job I gave you'll take?

PUBERT: I'd say… about… one minute.

BOB: *(To himself.)* Not long enough. *(To PUBERT.)* Okay, then, Pube. After you're through with that, then, I want you to… polish this phone.

PUBERT: Polish the phone?

BOB: Yeah. Just polish the phone, but don't pick up the receiver. Unless it rings, of course! If it rings, why, you just feel free to answer it.

PUBERT: Okay. You got a rag or somethin' I can polish this phone down with?

BOB: Uh… uh… uh… you can use this. *(Pulls the sandwich out of his pocket.)* The frog sandwich.

PUBERT: Polish the phone down with the frog sandwich.

BOB: And rig some cardboard under that table leg. That oughtta take a few minutes. Now, do a good job. And don't go nowhere. You hear me? Don't move a muscle from this spot until that job is thoroughly done.

PUBERT: I'd like to go get a rag to do the phone with.

BOB: No, no, use that sandwich. You take it from the old garbageman. That's recycling, that is. *(Exits.)*

PUBERT: Guy's fuckin' nuts. *(Pause.)* Okay, Cardboard. Cardboard.

(PUBERT looks around the room. Settles on the American flag set piece. Goes upstage and tears off a bit. He folds the piece up.)

PUBERT: This oughtta do 'er.

(PUBERT kneels down and begins fixing the cardboard under the table leg. Enter TOBY.)

TOBY: Hey, what're you're doing?

PUBERT: Oh, hey, Uncle Toby. I'm just fixin' this table leg here so it don't wobble.

TOBY: Oh.

(Phone rings.)

TOBY: I'll get it. *(Picks up the receiver.)* Hello?

RAY'S VOICE: Hiya, punk.

TOBY: I beg your pardon?

RAY'S VOICE: I said, "Hiya, punk."

TOBY: Who do you wish to talk to?

RAY'S VOICE: Oh, a certain punk. The punk who's been sniffin' around my woman.

TOBY: I think there must be some mistake.

RAY'S VOICE: You been spendin' a whole lotta time with a certain woman, a full-growed, older type woman?

TOBY: I'd like to take the Fifth on that one.

RAY'S VOICE: What's that? You want to drink a fifth?

TOBY: Never mind.

RAY'S VOICE: Now, you listen: You meet me at the town dump. In one hour. We'll see who… Never mind, you pimply ass punk. I'll beat your ass from sunup to sundown.

TOBY: Uh, I don't think—

RAY'S VOICE: Show up. Or I'm comin' lookin' for you. *(Hangs up.)*

TOBY: *(Pause.)* Ulp. *(Hangs the phone up.)*

PUBERT: Who was that?

TOBY: The library. I owe a rather large fine.

PUBERT: Go kick the bitch's ass!

(TOBY pulls his gun out of the closet.)

TOBY: All right. I will. *(Cocks the gun and leaves.)*

PUBERT: Whoa.

SCENE TWO

The town dump. Sound of seagulls. Enter TOBY, tiptoeing, with his gun. TOBY tiptoes off. Enter RAY.

RAY: All right, I'm here. Come on out, punk. Come out where I can kick your ass! Let's go, faggot! Let's go, you little wimp! Where I can kick your ass! I know you're here, chicken shit!

(Enter TOBY with the shotgun. TOBY cocks and aims to fire at RAY. Out of nowhere, CLAUDE appears and leaps into the path of the bullet, in slow motion.)

RAY: *(Voice slowed down.)* Nooooooooooo!

(TOBY fires and shoots CLAUDE. CLAUDE falls. There is a long pause.)

RAY: Claude!!!!!!!! Claude!!!!! *(He kneels to check CLAUDE's vitals. It is clear that he is dead. This should be played as a genuinely tragic moment.)* He's... you've... Claude!

TOBY: *(Coming forward.)* I'm sorry, I—

RAY: *(Savagely.)* Don't you touch him! You killed my Claude. The only thing I loved in the world. *(Sobbing over the body.)* And you killed him. You killed him. You killed him. You killed him. You killed him. You killed him. You killed him. You killed him. You killed him. You killed him. You killed him. You killed

him. You killed him.

TOBY: Sorry. *(Exits.)*

(Sound bite from King Kong*: "It wasn't the airplanes that killed him. It was beauty killed the beast.")*

SCENE THREE

The barn. Pentagram projected on back wall. Candles about. ANGEL lies sleeping with her goat head on. Enter HAYSEED with a machete.

HAYSEED: Kill the scapegoat. Kill the scapegoat.

(HAYSEED raises the knife to slay ANGEL. ANGEL suddenly stirs awake.)

ANGEL: Hey. 'S up?

(HAYSEED clutches his heart, has a heart attack, and drops to the floor.)

ANGEL: That does it. I'm goin' back to Charon.

SCENE FOUR

BOB:
 We fought and died in fourteen wars, sir,
 From Great Swamp to Desert Storm,
 We found ourselves within death's jaws, sir,
 We felt his breath, it was wet and warm.
 We volunteered to do our parts, sir,
 Uncoerced by the law or the lash.
 Just the stuff within our hearts, sir.
 Red blood, blue veins, and white trash.

Our noble forebears came from Brit-
ain,
Lived in castles and wore crowns.
On fancy thrones they all were sittin',
Had no hassles, no one puttin' 'em
down.
They were still unsatiated:
Crossed the sea for to make some cash.
Three hundred years degenerated.
Blue blood, red coats, and white trash.
Now, mister, I ain't sayin' we should
fly the flag at half mast
Maybe that's takin' things way too far.
But if you ask me, this country's mov-
ing way too fast.
Seems like no one, no one's drivin' this
car.
I see the people all around me,
Ain't no different from the ones be-
fore.
It never ceases to astound me.
Seems to me we oughtta be far more.
Must be somethin' in our diets,
White bread, grits, canned corned beef
hash.
Built this plane, but we can't fly it.
Blue skies, red eyes, and white, white
trash.

EPILOGUE

Church.

BOB: Without a soul, brother, we're just
cold, calculating matter:
treat animals like people, treat people like
animals,
and treat 'em both like stuff that goes
down the disposal—
biological matter, cells and DNA, same as
lettuce leaves.
Big germ robots.
The old folk culture had a soul, an
oversoul,
a spirit that bubbled up from the people

but that's gone. Gone the way of the dodo.
in its place is some kinda
electronic, amnesiac vacuum.
A daily tinselburg mind wash
that makes us little better than vessels
blank slates for the billboard writers to
write on
fictions, frictions, fragmentations
Waco, Oklahoma City, Columbine, Ruby
Ridge
Heaven's Gate, Guyana, the Manson family
some say we're goin to hell in a handbasket
but that ain't nothin' new really.
The Bible says it's been our lot since Lot's
wife.
God made Adam from a pile of dirt and
dirt we are.
Even science backs me up on that.
A white trash president once spoke of the
"better angels of our nature"
but them angels are trapped in the bodies
of killer apes.
One of them shot that president in the
head.
Jesused him with a peashooter right there
in the theatre.
Given half a chance its Eve and Cain we
are,
and that angel, that ideal, that thing we
are supposed to be,
oh that angel slumbers, it withers and
shrinks.
What becomes of "of the people, by the
people, for the people"
if "people" are craven, lazy, fat, hate-filled,
ignorant, violent, scheming, character-
less cavemen?
Where's the virtue in democracy if every
man's a bloodthirsty Caesar?
It all becomes meaningless
we all become zombies, pawns in some
weird and senseless cosmic game.
Is there a way out of that house of horrors?

Is there a way out of the House of Trash?
Friends, I'm just a garbageman moonlighting as Baptist preacher
but even I know
maybe especially I know that when these
hands get dirty
I can wash 'em.
Like Pilate, like Lady Macbeth in
Shakespeare

this foot-washin' Baptist can wash the past
off these hands,
Though I have tried and I have failed
and though I don't always have the courage of my convictions
I'm gonna keep trying! I'm gonna keep
trustin'!
That Life has a meaning!
That mankind has a purpose!
And that I am more than $1.98 worth of
chemi-cules.

Straight-Jacket

Richard Day

RICHARD DAY was born in San Francisco, California, in 1962. He has been writing and producing television comedy for more than ten years. He has been nominated for three Emmy Awards, most recently in the category of Outstanding Writing in a Comedy Series for his gay-themed episode of "The Larry Sanders Show." His other writing and producing credits include "Mad About You," "Ellen," "Spin City," "It's Garry Shandling's Show," and, most recently, a TV project with actor Alfred Molina. Day is presently writing two television comedy pilots, "Edgewood" for the Fox Network, and "Set for Life" for NBC. He lives in a Beverly Hills mansion with his dog Roscoe and a constant stream of muscular young men.

Straight-Jacket was first produced by Mike Sullo on June 18, 2000, at Playhouse 91, New York City, with the following cast and credits:

Trick (Mike, Jeff, Josh,* Salvation Army Man,
Furniture Delivery Man,* Ray Verrine,* Ron*) ...... Ron Matthews

Guy .... John Littlefield

Jerry .... Jackie Hoffman

Sally .... Carrie Preston

Saul .... Mal Z. Lawrence

Rick .... Adam Greer

Freddie* .... Stevie Ray Dallimore

Directed by: Richard Day
Scenic Designer: Ray Recht
Costume Designer: Gail Brassard
Lighting Designer: F. Mitchell Dana
Sound Designer: Peter Fitzgerald
Composer: Stephen Edwards
Production Stage Manager: Tamara K. Heeschen
Press: Cromarty & Co.

*Denotes role eliminated from the published version of the script.

Music for the song "Two Kinds of Love" by Stephen Edwards may be obtained by contacting Sixfeetfive Music at 310-230-9456 or visiting www.sourceinsync.com.

AUTHOR'S NOTE

Imagine a late fifties sex comedy that actually dealt with the thorny real-world issues of its era. Just as those frothy films glamorized and oversimplified subjects like the advertising world and bachelorette living, so this one would scrub clean and dumb down homophobia, sexism, and the blacklist. Of course the characters would speak exclusively in wisecracks, and by the last reel every problem, no matter how systemic or rooted in mass bigotry, would be vanquished by true love.

Straight-Jacket is that movie brought to the stage.

Pulling this off requires a tremendous balancing act on the part of a production. Some sort of quotation marks must be placed around the material, or audiences will believe themselves to be in the hands of a simple-minded playwright, which may well be true but there's no point in leading with it. Yet if you camp things up too much, the genuinely involving love story that drives the play will be lost to caricature.

The best advice I can offer on how to achieve the correct tone is this: The answers to all of your questions are contained within the movie *Pillow Talk*.

CHARACTERS

GUY STONE: Early thirties, an impossibly handsome gay movie star

JERRY ALBRECHT: Early forties, Guy's manager, does not suffer him gladly

SAUL ORNSTIEN: Late forties, worry-plagued owner of S-R-O Pictures

SALLY OLSEN: Early twenties, Saul's beautiful, virginal secretary

RICK FOSTER: Mid-twenties, an idealistic young novelist

TRICK: A part encompassing several roles, their unifying aspect being a sexual history with Guy

TIME

1957.

PLACE

Hollywood.

ACT I
SCENE 1

It is a late fall but nevertheless balmy Beverly Hills morning, and we are in the luxurious and impeccably appointed bedroom of movie star GUY STONE. There are three doors, one leading to the hallway, one to the closet, and a sliding glass door that opens onto a balcony. As the lights come up, GUY lies in bed, while MIKE (TRICK), his gorgeous young bedmate, watches him sleep. MIKE can't help but giggle at his enormous good fortune, which causes GUY to slowly stir.

MIKE: Hi Guy. Did I wear you out last night? That was so incredible. I mean, there's sex and then there's *that*, there's two people sharing everything, becoming the same person almost. You know?

(GUY smiles at MIKE for a beat.)

GUY: I'm sorry, I'm terrible with names.

MIKE: It's Mike, remember? "What's your name?" "Mike?"

GUY: Right.

MIKE: I can't believe I'm in bed with Guy Stone. I feel like Betty Bright.

GUY: You're not butch enough.

(MIKE playfully hits GUY with a pillow.)

MIKE: Me? You.

(MIKE laughs. GUY joins in, politely.)

MIKE: So what's it like to be a big movie star, anyway? My friend Brian? He says I could be one. But I don't know. For one thing, how do you remember all those lines?

GUY: I don't.

MIKE: Brian is so funny. He works at the May Company, in the tall and large de-

partment? Only he calls it the... I forget, the something something department.

(GUY manages another, identical laugh.)

GUY: I didn't realize it was so late.

MIKE: What time is it?

(GUY looks around, but he does not own a clock.)

GUY: Late. And I have a...

MIKE: Costume fitting?

GUY: Sure.

MIKE: Okay. But can't you stay in bed for just ten more minutes?

(MIKE begins kissing GUY's chest, then his abdomen.)

GUY: Oh, what the hell? It's Tuesday.

(MIKE disappears under the covers. JERRY, a no-nonsense tank of a woman, enters and quickly assesses the scene.)

JERRY: You know, some people have coffee in the morning.

GUY: It makes me jumpy.

(MIKE pokes his head out from under the covers.)

JERRY: Hey there, little fella. I'm Jerry.

MIKE: Mike.

(MIKE offers his hand, but JERRY withholds hers.)

JERRY: Soak it in bleach first.

(MIKE quickly throws on his shorts and sandals.)

MIKE: Are you his mom? Because we were just, you know, talking.

JERRY: I'm his manager. *(Leading out*

MIKE.) Now it's a beautiful day, Mike, run along and play with the other gay children.

(But MIKE crosses back to GUY, and hands him a card.)

MIKE: Here's my number. I hope you'll use it.

GUY: Of course I will. What do you think you are, some stranger I picked up off the street?

(MIKE collects his duffel bag and a large sandwich-board which reads, "MAPS TO STARS HOMES.")

MIKE: Well, bye Guy. Bye, Mrs. Stone.

(MIKE exits. GUY tosses the card into a goldfish bowl filled with them.)

JERRY: Why do you even save them?

GUY: For the raffle. Am I shooting today?

(GUY gathers some lotions and sex toys, and crosses to an open cabinet. He stows the items in it, then closes the cabinet to reveal that its door is in fact hidden behind a portrait of himself.)

JERRY: We have a meeting, remember? With Saul? The head of the studio?

GUY: Oh. Neat.

JERRY: What would you do without me?

GUY: Get someone else.

JERRY: Try.

(GUY exits into the closet.)

GUY: (Offstage.) I bet I know what this is about. Saul is going to offer me "Ben Hur."

JERRY: Don't hold your breath. Every actor on the lot is after that part.

GUY: I know. I feel bad for them.

JERRY: Guy, things don't always go your way.

GUY: (Poking his head out.) Yes they do.

JERRY: No, what happens is, I work around the clock like a dog—without so much as a thank you from you, might I add—to make things go your way.

(GUY enters, now wearing pants and a shirt, and carrying shoes and socks.)

GUY: Either way, the effect is the same. (Crosses to the bed, and begins putting on his shoes.)

JERRY: So did you meet Mike at that gay bar?

GUY: No. I met him on the way home.

JERRY: Guy—

GUY: I have to stop going there.

JERRY: You do. You're —

GUY: Too famous now.

JERRY: You are.

GUY: Well what's the point of being famous if you can't use it to get laid?

JERRY: That's very good. When this ruins your career, you can become the shallowest philosopher ever.

GUY: It's not going to ruin my career.

JERRY: One blabbermouth is all it would take. These new magazines will print anything. "Screen Stars" is even planting photographers outside certain motels.

GUY: Which is why I always bring my boys here. (Puts on a baseball cap left behind by MIKE.)

JERRY: Guy, I need to ask you a question.

GUY: The answer is yes, a little.

JERRY: What?

GUY: You are putting on weight.

JERRY: That wasn't my question.

GUY: Sorry.

JERRY: I was—

GUY: No, the hair doesn't work.

JERRY: Stop that.

GUY: Just trying to help.

JERRY: I was wondering how serious you are about becoming a movie star.

GUY: Becoming? I happen to be the number one box office draw at S-R-O Pictures.

JERRY: Well S-R-O Pictures isn't exactly M-G-M. Hell, it's not even Warner's. I want to see you doing important pictures with A-list directors.

GUY: So book me some.

JERRY: I've tried.

GUY: And what's the problem?

JERRY: I think you know.

GUY: The no-talent thing?

JERRY: Please, you and half of Hollywood. It's a small town, Guy. Word gets around. And people may say they don't care, but when the chips are down and John Huston has to choose between you and Montgomery Clift—

GUY: (Please.) Jerry.

JERRY: Oh, get out. Are you sure?

GUY: These are his socks. And by the way, his career is coming along nicely.

JERRY: Because he's discreet. Which re-

minds me, you have a date tonight with Holly Warren.

GUY: Again?

JERRY: Do you know how many men would kill to go out with her?

GUY: You, for one.

JERRY: I am not a lesbian.

GUY: Then neither is Agnes Moorehead. (Finished dressing, GUY rises.)

JERRY: Guy, you need to appreciate how serious this is. Your image is the all-American boy. And last time I checked, the all-American boy didn't suck dick.

GUY: I'll introduce you to some people.

(GUY blows past JERRY, and crosses to the door.)

SCENE 2

The office of SAUL ORNSTEIN, owner and president of S-R-O Pictures. There is a large desk, a conversation area, and, along the back wall, a small glass panel for a projector lens. Two doors lead to the outer office and a private bathroom. GUY sits at SAUL's desk, perusing the screenplay for "Ben Hur." JERRY sits in the chair opposite him.

GUY: Can I help cast the slave boys?

JERRY: Okay listen: If this is about "Ben Hur," don't get all excited. Our position is we'd need a lot of money, because big epics take forever to shoot, and moving to Italy would be a pain. Both of which are true, by the way.

GUY: I know. But gladiator movies have brought me so much pleasure, I feel I should give something back.

(SALLY, a whirlwind of virginal energy, enters with a pitcher of lemonade on a tray.)

SALLY: Who wants lemonade?

JERRY: I do.

(SALLY crosses to GUY and serves him some.)

SALLY: I made it myself. There's a lemon tree in my backyard.

(GUY takes his lemonade and crosses to the conversation area. SALLY follows, passing JERRY, who reaches in vain for a glass.)

JERRY: I do. Yoo hoo. Over here.

(SALLY quickly serves JERRY, then hurries back to GUY.)

SALLY: Well, it's not really my backyard, it's everybody's. I have an apartment. Can I tell you again how wonderful you were in "The Love Barrel?"

GUY: Please. I always say, without my fans, I'd be no better than they are.

SALLY: Oh, I'm much more than a fan. I know everything about you. You're thirty-one, your favorite color is blue—so masculine. And I love that you hunt.

GUY: (To JERRY.) I do?

JERRY: Read your bio.

SALLY: You know, I probably shouldn't tell you this, but you're sort of why I moved here from Nebraska. See, I read that article in "Screen Idols" magazine—"Guy Stone's Perfect Woman Checklist"? And I realized I had everything you were looking for, except one.

JERRY: That one's usually the deal-breaker.

(SAUL, blustery and aggressive to compensate for myriad insecurities, enters through the bathroom door, reading Variety.)

SAUL: Yul Reissman died. That's too bad.

JERRY: You always go straight to the obituaries.

SAUL: It's the only part of the trades I can read without getting jealous. (With outstretched arms.) Guy!

GUY: Saul!

(GUY and SAUL hug.)

SAUL: How's my box office quarterback?

(GUY pantomimes a baseball batter.)

GUY: Still swinging.

SAUL: Did you see the grosses for "Love is for Lovers?" We're cleaning up.

GUY: Is that the one with me and the Countess?

SALLY: No, that's "Lovers Love Love."

SAUL: Oh Sally, could you come here for a sec?

(SALLY crosses to SAUL.)

SALLY: Yes Mr. Ornstein?

SAUL: Just this.

(SAUL pinches SALLY's butt.)

JERRY: Charming.

SAUL: Hey, I gotta get it somewhere. Bernice gave herself to me exactly once, on our honeymoon, and then said, "that's the last time I screw you 'til the divorce."

SALLY: Well, guess I'll go perk some coffee. But I'll be right outside. (To GUY.) If you need anything.

(GUY smiles blandly at SALLY, who exits.)

SAUL: I've been trying to jump her bones since she started, and nothing. You she practically throws herself at.

GUY: The key is to appear uninterested.

SAUL: And be a movie star. I bet you get more tail in a week—

JERRY: We're on a schedule, so I'm going to pretend to be offended.

SAUL: Right, right, business. Which, your pictures aside, is for crap. I got the majors trying to squeeze me out, the Feds blacklisting half my directors, and TV. People only come out for big epics now, which is why I'm sinking my entire 1955 production budget into one spectacular picture, "Ben Hur."

GUY: And you wanted to see me about something.

SAUL: Yeah, Rosenthal just turned in this potboiler about a coalmine. I need you for the lead.

GUY: I'm sorry?

SAUL: "My Blood," or "Blood Mine," or something. It's nothing special, but we'll crank it out in three weeks, make some pocket change.

JERRY: Saul, Guy is not a pocket change actor anymore.

SAUL: So what, I'm supposed to just pay him to sit around until March fifth?

JERRY: What's March fifth?

SAUL: When we start "Ben Hur."

GUY: Really?

(JERRY motions for GUY to cool it, then faces SAUL.)

JERRY: Well, we're honored, naturally, but it really depends on the number. I mean, such a long shoot, and moving to Europe—

GUY: I get to be "Ben Hur!"

JERRY: How does a buck fifty sound?

SAUL: Congratulations, Guy.

(SAUL moves to hug GUY, when JEFF (TRICK), a young executive, rushes in with a manilla envelope.)

JEFF: Sir? Hi Guy.

GUY: (Meaningfully.) Jeff.

JERRY: You know, at this rate you're going to run out.

SAUL: Jeff, we're in a meeting here.

JEFF: I know, but this just came. It's kind of important.

(JEFF hands SAUL the envelope. SAUL pulls an 8×10 photograph from it and goes ashen.)

JERRY: Oh my God, what? (She peers over SAUL's shoulder.) Aw, hell.

GUY: What's the problem?

SAUL: You are!

(SAUL throws the photograph at GUY, who looks at it.)

GUY: This is a terrible picture of me.

JERRY: Yes Guy, that's why we're all so concerned.

SAUL: I have three Guy Stone pictures still in the can. I'm ruined. (To JEFF.) Who sent this?

JEFF: Photoplay. It's going to be their cover.

SAUL: What do they want, money?

JEFF: Or a trade.

SAUL: Fine, tell 'em Holly Warren is addicted to smack.

JERRY: Is that true?

SAUL: It will be once this kills her career. *(To JEFF.)* Now!

JEFF: Yes sir.

(JEFF rushes out. SAUL needs a minute to catch his breath.)

GUY: So. "Congratulations, Guy…"

JERRY: Guy.

SAUL: Congratulations nothing. This whole time, he's been sweet? I've hugged you!

JERRY: Okay, here's why this is good—

SAUL: This is good?

JERRY: Yes, because it's been taken care of, and it taught Guy he has to be careful, which means he won't make the same mistake when he's doing "Ben Hur."

SAUL: He's not doing "Ben Hur."

JERRY: Excuse me?

SAUL: I'm not sinking five million dollars into a vehicle for the new Miss America.

JERRY: But you killed the story.

SAUL: This story. I'm sorry, but it's too risky.

(JERRY begins to say something, but SAUL's look silences her. She turns to GUY, who is leafing through a magazine.)

JERRY: You know, Guy, if *my* career were over… Wait a second, you're my only real client. My career *is* over.

GUY: You'll think of something.

JERRY: Not—

GUY: This time.

JERRY: This time—

GUY: It's different.

JERRY: It is! You finally managed to screw things up so bad—

GUY: Don't push. It'll come.

JERRY: Right now I couldn't help you if you…

(JERRY trails off suddenly. GUY knows the look.)

GUY: See?

JERRY: What if he got married?

SAUL: Married? But he's a—

JERRY: America's most eligible bachelor. Can you imagine the publicity? Plus it'll K.O. any gay talk with one punch.

GUY: Very good.

JERRY: You don't deserve me.

SAUL: Wait, wait, slow down. First of all, marry who? Because I promise any two-bit starlet would stab us in the back.

GUY: What about Jerry? She's single.

JERRY: Bless your gay little heart.

(SALLY bursts in with coffee service on a tray.)

SALLY: Coffee time!

(JERRY, SAUL, and GUY stare at SALLY, all having the same brainstorm simultaneously. SALLY becomes self-conscious.)

SALLY: I'll just leave this here.

(SALLY sets down the coffee service, smiles at GUY, then exits.)

JERRY: We know her, she's trustworthy…

SAUL: She's not that kind of girl.

JERRY: Who says she has be in on it?

GUY: Wait, Jerry—

JERRY: What? She's obviously crazy about you.

GUY: Maybe, but—

JERRY: Definitely. *(To SAUL.)* Hell, she'd say yes if he asked her today.

SAUL: You think so?

JERRY: In a heartbeat.

SAUL: If he proposed right now.

JERRY: You saw.

SAUL: Deal.

JERRY: What?

SAUL: Stone proposes to her right now and she says yes, he can keep "Ben Hur." But she says no, you let me out of his contract.

JERRY: Saul, that's not fair.

SAUL: Fair is he's fired and you get nothing.

JERRY: So the deal is, Sally has to agree to marry him today.

SAUL: Today? Right now. *(Into intercom.)* Sally, we need you back in here.

JERRY: Oh, no. He at least gets to be alone with her.

SAUL: Fine. For five minutes.

JERRY: Ten.

SAUL: Six. *(Into intercom.)* Sally!

GUY: Jerry.

SAUL: Ten to one she got her necklace caught in the mimeo machine again.

(SAUL exits to retrieve her. JERRY whirls around to face GUY.)

JERRY: What?

GUY: You know perfectly well. Someone who's in on it is one thing, but I'd be living with her. Can you imagine spending day after day listening to some superficial ditz yammer on and on about me, me, me? *(Off JERRY's stare.)* Well it's your job.

(SALLY enters.)

SALLY: You wanted to see me?

JERRY: Yes. Guy has something he wants to ask you. Quickly. *(Gives GUY her most urgent stare, then exits.)*

SALLY: What is it?

GUY: Nothing. Sit down.

SALLY: *(Excited.)* Really? *(Sits on the sofa.)*

GUY: I just thought we could talk.

SALLY: What could I possibly have to say that would interest you?

GUY: I have no idea. What do you do for fun?

SALLY: Watch Guy Stone movies. And I cook, and I garden, and sew. I just started crocheting a pillow for my couch that says "Bless this Mess." *(Laughs, then.)* Though my home is actually quite clean.

(GUY tries to go forward, but discovers that he can't.)

GUY: All right, I'm just going to come clean here.

SALLY: Yes?

(He turns away from her, which puts him face to face with some "Ben Hur" storyboards on an easel.)

GUY: I love you.

SALLY: *(Giggling.)* Guy!

GUY: I mean it.

(SALLY giggles again, then suddenly stops.)

SALLY: You love me?

GUY: Ever since the day we met.

SALLY: July 16, 1953.

GUY: Right.

SALLY: At the commissary.

GUY: Right.

SALLY: You had the cold cut plate with—

GUY: Oh, for the love of God.

SALLY: Guy Stone loves me.

GUY: You must have suspected.

SALLY: No! I mean, I always hoped. But before today honestly I didn't even think you liked me.

GUY: How can you say that?

SALLY: Well, whenever you come to see Mr. Ornstein, you just walk right by me without looking.

GUY: It hurts too much.

SALLY: You don't even say "hi" on the phone.

GUY: I'm afraid I'll say "hi love you."

SALLY: Oh, Guy, I love you too. I always have.

GUY: So marry me.

SALLY: Guy!

GUY: Or don't you love me after all?

SALLY: No, I... It's just... We've never even been on a date.

GUY: But hasn't every one of my movies been a sort of date? *(Off posters.)* You've fought wars with me. You've been to Eu-rope with me. You've even... coached a chimp quarterback with me. How many more dates do we need to confirm what we both already know so well?

SALLY: My head is swimming. This is just like in "My Husband, The Ghost," where you ask Betty Bright to marry you from right there on the gallows.

GUY: That exactly how I feel now.

SALLY: What is it you say to her? "No, it's not sensible, but are roses? Or sunsets? Marry me, Countess, and I will love you senseless."

GUY: Right.

SALLY: *(Through tears of joy.)* That's the most beautiful proposal I ever heard.

(GUY and SALLY kiss. SAUL and JERRY enter.)

SAUL: Time's... *(Then, taking in scene.)* I don't believe it.

SALLY: Mr. Ornstein! Guy and I are getting married.

JERRY: *(To GUY.)* Congratulations.

SALLY: Thank you. I have to call my parents!

(SALLY rushes out. GUY wipes off her kiss.)

GUY: So do I get the part?

SAUL: You just want to wear the dress.

SCENE 3

Guy's bedroom, morning, a week later. GUY is asleep in bed. SALLY enters with two Sears bags. She smiles lovingly, moves to the bed, and gently blows on GUY. GUY stirs, sees SALLY, and screams.

SALLY: Good morning, my darling husband.

GUY: Your what?

SALLY: I know, I can't believe it either. I keep pinching myself to see if I'm dreaming.

GUY: Any luck?

(SALLY moves to the window and pulls open the drapes, blasting GUY with harsh sunlight. SALLY shows him the newspaper.)

SALLY: We're even in the paper. "Guy Stone Weds Ordinary Nobody."

GUY: When was this picture taken?

SALLY: At the reception, last night. Don't you remember?

GUY: Parts of it.

SALLY: I'll never forget a moment of the entire night. Especially the last part. You made me a woman, Guy.

GUY: I did?

SALLY: It was so wonderful. And you want to know why? Because I waited twenty-five years for it.

GUY: Well then, that's just the schedule we're going to stick to.

SALLY: Now up, up, up. Fast like a bunny.

(SALLY tickles GUY, who rolls out of bed to escape her. SALLY begins humming and making the bed as GUY puts on his robe.)

SALLY: No, Guy. I bought you all-new things.

(SALLY proudly shows GUY a hideous robe from a Sears bag.)

GUY: Good God.

SALLY: That'll be a quarter for the swear jar.

(GUY puts a quarter from his bed-table into the jar.)

GUY: What the hell is a—

(SALLY shakes the jar.)

SALLY: At this rate, I'll have that washer-dryer in no time.

(GUY puts another quarter into the jar. A SALVATION ARMY MAN (TRICK) enters.)

SALVATION ARMY MAN: Hi, Guy.

(GUY nods back.)

SALLY: You know the Salvation Army man?

GUY: I do a lot of charity work.

SALVATION ARMY MAN: Thanks a lot. (Takes two sculptures and exits.)

GUY: Wait—where is he going with my things?

SALLY: They're our things now, honey, though honestly trash is more like it. I'm giving it all away.

GUY: Without discussing it?

SALLY: Men don't know anything about decorating. Now come downstairs and I'll make you a nice chicken-fried steak.

(Overloaded, GUY collects his clothes.)

GUY: Actually, um… I have to go.

SALLY: To where?

GUY: Big Bear. I need to check on my place.

SALLY: You mean like a honeymoon?

GUY: Yes. But alone.

SALLY: Over my dead body.

GUY: I'm sorry?

SALLY: When you're not working, you're home with me. Marriage has rules, and if you aren't willing to follow them, we might as well just get an annulment right now.

GUY: No! No need to do anything rash. I'll stay. But I agree—marriage does have rules. In fact, I have a few of my own.

SALLY: Well of course you do. You wear the pants in this house.

GUY: That's right. Generally speaking. And rule number one is no redecorating.

SALLY: All right.

GUY: Just like that?

SALLY: The vow says "Love, honor, and obey." What else?

GUY: Rule number two, don't touch the cabinet. *(Indicates the portrait of himself.)*

SALLY: Cabinet?

GUY: Portrait. I don't like people touching pictures of me. Or me, for that matter, which brings me to rule number three: Separate beds. In fact, separate rooms.

SALLY: But why?

GUY: I just think a man and woman sleeping in the same bed is ungodly.

SALLY: Even once they're married?

GUY: I'm deeply religious.

SALLY: Then we should get to church.

GUY: Which is not to say a fanatic.

SALLY: Can we at least share a bed when we're trying to have children?

GUY: Absolutely. Rule number four: No children.

SALLY: Honey—

GUY: The Russians have the bomb. I will not bring new life into a world that's about to end.

SALLY: But I love children.

GUY: Do you love watching them melt?

SALLY: I just don't know what you expect me to do with all my time.

GUY: Well, you have your job.

SALLY: My only job now is housewife.

GUY: You can't just leave Saul in the lurch. At least finish out the fifties.

SALLY: I don't know…

GUY: Love, honor, and what?

SALLY: You're right, of course. Now if those are all the rules, how about you stay here and read the paper, and I'll bring breakfast up to you?

GUY: Really?

SALLY: Of course. That's what wives do, silly.

(GUY lies back down on his bed, opens the paper, and smiles.)

GUY: Women need a better agent.

SCENE 4

SAUL'S office, two weeks later, morning. SALLY is laying out contracts on SAUL's desk, while SAUL opens champagne and JERRY leafs through a stack of magazines. GUY lounges on the sofa in a coal miner's costume.

JERRY: I've never seen so many covers.

SAUL: And not just the fan mags, we got *Look, Redbook, Reader's Digest*. People can't get enough of you two.

SALLY: This morning in the supermarket I was nearly mobbed.

JERRY: *(To GUY.)* You make her do the shopping?

SALLY: Oh, I had to go out anyway to fetch his drycleaning.

JERRY: Guy, she's your wife, not your slave.

GUY: She enjoys it. Right, honey?

SALLY: I enjoy anything that makes my husband happy.

SAUL: She's like the camera negative of Bernice.

(SAUL begins pouring champagne. SALLY, who has finished laying out the contracts, hands GUY a pen.)

SALLY: Well, all ready… Mister Hur.

(GUY takes the pen, then turns to JERRY.)

GUY: Last chance to gouge him.

JERRY: Believe me, he's tapped.

(GUY signs the contract.)

GUY: Spletty… Abromowictz.

(SAUL passes out champagne.)

SALLY: Bottoms up!

(Everyone downs their champagne except SALLY, who sips.)

SAUL: Come on, sweetie—drink up so I have a chance.

SALLY: Mr. Ornstein, I'm a married woman.

GUY: That's right. Don't make me make Jerry defend her honor.

(SALLY collects the contracts, then hugs GUY.)

SALLY: Well, congratulations, honey. Can I celebrate with a new dress?

GUY: Absolutely.

(SALLY hurries out, bubbling over with happiness.)

JERRY: You have her buying your clothes, too?

SAUL: Oh, did I tell you? John Ford's people called. They want us to loan you out.

GUY: John Ford?

JERRY: I know!

GUY: No, I mean who is that?

SAUL: Even people who should know better are buying into this thing. 'Course it doesn't hurt to have Sally talking you up all over town.

GUY: She's like a second manager.

JERRY: Hey.

GUY: Relax. Five Sally's couldn't do the work of one lesbian.

JERRY: I'm not a lesbian.

GUY: Yet your favorite sport is…

JERRY: Plenty of women golf.

SAUL: I'm just saying, you could have done a lot worse.

JERRY: Well, if you'll excuse us, Guy is due back on the set.

SAUL: Actually, he's wrapped. I'm shutting that picture down.

GUY: What? Saul, I need to be making a picture. When I'm home too much, Sally… takes advantage.

SAUL: Yeah? What's she like?

GUY: Total bottom.

JERRY: Besides, what's the problem with "Blood Mine?"

SAUL: The problem is, I got Red hunters from Washington breathing down my neck, and it's just too lefty. We gotta tone down the script. *(Into intercom.)* Sally, is the writer here yet?

SALLY: *(Offstage.)* Yes, Mr. Ornstein.

SAUL: You can stay if you want.

JERRY: Please, Guy doesn't even look at his scripts until the day they shoot.

GUY: Sometimes not even then.

(GUY and JERRY begin out, just as the young, Bohemian RICK FOSTER enters.)

GUY: But you know what? I should take more of an interest.

JERRY: We have to go.

GUY: Bye.

SAUL: Who are you?

RICK: Rick Foster. Is this the meeting about "Blood Mine?"

SAUL: Yes. Only no one here ordered a pizza...

RICK: I'm the writer.

SAUL: I thought Rosenthal was on this one. What happened to him?

(JERRY taps SAUL's Variety.)

SAUL: Aw, that's too bad.

RICK: I wrote the novel.

(SAUL sighs, and presses his intercom button.)

SAUL: Sally, you want to get a couple of people from the phone book in here too?

SALLY: *(Offstage.)* Yes, Mr. Ornstein.

SAUL: *(To RICK.)* Sorry for the mixup. Tell the Valley I said hi.

GUY: He might as well stay, since he's here. After all, we could always use a fresh pair of blue eyes.

(GUY sits down on the sofa, and pats the seat next to him. JERRY does not like where this is heading.)

JERRY: Fine, let's do this then. What exactly needs toning down?

SAUL: What doesn't? The picture's a god-damned pinko tract. Why shoot the thing, we should just have angry dog-faced broads pass it out on street corners.

RICK: It's a balanced look at the labor movement.

SAUL: *(Into intercom.)* Sy, roll those rushes for me again.

(The lights dim, and a projector behind the back wall starts up. Everyone watches the unseen screen on the fourth wall, as the film's soundtrack plays from the back of the house—a dialogue between GUY and FREDDIE STEVENS (TRICK).)

FREDDIE: *(Offstage.)* Not only did our little cave-in silence the union boys, we don't even have to pay to have them buried.

(We hear male laughter, then a door burst open.)

FREDDIE: *(Offstage.)* Goodman!

(Watching himself, GUY mouths his screen dialogue.)

GUY: *(Offstage.)* Surprised to see me, Greid? Well it takes more than two hundred tons of coal to crush the worker spirit.

FREDDIE: *(Offstage.)* You'll never pin that on me. We rich types got Uncle Sam in our back pocket.

GUY: *(Offstage.)* Yeah? Well he'd better climb out of there before his nieces and nephews go looking for a new uncle.

FREDDIE: *(Offstage.)* And give up their precious freedom?

GUY: *(Offstage.)* Know why they call it freedom? Because nobody's free, and that's dumb.

(The projector stops and the lights come up.)

RICK: None of that is from my book.

GUY: Hey! Why don't we have Rick here do the revisions?

SAUL: We need a screenwriter.

RICK: I don't want the job anyway.

SAUL: What do you mean you don't want the job? This is a major motion picture.

RICK: It's a major piece of crap.

SAUL: No one says no to me! I'll ruin you. You'll never work in pictures again.

RICK: I don't want to work in pictures.

SAUL: Yeah? Well you're gonna.

RICK: I'd better leave while you still sound insane.

(RICK begins out. GUY stops him.)

GUY: He'll just get someone bad. This way you can protect your book.

(RICK takes a beat, though whether it's to consider GUY's point or GUY himself is unclear.)

RICK: I'm making a mistake.

(RICK exits. JERRY turns to GUY.)

JERRY: So are you. We have a good thing going here.

GUY: I'm only thinking of the script. Set up a meeting, I want to give him my notes.

JERRY: In fifteen pictures, the only note you've ever had is "more places where I take my shirt off."

GUY: Well I have it again. And since you brought it up, you don't suppose he's…

JERRY: No.

GUY: Then again, you don't think you are.

SCENE 5

GUY's bedroom, night. GUY is clearly primping for a date, while SALLY buzzes about, setting out refreshments and straightening up.

SALLY: The bedroom is certainly an unconventional place for a meeting.

GUY: It's a creative meeting, and the bedroom makes me feel more… creative.

SALLY: I know—I remember three weeks ago last Thursday.

(SALLY giggles. GUY sets a particular book prominently on a table.)

GUY: Well, you mustn't keep Bernice waiting.

SALLY: Oh Guy, I hate her stupid women's group. That awful Edith Head always makes fun of my clothes, and Barbara Stanwyck just stares at me. Can't I stay here with you?

GUY: You'd just be in the way. But I'll tell you all about it when you get home no earlier than midnight.

SALLY: All right. But will you miss me?

GUY: Let's see.

(GUY gives SALLY a peck on the cheek.)

SALLY: Honey, it has to last me the whole night.

(SALLY gives GUY a much longer kiss. RICK appears in the doorway.)

RICK: The maid said I should—

SALLY: Oh! My goodness, I could just die. But it's legal. *(Flashes her ring.)*

RICK: I was just about to call the cops.

GUY: Honey, this is Rick Foster. Rick, this is... um...

SALLY: Sally Stone. Sally Stone Sally Stone Sally Stone. I could say it a million times.

GUY: In the car.

(GUY shoos SALLY out.)

SALLY: Well, nice to meet you, Mr. Foster.

RICK: You too, Sally Stone.

(SALLY giggles, then exits.)

RICK: She's certainly in love.

GUY: What? Oh, that was mostly for your benefit, I'm afraid. Any passion we might once have shared is long gone. By this point, we're more roommates than lovers.

RICK: Wasn't your wedding five weeks ago?

GUY: Almost six. Are you married, Rick?

RICK: No.

GUY: Girlfriend?

RICK: No.

GUY: Really.

(RICK sits, and sees the book GUY set out earlier.)

RICK: Hey, you're reading my novel.

GUY: Sure. It was so sweet of you to dedicate it to your mother.

RICK: She really encouraged me. My whole life, she's been more like a best friend than a mom.

(Emboldened, GUY sits right next to RICK.)

GUY: I think Judy Garland is great, don't you?

RICK: She's like antique shopping and pool parties rolled into one.

GUY: Well, enough small talk. Let's get to work.

(GUY moves closer to RICK.)

RICK: Can I put on the game?

(GUY freezes in place.)

GUY: The game?

RICK: Isn't that a television?

(RICK points to an unseen piece of furniture. GUY shakes his head wanly.)

GUY: It's an early Deco credenza. *(Rises and fixes himself a drink.)*

RICK: You know, all you have to do is ask.

GUY: Ask what?

RICK: If I'm gay.

GUY: Are you gay?

RICK: I'm gay.

GUY: I'm gay.

RICK: *(Sarcastically.)* Really?

GUY: Hey, I act plenty straight. I even have a wife.

RICK: And what's that about?

GUY: It's Hollywood. So. We're both gay.

RICK: Custom dictates we have sex now.

GUY: Okay, then.

(GUY returns to RICK, who moves away.)

RICK: I was joking.

GUY: I don't get it.

RICK: Anyway, wouldn't that make working together kind of awkward?

GUY: There's only one way to find out.

(GUY advances on RICK again.)

RICK: I'm really not interested in having sex right now.

GUY: Are you sure you're gay?

RICK: Maybe you're just not my type.

GUY: Please, I'm everybody's type.

RICK: I can't believe you actually said that.

GUY: What? That's not vanity, it's professional pride. My job is to make every man, woman, and child in America love me to pieces. And I take it very seriously.

RICK: I can tell.

GUY: And don't pretend you're the only holdout, because I have a sense for these things.

RICK: Well either way, you're married.

GUY: What does that have to do with anything?

RICK: I guess it's a generational thing.

GUY: Excuse me?

RICK: How old are you?

GUY: I can play twenties.

RICK: A lot of people my age aren't interested in hiding who we are.

GUY: Are a lot of people your age movie stars?

RICK: Hey, how about we put the whole subject aside, and just focus on the script? I heard you had some notes for me.

GUY: Right. Um, more places where I take my shirt off.

RICK: So this whole meeting was really just about seducing me.

GUY: Duh.

RICK: Well the thing is, I really do need help. I got this memo today of changes the studio wants, and I don't know how to address them without ruining the picture.

GUY: I'm sure they're not that bad.

RICK: For Hollywood, probably not. *(Reading from memo.)* "Number Three: Eliminate all references to labor unions."

GUY: So?

RICK: Did you finish my book?

GUY: Not yet.

RICK: Where are you?

GUY: The dedication.

RICK: It's the story of coal miners struggling to unionize. Take that out and all that's left is the romance between you and the shop-girl, who, oh, they want to make a Countess.

GUY: So leave the labor stuff in, and just change the word "union" to "guild" or "league" or something.

RICK: They're stupid enough to fall for that? Wait, I forgot where I was.

GUY: You're kind of a hypocrite, aren't you?

RICK: Me? You're the one with a wife.

GUY: That's right. Fans want me straight, so I can either be straight or go into another line. Just like you can either consider yourself above Hollywood or take our money, but not both.

RICK: I didn't even want this job. You talked me into it.

GUY: I said two sentences. If you're that much of a pushover, we should be having sex now.

RICK: *(Caught off guard.)* You're actually very smart when you need to be.

GUY: I know. But it's so much work.

RICK: I don't understand this place.

GUY: Someone once said only a few people could hold the entire equation of Hollywood in their head.

RICK: *(Impressed.)* F. Scott Fitzgerald.

GUY: I guess that kid in the carwash men's room was a big reader.

(RICK actually laughs. GUY knows when to press his advantage. He begins moving about the room, dimming the lights, turning on music, and grabbing a bottle of champagne.)

GUY: So how about instead of trying to understand this place, we just sit back, drink some champagne, and enjoy it?

(GUY turns to the sofa, but RICK has moved to the door.)

GUY: Where are you going?

RICK: I don't mess around on the first date.

(RICK exits. GUY calls after him.)

GUY: Are you sure you're gay?

SCENE 6

SAUL's office, two weeks later. SAUL enters and can't help but notice the elaborate Hammond home organ set up in his office. He turns around and calls through the still-open door.

SAUL: Sally!

(SALLY enters.)

SALLY: Yes, Mr. Ornstein?

SAUL: What the hell is this?

SALLY: Oh, Guy's birthday present. I needed someplace to hide it.

SAUL: An entire lot full of empty stages, and you choose here.

SALLY: It's where they delivered it. I was going to move it myself, only it's too heavy, because I had it done in walnut because it's more masculine. Oh, do you think Guy will like it?

SAUL: Will Guy like a masculine organ? I think that's a safe bet.

SALLY: They're oodles of fun at parties. Plus I wanted to do something special for him. After all, he's done so much for me.

SAUL: You've done plenty for him, believe me.

SALLY: Hardly. Mr. Ornstein, can I ask you something? Once you've been married for a while, how do you keep it exciting?

SAUL: You don't.

SALLY: Oh, I could never believe that, not when there's love. But lately, I worry that Guy and I are drifting. He's always working with that writer, and even when we're together he seems preoccupied. Mr. Ornstein, you're a man. What can a girl like me do to turn a fella's head?

SAUL: You're doing it, Sally. Guy just can't see.

SALLY: But he has to. How can I… Well I hate to be blunt, but how can I get him in the mood for closeness?

SAUL: Okay, first go down to the film library, and bring home "Tarzan Goes to Boot Camp."

SALLY: Whatever for?

SAUL: The jungle. Trust me.

SALLY: Oh, listen to me go on. The simple fact is, my life is a dream come true. *(Re: organ.)* Hey, do you want to hear me play?

SAUL: Not even a little.

SALLY: Come on. Just to see what I remember.

(SALLY sits at the organ and turns it on. SAUL sighs and leans against his desk. SALLY flips a few switches on the organ, and a cheesy percussive track begins playing. She sings a few voice-clearing notes which are not particularly promising, then hits a few chords on the organ, also to no great effect. But unexpectedly, she finds a melody, and begins playing it fairly well. After a moment, she begins singing. Her voice is actually not bad.)

SALLY: *(Sings.)*
　　Two kinds of love, we're in two kinds
　　　of love
　　I have feelings for you,
　　I'll spend all my days with you.

(SALLY flips a few levers on the organ, which begins reproducing several more instruments.)

SALLY: *(Sings.)*
　　Two kinds of love, we're in two kinds
　　　of love
　　Even though now it seems, you're feel-
　　　ing no love for me,

(As SALLY segues into the chorus, she flips a few more levers, adding several more instruments and creating an improbably rich sound.)

SALLY: *(Sings.)*
　　Still I hope deep inside you'll change,
　　And I still fantasize a way,
　　For us to go on, in spite of
　　Two kinds of love!

(SALLY flips a few more levers, and dives into the keyboard with mad abandon. The organ's repertoire is revealed to be limitless: She calls upon horns, strings, even a vocal choir to create a rich tapestry of music, which builds to an enormous crescendo, then abates.)

SALLY: *(Sings.)*
　　You're never around, you're nowhere
　　　to be found.
　　Is it something I said? Or am I being
　　　misled?
　　Still I hope deep inside you'll change,
　　And I still fantasize a way,
　　For us to go on, in spite of
　　Two kinds of love!

(SALLY lets loose a final over-the-top flourish of all possible instruments simultaneously, then ends the song with a decisive chord. She switches off the organ, smiles mildly, and turns to SAUL, who is near tears.)

SALLY: Mr. Ornstein, are you all right?

SAUL: I have to call my wife! *(Rushes out of his office, sobbing.)*

SCENE 7

GUY's bedroom, later that day. The place has been ransacked by some vigorous, prolonged, and apparently just-completed sex. GUY is now putting his shoes back on; RICK, who is shirtless, puts on his pants.

RICK: Okay, that was the best sex I've had in my life.

GUY: Yeah, I get that a lot.

RICK: Shut up. *(Throws a pillow at GUY.)*

GUY: You hungry?

RICK: Sure, what do you got?

(GUY moves to a tray of covered food in the corner.)

GUY: Looks like lobster salad, a couple of steaks, and a big thing of… caviar.

RICK: Nice life you have going here.

GUY: I suppose. But the truth is, I'd give it up in a heartbeat for something even more lavish.

RICK: What do you think you would have done if the whole movie star thing hadn't worked out?

GUY: I don't know. Something fabulous.

RICK: You're right, aren't you?

GUY: Of course. Things always go my way.

RICK: Well, except you're gay.

GUY: That's a bad thing?

RICK: It's a crisis. When you realize you're something the rest of the world fears and oppresses? At least that moment must have been hard for you.

GUY: Sure. But fortunately my track coach was there to help me through it.

(GUY tries to pour wine for RICK, who covers his glass.)

RICK: Today I actually do have to work.

GUY: Another memo?

RICK: Now Saul says at the end the miners can't even join the labor… Oh, "guild" is a no-sale. I'm trying "coalition."

GUY: Do I still get the girl?

RICK: So far.

GUY: Then we're fine. People don't want politics, they want romance.

RICK: I don't even know anymore. It's starting to feel like we've changed so much, all that's left of my book is the title.

GUY: Well your book isn't changing, and the movie will draw attention to it.

RICK: That's true.

GUY: All the best rationalizations are.

(GUY wraps an arm around RICK. Suddenly we hear a door close downstairs.)

FEMALE VOICE: *(Offstage.)* Guy?

RICK: Is that Sally?

GUY: She's supposed to be at work.

(We hear footsteps coming upstairs. RICK begins looking around frantically.)

RICK: Where's my shirt?

GUY: There's no time. Hide.

(RICK heads toward the bathroom.)

GUY: Not there!

RICK: How about the closet? We can be together.

(RICK dives behind the bed, just as the door opens and JERRY enters.)

GUY: Jerry.

(JERRY sees the mess.)

JERRY: Couldn't find the last popper?

GUY: No, see we were…

JERRY: We?

(RICK appears from behind the bed.)

RICK: Hey, Jerry.

JERRY: I take it your meeting went well.

GUY: And we're kind of in the middle of another one, so…

JERRY: You may have to adjourn. The newsreel crew will be here any minute.

GUY: Newsreel crew?

JERRY: They need some "Guy and Sally at home" stuff for that piece they're doing. Which they're not planning to show on a bedsheet in some bank teller's apartment.

GUY: Relax. It's not like we were caught.

JERRY: Guy, I don't think you appreciate the stakes here. Occasional sex we can work around, but seeing someone on a regular basis—

RICK: So you're saying he can never fall in love?

JERRY: Hey, I don't make the rules.

RICK: But you do. We all do, with our actions.

JERRY: Okay, can I just say that is beautiful, and retarded. Maybe thirty years from now a gay actor will be no big deal, but if you think I'm going to sacrifice Guy to the cause—

RICK: I think you'll do whatever's expedient—

GUY: Rick, Jerry, please—I hate seeing the men in my life fight. Now I have a compromise. *(To JERRY.)* You leave, and Rick and I will have sex again. *(Off JERRY's look.)* Kidding. We'll straighten up, then he'll go too, now bye.

(GUY ushers JERRY out, closes the door, and turns to RICK.)

GUY: I was kidding about the kidding. Now where were we?

RICK: Hiding under your bed.

GUY: For three seconds.

RICK: It's all so easy for you. The compromises. The deceptions.

GUY: *(Pouring wine.)* Drink this wonderful elixir and it will be easy for you, too.

RICK: You know, this is not a virtue. The constant glibness?

GUY: Don't you think I'm funny?

RICK: Oh, you're funny. About everything. But not everything is funny. One of these days life is going to go serious on you, and you'll have no idea how to handle it.

GUY: So show me.

RICK: *(With irony.)* By my example?

GUY: Rick, I know all this is hard for you. I hate it too. But just be patient, and before you know it it'll be spring.

RICK: And you'll go to Italy.

GUY: And we'll go to Italy.

RICK: What?

GUY: Think about it. An oceanfront villa, no Sally, no reporters. Just you and me.

RICK: I don't know what to say.

GUY: Try "yes."

RICK: Okay. Yes.

GUY: Excellent! *(Kisses RICK.)* I love you!

RICK: I love you, too.

(RICK kisses GUY. The kiss grows more passionate. GUY takes RICK in his arms and dips him, turning around just in time to see SALLY enter. GUY hurls RICK away from him, onto the bed.)

GUY: Honey!

SALLY: *(Distracted by the mess.)* What happened in here?

GUY: We were... acting out the fight scene.

SALLY: Boys will be boys. *(Begins straightening up.)*

RICK: *(Overly butch.)* Well, I guess it's time to knock off.

GUY: I'm certainly spent.

(RICK collects his things, and heads out.)

SALLY: Goodnight, Mr. Foster.

RICK: Sally.

(RICK notices his belt draped over a chair, and grabs it.)

RICK: The fight scene gets pretty wild. *(Exits.)*

GUY: So how was work?

SALLY: Boring. I left early.

GUY: For the newsreel thing?

SALLY: No, I canceled that. We have the whole house all to ourselves.

GUY: Well that's nice, but I still have a lot of work to do.

SALLY: You may find it hard to concentrate... *(Produces a sexy negligee from her handbag.)*

GUY: I've never seen that before in my life.

SALLY: How could you have, silly? I just bought it. I was so embarrassed setting foot in that department, but I wanted to have on something sexy when I showed you your other surprise. *(Exits into the hallway, then quickly returns lugging two heavy film cases.)*

GUY: *(A kid on his birthday.)* "Tarzan Goes to Boot Camp?!"

SALLY: It was Mr. Ornstein's idea.

GUY: Aw, he's the best.

SALLY: Hey, why don't you set up the projector in here? That way, if you start feeling intimate...

GUY: Actually, it's that time of the month.

SALLY: Still?

GUY: You didn't think it happened to men at all. But listen, why don't you lug these to the screening room while I grab a quick bath?

SALLY: Would you like company?

GUY: No, but those wonderful salts...

SALLY: On my vanity.

GUY: Fabulous.

(GUY exits into the bathroom. SALLY stares after him, concerned, then rises and begins straightening up the room. She finds herself drawn to Guy's portrait, and notices a hidden handle under the frame. She pulls on it, opening the cabinet door and revealing a wall of drawers behind it.)

(SALLY steels herself, then opens a drawer. Seeing what's inside, she laughs, enormously relieved, and removes a pair of gym shorts from it. But closer examination reveals that the shorts have no ass. She throws them on the bed and opens another drawer. She pulls out several bodybuilding magazines and some gay pornography. Realizing what she's touching, she flings it away from herself reflexively, then opens another drawer. She takes several bottles of lotion from it, and some black leather studded underwear. She drops these items as well, then opens one of the double drawers, but pulls too far, causing a cornucopia of films, nude male posters, some black rope, and rubber toys to spill everywhere. SALLY screams. GUY runs back into the room, now in a robe.)

GUY: What's wrong? *(Then, seeing the bed.)* Oh.

SALLY: I didn't mean to… I know I promised… But the place was all… And you've been acting so… Guy, what are all these things?

GUY: You know. Stuff.

SALLY: What are you doing with it?

GUY: Oh, you think… Now *that's* funny. *(Forces a laugh.)*

SALLY: You can explain all this?

GUY: Of course I can. The, um, the creams and lotions are for my skin.

SALLY: But you have beautiful skin.

GUY: Because I keep it lubricated. Then the… fitness magazines I buy for the articles, and inspiration. One day *I'm* going to look like *that*.

(GUY indicates a picture of a burly young man in assless chaps. SALLY's eyes move to the objects on the floor.)

GUY: As for the rest of this stuff—the leather delicates and rubber novelties and cylindrical massagers—that happens to be a great story.

SALLY: I could use a laugh about now.

GUY: Then get ready. Because they, in fact, are actually…

SALLY: Yes?

GUY: Don't rush me.

SALLY: I'm going to mother's.

GUY: They're a joke. A joke gift from Charlton Heston. He sent the whole mess over when he heard we'd gotten married. In a big pink basket!

SALLY: But why?

GUY: Because I'm so *not gay*. Chuck is going to get the biggest kick when he hears what you thought.

(GUY laughs; SALLY joins in, then hugs him.)

SALLY: I'm such a fool.

(GUY nods, then breaks the hug. A strange feeling comes over him—empathy.)

GUY: Sally, actually—

SALLY: I gave myself quite a scare there. I mean, we would have had to divorce, and then the reporters would want to know why, and I just couldn't lie to them, not to protect a pervert. Thank goodness it was all my imagination.

(SALLY laughs. GUY joins in, hollowly.)

SALLY: Now come here, you.

GUY: But it's that…

SALLY: I know, but you've got that look on your face. I can tell nothing is going to keep you away from me. *(Lies back on the bed.)* I could resist, but you'd just over-power me.

(SALLY pulls GUY on top of her.)

GUY: You know me so well.

(SALLY starts kissing him, and doesn't stop.)

SCENE 8

SAUL's office, two weeks later. The lights are low, and the projector is running. RICK and SAUL are watching the final cut of "Blood Mine," specifically the big confrontation scene between GUY and FREDDIE.

FREDDIE: *(Offstage.)* So you're saying every single union organizer was in that mine?

(We hear a door burst open. GUY enters from the bathroom in time with it, and be-gins mouthing his dialogue.)

FREDDIE: *(Offstage.)* Goodson!

GUY: *(Offstage.)* Surprised to see me, Mr. Fatherman?

FREDDIE: *(Offstage.)* I'll say. I've been worried sick.

GUY: *(Offstage.)* Yeah? Well I had a lot of time to think while you spared no expense to rescue us, and I've been worried too—worried I hurt your feelings. We don't need to join that labor club.

FREDDIE: *(Offstage.)* You know what they say: If it ain't broke…

GUY: *(Offstage.)* It was probably made in America.

FREDDIE: *(Offstage.)* The Countess is a lucky woman.

(Music swells, then the film ends. The lights come up.)

GUY: I am so handsome.

SAUL: *(To RICK.)* I was wrong about you, kid—you pulled it off. All we need now is a new title.

RICK: How about "America Works!"

SAUL: Perfect. How'd you like to write the next "Captain Astro?"

(SAUL exits into the bathroom.)

GUY: Your first movie—and starring me.

RICK: It's a piece of crap.

GUY: But starring me. You must be so proud.

RICK: Doesn't it tear your guts out to see something like that?

GUY: So maybe it's not the best movie in the world. At least you have a credit.

RICK: The scary part is, I know what you mean. What happened to me? A month ago I sat right here making fun of you people.

GUY: It's the system.

RICK: No, Guy.

GUY: It is. You make the bad ones—

RICK: —so you can make the good ones, and we're just giving the people what they want, and they don't call it "show art." I've bought into every one of your stupid rationalizations, and all I've got to show for it is a fascist movie with my name on it, and a boyfriend I can only see at meetings.

GUY: Is that what this is about? It's just been harder to get away now that filming is over, especially since, um…

RICK: Sally.

GUY: Thank you, started getting suspi-cious. But once we're in Italy—

RICK: Sally is coming with you to Italy, Guy. We both know it. I'm through lying.

GUY: Well what do you want me to do, give up "Ben Hur?"

RICK: I want you to be honest about the fact that you're choosing "Ben Hur" over me.

GUY: I'm not. I want both.

RICK: You can't have both.

GUY: Yes I can.

RICK: How?

GUY: Because things always go my way.

RICK: Must be nice. *(Collects his knapsack.)* Well listen, I really hope "Ben Hur" makes you happy.

GUY: Rick, don't make this into one of your things.

RICK: I'm not. This isn't courage, Guy. I'm not being principled or resolute or brave. I just see where this is going, and I'm not afraid to face the truth, even if for the life of me I can't understand it. Because I'm real.

(SALLY enters with a pitcher on a tray.)

SALLY: Who wants lemonade?

RICK: Goodbye, Guy.

(RICK exits, near tears. GUY begins after him, but SALLY blocks his path by offering him the tray.)

GUY: No thanks.

(SALLY puts the tray down, then notices that GUY is near tears himself.)

SALLY: It's okay, hon, no one can see. *(Hugs GUY.)* I always cry at your movies, too.

(GUY stares after RICK, then grabs his wife tightly as the lights go down.)

ACT II
SCENE 1

GUY's bedroom, two weeks later, night. There's a punchbowl set up, and the bed is covered with coats and purses. GUY, in a tuxedo, lies underneath them. We hear laughter and music from a party downstairs, as SALLY enters, calling behind her.

SALLY: Thank you. It's from a pattern. *(Closes the door and sees GUY.)* Honey!

GUY: Are there still people here?

SALLY: Yes, there are still people here. We're entertaining, now up.

GUY: I don't feel like it.

SALLY: Please? It's my first party as Mrs. Guy Stone. I want everything to be perfect.

(GUY struggles to sit up, but doesn't quite make it.)

SALLY: What has gotten into you lately? All this sleeping, and moping. I bet it's the season. Growing up, winter would make me blue, too. And my mother would say, feelings are like treasures, so bury them.

GUY: *(Sitting up.)* I'm Guy Stone, happily married movie star.

SALLY: That's better. And you'll have fun once you're downstairs—everyone is here. Bing Crosby and Judy Garland and Charlton Heston. Who is not letting on about that gift basket, by the way. He looked at me like I was crazy.

(JERRY enters, looking uncomfortable in a nice dress, and calls behind her.)

JERRY: Yeah, that was funny in high school.

SALLY: Miss Albrecht, what are you doing up here? All the bachelors are downstairs.

JERRY: I know. They voted me out.

SALLY: That's no way to talk. *(Serving JERRY some punch.)* One day a man like Guy will fall for you, too.

JERRY: Oh, I'm sure of it.

(GUY has returned to the bed.)

SALLY: Honey…

JERRY: *(Off punch.)* What is this stuff?

SALLY: *Good Housekeeping's* Festival Punch. It's fruit juice, champagne, a pinch of brandy, and Wheat Chex.

JERRY: It's delicious.

SALLY: Guy…

(SALLY gives him an urgent "up" gesture, while JERRY pours her punch back into the bowl. SAUL enters, a little drunk, and sees SALLY.)

SAUL: There she is.

SALLY: Hello, Mr. Ornstein.

(SAUL kisses SALLY on the cheek. JERRY prepares for a kiss herself, but SAUL just nods.)

SAUL: Jerry.

SALLY: Whew—I can tell someone's been to the bar.

SAUL: Premiere nights always give me the jitters.

SALLY: Well I thought Guy's movie was wonderful. Didn't you?

JERRY: I loved it. And I know people are going to think I'm just saying that because

I'm his manager and I have to.

SAUL: Where is he, anyway?

(GUY gives a slight wave from the bed.)

GUY: Hey, Saul.

SAUL: Stone, I didn't pack this place with reporters so you could nap. I want you downstairs, and I want you smiling.

GUY: About what?

JERRY: He just needs perking up. *(Looking through purses.)* Which one of these is Judy's?

(SAUL pours himself some punch.)

SAUL: I'm about to risk five mil here, I don't want to worry if my star is gonna off himself.

JERRY: I meant to warn you about this. *(Leading SAUL out.)* See, Guy has been studying with a method acting coach, and tonight's premiere actually sent him back into character as the young coal miner trapped in a cave-in. I know that sounds like bullshit, because it is, I'll talk to him.

(JERRY pushes SAUL out the door.)

SALLY: More punch, Miss Albrecht?

JERRY: No, but you know what I'd like? What is that thing you have out back?

SALLY: The cookie tree?

JERRY: *(Leading SALLY out.)* Yes. Go pick me a nice cookie from the cookie tree. Thank you, sweetheart.

(JERRY pushes SALLY out as well, then closes the door and turns to GUY.)

JERRY: Okay sport, enough is enough.

GUY: I'm not going down there.

JERRY: I know this whole thing with Rick has been hard on you.

GUY: No, don't even try.

JERRY: But... Guy, listen. When you came to me five years ago and said you wanted to be a star, I told you there'd be some sacrifices.

GUY: And then I went that whole week without work.

JERRY: It may be time to make another one.

GUY: It's not fair. Nobody else has to sacrifice love.

JERRY: What? Please, you could count the happy couples downstairs on your fingers. Hell, so could Harold Russell. Fame destroys everyone's lives. You'd be just as miserable if you were straight, and you'd be wearing a much uglier tux.

GUY: And I'd be fat.

JERRY: There's the Guy Stone I remember. Now how about we go downstairs and show those losers a real movie star.

(GUY stands up, ready to do just that, and sees RICK in the doorway.)

GUY: Rick.

RICK: Hello Guy.

JERRY: Oh geez, who invites the writer?

GUY: Can you give us a minute?

JERRY: No, I'm staying right here where I can hold your pants up.

GUY: Please?

JERRY: Five minutes. Or I come back with a hose. *(Reluctantly exits.)*

GUY: Were you at the premiere?

RICK: I'd say I'm not that much of a masochist, but I'm here.

GUY: I'm glad. You look good.

RICK: You too. So? *(Looks quizzically into the punch bowl.)*

GUY: Wheat Chex. Rick, let's try again.

RICK: No.

GUY: It would be different.

RICK: What would be different?

GUY: Me. Rick, these past two weeks have taught me a lot. It turns out things don't always go my way. It turns out I can make mistakes which, if I don't correct, I'll regret for the rest of my life.

RICK: How many times did you rehearse that speech?

GUY: I've never rehearsed in my life.

(RICK laughs, then cuts it short.)

RICK: No. You're funny, I'm laughing, but when the chips are down you choke, and I can't go through that again.

GUY: You won't have to. I know I'm not the strongest person in the world, but Rick, if you take me back, I promise I will never hurt you again.

(RICK regards GUY for a moment.)

RICK: I just need to ask one question.

GUY: Anything.

RICK: When did Judy Garland get so fat?

(GUY smiles, and RICK and he hug. The lights in the bedroom go out, and come up on a small set meant to represent a corner of the party. There is another punch bowl here, and a glass door that leads to the backyard. SALLY emerges through the door, holding a

tree branch that has been adorned with cookies. She sees the back of a handsome man, JIM (TRICK), who is serving himself punch.)

SALLY: Guy?

(JIM turns around.)

SALLY: I thought you were my husband. Have you seen him?

JIM: Oh yes.

(SAUL enters from outside, even more drunk than before.)

SALLY: Getting some fresh air?

SAUL: Puking. Oh, I see you've met Tim Jully. Jim Tully. He's a reporter from "Screen Stars."

SALLY: *(Disapprovingly.)* "Screen Stars"?

SAUL: No, no, they're doing a nice piece on us. *(To JIM.)* And not just a blurb in your column, either—I want a two page spread and the cover.

JIM: Sure. How's this for a headline: "World's Dullest Party Bores Reporter to Death." *(Exits.)*

SALLY: It wouldn't be so dull if someone would play the organ.

SAUL: Don't worry, toots. People are having a blast. *(Serves himself more punch.)*

SALLY: I think you may have had too many blasts.

SAUL: Or maybe you could just use one.

SALLY: A good hostess allows herself one drink every ninety minutes.

SAUL: Where'd you read that, "Frigid Bitch" magazine?

SALLY: Mr. Ornstein, really.

SAUL: My wife is the editor. She does a regular column which is just the word no.

SALLY: Where is Bernice this evening?

SAUL: She went straight home from the flick. Her tuxedo was bothering her. It's funny, really. With you and Guy I thought, how could she not see something so obvious?

SALLY: How about I take you to the guest room?

SAUL: I thought you'd never ask.

SALLY: So you can rest.

SAUL: You and me are in a position to help each other. Wouldn't you say?

(SAUL moves closer to SALLY.)

SALLY: Miss Albrecht will be wondering about her cookies.

SAUL: Don't run off. You're a young vibrant woman, and I've got a good five minutes 'til I need to puke again.

(SAUL moves in closer still.)

SALLY: Mr. Ornstein, I'll scream.

SAUL: How about we both do?

(SAUL kisses SALLY, who waits a beat before moving away.)

SALLY: No! I have a husband.

SAUL: So do I.

(SAUL moves in again. SALLY beats him back with the cookie tree branch, and runs outside, then up some stairs. Lights up on the bedroom, where GUY and RICK are now half undressed and kissing. GUY kneels at RICK's crotch just as SALLY emerges through the balcony doors.)

GUY: Sally, you know Rick.

(SALLY screams and runs to the bedroom door, but it's locked. SAUL enters behind SALLY, and sees GUY and RICK.)

SAUL: A few more drinks and I'd join in.

(SALLY gets the door open, and JIM rushes in, camera poised.)

JIM: I heard a scream, and— *(Seeing GUY and RICK.)* Cha-ching! *(Takes a picture, and turns to SAUL.)* I don't think the cover will be a problem.

(JIM rushes out, passing JERRY, who enters and takes in the scene.)

JERRY: Okay, here's why this is good.

SCENE 2

RICK's apartment, a week later, evening. RICK's tiny hovel is furnished with mis-matched hand-me-downs, a few tacked-up posters providing the only decoration. There is at least one door and window. RICK is at the table, trying to write, but he's preoccu-pied. GUY enters carrying a paper bag.

GUY: Honey, I'm homo.

RICK: Where have you been? I was wor-ried.

GUY: I was just walking around. Is it me, or is everyone in this neighborhood gay except our landladies?

RICK: It's pretty friendly. So people left you alone?

GUY: One kid called me Guy Fag. Which I don't get—Gay Stone is such a gimme. *(Off bag.)* Hey, I bought dinner.

RICK: Not—

GUY: No, not steak. Chicken, and rice, and peas, and one bottle of swill beer.

RICK: I'm impressed.

GUY: You never really forget how to be poor. It's like riding a bicyclist.

RICK: Still, usually poor doesn't come after Beverly Hills.

GUY: The truth is I'm kind of enjoying it. It's charming.

RICK: *(Gesturing to the room.)* Charming?

GUY: Which doesn't mean I won't drag you to Malibu the second they let me at my money. *(Indicating typewriter.)* So how are we coming with my stage debut?

RICK: I think maybe okay.

GUY: Confidence. *(Takes the pages, and scans through them.)*

RICK: Writing that movie actually taught me a lot. *(Beat.)* You hate it.

GUY: No, it's good, it's good…

(RICK turns to a particular page.)

RICK: "Jess takes his shirt off."

GUY: You're a genius.

(The buzzer sounds. RICK and GUY look at each other.)

GUY: I'm going to guess… *Photoplay.* No, the *Times.*

RICK: While you were out. Twice.

(RICK answers the door. It's JERRY.)

JERRY: Thank God. It took me forever to find this place.

RICK: You've never been to Silver Lake?

JERRY: If I want to be around a bunch of men who have no interest in me, I can go anywhere.

GUY: Jerry. What are you doing here?

JERRY: Can't a manager check on her number one client?

GUY: Number one, huh? Still?

JERRY: Well, in the sense of biggest homo.

GUY: You met with Saul.

JERRY: Yes I did.

GUY: Guess I can forget about "Ben Hur."

JERRY: *(Nods.)* I might be able to get you "Cleopatra."

GUY: Moving to Italy would have been a pain, anyway.

JERRY: You've certainly changed.

GUY: Rick is a good influence. So how are you doing with all this?

JERRY: *(To RICK.)* Did he just ask how I was doing?

RICK: I think so.

JERRY: I need to sit down. *(Sits at the table.)*

GUY: Are you all right?

JERRY: Stop it! Change I can take. This is just creepy.

GUY: Hey, Rick is writing me a play.

JERRY: Oh goody. *(To RICK.)* Of course, the real money is in poems.

RICK: I can use that. It's about Hollywood.

(RICK scribbles something on a pad. JERRY reads the play's cover page.)

JERRY: "The Dream Crushers." So do you come down pro or con?

GUY: Once the divorce is final, I'm going to put it on.

JERRY: Right. Guy.

GUY: On the cheap. Don't worry, I know I just get half.

JERRY: Of what?

GUY: My money. I'm rich, remember? You saw how I lived.

JERRY: Exactly. You spent everything the minute it came in. Mostly on the house, but Sally gets that.

GUY: So how much do I have?

JERRY: Nothing.

GUY: What is that in dollars?

JERRY: I thought you knew.

GUY: So I'll go back to work. I know I can't star, but supporting. Television.

JERRY: Guy, there's nothing for you. And there won't be, ever again.

GUY: Jerry, I can't even go to restaurants. I made Rick take me to Musso's the other night, and we had to leave. Even then people followed us, calling me names which I laughed off because in my head I've already bought the Malibu beach house with the big gate to keep them all out.

JERRY: I'm sorry.

RICK: So, would you like to stay for dinner? *(Gestures to the unappetizing groceries.)*

JERRY: Actually, how about we… How about I pick us up some steaks?

GUY: Yes!

RICK: There's a place on Rowena, catty-corner to—

JERRY: I'm lost already.

RICK: I'll come with you. *(To GUY.)* You gonna be okay?

GUY: Sure. I'll teach the mouse some more tricks.

(JERRY and RICK exit. Left alone, GUY picks up the play manuscript again, and begins reading.)

GUY: "I'll tell you what stardom is like. It's being thirty-four and—" Thirty-four?

(GUY takes a pencil and makes a correction to the page. A MAN (TRICK) stealthily enters through the window, sneaks up on GUY, and shoves a handkerchief over his mouth. GUY struggles to free himself, clutching at his attacker.)

GUY: Bmmm! Nmmmm!

(GUY gets a handful of the MAN's large bicep.)

GUY: Mmmmmm…

(GUY falls unconscious.)

SCENE 3

A room in a mental hospital, indicated by a projection screen; a swivel chair, on which GUY sits wearing a straitjacket; and a small control panel on a stand. DR. MÜELLER (TRICK) fiddles with its buttons as he talks to GUY.

GUY: I want to go home.

DR. MÜELLER: *(Austrian accent.)* You are home, Mr. Stone. Your vife has committed you to ziss hospital, und it is your home until I deem you cured of your sexual disease.

GUY: Penicillin usually does the trick.

DR. MÜELLER: Yes, vit—zee homosexual substitute for courage. Ve've got our vork cut out for us.

GUY: Wait, I know that accent. The stairwell of the UCLA parking structure?

DR. MÜELLER: In my youss, I vas confused. But rasser zan give into my base urges, I developed a zerapy for overcoming zem. Und now I vould like to share it viss you.

(DR. MÜELLER connects a few wires to GUY, which lead to his control panel.)

GUY: What's that?

DR. MÜELLER: It iss called an agony bolt. It sounds more scary zan it iss.

(DR. MÜELLER turns GUY's chair away from us, so that it faces the screen, then presses a button on the control panel. A slide of a muscular young man in a fitness pose is projected onto the screen.)

DR. MÜELLER: Does ziss gentleman appeal to you?

GUY: Jeff? Yeah, one time—

(DR. MÜELLER moves a dial on his panel. GUY convulses in electric shock.)

DR. MÜELLER: A simple yess or no vill do.

(DR. MÜELLER changes the slide to one of another attractive man.)

DR. MÜELLER: Does ziss gentleman appeal to you?

GUY: Brian? Yes—

(DR. MÜELLER gives GUY another electric shock.)

GUY: Ironically, he would have gotten off on this.

(DR. MÜELLER changes the slide to one of a third attractive man.)

DR. MÜELLER: Does ziss gentleman appeal to you?

GUY: Um… no.

DR. MÜELLER: You are lying.

(DR. MÜELLER gives GUY an electric shock anyway.)

GUY: How do you know?

DR. MÜELLER: Look at him.

(The lights go momentarily to black, then come back up, to signify the passage of time. DR. MÜELLER shows GUY a slide of an attractive woman.)

DR. MÜELLER: Does ziss voman appeal to you?

GUY: Yes.

DR. MÜELLER: Vhat about her do you admire most?

GUY: *(Isn't it obvious?)* The blouse.

(DR. MÜELLER gives GUY another shock. Lights down, then back up. DR. MÜELLER shows GUY a slide of a badly decorated room, then a stunning one.)

DR. MÜELLER: You can liff in house A or house B.

GUY: Maybe *you* can live in house A…

(DR. MÜELLER shocks GUY. Lights down, then back up. DR. MÜELLER shows GUY a slide of Babe Ruth.)

DR. MÜELLER: Babe Ruth holds a record for most vhat? ·

GUY: Babe Ruth? He said his name was—

(DR. MÜELLER shocks GUY. The lights go down, and they stay down for the following.)

DR. MÜELLER: Do you find ziss woman appealing?

GUY: Why… yes. *(A revelation.)* I do. I really do.

(Lights up. DR. MÜELLER is showing GUY a slide of Judy Garland. DR. MÜELLER gives GUY an extended shock, and GUY screams an extended scream. The lights again go down, then come up one last time. GUY is now beaten down and exhausted. DR. MÜELLER shows him a slide of an attractive man.)

DR. MÜELLER: Does ziss man appeal to you?

GUY: Ramon? No.

(DR. MÜELLER changes the slide to one of an attractive woman.)

DR. MÜELLER: Und ziss voman?

GUY: Yes.

DR. MÜELLER: Particularly…?

GUY: Breasts.

(DR. MÜELLER changes the slide to one of a baseball bat.)

DR. MÜELLER: Ziss is a…?

GUY: Baseball bat.

DR. MÜELLER: It reminds you of…?

GUY: Nothing.

(DR. MÜELLER changes the slide to one of another hideous room.)

DR. MÜELLER: Vat vould you change about ziss room if you could?

(GUY squints at the slide as the lights go down.)

GUY: Men don't know anything about decorating.

SCENE 4

GUY's bedroom. GUY lies in bed, sleeping. SALLY enters with coffee, and holds it under his nose. GUY stirs.

SALLY: Well hello, sleepyhead.

GUY: Where am I?

SALLY: Home. Dr. Müeller said you're cured.

GUY: *(Beat, then.)* That's great.

SALLY: I'm sorry you were there so long. He said you were one of his most stubborn patients.

GUY: Well I'm glad he didn't give up.

SALLY: Not as glad as me.

(SALLY kisses GUY.)

GUY: You're breasts are large and therefore attractive.

SALLY: Thank you, honey. Is there anything special you'd like to do today?

GUY: I'd like to watch sports, eat poorly, and then badger you for oral sex.

SALLY: *(With mock disapproval.)* Honey!

GUY: *(Cheerfully.)* Women are whores.

SAUL: *(Offstage.)* Hello?

GUY: Is that Saul?

SALLY: He said he wanted to look in on you. *(Calling.)* Up here, Mr. Ornstein.

(SAUL enters.)

SAUL: So how's my box office quarterback?

GUY: Good, thank you. And yourself?

(GUY socks SAUL in the shoulder, hard.)

SAUL: Ow! *(Grabbing his shoulder.)* What the hell was that?

GUY: Nothing. We're men.

(GUY socks SAUL again, just as hard.)

SAUL: Ow! Knock it off.

SALLY: Dr. Müeller said it might take a while for everything to "click."

SAUL: Just so it doesn't take too long. Did you tell him?

SALLY: He just woke up.

GUY: Tell me what?

SAUL: "Ben Hur" is in trouble. It needs a big star, and no studio will loan me one. I want you back.

GUY: But everyone thinks I'm g— *(Cringes from a sudden pain, then.)* A fag.

SALLY: Not anymore.

(SALLY hands GUY a stack of magazines. GUY reads the cover of the first.)

GUY: "Guy Stone: Homo No Mo."

SAUL: Sally really went to bat for you.

SALLY: I told the reporters that I made the whole thing up because I'm… Wait, the publicity department gave me just the right words… a small-minded, jealous shrew with mental problems.

SAUL: I hope you appreciate what you've got here, Stone.

GUY: I will tonight.

(JERRY enters.)

JERRY: Is it still visiting hours?

GUY: Jerry!

SALLY: Miss Albrecht, I don't know if you should—

JERRY: *(Re: SAUL.)* Tell him. He called me.

SAUL: I need to make this deal so we can announce.

JERRY: Now both of you, out, so I can confer with my client.

SALLY: Well, just a few minutes. He's recuperating.

(SAUL puts a hand on SALLY's shoulder and leads her out.)

GUY: Hands to yourself, Saul.

(SALLY and SAUL exit.)

JERRY: Nice touch.

GUY: I don't trust him with her.

JERRY: It's fine, they can't hear. Oh, are you all right? When Rick and I got back and you weren't there, we went crazy. And please know we did everything we could to find you. I even hired a private dick to—

(GUY convulses in pain.)

JERRY: What's wrong?

GUY: Please don't say "dick."

JERRY: God, what did they do to you? I know Saul is behind this. He put all his eggs in one basket with "Ben Hur," and now he's... *(She notices GUY is in pain again.)* What, "eggs?"

GUY: "Basket."

JERRY: Anyway, I'm busting you out. The car's right outside. *(Looking out window.)* Can we climb down this trellis?

GUY: And ruin my bougainvillea.

JERRY: Get dressed.

(GUY doesn't move.)

JERRY: Hurry.

GUY: I'm not going.

JERRY: What? Oh, no.

GUY: It's strange to me, too.

JERRY: You're cured. Guy Stone, who's blown more guys than the Santa Ana winds—

GUY: I know. Listen, I don't remember half of what went on in that hospital, and what I do recall I wouldn't wish on anyone. I'm not saying sending me there was right. But I was there. They did those things. And now, for better or worse, I'm cured.

(JERRY regards GUY for a long moment.)

JERRY: Bullshit.

GUY: What?

JERRY: You heard me.

GUY: You think I'm faking?

JERRY: No, Guy, I think you're a happily married, dyed-in-the-wool heterosexual who like he-men everywhere frets over his bougainvillea!

GUY: I don't expect you to understand.

JERRY: Oh, I understand, Guy. Things do always go your way, don't they? The very moment it begins to dawn on you how much you'd given up, like the cavalry here comes Sally galloping over the hill with her "cure."

GUY: This isn't about my house. My career. I was willing to give up all that when I thought Rick and I could be together.

And I actually did think that. I thought, people may hate gays, but they love me. I even imagined I might show them that we aren't so scary after all, but at the very least I was sure they would let me live and love in peace. Then I got to see human compassion and understanding in all its actual glory, and you know what? I *am* cured.

JERRY: Yeah, well Rick's not.

GUY: Jerry? Don't.

JERRY: He's in the car. Busting you out was his idea. Which is illegal, even if you want to go. But his feelings for you were too strong—

GUY: You're going to lecture me on integrity.

JERRY: Guy, he's worth whatever it costs—

GUY: On being true to my feelings.

JERRY: He's special. And he loves you. And if you let him go now—

GUY: You're a lesbian, Jerry. You are. And you've made every possible compromise, right down the line, but you're saying I should follow my heart?

JERRY: I'm saying don't make my mistakes all over.

(*SALLY enters.*)

SALLY: Can I have my husband back?

(*JERRY searches GUY for any sign that she's gotten through.*)

JERRY: He's all yours. (*Exits.*)

SALLY: You know, I was thinking—When you get tired of the movies, you should run for president. Wouldn't I make a good First Lady?

GUY: I suppose, although Oleg Cassini would kill himself.

SALLY: Guy! Men don't know anything about clothes.

(*GUY regards SALLY. A calm comes over him.*)

GUY: Honey, this life you have planned out for us, there's just one problem. I don't love you.

SALLY: It must be time for your pill.

(*SALLY searches through the bottles on his bed-table.*)

GUY: What's more, you don't love me.

SALLY: Of course I do.

GUY: You don't. You love Guy Stone, the movie star who hunts and wears plaid. You love my bio.

SALLY: I'm calling Dr. Müeller.

GUY: If you want. Maybe you can even force me to stay here. God knows I deserve it, after all I've done to you. But we'll never have real love, and trust me, it's not something you trade off.

(*RICK climbs over the balcony railing, and storms in.*)

RICK: Jerry said you aren't coming. Jerry said—

(*RICK trails off, too emotional to continue. GUY crosses to RICK and holds him.*)

GUY: I promised I would never hurt you. Don't you listen?

(*GUY and RICK share a smile. GUY becomes aware once more of SALLY and returns to her.*)

GUY: You okay?

SALLY: I only ever wanted you to look at me that way.

(*SAUL storms in with a head of steam.*)

SAUL: Okay, forget it. Deal's off.

GUY: But—

SAUL: I don't want to hear it. This whole business has been tearing me up inside since day one, and it stops now. Sally, you're a beautiful girl. More than that, you've got a pure heart like I've never seen, and you deserve better than some sham marriage to a fruitbasket. I love you.

SALLY: Mr. Ornstein!

SAUL: That's right, I love you, and get used to hearing it, because I want to marry you. 'Course it means "Ben Hur" is back in the crapper, and Bernice will probably get the studio, but none of that matters if I can have you.

(*SALLY is flustered, but clearly flattered by the attention.*)

SALLY: This is all so sudden. You really love me?

SAUL: Judge for yourself.

(*SAUL kisses SALLY. Unlike his earlier passes, this is a kiss of real tenderness, and it sends SALLY swooning. Just as they part, JERRY struggles over the outside railing, and falls to the balcony with an ungraceful thud. She enters, pulling strands of bougainvillea off herself.*)

JERRY: (*To GUY, re: bougainvillea.*) Sorry. (*To RICK.*) What's taking so long?

(*GUY looks at JERRY, then at SALLY and SAUL, and finally at RICK, whom he rests an elbow on as he begins to laugh.*)

JERRY: What?

GUY: Jerry, how do you feel about Bernice?

(*Blackout.*)

ABOUT THE AUTHOR

MARTIN DENTON is executive director of The New York Theatre Experience, Inc. He is the founder, reviewer, and editor of nytheatre.com, one of the premier sources for theatre reviews and information on the Internet since 1996. Denton is a member of the American Theatre Critics Association and The Drama Desk. He is the author of *The New York Theatre Experience Book of the Year 1998* and the editor of *Plays and Playwrights for the New Millennium*. He is passionately committed to discovering and fostering interesting new American drama wherever it can be found. He lives in New York City with his two Siamese cats, Logan and Briscoe.

THE NEW YORK THEATRE EXPERIENCE

The New York Theatre Experience, Inc., is a nonprofit New York State corporation. Its mission is to promote and increase awareness of and interest in theatre and the performing arts locally, nationally, and globally in order to inspire more people to attend and support live performance theatre. The principal activity of The New York Theatre Experience is the operation of a free website (http://www.nytheatre.com) that comprehensively covers the New York theatre scene—on, off, and off off Broadway. The New York Theatre Experience also publishes books of theatre reviews and features as well as newly written and produced plays.

If you would like to contact Martin Denton or would like to know more about the current and future plans of The New York Theatre Experience, Inc., please send an e-mail to mddenton@botz.com.

PLAYS AND PLAYWRIGHTS
for the
NEW MILLENNIUM

Edited by Martin Denton

A collection of eight exciting new plays which electrified audiences in New York City throughout 1998 and 1999. These gifted and talented young playwrights are boldly pushing contemporary theatre into the 21ˢᵗ century, helping to shape and define the themes and structures of the next wave of American drama.

Midnight Brainwash Revival by Kirk Wood Bromley — a revel for the new millennium.

Horse Country by C.J. Hopkins — a dizzying joyride through the American landscape.

When Words Fail... by David Dannenfelser — a tender comedy of the human spirit.

Making Peter Pope by Edmund De Santis — an epic comedy of a young gay man.

Crunching Numbers by Lynn Marie Macy — three linked one-acts about turning thirty.

Café Society by Robert Simonson — a cockeyed satire of contemporary urban America.

"So I Killed a Few People..." by Gary Ruderman & David Summers — a serial killer's chilling monologue.

Are We There Yet? by Garth Wingfield — a comic drama of renewal and rebirth.

Retail: $14.00

Additional information can be found on the web at http://www.nytheatre.com/newpromo.htm

Available in bookstores and on line or order directly from the publisher

Send a check or money for $14 (plus $3.50 for priority mail) to:

The New York Theatre Experience, Inc.
P.O. Box 744, Bowling Green Station
New York, NY 10274-0744